Woodrow Wilson:
The Years of Preparation

Supplementary Volumes to
The Papers of Woodrow Wilson
Arthur S. Link, Editor

A list of volumes in this series will
be found at the back of the book.

Woodrow Wilson

The Years of Preparation

JOHN M. MULDER

PRINCETON UNIVERSITY PRESS
Princeton, New Jersey

Library of Congress Cataloging in Publication Data will be
found on the last printed page of this book
This book has been composed in VIP Times Roman
Printed in the United States of America by Princeton
University Press, Princeton, New Jersey

For Mary

Contents

List of Illustrations

FOLLOWING PAGE 157

Preface

This study attempts to shed light on a number of questions, all far broader than the scope of this work. The first involves the often observed sense of American exclusivism, mission, and vocation, a national obsession with defending the exercise of power in moral terms. Although these concepts have been secularized to a large degree, American political ideology has been significantly influenced by religious ideas, particularly those arising out of the Protestant and Calvinist traditions. In recent years, this fusion of religion and politics in America has been described as a "civil religion," and it is clear that Woodrow Wilson's political thought and career demonstrate a significant example of the way in which religion interacted with politics in defining the goals of an individual and national policy.

Another purpose of this study was prompted by my dissatisfaction with certain types of American intellectual and religious history. Too often, it seemed, historians approached the intellectual development of a given period in terms of certain ideas which gained currency and others which had significance precisely because they were rejected. Insufficient attention was paid to the interaction of experience with ideas, the way in which thought influenced and was influenced by the events of individuals' lives and the society around them. While this study is an intellectual biography, it attempts to strike a balance between discussion and analysis of Woodrow Wilson's ideas and the events of his life.

In addition, American religious history has been written almost exclusively in clerical terms—what ministers thought, what they did, what they wrote. This examination of Wilson's intellectual development focuses on a layman's religious thought, expression, and experience, and in doing so, my hope is that it will contribute to a larger understanding of the American religious tradition, formed not only by the Jonathan Edwardses and Henry Ward Beechers but the Abraham Lincolns and Woodrow Wilsons. A still larger task remains—namely, the description of popular piety and the religious experience of those men and women who paid ministers' salaries, listened to sermons, prayed, and read and understood their Bibles in their own particular ways.

In treating Woodrow Wilson's life prior to his entry into politics, I have further tried to illumine a problem in late nineteenth- and early twentieth-century political history. Like many other middle-class Americans, Wilson had few apprehensions about the deleterious effects of America's rapid industrial and economic expansion during the late nineteenth century. Gradually, under the impact of the depression of the 1890's, labor unrest, exposés of corporate malfeasance, and social disruption, Wilson began to change his ideas about the role of government in American society. Laissez-faire individualism, which had sanctioned economic growth without governmental interference or regulation, was increasingly called into question.

Wilson sought to understand the forces which were transforming American society and to suggest and implement the ideas, values, and programs which would preserve a degree of order amidst social disintegration. In 1889, he asked, "Why may not the present age write, through me, its political *autobiography*?" and to some degree it did. Out of his own experience, Wilson provided the leadership which profoundly altered many traditional assumptions about the role of government in American society and the nation's responsibilities in world affairs.

This study ends with Wilson's nomination as governor of New Jersey. Wilson's ideas did undergo significant alterations during his political career, but his basic "principles" and attitudes remained substantially unchanged as governor of New Jersey and President of the United States. Wilson himself wrote of Abraham Lincoln that he could "be known only by a close and prolonged scrutiny of his life before he became President. The years of his presidency were not years to form, but rather years to test character." Or, as Ray Stannard Baker has written, "The first fifty-four years of Wilson's life were all preparatory: when he came to the New Jersey campaign, . . . he was made, intellectually and morally."

Several problems made this examination of Wilson's thought exceedingly difficult. The first is the endemic problem of relating ideas to events, motives to actions. That is mitigated in part by Wilson's constant and consistent expression of the values or purposes which he saw as the basis of his policies and programs. The second is the problem of interpreting the inherent tension between any personal faith and the compromises involved in its application. Religion, as well as ideology, can serve as both a powerful motivating stimulus but also an attractive means of rationalization. The task of the historian becomes one of maintaining a tension between sympathetic awareness of the importance of an individual's religious values and cautious suspicion of his use of them in explaining his own behavior.

In trying to describe the relationship of Wilson's religious faith and his political and educational thought, I have also encountered difficulty in defining Wilson's religion. Because he rarely used specific theological ideas and because his mind resisted formulating problems in theoretical terms, his religious faith cannot be described accurately as only an intellectual matter. Instead, for Wilson, religion was a series of values, assumptions, and attitudes, a way of perceiving the world and understanding his place within it. These "principles," as he called them, were so fundamental to his thought and behavior that although they did mature and develop, Wilson refused to see them as subject to intellectual challenge. As he once commented to his White House physician, "So far as religion is concerned, argument is adjourned."

As the following narrative attempts to demonstrate, Wilson was profoundly influenced by the Presbyterian covenant religious tradition, particularly as conveyed by his minister father. I have tried to describe in Chapters I and II the father's religious influence on Wilson, but in utilizing the term, "covenant theology," certain obstacles arise. The covenant theology developed in the late sixteenth and early seventeenth centuries out of the European reformation, but in New England it lost much of its vitality by the end of the eighteenth century. However, in the South and to a lesser extent in the Middle Atlantic States, the covenant theology continued to be the prevailing theological mode of expression, particularly among southern Presbyterians.

Fred J. Hood's superb study of Presbyterianism during the early nineteenth century suggests that the theological history of this period cannot be written solely in terms of New England ("Presbyterianism and the New American Nation, 1783-1826: A Case Study of Religion and National Life," unpublished Ph.D. dissertation, Princeton University, 1968). Presbyterians continued to formulate a theology that retained a large degree of continuity with the prior covenant tradition, especially as developed earlier in Scotland and at Princeton under John Witherspoon and Samuel Stanhope Smith. As Hood demonstrates, the experience of nationhood prompted Presbyterians to secularize certain aspects of God's covenant with the nation. God still controlled the destiny of the people, but the nation was bound, not by a divine moral law, but by the natural law. Providence, rather than God, became the guardian of national prosperity, and individuals possessed a special responsibility for maintaining obedience to the natural law. True religion was identified with ardent patriotism, for without the assurance of righteousness, the nation would no longer enjoy the blessings of Providence. It thus became possible for Presbyterians to continue to talk of a nation bound by covenants in terms which no longer necessitated a particular or well-defined conception of God.

What seems clear is that Wilson's father and Wilson himself experienced and appropriated this Presbyterian ethos. Wilson especially utilized this covenant mode of thinking to understand his life and ambitions, his relationship with his wife and American society, and he did so usually without specific reference to God. It provided a comprehensive view of the world and the individual's place within it, and for Wilson, it was most frequently employed to provide structure and wholeness in the midst of personal and social disorder. Because his covenant theological heritage had been somewhat secularized, it was sufficiently vague, ambiguous, and flexible to be applied to virtually any area of human life. It became part of Wilson's basic attitudes and assumptions, and his intellectual development is notable for his attempt to use covenant ideas in myriad ways. Furthermore, the covenant tradition's influence on Wilson's political thought and his appeal to the American public in the late nineteenth and early twentieth centuries suggest the pervasive and tenacious impact which these ideas retained in a much more secular age.

In preparing this study, I have incurred an indebtedness to many people. The thoughtful criticism and advice of Lefferts A. Loetscher have played a large role in shaping my thinking about the relationship between Wilson's religious and political thought, and he has read the text of this study in its various forms. In addition, I have gained considerable insight from the remarks and criticisms of E. David Cronin, Edward A. Dowey, James E. Loder, Martin E. Marty, James I. McCord, Randall M. Miller, and James H. Nichols. John F. Wilson and Nancy J. Weiss helped me clarify my ideas, and both offered a large measure of support and encouragement during the preparation.

Any student interested in Wilson owes an enormous debt to the editors of *The Papers of Woodrow Wilson*—Arthur S. Link, David W. Hirst, John E. Little, John Wells Davidson, M. Halsey Thomas, Jean MacLachlan, Sylvia E. Fontijn, and others. For two years while completing my research, I enjoyed the privilege of working with this staff and sharing my ideas with them. Their work in compiling and superbly editing a comprehensive documentary account of Wilson's life makes the task of research practically a pleasure. David W. Hirst and John E. Little generously shared their time and insight into Wilson, and I have benefited from their careful reading of my manuscript. To Arthur S. Link, who supervised this study in its earlier form as a doctoral dissertation, I owe a special debt of gratitude. For many years, he encouraged my work on Wilson and assisted me in numerous ways. He has been a constant but unfailingly charitable critic, and his suggestions have improved the text considerably. More than a teacher and adviser, he has been a warm friend, providing hours of discussion about Wilson and encouragement in my research. It is a special honor and privilege for me to have this book appear as a supplementary volume to the distinguished series of Wilson papers.

The library staffs of Princeton Theological Seminary, Princeton University, the Library of Congress, and the Presbyterian Historical

Society have been helpful at various stages of my research. I am especially grateful to Mrs. Mary G. Lane of the Historical Foundation in Montreat, North Carolina, for her assistance in uncovering many aspects of Wilson's father's life. Chapter I on Wilson's father appeared in a slightly different version in the *Journal of Presbyterian History, LII* (1974), 245-71, and it appears here with permission of the Presbyterian Historical Society. I want to thank Princeton Theological Seminary for secretarial assistance and Teri Betros, who typed the manuscript with speed, accuracy, and good humor. Miriam Brokaw has been a consistently helpful and patient editor, steering this book to publication.

My parents encouraged me throughout my work, and their influence is reflected in this study. As freely admitted Dutch Calvinists, they have placed a high value on the intellectual and religious development of their children and on serving society, giving their love and trust freely and openly. To my wife Mary I owe gratitude for so many things, large and small, that they cannot be mentioned. In addition to her heavy teaching responsibilities, she assisted in many of the more tedious aspects of finishing this study, and during periods of intense work and pressure, she demonstrated abundant patience and sympathy. Her love and support reminded me of what was important. Fortunately, our son Aaron arrived in time to enjoy the happiness of this book's completion and not endure the pressure of its preparation.

Abbreviations in the Notes

WW   Woodrow Wilson
JWW   Janet Woodrow Wilson
JRW   Joseph Ruggles Wilson
ELA   Ellen Louise Axson
EAW   Ellen Axson Wilson
DLC   Library of Congress
WP   Wilson Papers
HF, NC   Historical Foundation of the Reformed and Presbyterian Churches, Montreat, North Carolina
UA, NjP   University Archives, Princeton University Library
WWLL   Ray Stannard Baker, *Woodrow Wilson: Life and Letters*, 8 vols. (Garden City, N. Y., 1927-1939).
PWW   Arthur S. Link, David W. Hirst, John E. Little, John Wells Davidson *et al.*, eds., *The Papers of Woodrow Wilson*, 23 vols. to date (Princeton, N. J., 1966-1977).

In order to avoid cluttering the text with [*sic*], I have refrained from using it except when necessary to clarify meaning, and I have followed the text of *The Papers of Woodrow Wilson*. Italics are those of the author or speaker, unless otherwise indicated. Some care should be exercised in interpreting Wilson's use of italics. In many cases, the citations are from speech notes, and his underscoring may have been designed to guide his eye rather than emphasize certain words or phrases.

Woodrow Wilson:
The Years of Preparation

I

Joseph Ruggles Wilson

"My incomparable father," Woodrow Wilson called him and confessed, "If I had my father's face and figure, it wouldn't make any difference what I said."[1] History has issued a different verdict, for Joseph Ruggles Wilson has been known only as Woodrow Wilson's father, his early teacher, and the most formative single influence on his thought and personality.[2] And yet Woodrow Wilson's estimation of his father was not unjustified, for Joseph Ruggles Wilson stands as an important figure in his own right within the history of the southern Presbyterian Church. Indeed, he was one of its founders, and the first General Assembly of the Presbyterian Church in the Confederate States of America was held in his church in Augusta, Georgia, in 1861. At that meeting he was elected Permanent Clerk of the General Assembly and was soon promoted to Stated Clerk in 1865, a post he held until 1898. In addition to being one of the most important and highest church officials during the crucial early decades of the Presbyterian Church in the United States, the Rev. Dr. Wilson was renowned as a powerful and eloquent preacher and held important pulpits throughout the church. As a professor, he influenced generations of students and shaped the future leadership of the church.

Joseph Wilson's roots were not, however, in the South. He was born in Steubenville, Ohio, on February 28, 1822, the son of James and Anne (or Ann) Adams Wilson.[3] Both were Scotch-Irish immigrants

---

[1] Woodrow Wilson to Joseph Ruggles Wilson, Dec. 16, 1888, *The Papers of Woodrow Wilson,* Arthur S. Link, John Wells Davidson, David W. Hirst, John E. Little *et al.* (eds.) (Princeton, N. J., 1966—), VI, 30; hereinafter cited as *PWW.* Ray Stannard Baker, *Woodrow Wilson: Life and Letters,* 8 vols. (Garden City, N. Y., 1927-39), I, 31, hereinafter cited as *WWLL.* The following abbreviations for individuals will also be used in the notes: JRW—Joseph Ruggles Wilson, JWW—Janet Woodrow Wilson, WW—Woodrow Wilson, ELA—Ellen Louise Axson, EAW—Ellen Axson Wilson.

[2] See for example, *PWW,* I, 3-4, n. 1; Arthur S. Link (ed.) *Woodrow Wilson: A Profile* (New York, 1968), p. ix; *WWLL,* I, 30.

[3] Much biographical data on JRW has been collected by L. Joel Swabb, Jr., in "The Rhetorical Theory of Rev. Joseph Ruggles Wilson, D.D." (unpublished doctoral dissertation, Ohio State University, 1971), and I want to record my gratitude to him for his help in my own research. Other valuable sources are Francis P. Weisenburger, "The Middle Western Antecedents of Woodrow Wilson," *Mississippi Valley Historical Review,* XXIII (1936), 375-90; George C. Osborn, "The Influence of Joseph Ruggles Wilson on His Son Woodrow Wilson," *North Carolina Historical Review,* XXXII (1955), 519-43, and *Woodrow Wilson: The Early Years* (Baton Rouge,

who came over together and were married in the United States. James
Wilson settled first in Philadelphia, plying his trade as a printer with
the virulently Jeffersonian paper, the *Aurora*. Within five years he
was virtually the head of the paper, though it was nominally edited by
William Duane. In 1815 he moved to Steubenville, Ohio, to become
editor and proprietor of the *Western Herald and Steubenville Gazette*,
the motto of which was "Principles, Not Men." Quickly becoming
embroiled in Ohio politics and bitter partisan fights, he attacked Andrew Jackson and enlisted his paper in the antislavery cause.[4] He
served as a Whig member of the Ohio legislature and as an associate
judge of the Court of Common Pleas, despite the fact that he was not a
lawyer.

Joseph Ruggles was the youngest of seven boys in a family of ten
children. Ray Stannard Baker suggests that he was the favored son of
the family because he was given an education to become a minister.
However, other evidence indicates that this youngest son failed to
share equally in his father's efforts to secure a prominent and established career for his many sons.[5] He began his educational training at
the Steubenville Academy and attended Jefferson (now Washington
and Jefferson) College, being graduated as valedictorian in 1844. He
taught briefly at Mercer, Pennsylvania, and then attended Western
Theological Seminary (1845-1846). He studied under Charles Hodge
for one year at Princeton Theological Seminary (1846-1847) and returned home to teach at the Steubenville Male Academy until 1849.
During this time (1848), he was licensed by the Steubenville Presbytery and ordained and installed in the Presbyterian Church of Chartiers,
Pennsylvania, by the Presbytery of Ohio in 1849.

Within weeks after his ordination, he married eighteen-year-old
Janet, or Jessie as she was usually called, Woodrow on June 7, 1849.
The Woodrows, as Baker has said, were "a more distinguished stock"[6]
than the Wilsons, tracing their ancestry to prominent Scottish divines
across six generations. The family emigrated from Carlisle, England,
where Jessie's father, the Rev. Thomas Woodrow, was pastor of an
independent church and a member of the Congregational Union. They
settled first in Poughkeepsie, New York, and then Brockville, Ontario,
during 1836-1837. The long journey proved too much for Thomas
Woodrow's wife, Marion, who died in 1836. Her sister Isabella helped

La., 1968), pp. 3-46; *PWW*, I, 3-4, n. 1; *WWLL*, I,1-80; J. H. McNeilly, "The Rev. Joseph R.
Wilson, D.D.," *Southern Presbyterian*, May 18, 1899; and the Wilmington *North Carolina
Presbyterian*, Jan. 30, 1896.

[4] Weisenburger, "Middle Western Antecedents of Wilson," pp. 376-77; Randall M. Miller,
"The Union Humane Society," *Quaker History*, LXI (1972), 93, 99-100.

[5] *WWLL*, I, 12; Weisenburger, "Middle Western Antecedents of Wilson," pp. 385-87.

[6] *WWLL*, I, 14.

to raise the family of eight children, of whom Jessie was the fifth and which included James Woodrow, prominent theologian of the Southern Presbyterian Church.

In 1837, Thomas Woodrow settled in Chillicothe, Ohio, where he served as pastor of the First Presbyterian Church until 1848. He resigned because of supposed ill health but lived almost thirty years thereafter. He moved to Worthington, Ohio, serving as minister there until 1857, and then transferred to Nicholasville, Kentucky, where he labored until the onset of the Civil War. In 1861, he returned to Ohio where he served as stated supply (temporary pastor) in various churches until ill health compelled his retirement in 1865. During these convulsive years in American Presbyterianism, Woodrow sided with the Old School Presbyterians in 1837 and the northern church in 1861, but he is known to have voted against antislavery resolutions in the Chillicothe Presbytery.[7]

The Woodrow children remained close, perhaps because of the travail of immigrating to the United States and the loss of their mother while they were all quite young. In addition, their father seems to have lost some interest in them, for he remarried and at the time of his death in 1877 did not remember any of the children of his first marriage in his will.[8] Moreover, Jessie made only one brief and curiously restrained mention of her father's death in letters to her son Woodrow.[9]

With his wife, Joseph Ruggles Wilson began his long ministry in the church. Initially it was an uncertain and itinerant life. He served the Chartiers church for only two years, 1849-1851, and supplemented his small salary as Professor Extraordinary of Rhetoric at Jefferson College, which involved tutoring students at their own expense. In 1851, he moved to the South, settling at Hampden-Sydney College in Virginia, where he became Professor of Chemistry and Natural Science[10] and served as stated supply at nearby Walker's Church. Wilson remained at Hampden-Sydney for four years until he received a call from the First Presbyterian Church in Staunton, Virginia. Accepting the invitation in December 1854, he was eventually installed on June 24, 1855. This church had a prominent pulpit, its 168 members making it one of the largest churches in the Presbytery of Lexington.[11]

[7] Weisenburger, "Middle Western Antecedents of Wilson," pp. 387-90.

[8] He did remember the six children by his second wife, Harriet Renick, who had also predeceased him. *Ibid.*, p. 390; Osborn, *Woodrow Wilson*, pp. 6-7.

[9] See her letters for April and May, 1877, in *PWW*, 1, and JWW to WW, May 3, 1877 (Wilson Papers, DLC). The break, however, was never complete, for as Baker points out, Thomas Woodrow visited the Wilsons in Augusta and preached in JRW's pulpit. *WWLL*, 1, 19.

[10] Alfred J. Morrison, *The College of Hampden-Sydney: Calendar of Board Minutes, 1776-1886* (Richmond, Va., 1912), pp. 139, 141.

[11] *Minutes of the General Assembly of the Presbyterian Church in the United States of America* (Philadelphia, 1855), p. 430.

The Staunton church provided a new, capacious manse, badly needed for Wilson's growing family. Marion Williamson was born in 1851 in Chartiers; Annie Josephine arrived in 1853 in Hampden-Sydney; and Thomas Woodrow was born on December 28 (or 29), 1856, in the Staunton manse. Wilson's tenure of two years in Staunton was brief but productive. He served for one year as principal of the Augusta Female Seminary (later Mary Baldwin College), located next to the church, and presided over the expansion of the seminary's buildings. During his pastorate, the church vestibule was added and other improvements were made.[12] He also took an active role in the affairs of the Presbytery of Lexington, serving as moderator, clerk, and treasurer, and preaching occasionally at its regular meetings. As chairman of the special presbytery committee, he aided in the establishment of the Mt. Horeb Presbyterian Church.[13]

Wilson remained restless, eager to establish himself in this new area of the country, ambitious for recognition within the church. Just as his father had battled his way to political and financial success in a new and foreign land, so too his son proposed to achieve prominence within the church and in another area of the country. Wilson's ambition is revealed in his first published sermon or address, *The True Idea of Success in Life*, delivered on June 10, 1857, before the Union and Philanthropic Societies of Hampden-Sydney College. Wilson indicated his growing accommodation with the southern point of view on slavery, declaring that he would "love to swing a flail of rebuke over the heads of fanatical men, who, among the ices of the North, can talk deliberately of quenching here those bright domestic fires which are kept a-burning, as they were kindled, in the mutual good will of white and black!"[14]

But instead of pursuing that theme, Wilson chose to examine the problem of individual success. He denied that it was due to mere good fortune; that it was based on the acquisition of property; or that it had to be recognized. Rather, he linked success to happiness and described "the pursuit of *real happiness* to be nothing else than the pursuit of *real success*." Happiness, in turn, depended on the individual's sense of "a personal worth," but was not achieved by staying aloof and pure

[12] Howard McKnight Wilson, *The Lexington Presbytery Heritage* (Verona, Va., 1971), pp. 114, 244, 420, 429; Arista Hoge, *The First Presbyterian Church, Staunton, Virginia* (Staunton, Va., 1908), pp. 36-37; *Hand-Book of the First Presbyterian Church, Compiled by the Committee on Printing* (Staunton, Va., 1903), pp. 50-51; "Minutes of the Session of the First Presbyterian Church, Staunton, Virginia," 1855-57 (Historical Foundation, Montreat, N. C.), *passim.*

[13] "Records of Lexington Presbytery, Synod of Virginia," 1855-57 (Historical Foundation, Montreat, N. C.), *passim.*

[14] *The True Idea of Success in Life. An Address Delivered Before the Union and Philanthropic Societies of Hampden Sydney College, June 10, 1857 . . .* (Richmond, Va., 1857), p. 7.

from the world. Life was a gift from God and involved moral exertion and ethical achievement. Drawing on the familiar strains of the Protestant ethic, Wilson declared that life is not something "we are to *endure*, but to use, to improve, to make the most of." "Life," he continued, "is not a season through which the soul is to dream. It is a day in which the soul must act." The source of strength for such action was God alone. "There must be a *God* presiding over and through all truly successful enterprise," he concluded.[15]

Eager to improve his own life, Wilson's opportunity came quickly. In the summer of 1857 he traveled to Augusta, Georgia, to perform the wedding ceremony for his brother-in-law, James Woodrow.[16] There he preached at the First Presbyterian Church, and the congregation, impressed by the eloquence and power of his sermon, issued a call to him on December 18, 1857. He preached his first sermon on January 10, 1858, and was installed on May 2, 1858.[17] Like his father who was adept in the ways of political patronage, Wilson knew how to extend his contacts throughout the church, and he asked Samuel K. Talmage, president of Oglethorpe University, to participate in the installation service.[18] Through the good offices of Talmage, and possibly through the influence of James Woodrow, then a member of the Oglethorpe faculty, Wilson was honored with the Doctor of Divinity degree from Oglethorpe at the commencement exercises in 1858.[19]

Duly tagged as one of the leaders in southern Presbyterianism and occupying one of the most important pulpits in the southern church, Wilson had achieved a substantial degree of prominence in the South within the short space of seven years. In Augusta he ministered to a congregation of 224 souls[20] and resided in a large, comfortable manse with slaves to serve him and his family. His fame as a preacher of arresting rhetoric and cogent thought spread throughout the church, and he demonstrated a clear acceptance of southern ideals and thinking.

Wilson shared with his southern Presbyterian colleagues an adherence to the Scottish covenant, or "federal," theology, particularly as it was developed in the South by James H. Thornwell and others. According to this theological point of view, God had established a covenant of grace with people, offering them forgiveness from their sins in exchange for obedience to the divine will. A further covenant, one of

[15] *Ibid.*, pp. 15, 22, 29.   [16] Osborn, *Woodrow Wilson*, p. 8.

[17] Augusta, Ga., *Chronicle & Sentinel,* Jan. 10, 1858; Augusta, Ga., *Daily Constitutionalist,* Jan. 10 and May 2, 1858.

[18] Augusta *Daily Constitutionalist,* May 2, 1858. Isaac Stockton Keith Axson, Woodrow Wilson's future grandfather-in-law, also took part in the service.

[19] Allen P. Tankersley, *College Life at Old Oglethorpe* (Athens, Ga., 1951), p. 94.

[20] *Minutes of the General Assembly of the Presbyterian Church in the United States of America* (Philadelphia, 1858), p. 448.

nature, had also been established by God, in which the affairs of this world—its laws and its government—were conducted according to God's moral law. The essential thrust of the covenant theology was to provide a comprehensive theological view of the individual, the church, and society, each with its own function and place within the divine scheme of government of the world. It was, as many scholars have observed, a "theology of politics,"[21] which gave rational and predictable "government" to every aspect of human life.

Wilson's adherence to this covenant theology, with its conception of a stratified society, coalesced easily with a southern society based on slavery and the clear definition of the roles of men and women. In a sermon, *Female Training,* delivered before the students and friends of Greensboro Female College in Greensboro, Georgia, on May 23, 1858, Wilson outlined the respective positions of the two sexes: "the one ruling at the head, and the other subject to that head." Man was meant for the struggle of life in the world at large, carving out his own measure of success; woman's place was in the home, "away from the rush and storm of life." But her role was not necessarily one of inferiority; rather, she was intended to be man's partner in the world, exercising through her "physically weak" nature her ordained endowment of love, endurance, and devotion within the home. Wilson did, however, emphatically reject the prevalent conception that woman's role necessitated no formal education. "It cannot be doubted," he proclaimed,

. . . that the community which has not made adequate provision for the right education of its daughters, is in a sadly self-ruinous condition—and that those parents who will not sacrifice much to place their female children within the reach of a first-rate education, are failing in one of their highest duties; and that even that Church membership, which fails, by properly directed effort, to secure a religious training for girls connected with their families, appropriate to their received standards of Bible truth, must be considered false to their own belief, disregardful of the future of their children, and greatly deficient in intelligent zeal for the welfare of their fellow men.[22]

[21] The literature on covenant theology is voluminous, but some of the more helpful contributions to this study are Michael Walzer, *The Revolution of the Saints: A Study in the Origins of Radical Politics* (Cambridge, Mass., 1965); James B. Torrance, " 'Covenant or Contract' A study of the theological background of worship in seventeenth-century Scotland," *Scottish Journal of Theology*, XXIII (Feb. 1970), 51-76; Sidney A. Burrell, "The Covenant Idea as a Revolutionary Symbol: Scotland, 1596-1637," *Church History*, XXVII (1958), 338-50; Leonard J. Trinterud, "The Origins of Puritanism," *Church History,* XX (1951), 37-57; H. Richard Niebuhr, "The Idea of Covenant and American Democracy," *Church History,* XXIII (1954), 126-35; Perry Miller, *The New England Mind.* 2 vols. (New York, 1939 and 1953), and *Errand Into the Wilderness* (Cambridge, Mass., 1956).

[22] *Female Training. A Sermon Delivered in the Union Church at Greensboro, Ga., before the*

Only through such education could a woman realize the power of religion—her *"peculiar ornament*, as it is the right foundation of her *peculiar influence.*"[23] Nearly thirty years later, Woodrow Wilson's fiancée, Ellen Louise Axson, said that she had read the sermon "with real pleasure—for it is as 'timely' now as then, and not at all too 'old fashioned' to suit us." Her only objection was that "he calls women 'our females' !"[24]

If God had established and circumscribed a role for women in Wilson's theology, the place of black slaves was even more clearly defined by divine decree. On January 8, 1861, Wilson delivered to his Augusta congregation the last of a series of sermons on "Family Government," dealing with masters and slaves. The sermon was immediately published, and in a prefatory letter Wilson explained that he did not prepare it "with *exclusive* reference to the present unhappy agitations of the popular mind." Nevertheless, he declared, "it is surely high time that the Bible view of slavery should be examined, and that we should begin to meet the infidel fanaticism of our infatuated enemies upon the elevated ground of a divine warrant for the institution we are resolved to cherish."[25]

Wilson argued that there was a divine sanction for slavery on the basis of the silence of scripture (it "is never once condemned, never once even discountenanced") as well as the explicit provisions for it. Drawing on the covenant theology, he declared that slavery is

> found imbedded in the very heart of the *moral law* itself—that law which determines the *principles* of divine administration over men—a law which constitutes, if I may so speak, the very *constitution* of that royal kingdom whose regulations begin and end in the infinite holiness of Jehovah, and whose spread through the universal heart of the race is the aim of all Scripture.[26]

Indeed, Wilson maintained that God had "included slavery as an organizing element in that family order which lies at the very foundation of Church and State." The fundamental problem was that neither slaves nor masters were living in obedience to that law contained in the scriptures. He heralded the time when through proper obedience by masters and slaves, slavery would be recognized as "that scheme of politics and morals, which, by saving a lower race from the destruction

---

Friends of the Greensboro Female College, May 23, 1858 . . . (Augusta, Ga., 1858), pp. 6, 8, 10.

[23] *Ibid.*, p. 15.

[24] ELA to WW, May 10, 1885, *PWW,* IV, 579.

[25] *Mutual Relation of Masters and Slaves as Taught in the Bible* . . . (Augusta, Ga., 1861), p. 3.

[26] *Ibid.*, pp. 11, 15.

of heathenism, has under divine management, contributed to refine, exalt, and enrich its superior race!"[27]

Wilson's vision was never to be realized, and the slavery issue tore apart the nation, Old School Presbyterians, and Wilson's own family. In May 1861, soon after the attack on Fort Sumter, the Old School Presbyterians gathered in Philadelphia. The passage of the Spring Resolutions left the Old School Southerners embittered,[28] and presbyteries throughout the South responded by withdrawing from the Presbyterian Church in the United States of America. A convention was set for August 15, 1861, in Atlanta, Georgia, for delegates from the southern presbyteries, and a General Assembly meeting was scheduled for December 4 in Augusta, at the invitation of Wilson. At this first meeting of the General Assembly of the Presbyterian Church in the Confederate States of America, held in Wilson's church from December 4-16, 1861, Wilson was elected Permanent Clerk, John N. Waddell became Stated Clerk, and Benjamin M. Palmer was unanimously chosen Moderator.[29]

This was the beginning of Wilson's long service in the hierarchy of the southern church, and in 1865 he was elected Stated Clerk. Because of the decentralized organization of the southern Presbyterian Church, the office of Stated Clerk carried with it relatively little power. However, it did bring several significant responsibilities. It involved serving as ex-officio Treasurer of the General Assembly, ruling on points of procedure at General Assembly meetings, carefully preparing the minutes of the Assembly's meetings (a task often made easier by the assistance of his son Woodrow), and facilitating the smooth functioning of the church polity on the synodical and presbytery levels.[30]

Led by James H. Thornwell, the Augusta Assembly declared that its

---

[27] *Ibid.*, pp. 7, 21. Ellen Louise Axson, commenting on this sermon many years later, called it "a thoroughly *Southern* sermon, and a very strong presentation of that side: . . . though it *is* an outworn subject now." ELA to WW, May 10, 1885, *PWW*, IV, 579.

[28] These resolutions, sponsored by Gardiner Spring of the Brick Presbyterian Church in New York City, called for a day of national prayer and repentance on July 4, 1861, declared "unabated loyalty" to the Constitution of the United States, and acknowledged responsibility for promoting and perpetuating the integrity of the United States. *Minutes of the General Assembly of the Presbyterian Church in the United States of America* (Philadelphia, 1861), pp. 329-30.

[29] For discussion of the division of 1861 and the General Assembly of the Presbyterian Church in the Confederate States of America, see Lewis G. Vander Velde, *The Presbyterian Churches and the Frederal Union, 1861-1869* (Cambridge, Mass., 1932); William Junius Wade, "The Origins and Establishment of the Presbyterian Church in the United States" (unpublished Ph.D. dissertation, University of North Carolina, 1959); Thomas C. Johnson, "History of the Southern Presbyterian Church," *American Church History Series* (New York, 1894), XI, 311-479; Robert Ellis Thompson, *A History of the Presbyterian Churches in the United States* (New York, 1895); *Minutes of the General Assembly of the Presbyterian Church in the Confederate States of America* (Augusta, Ga., 1861), hereinafter cited as *Minutes*, with the Assembly year in parentheses; Augusta *Chronicle & Sentinel* and Augusta *Daily Constitutionalist*, Dec. 4-17, 1861.

[30] One major difficulty in assessing JRW's role as Stated Clerk is the absence of records for his

justification for separating from the northern church was based on the spirituality of the church and the separation of church and state. "We are neither the friends nor the foes of slavery," the Assembly stated; "that is to say, we have no commission either to propagate or abolish it. The policy of its existence or non-existence is a question which exclusively belongs to the State."[31] Twenty-five years later, Wilson recalled the scene in Augusta. The Assembly convened, he said, "under extraordinary circumstances, when the opening roar of such a civil war as the world had not hitherto beheld was causing all the land to quake with indefinable apprehensions." Thornwell commanded the rapt attention of the Assembly. "Every eye was upon him, and every interrupting sound was hushed as by a spell; and whilst for forty minutes, this Calvin of our modern Church poured forth a stream of elevated utterance such as he of Geneva never surpassed." While the war was lost, Wilson concluded, the principles of the southern church, and even the church itself, had endured.[32]

And yet the war took its toll on the church, particularly Wilson's church in Augusta. After the battle of Chickamauga in 1863, it was used as a hospital and the churchyard as a detention camp for Union prisoners. The damage to the church was considerable, and the congregation eventually received $2,000 from the Confederate government.[33] During that summer, Wilson labored as an army chaplain under the Presbyterian Board of Home Missions,[34] and throughout the war he served as chairman of the Executive Committee of the Georgia Relief and Hospital Association. The organization assisted in forwarding clothing and supplies to indigent soldiers as well as organizing medical and relief efforts.[35] In addition, he purportedly dismissed his congregation one Sunday morning with the injunction that they were to help in the undermanned Confederate arsenal at Augusta to provide supplies for the army.[36]

---

tenure in that office. He certainly must have kept correspondence and records, but since there was no permanent Office of the Stated Clerk, everything traveled with him, and after his retirement, all of it was probably lost or destroyed.

[31] *Minutes* (1861), pp. 55-56.

[32] "Memorial Address," in *Memorial Addresses Delivered Before the General Assembly of 1886, on Occasion of the Quarter-Centennial of the Organization of the Southern Assembly, in 1861* (Richmond, Va., 1886), pp. 9, 13, 14-19.

[33] Georgia Historical Records Survey and Works Progress Administration Survey of State and Local Historical Records, "History of the First Presbyterian Church, Augusta, Ga.," *Inventory of the Archives of Georgia: Presbyterian Churches* (Philadephia, 1969), p. 299; Augusta *Daily Constitutionalist,* Dec. 16, 1863; *Memorial of the Centennial Anniversary of the First Presbyterian Church, Augusta, Georgia* (Philadelphia, 1904), p. 44.

[34] *Ibid.*, p. 43.

[35] Augusta *Daily Constitutionalist*, Dec. 8, 1861; Augusta *Chronicle & Sentinel*, March 17, 1863.

[36] *WWLL*, I, 51.

All this exacted a physical price from Wilson. At the General Assembly of 1864 he was described as "a tall, pale, thin, intellectual looking young man of thirty-five [*sic*]. His dark eye beams with intelligence, his sunny smile is strongly suggestive of fun and good humor, but he has the appearance of being overworked. But for the blockade, it would be a capital idea for his people to give him a holiday, and let him travel in Europe and the Holy Land for six months or a year."[37] The war also isolated Wilson from his family; two of his brothers were generals in the Union Army, and although he invited his father-in-law to preach in his Augusta pulpit,[38] Wilson had virtually no further contact with his brothers or sisters after the war.

Despite the war, Wilson's years in Augusta were rewarding, characterized by the growth of his congregation from 224 to 400 members,[39] active participation in the business of Hopewell Presbytery and civic affairs in Augusta,[40] and growing prominence in the southern church. In 1863 he was elected by the General Assembly to the Board of Trustees of Columbia Theological Seminary and reelected in 1867.[41] He was also regularly elected to the executive committees responsible for foreign missions, domestic missions, and sustenation, and was chairman of the committee dealing with revisions in the *Book of Order*, or church constitution.[42] He briefly joined James Woodrow and others in reviving *The Southern Presbyterian Weekly* after the war, but soon withdrew because of the financial pressures.[43] His ministry in Augusta was later described as "perhaps the most fruitful years of his pastoral and pulpit work," and he was remembered by his parishioners as "a man of literary tastes—always a student."[44]

In 1870, while Wilson was serving as chairman of the Columbia Theological Seminary Board of Trustees, the Board and Faculty requested that the General Assembly elect a Professor of Pastoral and

[37] Charlotte, N. C., *Daily Bulletin*, May 15, 1864.

[38] Arthur Walworth, *Woodrow Wilson* (Baltimore, 1965), p. 7.

[39] *Minutes of the General Assembly of the Presbyterian Church in the United States of America* (Philadelphia, 1858), p. 448; *Minutes* (1870), p. 585.

[40] See for example, "Minutes of Hopewell Presbytery," Nov. 22, 1858, April 6 and Oct. 10, 1859, April 3, Sept. 19 and 21, 1861, and *passim* (Historical Foundation, Montreat, N. C.).

[41] *Minutes* (1863), p. 149; *ibid.* (1867), p. 137.

[42] For Assembly actions regarding JRW, see *ibid.* (1863), p. 141; *ibid.* (1864), pp. 266, 278, 286; *ibid.* (1865), pp. 352, 369, 373; *ibid.* (1866), pp. 34-35, 72-76; *ibid.* (1867), pp. 129, 149; *ibid.* (1868), p. 275; *ibid.* (1869), pp. 383, 393; *ibid.* (1870), pp. 507, 509-10, 515, 517, 535. For JRW's account of the 1862 General Assembly, see "The General Assembly of 1862," *Southern Presbyterian Review*, XV (1862), 52-60.

[43] John B. Adger, *My Life & Times* (Richmond, Va., 1899), pp. 228-29.

[44] *Presbyterian Standard*, XLIV (Feb. 11, 1903), 16; *Memorial . . . of the First Presbyterian Church, Augusta, Ga.*, pp. 44-45.

Evangelistic Theology and Sacred Rhetoric, since they were confident that the means of his support could be provided.[45] Wilson was nominated and elected to the new chair by an overwhelming margin.[46] This was the culmination of his long fight for success and preeminence in the southern church. At the age of forty-eight, he joined the ranks of a distinguished faculty—George Howe, John B. Adger, James Woodrow, and William S. Plumer. Because of the financial plight of the seminary after the war, Wilson supplemented his salary after 1870 as stated supply in the First Presbyterian Church of Columbia, South Carolina, for which he received a generous $1,500 a year.[47]

Wilson clearly intended to make the move to Columbia his last, to end his ministry with long service as a professor of theology. The Wilsons purchased a lot and constructed a comfortable home in 1872 for the family of two girls and two boys, Joseph R. Wilson, Jr. having been born in 1866. With two sources of income, they lived comfortably in the midst of war-ravaged Columbia. Wilson, in fact, showed a distinct affection for the comforts of this world, taking his summer vacations alone and usually at Saratoga, New York.[48] Once when he bought some clothing for a very low price, his wife exulted in a letter to Woodrow: "Something new for him to get bargains you know."[49] For his day, Wilson was something of a liberal, and he enjoyed billiards, chess, English novelists, and on occasion "a good nip of Presbyterian scotch," according to William Allen White.[50] He drew the line at cards and dancing, but he faithfully supported one of the South's principal industries, tobacco, and found it absurd that anyone could describe smoking as a sin: "Everyone must admit that there is something to be said against the use of tobacco, considered as a matter of taste, or as a question of cleanliness. But, to make it a sin!"[51]

He was extremely popular as a professor, in part because he and James Woodrow were the only two relatively young men on the faculty. Samuel L. Morris, a former student, described Wilson and Woodrow as "great teachers" and the others as "superannuated."[52] Despite the title of his chair, Wilson was, in no strict sense of the

[45] *Minutes* (1870), p. 509.

[46] *Ibid.*, pp. 515, 517; *Southern Presbyterian*, June 16, 1870.

[47] *WWLL,* I, 58-59; W. A. Clark, "A Brief History of the First Presbyterian Church, Columbia, South Carolina," *Presbyterian of the South,* LXXXVI (Oct. 30, 1912), 2.

[48] See JRW to WW, Aug. 11, 1875, and Aug. 16 and 24, 1878, *PWW*, I, 71, 397, 398; Sept. 3, 1881 and Sept. 4, 1883, *ibid.*, II, 79-80, 418-19; June 17, 1889, *ibid.*, VI, 323.

[49] JWW to WW, April 1, 1879, *ibid.*, I, 473.

[50] William Allen White, *Woodrow Wilson* (Boston and New York, 1924), p. 16; Henry W. Bragdon, *Woodrow Wilson: The Academic Years* (Cambridge, Mass., 1967), p. 5.

[51] "A Sinless Sin," *North Carolina Presbyterian,* July 19, 1876.

[52] Samuel L. Morris, *An Autobiography* (Richmond, Va., 1932), p. 53.

word, either a theologian or a scholar, although his contemporaries frequently used the latter term to describe him.[53] He never produced a scholarly work of note and often shied away from discussing complex theological issues.[54] His reading interests were not restricted to theology, ranging from literature to politics and science.[55] He felt disdain for pedantry and the mere accumulation of information. Woodrow Wilson was fond of quoting his father's insistence that "the mind is not a prolix gut to be stuffed."[56]

His forte was rhetoric, written and spoken, and his primary skill was as a teacher of preaching.[57] He described the homiletical office as "an institution ordained of *God*" and conceived of it in exalted, powerful, even masculine terms. The pulpit, he declared in his inaugural address as professor at Columbia, "has, under the directing hand of God, made all Protestant countries what they are. It has raised all civilisation to the position it now occupies." He longed for the day when the pulpits of the world would be occupied by " 'men of God' in the highest sense; of zeal, apostolic; of intelligence, the most masculine, transfused with a love and faith the most energetic and vital; fountains of light; centres of power; men whose speech, fired from heaven, shall be felt to be genuine, true, humane, suggestive, pregnant, creative of all good."[58] He also saw preaching in a highly personalized way, for he argued that "there is a sense in which the preacher preaches *himself*." He criticized any demonstration of "ministerial arrogance," but for the preacher truly to communicate the gospel, he must recognize that "it is not Christ *only* that he preaches, but Christ *in him*; and this gives to his preaching a vital energy which the dead letter of a book—even though that book be the Bible—does not and cannot possess."[59]

Self-assured, self-confident, recognized as one of the great leaders

[53] See, for example, Alfred Nevin (ed.), *Encyclopedia of the Presbyterian Church in the United States of America: Including the Northern and Southern Assemblies* (Philadelphia, 1884), p. 1,018.

[54] See JRW's article, "Presbyterianism and Education," *Presbyterian Quarterly*, III (1889), 321-33. The only article he published which bordered on a scholarly theological argument was "The Doctrine of Hell," *Southern Presbyterian Review*, XXIX (1878), 459-74. This was, however, originally a sermon or series of sermons delivered in Wilmington. Wilmington, N. C., *Morning Star*, Feb. 10, 17, 1878; Wilmington, N. C., *Daily Review*, Jan. 28, Feb. 11, 1878.

[55] An indication of his broad reading interests is contained in his article, "The Life of Joseph Addison Alexander," *Southern Presbyterian Review*, XXI (1870), 389-410.

[56] "The Young People and the Church," Oct. 13, 1904, *PWW*, XV, 513.

[57] For an extended discussion of JRW as a rhetoretician, see Swabb, "The Rhetorical Theory of Rev. Joseph Ruggles Wilson, D.D."

[58] "Inauguration of the Rev. Dr. Wilson," *Southern Presbyterian Review*, XXII (1871), 417, 424, 427.

[59] "In What Sense are Preachers to Preach Themselves," *Southern Presbyterian Review*, XXV (1874), 350, 351, 355.

and preachers of the church, Wilson was soon shattered by his devastating experience at Columbia. In February 1871, he began his service as stated supply in the First Presbyterian Church,[60] but after only a year and a half, a paper was presented to the session in October 1872, urging selection of a full-time minister. Wilson resigned in July 1873 "to relieve the Session of all embarrassment."[61] When the seminary reconvened in the fall of 1873, Wilson and John B. Adger led a movement in the faculty to institute compulsory Sunday chapel services at the seminary at 11 A.M., in obvious conflict with the services at the First Presbyterian Church.

Wilson's motivation was, no doubt, partially personal pique at the loss of a necessary source of income, but Adger insisted later that the initiative for these services had come in September from the students, who later changed their minds.[62] The proposal was stymied by a tie vote in the faculty, George Howe and William S. Plumer vetoing the idea because it would compete with the services at the First Presbyterian Church. In November, James Woodrow returned from Europe, sided with Wilson and Adger, and the services were instituted in January. Whether intentional or accidental, the timing was unfortunate because the services were initiated one week after the installation of the new minister of the First Presbyterian Church, John H. Bryson. The students rose up in anger, protesting "this as an interference with their personal liberty of worshiping where they chose."[63] Eventually, thirteen students were suspended for refusing to attend the services in the chapel.

The conflict raged throughout the spring, pitting Wilson, Woodrow, and Adger against Plumer and to a lesser extent Howe. The board met and supported the faculty's action, but the people of First Church and other churches in Charleston Presbytery were furious. Wilson attempted to run for commissioner to the General Assembly but could only muster three votes.[64] The chairman of the Board of Trustees, John O. Lindsay, was the only one who voted against the faculty's action,

[60] Fitz Hugh McMaster, *History of the First Presbyterian Church and Its Churchyard* (n.p., n.d.), p. 3. The pulpit became vacant in January 1871, upon the resignation of the regular minister, William Ellison Boggs.

[61] "A Brief History of the First Presbyterian Church, Columbia, South Carolina," p. 2.

[62] The following account of this fracas is based on John B. Adger's article, "A Card," published in *North Carolina Presbyterian*, July 22, 1874; *Southern Presbyterian*, July 16, 1874; and *Christian Observer*, July 22, 1874; and the General Assembly debate, especially William S. Plumer's speech, all covered in *Southern Presbyterian*, June 11 and 18, 1874; *Christian Observer*, June 3, 1874; and *North Carolina Presbyterian*, June 17 and 24, 1874. Also valuable are Louis C. La Motte, *Colored Light: The Story of the Influence of Columbia Theological Seminary, 1828-1936* (Richmond, Va., 1937), pp. 146-47, and Morris, *An Autobiography*, p. 54.

[63] *Ibid.*   [64] *Christian Observer*, June 3, 1874.

and when the report on theological seminaries came before the General Assembly, he moved to make the chapel services voluntary. "The meanest negro in Columbia can choose the place where he will worship God on the Sabbath day," he protested, "a privilege that is denied to the theological students, some of whom are licensed preachers of the gospel."[65]

For three days, the issue was angrily debated, interrupted only by ice cream, meals, sleep, docketed business, and the customary worship services. On the third day, Wilson was permitted to speak by a special vote of the Assembly. He described Plumer's account of the debates in the faculty as "a congeries of half truths" and vehemently defended his own motives and actions. "Let them bandy my name about," he cried. "I know, I know, I know, (with more and more emphasis,) that I have done right, and by that right I will stand to the end. . . . If you do not like the way in which we have managed the seminary, say so, and we will no longer trouble you." In reporting the debate, the *Christian Observer* noted: "Dr. Wilson is not a very effective debater. He had a great opportunity, but the debate resumed its course after his speech."[66]

The issue primarily involved the faculty's wisdom, morality, and authority in compelling the students to attend the chapel services. Wilson fused the issues of authority and morality, personalized them, and became absolutely intransigent. The Assembly voted to express its confidence in the faculty but recommended that attendance at the services be made voluntary. The vote was extremely close, 60 to 53,[67] and immediately after the tally was announced, Wilson submitted his resignation to the Assembly. Adger sent word later that he too was resigning. Wilson explained that he had submitted his resignation earlier to the board, which refused it because it cited no reasons. Now, however, he said, the Assembly had given him "light and guidance." Its action was an implied censure, and "if you refuse my resignation, you send me back to Columbia with the responsibility, but without the power to fulfill it, a position which no sane man will undertake. It is impossible for me to do it."[68] When some commissioners still protested against his resignation, he cited a schism in the faculty that made cooperation impossible and a desire to return to pastoral duties.[69] Woodrow Wilson later commented that his father "left Columbia Seminary . . . because the Gen[eral]. Assembly sustained the self-will of the students against

[65] *Ibid*.

[66] *Ibid*. Parenthetical comment is part of the text. See also the coverage of JRW's speech in the *North Carolina Presbyterian*, June 17, 1874, and the *Southern Presbyterian,* June 18, 1874.

[67] *Minutes* (1874), pp. 493-94.   [68] *Christian Observer*, June 3, 1874.

[69] *Ibid*.

the discipline of the faculty, and not because he was at all dissatisfied with his work."[70]

The controversy continued unabated for some months after the Assembly meeting,[71] and it was in fact one round in the long struggle for control of Columbia Theological Seminary.[72] Its immediate impact on the seminary was devastating. Enrollment shrank practically in half; three men refused to accept Wilson's vacant chair; and the seminary was finally forced to close temporarily in 1880 because of financial difficulties.[73]

Immediately after his defeat, Wilson accepted the call of the First Presbyterian Church of Wilmington, North Carolina, a lucrative pastorate paying $4,000 per year. The family tried to put a brave face on the move,[74] but the congregation of 169 communicants was substantially smaller than his Augusta charge, and the rough life of this seaport town was not congenial to Wilson's intellectual and social tastes.[75] His self-confidence was thoroughly shaken and his self-esteem badly battered. Throughout his long ministry in Wilmington, he suffered frequently from periods of depression and feelings of inferiority. His wife told Woodrow in 1876, "Your father is very blue this week. I don't think he will ever be quite happy here. I knew beforehand that he would not."[76] Wilson called solitude his "principal disease" and confessed to his son, "My life might have been greatly stronger by being greatly happier. But, mistakenly, I have nearly always chosen the dark sides of probabilities at which to look. It will not do. It is irrational. It

[70] WW to ELA, Oct. 12, 1884, *PWW*, III, 349.

[71] See, for example, *North Carolina Presbyterian,* July 8, 1874; *Christian Observer*, June 10, July 15, Aug. 5 and 12, and Oct. 7, 1874; *Southern Presbyterian*, June 11 and 25, and Oct. 1, 1874.

[72] The seminary had been controlled by the General Assembly since 1863. In 1881, control was restored to the Synods of South Carolina, Georgia, and Alabama, with the Synods of South Georgia and Florida cooperating and the General Assembly retaining the right of review. W.A. Alexander and G. F. Nicolassen, *A Digest of the Acts and Proceedings of the General Assembly of the Presbyterian Church in the United States* (Richmond, Va., 1911), pp. 125, 142, 309.

[73] Morris, *An Autobiography*, p. 54; *Christian Observer*, Aug. 19 and Oct. 7, 1874; F. D. Jones and W. H. Mills, eds., *History of the Presbyterian Church in South Carolina Since 1850* (Columbia, S. C., 1926), pp. 421-25.

The bitter outcome had an ironic twist for JRW. Plumer, whose academic competence as professor of theology had been in dispute, resigned his chair in theology in 1875, and he assumed JRW's old chair in pastoral theology. John Lafayette Girardeau, who had resigned from the Columbia Board of Trustees in protest over the 1874 General Assembly action, took Plumer's place as professor of theology. See Ernest Trice Thompson, *Presbyterians in the South*. 3 vols. (Richmond, 1963-73), II, 369-70.

[74] JWW to WW, May 20, 1874, *PWW*, I, 50; May 26, 1874, *ibid.*, VI, 694-95.

[75] *Minutes* (1874), p. 645; JWW to WW, April 11, 1877, *PWW*, I, 257-58; Dec. 31, 1884, *ibid.*, III, 574-75; and WW to ELA, Oct. 12, 1884, *ibid.*, 349-50.

[76] JWW to WW, Dec. 21, 1876, *ibid.*, I, 235.

is sinful, even."[77] He further confided that his life had been "too-much one of self-depreciations, and I deeply regret that it has been so. Both my usefulness and my happiness would have been furthered and augmented by an opposite course of feeling."[78]

Wilson's sermons in Wilmington reveal the pervasive influence of the covenant theology interacting with his own struggle to understand what had happened to himself and southern society. His sermons repeatedly focused on the problem of reconciling the covenant theology's idea of a God who governed the world through unlimited power and the fact of human suffering and perversity. "God is not merely the affectionate head of a *family*," he argued; "he is also and principally, the sovereign head of a *government*; a government not of arbitrary, although of absolute, will."[79] Despite God's power, Wilson admitted, a person does not feel secure, "so constant are the assaults of Sin, so tremendous, are, occasionally, the onsets of Satan."[80]

Life often seems capricious, he confessed to his congregation, and he described phenomena with which they as Southerners were all familiar—sickness, death, families scattered, fortunes destroyed, honors and reputations lost. "The pendulum of *every* clock of human life is liable to swing away—or to stop altogether—when least looked for—so that what was all right when 12 o'clock rang its bell has gone all wrong before the stroke of one. What, then, it may be asked, *is life worth*, taken at this gloomy rate [?]"[81] The value of life, he countered, was only established by faith in God who provides happiness to those who trust in him. "But now the question arises," he realized,

> does *God* make happy those who trust in him? I confess that it does not always *look* as if he did. It must be acknowledged that he leaves many of his trusters poor and forlorn, tossed and torn; and that there is not one of them, however favored in a worldly point of view, who does not have reason, daily, to shed tears of more or less racking grief, or utter groans of more or less remorseful sorrow. . . . Were

[77] JRW to WW, July 7, 1877, and Jan. 27, 1880, *ibid.*, pp. 278, 596-97.

[78] JRW to WW, Oct. 21, 1882, *ibid.*, II, 146. For other examples of JRW's feelings of depression and inferiority, see JRW to WW, Jan. 25, 1878, and April 10 and Nov. 19, 1879, *ibid.*, I, 346, 476, 585-86; and JWW to WW, June 5, 1880, *ibid.*, p. 659.

[79] "The Doctrine of Hell," p. 467.

[80] "The Heavenly Farmer," Matthew 3:12, February 5, 1882 (Wilson Papers, Library of Congress). All further references to this collection of seventeen manuscript sermons will be hereinafter cited as WP, DLC. The date assigned to unpublished sermons is the earliest date of delivery listed by JRW.

[81] Sermon on Phillippians 2:23, Dec. [?], 1883 (Historical Foundation, Montreat, N. C.). Further references to this collection of nine complete and five incomplete sermons will be hereinafter cited as HF, NC.

there no other answer to such a question, might we not rest the whole matter on this: *He has said so:* and does He not *know*?[82]

Wilson's resolution of this dilemma involved more than merely falling back on God's decrees and omnipotence. His Wilmington sermons increasingly focused on a God of love and grace, who suffered for people and offered them forgiveness from sin and release from death.

He ruled out an arbitrary God, insisting that God does not afflict people "because he likes to do so,"[83] and he rejected a God who merely issued laws and demanded obedience. "God has resolved not to be *forever misunderstood*," he proclaimed, "and, accordingly places Himself in an altogether new light . . . the soft, the subduing, the satisfying light of the *gospel*, the beamings of his reconciled face. . . . His throne has been transformed from smoking Sinai to smiling Sion; and the banners that wave before Him are not those of conquering battle but of victorious beneficence."[84] God rid the world of sin's power, according to Wilson, "by introducing a new law into the administration of his government—the amazing law of substitution,"[85] Jesus Christ for human sins. When God thus considers people, his best thoughts are thoughts of forgiveness, and Wilson offered his congregation an eloquent portrayal of God's sacrifice: *"the blessed Jesus:* that sum and substance of God's completed thoughtfulness for them who hurt Him: —there it is in all its fairness! God's thoughts are thus His best thoughts of pardon and peace."[86]

Wilson's religion became, as he put it, "essentially an affair of the heart," and God became the "loving authority." Sin was not merely disobeying a law, it was rejecting both God's love and his authority. "You may be as sure of His everlasting favor," Wilson comforted his congregation, "as He is of your place in His unforgetting memory."[87] And yet, Wilson's new emphasis on God's grace and the transformation of the individual did not mean a quiescent piety, for he constantly stressed the connection between faith and works. "The *inactive* [Christia]n is the doubting [Christia]n," he asserted, and added with perhaps a thought to himself, "The listless believer is the depressed and gloomy believer."[88] The Christian's mission in the world was there-

[82] Sermon on Psalm 118:8, 9, Oct. [?], 1881 (HF, NC); later published as "Trust in the Lord," *Southern Presbyterian Pulpit: A Collection of Sermons by Ministers of the Southern Presbyterian Church* (Richmond, Va., 1896), pp. 364-73, esp. pp. 370-71.

[83] Sermon on Ecclesiastes 7:13, Nov. [?] 16, 1884 (WP, DLC).

[84] Sermon on I John 4:19, Jan. [?], 1898 (HF, NC).

[85] "The Doctrine of Hell," p. 469.

[86] Sermon on Psalm 40:17, March 1, 1885 (WP, DLC).

[87] Sermon on Malachi 3:17, Nov. 7, 1880 (WP, DLC).

[88] Sermon on Genesis 47:8, sometime during 1878 (HF, NC).

fore clear: "Sow yourselves . . . in its every field of influence. Knead yourselves into its every possible loaf of soul-nourishing bread. Be vitalizing wheat, indeed, in all that the word implies."[89] He cautioned that such a calling was not easy. "It is often uphill. It is through an enemy's country. It is a running fight all along."[90] And yet individuals could be assured of success if they had "character" and received the blessing of God.[91]

It was one thing for Wilson to preach a gospel of love, forgiveness, and trust which called Christians to immersion in the affairs of this world and assured them success. It was quite another for him to feel the impact of that message in his own life. His feelings of inferiority and depression persisted, despite the fact that his years in Wilmington saw little diminution of his prestige within the church, and new responsibilities were constantly given to him.

On June 21, 1876, he became editor of one of the southern church's most influential newspapers, the Wilmington *North Carolina Presbyterian*, and its columns gave him an opportunity to vent his opinions on a wide range of questions. Shortly after the critical election of 1876, he urged the North not to be punitive toward the South and suggested to his readers that God was perhaps punishing the South in order to purify her and make her better.[92] He supported closer relations with the northern Presbyterian church but denounced the idea of union as something "no one wants."[93] He opposed Negro suffrage, defended the right of religious newspapers to be controversial, scorned the idea of woman preachers, and repeatedly returned to one of his favorite topics—the low salaries of ministers and the parsimonious giving of church members.[94] Yet Wilson found this position of influence a burden and resigned with the March 14, 1877 issue. "I am at last out of that editorial entanglement—much to my joy as you may imagine," he wrote Woodrow, and he explained to his readers that he had accepted the position only "as a temporary measure to preserve the paper from serious embarrassment and certain loss."[95]

Finally, in 1879, the southern church gave Wilson its highest recognition—the office of Moderator of the General Assembly. His mod-

[89] Sermon on Matthew 3:12, Feb. 5, 1882 (WP, DLC).

[90] Sermon on Mark 14:50, n.d. (WP, DLC).

[91] See the reports of sermons and public lectures on success and enjoyment printed in Wilmington, N. C., *Morning Star*, Dec. 16, 1874, Dec. 21, 1875, and April 11, 1883; Wilmington, N. C., *Daily Review*, March 9, 1880; and the *North Carolina Presbyterian*, May 3, 10, 1876.

[92] *North Carolina Presbyterian*, Nov. 29, 1876 and Feb. 28, 1877. See also a report of his sermon on the law of retaliation, printed in the Wilmington *Morning Star*, Feb. 20, 1877.

[93] *North Carolina Presbyterian*, June 21 and Aug. 16, 1876.

[94] *Ibid.*, July 5, Sept. 20, Oct. 11, Nov. 1 and Nov. 15, 1876; Jan. 3, 10, and 17, 1877.

[95] JRW to WW, March 15, 1877, *PWW*, I, 252; *North Carolina Presbyterian*, March 14, 1877.

eratorial sermon, which recalled the church to its historic faith, was hailed as "an admirable discourse in every way" and "a masterpiece of thought and expression."[96] His election brought jubilation from his wife. "Well—now we ought to be satisfied, I think," she wrote to Woodrow, "for the Church has now conferred upon your father *every honor* in her gift."[97] Wilson told the General Assembly that he would count his election "not as the highest honor merely of my life, but as the sweetest joy."[98] The Louisville *Courier-Journal* commended the way in which he presided, stating that "his rulings were prompt, and were always decided in his favor, and the sting was taken from them by that inexhaustible fund of rich humor which was cropping out on all proper occasions."[99]

In addition to the honor of the moderatorship, Wilson was regularly called upon to participate in limited ecumenical activities as one of the southern Presbyterian Church's representatives. In 1876, he was elected a delegate to the General Council of the Alliance of the Reformed Churches Holding the Presbyterian System and reelected in 1880 and 1884. He took part in only the 1880 proceedings, in Philadelphia, where he delivered a paper, "Evangelists and Evangelistic Work." The criterion for evaluating evangelistic work, he argued, was success. "That church, . . . which has no success in proclaiming God's saving grace, ought to have no place among the acknowledged representatives of Christianity; whilst the Church which publishes this grace the most effectually, ought to be thought of as occupying the foremost place of all." He insisted on the need for trained evangelists, commissioned by the church, to complement the role of the parish minister and compete with lay evangelists.[100]

At this meeting, Wilson was appointed to the important Committee on the Consensus of the Reformed Confessions, and though he contributed to its work, he did not go to Belfast in 1884 to participate in its presentation.[101] Mixing in high ecclesiastical circles did not satisfy him, for he wrote to Woodrow, "The Council . . . is a great bore, and

[96] The text of Wilson's sermon is published in the *North Carolina Presbyterian*, May 21, 1880; see the *Southern Presbyterian*, May 27, 1880, and the Wilmington *Morning Star*, May 24, 1880, for comments on it. The Moderator was elected to a one-year term. His chief reponsibility was presiding over the General Assembly.

[97] JWW to WW, May 23, 1879, *PWW*, I, 484.

[98] *North Carolina Presbyterian*, June 4, 1879.

[99] Quoted in the Wilmington *Morning Star*, May 30, 1879.

[100] "Evangelists and Evangelistic Work," *Report of Proceedings of the Second General Council of the Presbyterian Alliance* . . ., John B. Dales and R. M. Patterson, eds. (Philadelphia, 1880), pp. 447-51. Alarm over lay evangelists was one of Wilson's continuing concerns. See the *North Carolina Presbyterian*, Nov. 22, 1876, and Jan. 31 and Feb. 7 and 14, 1877.

[101] *Minutes and Proceedings of the Third General Council* . . ., George D. Mathews, ed. (Belfast, 1884), pp. 31-36; Appendix, pp. 1-8.

it gives literally no chance for conspicuousness—for all its proceedings are cut & dried, and its debators chosen beforehand."[102] His son, however, sensed the real reasons for his father's decision. "He has always underestimated his own abilities in a most provoking manner," Woodrow Wilson wrote to his fiancée, "and cannot yet be convinced that his services in the Council would be of any value."[103]

Despite his reservations, Wilson did accept a moderate ecumenism and urged cooperation and communication between denominations. "Sectarian wrangling is a curse to the Church," he declared in the *North Carolina Presbyterian*, and he further condemned the "detestable practice of luring weak members of other denominations."[104] Having urged closer relations with the northern Presbyterian Church, Wilson served as chairman of the conference committee of the northern and southern churches which met during 1888-1889. "We accomplished nothing, or nearly nothing," Wilson reported after a meeting in New York, "and are to meet again, on the 17th of April at Atlanta, in order to emphasize the non-doing[.]"[105] His pessimistic assessment was borne out in the final report, which made innocuous recommendations for reducing friction in common enterprises in the United States and abroad. The committee also failed to agree on the sensitive question of the evangelization of blacks and their place within the two denominations.[106] Wilson further served as a delegate to confer with the Reformed Church in America, while on the local level his congregations frequently united with Methodists, Baptists, and Lutherans in worship services.[107]

Prominence and prestige in Wilmington did not make Wilson happy, and his letters to his son reveal his deep dissatisfaction with his ministry there. He enjoyed preaching but found visiting his parishioners a burden. "They want a gad-about gossip," he complained to Woodrow.[108] The family found the city dull and the church cold,[109] but the most persistent source of irritation was the session's failure to pay Wil-

---

[102] JRW to WW, April 22, 1884, *PWW*, III, 143.

[103] WW to ELA, April 13, 1884, *ibid.*, p. 127.

[104] *North Carolina Presbyterian*, Nov. 1 and Aug. 9, 1876.

[105] JRW to WW, Jan. 5, 1889, *PWW*, VI, 39.

[106] See *Minutes* (1889), pp. 650-55, and *Minutes of the General Assembly of the Presbyterian Church in the United States of America* . . . (Philadelphia, 1889), pp. 69-74.

[107] See Wilson's speech in 1872 to the General Synod of the Reformed Church in America, printed in *A Letter by the Rev. S. S. Laws, LL.D., to the Synod of Missouri (O.S.)* . . . (New York, second edition, 1873), pp. 95-97. For his local ecumenism, see the Augusta *Chronicle & Sentinel*, Jan. 29, 1860; Augusta *Daily Constitutionalist*, Nov. 28, 30, 1860; and Wilmington *Morning Star*, Sept. 13, 1874 and Dec. 2, 1877.

[108] JRW to WW, Oct. 21, 1882, *PWW*, II, 147.

[109] JWW to WW, April 11 and June 6, 1877, *ibid.*, I, 257, 272-73.

son on a regular basis. "The Church treasury here is so far in arrears that I am becoming embarrassed pecuniarily," Wilson grumbled in 1879. His wife also fretted, "Your father seems to have an utter distaste for the whole affair—and would leave them if he could."[110] The session fell as much as three months behind, and when Wilson decided to resign in 1885, the news of his treatment by the session left a divided church in his wake.[111] Recurring ill health for both Wilson and his wife only reinforced his feelings of depression, and during his later years in Wilmington he dreamed of some avenue of escape. Bemoaning his lack of influence in trying to secure Woodrow a teaching position in the South, he even suggested to his son that they start their own college. His dream was that they could both teach at the same institution, but, he said, "it is too good to think about."[112]

Finally, when a teaching position opened up at the struggling theological school of the Southwestern Presbyterian University in Clarksville, Tennessee, Wilson jumped at the chance to return to the classroom. Woodrow Wilson hailed the change in occupation, writing to his fiancée that his father "was not *meant* for a pastor—despite the testimony of his splendid pulpit powers,—but he is of the stuff of which the greatest teachers are made."[113] Wilson did feel some apprehension about his new duties, and he solicited Woodrow's help in the preparation of his inaugural address.[114] In this speech, Wilson called for a theology which was biblical, Calvinistic, conservative, and yet progressive, and suggested that theological education be broadened to include not only those who chose the ministry as a profession but also those who chose other occupations as well.[115]

The move to Clarksville was something less than felicitous. Wilson was plagued by ill health, and his wife died in 1888; two years later, his daughter Marion died.[116] Wilson was not stimulated by his teaching responsibilities and complained about "the heavy dullness of the life" he was compelled to lead. His students were poor, and he described his work as "ding-donging theology and Greek exegesis into dull brains—

---

[110] JRW to WW, Feb. 19, 1879, *ibid.*, p. 458; JWW to WW, Feb. 4, 1879, *ibid.*, p. 452.

[111] JRW to WW, Dec. 17, 1884, *ibid.*, III, 549; March 2, 1885, *ibid.*, IV, 323.

[112] JRW to WW, Nov. 6, 1883, *ibid.*, II, 520; March 10 and May 6, 1884, *ibid.*, III, 73-74, 166.

[113] WW to ELA, Oct. 12, 1884, *ibid.*, pp. 349-50.

[114] JRW to WW, Jan. 15, 1885, and Dec. 17, 1884, *ibid.*, pp. 613, 549.

[115] *Inaugural Address Delivered Before the Board of Directors of the S.W.P. University . . .* (Clarksville, Tenn., 1886). Incidentally, Wilson's near-unanimous approval as Professor of Didactic, Polemic, and Historical Theology by the Southwestern Board was opposed only by John H. Bryson, Wilson's successor at the First Presbyterian Church in Columbia, S. C. See JRW to WW, Oct. 9, 1884, *PWW*, III, 343-44, n. 2.

[116] JRW to WW, June 28, 1888, *ibid.*, V, 743; Aug. 16, 1890, *ibid.*, VI, 690.

and sighing over the poor prospects of the church's oncoming ministry." The church, he commented, was "a miracle of endurance, with such ministers of her mysteries as she is compelled to put up with."[117] The enrollment was erratic but usually low, due to competition from Union and Columbia Seminaries, and later the new Louisville Seminary. In 1890, Wilson pronounced it "a farce" to continue the theological school at Southwestern and felt embarrassed at drawing a salary for so few students.[118] He interrupted his teaching with an occasional sermon or lecture, and in one address, later published as "Presbyterianism and Education," he attempted "to illustrate the proposition that Presbyterianism is precisely such a leading representative of the church as to be, in all its make-up, an educational power than which there is none mightier."[119]

His poor health, grief, loneliness, and discouragement with his teaching brought on frequent bouts of depression. He lived, he told Woodrow, in the "cellar" and "sub-cellars" of his mind and confessed that teaching had become a tax upon his nerves, "especially as stupidity is the pupil." He was faintly jealous when Woodrow received an LL.D. from Wake Forest College and irritated when he was beaten out for the chancellorship of the University of Georgia.[120] In 1893, he finally retired from Southwestern.

Throughout his long ministry, Wilson tenaciously held on to his position of prominence and prestige—the Stated Clerkship of the General Assembly. He successfully warded off two attempts, in 1877 and 1887, to elect Stated Clerks more often, but gradually he found his duties more onerous and burdensome. "How glad I shall be to get rid of the entire concern!"[121] he told Woodrow in 1887, and he became increasingly exasperated with church affairs. During James Woodrow's long fight over his teaching of evolution at Columbia Seminary, Wilson exclaimed, "What asses Presbyterians are capable of becoming—whose ears extend to all the earth!"[122] He bemoaned "the fearful

[117] JRW to WW, Dec. 5, 1889, *ibid.*, p. 450; Jan. 12, 1887, *ibid.*, v, 431; Jan. 13, 1890, *ibid.*, VI, 475.

[118] JRW to WW, March 5, 1888, *ibid.*, v, 706-707; Sept. 15, 18?0 and Oct. 25, 1890, *ibid.*, VII, 10-11, 52-54. JRW temporarily fought off an attempt by the Synod of Kentucky to solicit support of the Louisville Theological Seminary from neighboring synods. See JRW to WW, Nov. 7, 1891, *ibid.*, pp. 322-24, esp. n. 2.

[119] "Presbyterianism and Education," p. 322. See JRW to WW, Oct. 24, 1887, *ibid.*, v, 621.

[120] JRW to WW, June 11, 1887, *ibid.*, v, 516; Oct. 10, 1888, *ibid.*, VI, 14. William Ellison Boggs, Wilson's predecessor at the First Presbyterian Church in Columbia, S. C., was chosen Chancellor.

[121] JRW to WW, April 29, 1887, *ibid.*, v, 500. See also JWW to WW, Oct. 26 and Nov. 16, 1877, *ibid.*, I, 305-306, 320.

[122] JRW to WW, Oct. 25, 1890, *ibid.*, VII, 54.

monotonies of Gen. Ass. commonplace," and when the northern and southern churches met for a centennial celebration in Philadelphia, he used the opportunity to visit Woodrow and his family, rather than "listening to dreary gush-voicings in the Academy of Music."[123] In 1898, he finally resigned as Stated Clerk, and the Assembly recorded its "appreciation of his services, expressing the thanks of the church to her loyal servant, and invoking upon him during all the remaining years of his life the blessing of Almighty God."[124]

During his retirement, Wilson led an itinerant life, residing in Columbia, South Carolina, Richmond, Virginia, and Princeton, New Jersey, with summers in Saratoga, New York. He preached occasionally and was invited to deliver the seventy-fifth anniversary sermon by his old Wilmington congregation, which seemingly remembered him more warmly in his absence than his presence. "The people did every thing except *sleep* with me!" he wrote Woodrow.[125] As a widower, he established warm friendships with a number of women, but especially the widow Elizabeth Bartlett Grannis, editor of the New York *Church Union* for twenty-three years and active in the movement for the sterilization of habitual criminals and mental defectives. He stayed with her frequently in New York, where he enjoyed her "loving ministries."[126] Woodrow was initially noncommittal about his father's relationship with Mrs. Grannis, but as it continued he found her highly objectionable. She "is about as undesirable a companion as one could find in the ranks of chaste women,—as demoralizing as anyone could well be to one's manliness and self-respect,"[127] he exploded in a letter to his wife.

Wilson's deteriorating health ultimately necessitated his moving to Princeton in the spring of 1901 to live with his son and family until his death. The arrival of the infirm father produced a decided change in the Wilson family life, for Woodrow spent his evenings reading to his father rather than with the whole family.[128] The white-haired grand-

[123] JRW to WW, May 25, 1892, *ibid.*, p. 636; Oct. 24, 1887, *ibid.*, v, 620.

[124] *Minutes* (1898), p. 226.

[125] JRW to WW, Dec. 18, 1892, *PWW*, viii, 59. His sermon was published as "Yesterday, To-Day and Forever," *Memorial of the First Presbyterian Church, Wilmington, N. C.* (Richmond, Va., 1893), pp. 68-76.

[126] JRW to WW, July 25, 1889, *PWW*, vi, 358, n.1; Sept. 2, 1891, *ibid.*, vii, 285. JRW did not remember her in his will, but he did leave bequests of $250 each to two other women friends, Belle R. Robinson of Wilmington, N. C., and Hattie T. Tennent of Spartanburg, S. C. His entire estate amounted to $19,412.50, most of which was in cash. He stipulated that it should be divided evenly between Woodrow, Annie, and Joseph R. Wilson, Jr. The will, dated Sept. 11, 1902, is in WP, DLC.

[127] WW to EAW, Feb. 1, 1895, *ibid.*, ix, 149.

[128] "Recollections of Mary Hoyt" (R.S. Baker Coll., DLC).

father frightened the Wilson girls with his sharp tongue, and when his son was elevated to the presidency of Princeton University in 1902, he drew his granddaughters into his room and gravely admonished them, "Your father is a very great man."[129]

On January 21, 1903, Wilson died in his son's home and was carried south and buried next to his wife in what they had always hoped would be their home—Columbia, South Carolina. Woodrow provided the epitaph:

> Pastor, teacher, ecclesiastical leader[.] For thirty four years Stated Clerk of the General Assembly of the Presbyterian Church of the United States. Steadfast, brilliant, devoted, loving and beloved. A master of serious eloquence, a thinker of singular power and penetration, a thoughtful student of life and God's purpose, a lover and servant of his fellow men, a man of God.[130]

Newspapers noted his death with eulogies on his career. The Columbia, South Carolina, *State* hailed him as one of the founders of the southern Presbyterian Church, and the *Presbyterian Standard* praised his long service as Stated Clerk: "He was the soul of wit, an inveterate punster, the best company in the world at dinner, and he made even a Stated Clerkship a source of joy. He could kill an unwise overture by the way he would read it and then glare at the Assembly as if lost in wonder that any such thing had ever been thought of. His pleasantries brought the ripples of laughter that are so often a safety valve in strenuous times. And yet there was no poison in his shafts of wit." The Presbytery of Nashville described him as a man of "strong intellect, which placed him in the front rank with the great ministers of the church."[131]

The question of Joseph Ruggles Wilson's influence on his son Woodrow should be clarified by an analysis of the father's ministry and career. Like so many of his Gilded Age contemporaries, both in the pulpit and the pew, Wilson's father subscribed to the "gospel of wealth"—a nineteenth century version of the old deuteronomic formula that piety and personal prosperity were inextricably linked. Confronted with the travail of southern defeat in the Civil War and his depression over his own fortunes within the church, Wilson's father was

---

[129] R. S. Baker, Memorandum of an interview with Mrs. William G. MacAdoo and Mrs. Francis B. Sayre, May 30, 1926, *ibid.*

[130] Swabb, "Rhetorical Theory of Rev. Joseph Ruggles Wilson," pp. 93-94.

[131] Columbia, S. C., *State*, Jan. 24, 1903, printed in *PWW*, XIV, 331-33; *Minutes of the Presbytery of Nashville* (McMinnville, Tenn., 1903), pp. 38-39; *Presbyterian Standard*, XLIV (Feb. 11, 1903), 16.

forced to deal with suffering in much more immediate terms than his northern counterparts.[132]

Some interpreters have portrayed Wilson's father as a strong, self-assertive, and self-assured man who dominated his son and produced within Woodrow repressed feelings of hostility.[133] They have failed to appreciate the destructive effect of the father's experience at Columbia Theological Seminary, his subsequent discouragement and bouts with depression, and his dependence on Woodrow for strength, encouragement, love, and even identity.

By mid-career, Joseph Wilson was in some ways a broken man, struggling to overcome his feelings of inferiority, trying to reconcile a God of love with the frustration of his ambition for success and prominence within the church. Erik Erikson has defined this experience as the crisis of integrity—a confrontation which frequently occurs during the height of an individual's professional career. Erikson suggests that this crisis resolves itself either in terms of a more mature emotional integration or manifests itself in individual disgust and despair. "Such a despair," Erikson writes, "is often hidden behind a show of disgust, a misanthropy, or a chronic contemptuous displeasure with particular institutions and particular people—a disgust and a displeasure which, *where not allied with the vision of a superior life*, only signify the individual's contempt of himself."[134]

Viewed in these terms, Joseph Wilson's crisis of integrity resolved itself in two ways, neither one of which was wholly successful. The first was his theological struggle in Wilmington to understand and interpret a God of love within the context of human suffering, and it is here that what Erikson calls "the vision of a superior life" had its most conspicuous and complete expression. The elder Wilson's depression cannot be underestimated or ignored, but the resources of his own faith helped him to come to terms with his experience and make a partial adjustment to it. The second way in which he attempted to deal with his personal failure was by seeing in his son the opportunity to achieve the success that he had sought in vain. Throughout Woodrow Wilson's late adolescence and early manhood, Joseph Wilson increasingly began to identify with his son, lavishly showering affection on him,

[132] See Paul A. Carter, *The Spiritual Crisis of the Gilded Age* (DeKalb, Ill., 1971), pp. 85-107, 133-53; William G. McLoughlin, *The Meaning of Henry Ward Beecher: An Essay on the Shifting Values of Mid-Victorian America, 1840-1870* (New York, 1970), pp. 98-118.

[133] See Sigmund Freud and William C. Bullitt, *Thomas Woodrow Wilson: A Psychological Study* (Boston, 1967); Alexander L. and Juliette L. George, *Woodrow Wilson and Colonel House, A Personality Study* (New York, 1956).

[134] Erik H. Erikson, *Identity: Youth and Crisis* (New York, 1968), pp. 91-141, especially pp. 139-41. Italics mine.

expressing boundless confidence in his abilities, and advising him to avoid the pitfalls which had plagued his career in the church.

Freudian interpreters have customarily seen identity formation as a process of the child absorbing the goals, values, and assumptions of a parent, and while Woodrow Wilson unquestionably adopted many of his father's ideas of the world, a reverse process also took place. This involved the regression of Joseph Wilson into a subordinate position in the father-son relationship, fulfilling his ego and preserving his identity through the career of his son.[135]

The disastrous experience at Columbia chastened Wilson's father, and when he later spoke of success and ambition, he did so in terms that were not only eloquent but prophetic of his own life and his son's:

> So the ambitious man trusts to the people to lift him into the eminence of position. They raise him as high as he wished, higher even than once he had dreamed. They lavish upon him their honors and their stations. They place him at the very top. He is grateful; but, as he quaffs the bowl of their laudations, he by-and-by becomes conscious of a want that he had fondly hoped would also be met in the wine-taste of his gratified desires. Elevation has not made him happy; it has only made him cold and lonely, and envied—maybe hated—by some. The people had not that to give which comes exclusively from a satisfied mind, a mind restful, as on a rock of security; and, this being absent, all the rest resembles ashes. He evidently needs to go to a source of power higher still. People and princes can confer many favors upon those whom they greatly regard, and who know how to trust or to court them; but they cannot confer that smile which lights up the living-room of the soul, where the man is at home with his own thoughts, and where he holds converse with his immortality; and if that room remains dark, no lamps burning in any or in all of the other rooms can suffice to illumine the great house.[136]

Like his own father, Joseph Ruggles Wilson ardently pursued William James' bitch-goddess of success. When it eluded him or failed to bring him the happiness he saw as its necessary complement, he turned in large measure to his son Woodrow, and experienced vicariously the joy of becoming "a very great man."

---

[135] Talcott Parsons, *Social Structure and Personality* (New York, 1964), pp. 78-111; Nevitt Sanford, *Self & Society: Social Change and Individual Development* (New York, 1966), pp. 98-112.

[136] "Trust in the Lord," *Southern Presbyterian Pulpit*, pp. 368-69.

II

Boyhood and Student Days, 1856–1879

By Woodrow Wilson's own admission, his boyhood and family life exerted a powerful influence over his development, shaping and molding his personality and defining and clarifying some of his basic ideas about the world and his ambitions. "A boy never gets over his boyhood," he once confessed, "and can never change those subtle influences which have become a part of him, that were bred in him when he was a child."[1] That boyhood began in Staunton, Virginia, where Wilson was born in the manse near midnight on December 28-29, 1856. His parents were delighted with their new child and first son and named him Thomas Woodrow after his maternal grandfather. His mother described him as "a fine healthy fellow . . . and just as fat as he can be, . . . as little trouble as it is possible for a baby to be."[2] His uncle James Woodrow observed the future President but predicted a different future: "That baby is dignified enough to be Moderator of the General Assembly."[3]

Although Wilson was later proud of his Virginia roots, he lived there for only about a year, for his father moved in late 1857 or early 1858 to Augusta, Georgia. There Wilson spent his boyhood until 1870, when the family moved to Columbia, South Carolina. Wilson's most impressionable years were filled with conflict and war in the world around him. "My earliest recollection," he remembered, "is of standing at my father's gateway in Augusta, Georgia, when I was four years old, and hearing some one pass and say that Mr. Lincoln was elected and there was to be war."[4] He ran into the house to get an explanation from his father. The Civil War was an important part of Wilson's early experience; in addition to observing his father's service as an Army chaplain and coordinator for local Army relief efforts, Wilson witnessed at first hand the wounded soldiers hospitalized in the sanctuary of his father's church and Union soldiers imprisoned in the churchyard. His father took him to the Confederate ordnance factory to watch the production of munitions, and his early lessons were of warfare and bloodshed, enemies and allies, victory and defeat.

[1] "Robert E. Lee: An Interpretation," Jan. 19, 1909, *PWW*, xviii, 631.

[2] JWW to Thomas Woodrow, April 27, 1857, *ibid.*, i, 7.

[3] Quoted in WW to EAW, July 20, 1902, *ibid.*, xiv, 29.

[4] "Abraham Lincoln: Man of the People," Feb. 12, 1909, *ibid.*, xix, 33.

While an atmosphere of conflict and death surrounded him, Wilson's family was his haven, an insulation against an alien and antagonistic world. His parents showered love and affection on him, and throughout their lives he was clearly the favored one among the four children. In material terms, the Wilson family does not seem to have suffered much from the Civil War, but the permanent alienation from the Wilson side of the family in the North and the temporary separation from most of the Woodrows drew Wilson's parents toward their own children and united the family. Wilson's mother, in particular, tried to shield her son from the world of violence and war by lavishing love and affection on him. To her friends she was known as reserved and sedate, but to her son she was warm, loving, solicitous of his health and welfare, and perhaps overprotective. Often beginning her letters to him with "My precious Son" or "My Darling Son," she wrote to assure him constantly of her love: "God bless you, darling boy. You have never been anything but a comfort to me all your life!"[5] When Wilson did not earn the grades at Princeton that he and his parents expected, his mother assured him that it was certainly due to the professors' injustice, and when he was disciplined for too many absences at the University of Virginia, his mother once again comforted him with her belief that the professor had been unjustifiably harsh in admonishing Wilson.[6]

Wilson depended heavily on his mother's affections. She was subject to frequent illnesses, and during his early years he sought out his mother more than his father. "I remember," he later told his wife, "how I clung to her (a laughed at 'mamma's boy') till I was a great big fellow: but love of the best womanhood came to me and entered my heart through those apron-strings."[7] He viewed his mother as reserved but a constant source of uncritical, faithful love, and he felt determined not to disappoint her. In an essay on the duty of a son to his parents which Wilson wrote shortly after leaving home for Princeton, he asked rhetorically, "Your mother, who brought you forth, nourished you in your helplessness, loves you as only a mother can—who will trust you when all others forsake you, and is ready to give her all to make you happy—are you to do nothing for her?"[8]

Nearly thirty years after her death he described his love for her in vivid terms. "It is very hard for me to speak of what my mother was without colouring the whole estimate with the deep love that fills my heart whenever I think of her. . . . She was one of the most remarkable

[5] JWW to WW, June 13, 1882, *ibid.*, II, 133.

[6] JWW to WW, Jan. 20, 1879, and June 18, 1880, *ibid.*, I, 448, 661.

[7] WW to EAW, April 19, 1888, *ibid.*, V, 719.

[8] "One Duty of a Son to His Parents," Oct. 8, 1876, *ibid.*, I, 206.

persons I have ever known. She was so reserved, that only those of her own household can have known how lovable she was, though every friend knew how loyal and steadfast she was. I seem to feel still the touch of her hand, and the sweet steadying influence of her wonderful character. I thank God to have had such a mother!'"[9]

Her influence left a deep impression on Wilson's emotional life. In his marriage with Ellen Louise Axson, Wilson craved and sought the same supportive love and tried to create the same sense of intimacy and privacy in his own family. Jessie Wilson's solicitous, protective affection also tended to make Wilson introspective and melancholy, a condition he often tried to remedy by furious bursts of activity and work. "Outside Mr. Tommy was his father's boy," a former butler in the Wilson house noted. "But inside he was his mother all over."[10]

If Wilson's mother to a large extent molded and influenced his early emotional life, Joseph Ruggles Wilson was unquestionably the most important influence in his intellectual life, particularly in the formation and development of his religious faith and early political ideas. Link has concluded that "this relationship was indubitably the most important force during the formative years of Woodrow Wilson's life," and Baker considerably stretched the case by arguing that "until after he was forty years old, Woodrow Wilson never made an important decision of any kind without first seeking his father's advice."[11]

In contrast to his mother, Wilson's father was outgoing, gregarious, and virile, with a commanding appearance and a gift for facile expression. He dominated the atmosphere of the Wilson home, reading to his children, leading their instruction, and prodding the somewhat withdrawn Woodrow into self-assertion. In the aftermath of the Civil War, southern education was slow in reviving, and Wilson's father became his chief teacher until he left for college. He apparently was not particularly eager that his son learn to read, for Woodrow did not master his letters until he was nine and did not acquire the fundamentals of reading until he was eleven.[12] His father was concerned that his son master the art of self-expression, and family life often consisted of verbal training of various types. When his son fumbled in the middle

[9] WW to the Rev. William J. Hampton, Sept. 13, 1917; quoted in *WWLL*, I, 34.

[10] William Allen White, *Woodrow Wilson* (Boston and New York, 1924), p. 59.

[11] Link (ed.), *Woodrow Wilson: A Profile*, p. ix; *WWLL*, I, 30.

[12] William Bayard Hale, *Woodrow Wilson: The Story of His Life* (Garden City, N. Y., 1912), p. 46; *WWLL*, I, 36. The Georges have argued that Wilson's slow acquisition of reading skills was a sign of rebellion and resentment against his father's demands. It is equally possible that due to the exigencies of the Civil War, which did not end until Wilson was nearly nine, no schools were open in Augusta. Moreover, because of his heavy parish responsibilities during the war, Wilson's father was not able to undertake a more systematic training of his son. Georges, *Woodrow Wilson and Colonel House*, pp. 6-8.

of a sentence, his father would inquire, "What do you mean by that?" The explanation would be greeted by the curt question, "Then why don't you say so?"[13] Woodrow received regular writing assignments from his father, who corrected them and had his son rewrite them until his style and expression were sufficiently clear. Dr. Wilson's own gifted tongue could also be used sharply, and his son was the occasional object of a particularly pointed shaft of his wit. "He was proud of WW," Wilson's cousin Helen Bones recalled, "especially after his son began to show how unusual he was, but only a man as sweet as Cousin Woodrow could have forgotten the severity of the criticism to the value of which he so often paid tribute, in after life."[14]

But to focus exclusively on Wilson's father as a demanding, caustic critic of his son seriously distorts the nature of their relationship. His father's criticism was meted out with large doses of love and affection, and father and son became constant companions and even co-workers. Wilson aided his father in the preparation of the General Assembly minutes and conducted his correspondence when he was absent.[15] He accompanied his father on pastoral calls and sent him regular "Assembly letters" when Dr. Wilson was away for the southern Presbyterian Church's annual meeting.[16] His father reciprocated by giving his son constant encouragement throughout his career, reminding him frequently of his faith in Woodrow's abilities and his confidence that he would succeed. Their correspondence, Baker has said, "can be called nothing but love letters,"[17] and after Wilson left home and established a career and family of his own, his father exclaimed how he "longed for the presence of that dear son in whose large love I trust so implicitly and in the wealth of whose gem-furnished mind I take such delight: him in whom my affections centre as my child, and my confidences as my friend."[18]

Wilson's father gave him an enduring fondness for English literature and political institutions. He introduced him to English writers— Burns, Tennyson, Wordsworth, and Dickens—and the reading table was covered with the *Edinburgh Review* and the New York *Nation*.[19] He also imparted to his son part of his own affection for their Scotch-Irish heritage. To a class of students at Bryn Mawr, Wilson quipped

[13] *WWLL*, I, 38.

[14] Helen Bones to R. S. Baker, July 2, 1925 (R. S. Baker Coll., DLC); Georges, *Woodrow Wilson and Colonel House*, p. 8.

[15] Wilson's Diary, July 13 and Aug. 12, 1876, *PWW*, I, 153, 178; WW to ELA, March 23, 1884, *ibid.*, III, 95.

[16] Diary, July 19, 1876, *ibid.*, I, 156; WW to JRW, May 23, 1877, *ibid.*, I, 265-66; JRW to WW, May 22, 1893, *ibid.*, VIII, 216-17, n. 1.

[17] *WWLL*, I, 40.   [18] JRW to WW, March 6, 1889, *PWW*, VI, 137.

[19] Bragdon, *Wilson: The Academic Years*, p. 10.

that "no one who amounts to anything is without some Scotch-Irish blood" and frequently praised "that adventurous, indomitable people, the Scots-Irish."[20] In later life he reveled in the sense of freedom and abandonment which he attributed to his father's inheritance. "I myself am happy that there runs in my veins a very considerable strain of Irish blood," he once remarked. ". . . There is something delightful in me that every now and then takes the strain off my Scotch conscience and affords me periods of most enjoyable irresponsibility when I do not care whether school keeps or not, or whether anybody gets educated or not."[21]

He likewise adopted his father's allegiance to the South, declaring later in life that "the only place in the country, the only place in the world, where nothing has to be explained to me is the South."[22] Before an audience of professional historians in 1896, he insisted that there was "nothing to apologize for in the past of the South—absolutely nothing to apologize for."[23] Throughout his life he demonstrated a southern attitude toward women, and, although shedding some of his father's more blatant racist views, he exhibited a paternalistic attitude toward Negroes. Yet he was no devotee of the Lost Cause, and as early as 1880 he declared, "I yield to no one precedence in love for the South. But *because* I love the South, I rejoice in the failure of the Confederacy."[24] His historical writing at times displayed a southern bias, but his *Division and Reunion* was one of the first efforts to treat the Civil War and Reconstruction with a modicum of impartiality. As Link has noted, his affection for the South waned in the 1890's under the challenge of populism but flowered again as Wilson became a progressive and made his entry into politics.[25]

Although Wilson's early education and relationship with his father contributed to many of the attitudes and ideas that were to endure in his thinking for the rest of his life, perhaps the most important contribution of his home was the deep religious faith and activities that pervaded the Wilson family life. Daily devotions, Bible reading and prayers, characterized the Wilson home. Sundays were spent going to hear Dr. Wilson preach; Woodrow and the other children attended Sunday School; and in the evening the family would either attend a second worship service

[20] *WWLL*, I, 5; WW, *A History of the American People*. 5 vols. (New York, 1902), II, 60.

[21] Address to the Friendly Sons of St. Patrick in New York City, March 17, 1909, *PWW*, XIX, 103.

[22] "Robert E. Lee," Jan. 19, 1909, *ibid.*, XVIII, 631.

[23] Remarks on a paper by Frederick Jackson Turner, "The West as a Field for Historical Study," Dec. 31, 1896, *ibid.*, X, 93.

[24] "John Bright," March 6, 1880, *ibid.*, I, 618.

[25] Arthur S. Link, "Woodrow Wilson: The American as Southerner," in *The Higher Realism of Woodrow Wilson* (Nashville, Tenn., 1971), pp. 21-37.

or gather at home to sing hymns. Wilson was very fond of hymn singing and developed a strong tenor voice. Some of the hymns moved him
to tears, and he found special comfort in the communion service.[26]
This reverence for Sunday as a holy day to be spent in worship of God,
family activities, and rest stayed with Wilson for the remainder of his
life. Even as President, he reportedly refused to attend an opera at La
Scala until he was assured that he was going to a religious service.[27]
Although he was never a rabid sectarian, he preferred the austere style
of Presbyterian worship, calling the Episcopalian service "a ridiculous
way of worshiping God" and terming revival meetings *"flirting made
easy."*[28]

But it was Wilson's experience in the southern Presbyterian Church,
and above all the influence of his father, which left the characteristic
stamps on Wilson's religious faith for the rest of his life. It was a singularly Presbyterian faith that Wilson inherited, strongly affected by the
ethos of the southern Presbyterian Church and its covenant theology.
This theology, as noted before, was concerned primarily with the distribution of power, divine and human, in the world; and in its comprehensive view of the individual's relationship to God and other people,
it imposed a comprehensible pattern—orderly, predictable, and
permanent—upon the transient character of human affairs. Particularly
in its formulation by Joseph Ruggles Wilson, the covenant theology
forged a union of God's authority and God's love, making God absolutely sovereign over the affairs of this world, but relating to people in
love, not arbitrary power. In its doctrine of election, it was an activistic
creed, calling the individual to be God's agent in the world, realizing
the divine will. Human activity was supervised and blessed by God,
and the individual could therefore be assured of success. That success,
according to Wilson's father, was never a personal achievement or
self-fulfillment, for that was the sin of self-seeking. Rather, success
was always seen as serving God and obeying the divine law which
governed human life.

In making obedience central to a person's relationship to God,
Joseph Ruggles Wilson's covenant theology made the world an alien
and hostile environment in which faithfulness to God was always being
undermined. Steadfast allegiance was imperative; compromise could
not be tolerated. Simultaneously, this view saw conflict in the world
not as a struggle between people but as a struggle between contending
principles—good and evil, right and wrong. Consequently, one did not

[26] *WWLL*, I, 36, 47; WW, Diary, Oct. 1, 1876, and June 3, 1877, *PWW*, I, 202, 272.

[27] Arthur S. Link, "Woodrow Wilson and His Presbyterian Inheritance," in *The Higher
Realism of Woodrow Wilson,* p. 12.

[28] Diary, June 11, 1876, *PWW*, I, 138; WW to Robert Bridges, Aug. 10, 1878, *ibid.*, p. 395.

fight others but their ideas. The human element was rejected, eliminated from a larger fight for the preservation and realization of God's order on earth.

God's will for the world as complete, certain, and unchanging, God as both total love and absolute authority, human responsibility for God's work, obedience as a duty, service of God rather than others, no compromise of principles, the world as the arena for the battle between good and evil—these were the hallmarks of Wilson's father's covenant theology, and they appear repeatedly in his sermons and letters to his son. God's law, he was fond of saying, was the divine constitution for the world, and the Bible was not merely the revelation of God but "a *guide to the entire life*, and must therefore prove *attractive* to the soul who would learn to practise its lessons."[29] Like an old Puritan divine, he could portray God as "that infinite, that holy, that tremendous, that all controlling Being" and graphically describe "His thunderings in the law as He descends to execute its penalties" or "the *remorseless* tramplings of His will in the woes and wailings of dying sufferers."[30] On the other hand, Dr. Wilson could reassure his son of "the smile of God" which obliterated sin and remind his congregation that God's thoughts were "His best thoughts of pardon and peace."[31]

Fundamentally, the God proclaimed by Wilson's father was a "loving authority." He often drew similarities between divine and paternal love and utilized the motif of father and son throughout his sermons. "There is surely nothing in the nature of God more touching or more inviting than *His fatherliness*," he declared and outlined three different kinds of God's children—obedient, insubordinate, and defiant. But "the parental relation is not *destroyed*," he argued, "however it may be *shocked*—by the child's wicked conduct."[32] And, in a colorful passage, Wilson's father gave explicit testimony of his conception of God as the divine parent who exhibited both love and authority toward the children of God:

> God is this Highest One, and His principal decoration is upon His Person where, as a *Parent*, He shall appear with sons & daughters unnumbered but yet without one absent, with their love for Him fully a-light—flaming in unison with His for them; or when as a king He shall seat Himself amid His completed court, to cast His eye over

[29] *Mutual Relation of Masters and Slaves, passim;* sermon on James 1:25, Nov. 10, 1878 (WP, DLC).

[30] Sermon on I Timothy 4:12, April 10, 1898 (WP, DLC); sermon on I John 4:19, Jan. [?], 1898 (HF, NC).

[31] JRW to WW, March 27, 1877, *PWW*, I, 254; sermon on Psalm 40:17, March 1, 1885 (WP, DLC).

[32] Sermon on Matthew 21:28, Feb. 9, 1897 (HF, NC).

a vast-crowded scene where from no voice is raised but the voice of adoration from tongues as true as His own, and no hand is uplifted but the hand of allegiance moved by oathful hearts as faithful as even He could demand.[33]

One could not accept such love without submitting to divine authority, and complete obedience was the Christian's response. "The subject must forsake *all* opposition to his king," Wilson's father insisted and flatly concluded that to follow Christ meant "to accept of His love, and then to accept His law; to cast yourself upon His redeeming work, and then to permit Him to fix upon you His requiring will."[34]

Because of the power of evil in the world, obedience was never easy, but believers could clearly know God's law and will for their lives. "Whatever *God* says is to them absolute truth," Wilson's father confidently proclaimed. "Whatever God commands is to them absolute duty; whatever God covenants to give is to them absolute certainty."[35] In fact, the test of faithfulness was nothing less than obedience in action. "All His believers are . . . His obeyers," he maintained. "It is in what we *do* for Christ that we discover our faith in Him."[36] The Protestant ethic thus became blessed with divine authority, and Wilson's father consistently impressed upon his son that hard work was a fulfillment of his duty to God and would receive divine blessing. When his son's interest in study waned at Princeton, his father advised, "Through this work success comes—and comes as a *matter of law*—therefore, *must* come."[37]

This was a heady, powerful creed. Its scope covered the entire range of human affairs, and God's covenant with people—the divine constitution—provided a comprehensive understanding of the world and Woodrow Wilson's place in it. It encouraged a basic confidence in him that although the world might be against him, God was with him and his efforts would be blessed with divine approval. It assured him that both love and authority were unified in God and impressed upon him the Calvinistic sense of his duty to be obedient to God's certain and unchanging law. His father's covenant theology also influenced him to see that ambitions were only true if they were defined in terms of God's service, not in terms of selfish desire. When conflicts would arise in Wilson's life, he could be confident of his obedience to God's law, reject compromise as halfhearted obedience, and interpret the conflict

---

[33] Sermon on Malachi 3:17, Nov. 7, 1880 (WP, DLC).

[34] Sermon on Luke 5:11, sometime during 1882 (HF, NC); sermon on Matthew 9:9, April 3, 1881 (WP, DLC).

[35] Sermon on I Timothy 4:12, April 10, 1898 (WP, DLC).

[36] *Ibid.*; sermon on Genesis 47:8, sometime during 1878 (HF, NC).

[37] JRW to WW, Jan. 25, 1878, *PWW*, I, 346.

not as a personal one but as the clash of antagonistic principles. Such attitudes, of course, did not emerge full-blown, but they were inherent in the Presbyterian legacy of Wilson's home and his father's own theology.

In 1870, Wilson's family moved to Columbia, South Carolina, and his father began his duties as professor at Columbia Theological Seminary. Wilson's father eagerly accepted the new position, but it came at an unfortunate time for his son who was just entering adolescence. He apparently had some difficulty making friends there, for on the eve of their departure from Columbia, his mother reassured him that he did have many friends in Columbia and would find even more in Wilmington.[38] A schoolmate remembered him as "extremely dignified" and said, "He was not like the other boys. He had a queer way of going off by himself."[39] Nevertheless, Wilson himself recalled "my own very happy boyhood in Columbia."[40]

Baker called the years in Columbia "among the most important of his whole life. It was the period of his spiritual awakening: of dreams that became visions, of hopes that became purposes."[41] It was, in fact, a time of profound personal and religious turmoil for the young Wilson. His father probably intended that his son should follow in his footsteps and enter the ministry. In a sermon in the summer of 1872, Wilson's father preached on the theme of being the sons of God and proclaimed that all God's sons were made with potential. Then, with an obvious thrust at his young son in the congregation, he declared, "Ignorant as now he [the son] is, he may become one of the Church's rarest scholars, highest in her schools of divinity, or one of her most illustrious reformers, the light of generations, or one of her grandest orators." Wilson's father had high expectations for his son, for he had penciled in the names of Luther, Latimer, and Knox in the manuscript but apparently reconsidered and crossed them out.[42] Wilson made an initial step toward the career his father had expected him to pursue by attending his lectures at the seminary and listening to his father's conversations with other seminary professors in their home.[43]

But Wilson's deepest religious experience did not come through his father. During the winter of 1872-1873, a young student, Frank J. Brooke, began holding religious meetings in his room, and Wilson attended. Brooke was poorly prepared for his theological training, but what he lacked in knowledge he made up with zeal. Soon the meetings moved from Brooke's room to a small stable which had been converted

[38] JWW to WW, May 20, 1874, *ibid.*, p. 50.   [39] William Barnwell in *WWLL*, I, 59.

[40] WW to David Clymer Ward, Dec. 14, 1914, in *ibid.*, p. 72.

[41] *Ibid.*, p. 57.   [42] Sermon on I John 3:2, July 21, 1872 (WP, DLC).

[43] *WWLL*, I, 61-64.

to the seminary chapel. On one occasion, Brooke asked everyone who accepted Christ to come forward to a seat on the front bench, and Wilson made the trip to the front of the chapel.[44] Many years later when he visited Columbia as President, he stopped at the chapel. "I feel as though I ought to take off my shoes," he commented. "This is holy ground."[45]

Wilson's conversion experience was clearly one of intensity. Despite his father's deteriorating relationship with the First Presbyterian Church of Columbia throughout the early part of 1873, Wilson obviously felt a compulsion to join the church. The session's minutes of July 5, 1873, duly recorded that Wilson and two other boys "after a free conversation during which they severally exhibited evidences of a work of grace begun in their hearts—were unanimously admitted into the membership of this church."[46] That same month, Wilson's father terminated his service as stated supply of the church.

In the fall of 1873, Wilson set off for Davidson College in North Carolina with his friend Brooke, as Baker has said, "with the general understanding on the part of his family that he was to study for the ministry."[47] At Davidson he was a fairly good student, scoring highest in composition and English and lowest in mathematics.[48] His performance was even outstanding, considering his relative lack of formal educational training. In Augusta, he had attended briefly the school run by Joseph T. Derry, a former Confederate officer, and in Columbia he went to a slightly better "classical" school conducted by Charles H. Barnwell.[49]

At Davidson, Wilson played second base for the freshman baseball team, but his chief interest was the campus debating club, the Eumenean Society. Although only a freshman, he was called upon to offer the prayer which opened one meeting, but at times he was disciplined and fined for "improper conduct," "talking," and "sitting on the rostrum." Wilson and two other members were asked on one occasion to judge a debate on the question, "Is a mob ever justified in taking the life of a king who is a tyrant and usurper?" The judges decided in favor of the negative, but the rest of the house reversed them. Most striking is Wilson's interest in the constitution of the Eumenean Society, for while he did not rewrite or restructure this document as he did others

[44] *Ibid.*, pp. 66-67; La Motte, *Colored Light*, p. 149.

[45] *WWLL*, I, 67.

[46] Minutes of the Session of the First Presbyterian Church, Columbia, S. C., July 5, 1873, *PWW*, I, 22-23.

[47] *WWLL*, I, 71-72.

[48] John Rennie Blake to Whom It May Concern, June 25, 1875, *PWW*, I, 67, n. 1.

[49] *WWLL*, I, 42, 59.

later, he did assume the onerous task of recopying the constitution into the formal records.[50]

At Davidson Wilson was remembered as "witty, genial, superior, but languid,"[51] and his enervation may have been due to the intensification of his religious turmoil. Wilson's conversion experience and subsequent admission into the church had not quieted his spiritual ferment, which seems to have grown greater in his absence from home. At precisely the same time that his father was becoming more deeply embroiled in the controversy in Columbia, Wilson was becoming more confused and shaken. In November, he copied into his notebook a poem entitled "The Prayer," which apparently struck him deeply. The poem read in part:

> The way is dark, my Father! Cloud on cloud
> Is gathering thickly o'er my head, and loud
> The thunders roar above me. See, I stand
> Like one bewildered! Father, take my hand,
>   And through the gloom
>   Lead safely home
>   Thy child. . . .
>
> The way is long, my Father, and my soul
> Longs for the rest and quiet of the goal:
> While yet I journey through this weary land,
> Keep me from wandering, Father, take my hand,
>   Quickly and straight,
>   Lead to heaven's gate
>   Thy child.

The second half of the poem consisted of an assuring answer that "at thy side/Thy Father walks." "The cross is heavy, child, yet there was One/Who bore a heavier for thee—My Son,/My well beloved."[52] The prevailing theme of father and son, whether divine or human, may merely suggest Wilson's homesickness for his "incomparable father." But the poem may also indicate even more poignantly Wilson's feeling of isolation from his father, who was enduring the greatest crisis of his ministry. It would be simplistic to argue that Wilson identified his own father with God, despite his father's use of parental imagery to describe God. Yet with Dr. Wilson under attack, his son's own sense of

---

[50] WW Notebook, c.May 1, 1874; Minutes of the Eumenean Society, March 28 and Jan. 31, 1874, Nov. 15, 1873, March 27 and May 9, 1874, *PWW*, I, 47, 43, 39-40, 36, 42, 49.

[51] A. M. Fraser to R. S. Baker, *WWLL*, I, 74.

[52] "The Prayer," c. Nov. 6, 1873, *PWW*, I, 33-35.

confidence and assurance about himself and his spiritual health was undermined.

His spiritual turmoil persisted throughout the academic year, and in May 1874, he jotted in one of his notebooks a revealing confession of his sense of sin and unworthiness. "I am now in my seventeenth year," he wrote,

> and it is sad, when looking over my past life to see how few of those seventeen years I have spent in the fear of God, and how much time I have spent in the service of the Devil. Although having professed Christ's name some time ago, I have increased very little in grace and have done almost nothing for the Savior's Cause here below. O, how hard it is to do that which ought to be my greatest delight! *If God will give me the grace I will try to serve him from this time on, and will endeavour to attain nearer and nearer to perfection.*[53]

He also confided to his notebook that he had heard a sermon by a minister that made him "think all the trouble is within," and in his notes on the discourse Wilson recorded his feeling that the chief characteristic of a Christian was humility before God.[54] Wilson's uncertain spiritual health was matched by reversals in his physical health,[55] but he recovered, completed his exams, and when he left the campus he fully expected to return and complete his degree.[56] His father's dramatic resignation from Columbia Seminary and the family's sudden move to Wilmington, North Carolina, altered the picture, and his parents kept him at home in Wilmington for a year.

What happened to Wilson from late 1872 through 1874 can never be known with any confidence, but it was obviously a time of confusion and spiritual difficulty for this child of the Presbyterian manse. It is likely that Wilson underwent the common adolescent conversion experience,[57] and that his separation from home, coupled with his father's ordeal in Columbia, intensified his uncertainty about God's love and forgiveness and his own feelings of unworthiness. However, it is also clear that Wilson was beginning to realize that he wanted to make politics, not the ministry, his vocation. At about this age, he purportedly hung a portrait of Gladstone above his desk at home and announced to his inquiring cousin: "That is Gladstone, the greatest statesman that ever lived. I intend to be a statesman, too."[58] Part of Wilson's spiritual

---

[53] Journal, May 3, 1874, *ibid.*, vi, 693.

[54] Journal, April 26, 1874, *ibid.*, pp. 691-92.

[55] JWW to WW, May 20, 1874, *ibid.*, i, 50; Minutes of the Eumenean Society, May 22 and 29, 1874, *ibid.*, pp. 50-51, 52.

[56] WW Notebook, *c.* June 1, 1874, *ibid.*, p. 53.

[57] See Gordon Allport, *The Individual and His Religion* (New York, 1950), pp. 36-40.

[58] Jessie Bones Brower to R. S. Baker, *WWLL*, i, 57.

crisis might therefore have been his unwillingness to become a minister as his father wished. At Davidson his feelings of guilt were heightened as he realized he might be disappointing his father, especially in a time of personal crisis.

There is very little subsequent evidence that Wilson's father was disappointed in his son's choice of career or that he tried to dissuade him from studying politics. He is supposed to have exclaimed after hearing his son read one of his essays, "Oh, my boy, how I wish you had entered the ministry, with all that genius of yours!" And when Wilson was ordained as an elder in the Presbyterian Church, his father commented that he would rather have him be an elder than President of the United States.[59] Nevertheless, Wilson's father supported his son in his decision, both morally and financially, and however great the initial blow to the elder Wilson's dreams, he adjusted and encouraged his son in everything he attempted. In this respect, Wilson's father's disastrous experience at Columbia was providential, for his subsequent discouragement and disillusionment undoubtedly eased the conflict over his son's vocational choice. After he left Columbia, Wilson's father was hardly in a mood to insist dogmatically on the virtues of a church vocation. His son was thus able to establish his own identity and independence apart from his father, and he did so gradually, without a decisive break with the parents he so dearly loved.

Wilson's year in Wilmington with his parents was a dreamy, introspective one, spent in part preparing for his entry into Princeton. He also acquired and mastered shorthand skills which he would profitably use for the rest of his life.[60] Above all, it was a year in which Wilson nurtured his love for the sea in the port city of Wilmington, visiting the docks, sketching ships, even climbing aboard and injuring himself in a fall into a ship's hold.[61] The sea fired his imagination, and he set up a Royal United Kingdom Yacht Club with "Lord Thomas W. Wilson, Duke of Carlton, Admiral of the white, Royal Navy, &c. &c." in the position of leadership as commodore. Even an imaginary world needed order and structure in Wilson's mind, and he constructed an elaborate constitution for the Yacht Club with officers and meetings and procedures to be followed. Races between the member yachts were stipulated and prizes awarded by "Lord T. W. Wilson," owner of two 280-ton English ships, *Eclipse* and *Sea Bird*.[62]

Wilson apparently wrote an even earlier constitution in Augusta for

[59] *Ibid.*, p. 89; A.D.P. Gilmore, *Woodrow Wilson—The Christian* (Wilmington, N. C., 1924), p. 12.

[60] See the Editorial Note, Wilson's Study and Use of Shorthand, 1872-1892, *PWW*, I, 8-19.

[61] Jessie Bones Brower to R. S. Baker, *WWLL*, I, 60-61.

[62] Constitution for the Royal United Kingdom Yacht Club, *c.* July 1, 1874, *PWW*, I, 54-56; Editorial Note, Wilson's Imaginary World, *ibid.*, pp. 20-22.

"The Royal
United Kingdom Yacht Club"
Vessels

Name	tonnage	owner	Nationality
1. Eclipse,	280,	Lord Thomas W. Wilson,	English
2. Foam,	280	" W. P. Hutchinson,	"
3. Albatross,	280	" L. D. Alexander,	"
4. Osprey,	280	" C. R. Shields,	Irish
5. Sea Bird,	280	" J. W. Wilson,	English
6. Circe,	270	Sir J. Warren,	"
7. Dauntless,	270	Mr. S. W. Beach,	Scotch
8. Renown,	270	" N. Harrington,	"
9. Gazelle,	269	Lord C. C. McCarthy,	Irish
10. Aurora,	268	Mr. A. C. O'Brien,	"
11. Beatrice,	265	" C. W. Fletcher,	English
12. Enterprize,	260	" J. Mc. Campbell,	Scotch
13. Independent,	260	Sir J. Wm Leckie,	Irish
14. Imogen,	260	" C. Cunningham,	English
15. Kestrel	260	" J. P. Clarence,	"
16. Magic	250	Mr. L. C. Evans,	"
17. Naiad	250	" Alex J. Smith,	Scotch
18. Orion	250	" James "	"

Wilson's first constitution, written when he was
17 years old. *Library of Congress*

a baseball association, the Lightfoot Club, and he conducted meetings in the loft of a barn under a red portrait of the devil.[63] The constitution of the Royal United Kingdom Yacht Club is significant in its demonstration of Wilson's immersion into a dream world after his difficult year of spiritual upheaval at Davidson and for its revelation of his early and deep admiration for British life. This desire for order and structure may have been a means of compensating for the sudden and unhappy move by the Wilson family to Wilmington. It may also have been prompted by a lingering sense of uneasiness about his desire to study politics instead of theology.

More importantly, the constitution reveals Wilson's "passion, even at an early age, for constitutional order,"[64] a passion stimulated and influenced in large degree by his covenant theological heritage. The corollary to God's structuring and ordering of the world by divine law was the human attempt to arrange the world with covenants or constitutions. Such a conception of the world subjected even an illusory world of the imagination to the mastery of the writer of the constitution; it tamed a threatening environment and made its uncertainties predictable and comprehensible.

After a year of reading and of flights into his imaginary world, the eighteen-year-old Wilson departed from Wilmington for his first year at Princeton. As a freshman he made a fairly good record, indicating that his preparation in Wilmington had reaped good results. He found his studies difficult at first, particularly Greek and mathematics, but gradually developed more confidence in his intellectual skills. He soon impressed his fellow students with the quality of his mind and power of expression, for a classmate recalled that "everyone soon began to look upon him as one of the most original and superior men in the college." Another remembered Wilson as a student of clear resolution and goals. "We went to college without an objective, but Wilson always had a definite purpose."[65]

He arrived on the campus a transplanted Southerner and soon found antagonists with whom to discuss the conflict of North and South and the policies of Reconstruction. On occasion the arguments would last until dawn, Wilson growing "quite bitter" and appearing "full of the South and quite a Secessionist."[66] He suffered from the political taunts of his northern friends, often suppressing with difficulty an urge to retaliate physically, but his mother constantly warned him to avoid any

[63] WWLL, I, 29, 45.

[64] Constitution for the Royal United Kingdom Yacht Club, c. July 1, 1874, PWW, I, 56. n. 1.

[65] Albert Wylly to R. S. Baker, WWLL, I, 85; Baker memorandum of interview with Hiram Woods, Dec. 9, 1925 (R. S. Baker Coll., DLC).

[66] Henry W. Bragdon interview with Robert H. McCarter, July 15, 1940, quoted in Bragdon, Wilson: The Academic Years, p. 21.

altercation.[67] After the election of 1876, he was plagued by "harrowing suspense" for weeks until the victory of Hayes was assured.[68] Despite these political differences, he soon developed strong friendships with a number of his classmates from the North, friendships which he cultivated and preserved throughout his life. These relationships were formed primarily with some of the wealthier and more worldly members of the Class of 1879, as Henry W. Bragdon has pointed out. Wilson's cronies in Witherspoon Hall, known as the Witherspoon Gang, as well as his fellow "Alligators," a rather well-to-do eating club, were conspicuous by the absence of preministerial students which abounded in the Princeton student body.[69] Wilson moved easily in this crowd, usually occupying some of the most comfortable and expensive quarters. He regularly relied on his parents' effusive love and his father's comfortable salary in Wilmington for financial underwriting of his needs. What he wanted he asked for and received, causing his father to exclaim: "I am goose enough to send you the money you order!"[70]

When Wilson entered Princeton, the college was pervaded by a conscious religious tone. Every president had been a Presbyterian minister, and presiding over the college in 1875 was James McCosh. In Wilson's Class of 1879, only two students declared that they were not members of a church, and the leaders of every class organized prayer meetings which were held twice a week.[71]

In the spring of 1876, the college was swept by a revival, and the primary impetus for it seems to have come from the students themselves. After four weeks, 115 conversions were reported in the student body, and President McCosh called in Moody and Sankey, as well as other ministers, to keep the revival alive. Voluntary prayer meetings were held every night during this period, and occasionally at noon as well.[72] As a regular participant in the class prayer meetings, Wilson was presumably a part of the revival, but there is no documentary evidence of his involvement. He may have even begun to tire of these regular inquiries into the state of his immortal soul, for he was later fond of telling about a student at Princeton who, in the midst of the

[67] JWW to WW, Nov. 8 and 15, Dec. 1, 1876, *PWW*, I, 223, 228, 233.

[68] WW Shorthand Diary, Nov. 6, 7, 8, 9, 10, 11, 13, 22, 1876, *ibid.*, pp. 221-25, 230.

[69] Bragdon, *Wilson: The Academic Years*, pp. 27-30. Among Wilson's lifelong friends in the Class of 1879 were Robert Bridges, Cyrus H. McCormick, Cleveland H. Dodge, Cornelius C. Cuyler, Edward W. Sheldon, Charles A. Talcott, and Hiram Woods. Not all of these friendships developed during Wilson's undergraduate years; those with McCormick and Dodge, in particular, do not seem to have blossomed until many years after graduation.

[70] JRW to WW, Nov. 3, 1876, *PWW*, I, 219.

[71] Bragdon, *Wilson: The Academic Years*, p. 18.

[72] *Ibid.*

religious fervor, posted a sign on his door which read: "I am a Christian, but studying for exams."[73]

During his freshman year, Wilson began an "Index Rerum," or commonplace book, consisting of an alphabetized collection of sayings and quotations which he transcribed for future use. In recording Wilson's reading interests and ideas, the notebook is the first concrete indication of his desire to study history and political affairs. Most of the quotations reveal Wilson's affection for English life and letters and come largely from historians or politicians, including Burke, Carlyle, and Macaulay, but also Daniel Webster and Andrew Jackson. There is also a significant representation from English literary figures—Milton, Pope, Spenser, Goldsmith, Cowper, and others.[74] Wilson's choice of quotations is a striking reflection of his moral values as a student and his focus on principles in political affairs.

For example, Wilson quoted Goldsmith on the pursuit of truth as a journey toward ideals: "In every duty, in every science in which we would wish to arrive at perfection, we should propose for the object of our pursuit some certain station even beyond our abilities; some imaginary excellence, which may amuse and serve to animate our enquiry."[75] Similarly, he excerpted a passage from one of Spurgeon's sermons or essays which emphasized the necessity for staying faithful to one's ideals, even at the expense of friendship: "Leave consequences to God, but do right. Be genuine, real, sincere, true, be right, God-like. . . . If in the course of duty you are tried by the mistrust of friends, gird up your loins and say in your heart, 'I was not driven to virtue by the encouragement of friends, nor will I be repelled by their coldness.'"[76] The young Wilson, developing his own study habits, also emphasized his need for discipline and for breaking habits. "Keep busy; idleness is the strength of bad habits," he copied into his notebook as he appropriated the Protestant ethic. "Do not give up the struggle when you have broken your resolution once, twice, ten times, a thousand times. That only shows how much need there is for you to strive."[77]

His father's letters sounded the same themes and reinforced Wilson's determination to achieve prominence in the world. When the boy's dreams outpaced his capacity for work, his father admonished him to pay more attention to his studies. "Dismiss *ambition*—and replace it with hard industry, which shall have little or no regard to

---

[73] News report of a speech to the Private Secondary School Association of Philadelphia, March 10, 1906, *PWW*, xvi, 328.

[74] Index Rerum, Feb. 22, 1876-c.Nov. 15, 1876, *ibid.*, i, 87-127.

[75] *Ibid.*, p. 110.   [76] *Ibid.*, p. 124.   [77] *Ibid.*, p. 90.

present triumphs, but which will be all the time laying foundations for future work and wage."[78] And when Wilson lapsed into adolescent introspection, his father implored him not "to dwell upon *yourself*," adding, "Concentrate your thoughts upon *thoughts* and *things* and *events*. . . . Go out from your own personality. Do not regard ego as the Centre of this universe." He assured his son that he had superior abilities, perhaps even genius, but "what is the secret heart of genius? the ability to work with painstaking self denial."[79]

Such injunctions encouraged high ambitions and a driving intensity which inevitably brought disappointments to Wilson. Both father and mother were quick to reassure him. His father, with more than a casual awareness of defeat and its effects, insisted that his son not let depression overcome him. "I beg of you . . . ," he implored, "that you will strive ag't. despondency as you would with a deadly foe: aye, pray against it as you would for some great salvation." He urged him to fight depression as "your greatest foe—and fight to conquer."[80] His mother urged him to lower his sights; "don't be too ambitious, dear—for that kind of ambition brings *only* worry—unhappiness."[81] Even his father inquired, "Dearest boy, can you hope to jump into eminency all at once?"[82] His father's cure for depression was ever the same: hard work and trust in God. "You ought to throw, to pour yourself into your daily studies as if they were your very life," he admonished, "thinking of almost nothing besides except God and your friends." "Expect success and not failure. Say to the future, 'others have conquered you and so will I—God helping me, the odds shall be on my side.' "[83]

The ideal of work surrounded Wilson on all sides. The way to success was hard work; the answer to defeat was more work. Even when his grades were satisfactory, his father praised him but always held before him the ideals that were as yet unrealized. "You have so far justified our expectations," he wrote him, "but not *more* than justified them—for we know what you *could* do. And we as well know that what you have achieved is nothing to what you can accomplish. Modest energy spurred by Christian principle may properly lay claim to every rightful honor."[84] When his father's injunctions and criticisms bore too heavily upon Wilson, his mother would intercede to shore up his flagging spirits. "If anybody deserves to succeed *you do*,"[85] she

[78] JRW to WW, Dec. 22, 1877, *ibid.*, p. 332.
[79] JRW to WW, Jan. 25, 1878, *ibid.*, pp. 346.
[80] JRW to WW, Jan. 27, 1880, *ibid.*, p. 597; Dec. 17, 1884, *ibid.*, III, 549.
[81] JWW to WW, Jan. 22, 1878, *ibid.*, I, 342.
[82] JRW to WW, Dec. 22, 1877, *ibid.*, p. 332.
[83] JRW to WW, Jan. 27 and Oct. 19, 1880, *ibid.*, pp. 597, 685.
[84] JRW to WW, March 27, 1877, *ibid.*, p. 254.
[85] JWW to WW, Nov. 26, 1879, *ibid.*, p. 587; April 2, 1884, *ibid.*, III, 110.

comforted. Even his father was careful not to leave the impression that his criticisms obliterated his love. "Write me freely, my darling, as to all your feelings," he assured him, "and trust us both, in the future as in the past, with all your secret desires—being *sure* that we are your truest friends."[86]

This carrot-and-stick approach—confidence in Wilson's ability and future and calls to unflagging labor—was matched by Wilson's father with a persistent concern for his son's spiritual health. "God bless you, my boy," he told him. "Do not forget to ask His blessing upon your efforts."[87] In Dr. Wilson's view, prayer and a healthy relationship with God were essential for the proper development of character, and during Wilson's years at Princeton, he expressed the hope that "if you come out from college, darling son, with a character unimpaired and untainted our gratitude will know no bounds. I trust, therefore, that you are often in the attitude of prayer to Him who alone can keep you amid multiplied temptations. . . . God bless you sweet one."[88]

Dr. Wilson need not have worried; his son's diary at Princeton was filled with Wilson's own concern for his spiritual life and his desire to have a close relationship to God. The diary, which he kept in short-hand and maintained intermittently from June 1876 until early in his senior year, regularly concluded the survey of each day's activities with a short prayer of gratitude for God's blessing to him and his family. "Thank God for health and strength through another day!" "The blessings of another day are added to my load of gratitude to God." "God bless all that are dear to me and continue to bless them and me as He has in the past!" "Thank God for health and strength and privileges of another sabbath." "I am, thank God, still free[,] happy and perfectly healthy. I cannot be too thankful for all God's mercies to me." "Went to bed happy and thankful for all His mercies."[89]

Wilson further confided to his diary that he found praying out loud a more satisfying religious experience than praying silently, and in the contractual spirit of the covenant theology, he resolved to make God "some slightly better return for His many mercies."[90] This diary, ranging from critical comments on sermons to prayers about his erratic health, reveals the importance Wilson ascribed to his religious faith and life. While there are confessions of his inability to live up to what he saw as the requirements of the Christian faith, his Princeton diary is

---

[86] JRW to WW, Jan. 25, 1878, *ibid.*, I, 346.

[87] JRW to WW, Feb. 25, 1879, *ibid.*, p. 460. See also JRW to WW, Nov. 3, 1867 and Jan. 30, 1877, *ibid.*, pp. 220, 240.

[88] JRW to WW, April 13, 1877, *ibid.*, pp. 258-59.

[89] Diary, June 7, 8, 10, 25, 19, and 27, 1876, *ibid.*, pp. 135-37, 143, 146.

[90] Diary, Sept. 23, 1876, *ibid.*, p. 198.

notable for a new sense of confidence and an absence of the brooding introspection about his sinfulness which characterized his religious experience at Davidson.

This confidence, as well as his indebtedness to his father's theological influence, is also reflected in a series of essays which Wilson wrote during the summer and fall of 1876. They were published in the Wilmington *North Carolina Presbyterian*, then under his father's editorial leadership. His first essay, "Work-Day Religion," was a characteristic statement of the Calvinistic, activistic creed of immersion into an evil world to realize God's will. "Life is a work-day," Wilson declared.

> . . . We should perform every act as an act of which we shall some day be made to render a strict account, as an act done either in the service of God or in that of the Devil. . . . The Christian character is not one to be assumed only upon the Sabbath or other stated occasions, but is a character which is perfected only by that work-day religion—a religion pervading every act—which is carried with us into every walk of life and made our one stay and hope. The armor of God is not for a parade one day every week, but for constant use in warding off the attacks of the evil one, and thus for the securing of perfect safety.[91]

Wilson further argued that the devil could only be fought by constant attention to one's duty, not by a pietistic withdrawal from the world or tiring "every one with untimely quotations from the Bible, or long discourses upon topics which concern none but Theologians." The call was to action, to the performance of good works in the world.[92]

The martial theme of battling for God and against the devil was sounded even louder in Wilson's second essay, "Christ's Army." Just as his father had emphasized life as a struggle between good and evil, the necessity of fighting for God, and the obligation to remain true to God's law, Wilson stressed the responsibility of each Christian to wage the righteous fight against the devil. "Surely in this great contest there is a part for every one, and each one will be made to render a strict account of his conduct on the day of battle," Wilson insisted. He went on to ask, "Will any one hesitate as to the part he shall take in this conflict? Will any one dare to enlist under the banners of the Prince of Lies, under whose dark folds he only marches to the darkness of hell? For there is no middle course, no neutrality."[93]

The problem was, as Wilson realized, how individuals could know that they belonged to Christ's army. In classic Calvinistic terms, Wil-

[91] "Work-Day Religion," Aug. 11, 1876, *ibid.*, pp. 177-78.

[92] *Ibid.*, p. 177. See also WW's essay, "The Positive in Religion," Oct. 15, 1876, *ibid.*, pp. 211-12.

[93] "Christ's Army," Aug. 17, 1876, *ibid.*, p. 181.

son raised the question of how people knew they were in the elect, but rather than answering it in terms of God's grace, Wilson again emphasized moral deeds as the assurance of salvation and membership in Christ's army. "One who . . . faithfully does his duty and purifies himself in the smallest things has little to fear from the foe," Wilson argued, "and, if he withal leads others by his example and precept to do likewise, and fears not to warn the enemies of the Cross to turn from the error of their ways, he may rest assured that his name is enrolled among the soldiers of the Cross."[94] Throughout his life during crises or periods of stress, Wilson at times reverted to this dualistic and rigidly moralistic view of the world and human activity in it. In the midst of the fight over Senate ratification of the Versailles Treaty, he remarked to his physician about his opponents, "Doctor, the Devil is a busy man."[95]

The moralistic and legalistic character of Wilson's religious faith is also illustrated by his treatment of the Bible. He essentially viewed it as "the most perfect rule of life" and noted that "at no time can any nation be prosperous whose laws are not founded upon [the Bible's] eternal principles of right and wrong, of justice and injustice, of civil and religious liberty." Wilson understood the Bible as basically a rule book in which people could find a clear definition of the moral law for the world, and the rest was their responsibility. By obeying the law, he could gain "for himself an assurance of everlasting life." Wilson showed no awareness of problems in the Bible or controversies surrounding interpretation of its passages, and he demonstrated little sensitivity to the Bible as a record of God's grace toward people when the rules were broken. Nevertheless, he did appreciate the Bible in dynamic and historical terms, seeing it as "this old and yet ever new volume" whose lessons of the past could be utilized and made relevant for the present.[96]

Throughout his years as an educator and even after he entered political life, Wilson retained a profound conservatism that tested the ideas and institutions of the past against the needs and demands of the present. This basic attitude was rooted in and reinforced by several factors, but chief among them was Wilson's understanding of God's law and will as recorded and permanently preserved in the Bible. With such a standard, a person could measure history and withstand the buffetings of social change. Even more, the task of rooting out evils became for Wilson a task of restoration and reformation, not revolution.

By the beginning of Wilson's sophomore year, he had decided to

---

[94] *Ibid.*

[95] Cary T. Grayson, *Woodrow Wilson: An Intimate Memoir* (New York, 1960), p. 106.

[96] "The Bible," Aug. 25, 1876, *PWW*, I, 185. For another example and elaboration of these themes, see WW's essay, "Christian Progress," Dec. 20, 1876, *ibid.*, pp. 234-35.

become a lawyer,[97] and in an especially significant essay on "The Christian Statesman," Wilson worked out his justification of politics as a divine vocation. He rejected the idea that Christian service could only be expressed in certain professions and regretted that there was "a growing tendency to confine religion to certain walks of life." Following his father who called the ordinary believer a statesman of God,[98] Wilson argued that the Christian faith was "the first requisite for a statesman, upon whom rests so heavy a responsibility." He characteristically emphasized the need to remain faithful to principles, "irrespective of party," and silence or inaction did not release the statesman from responsibility. He also sounded the familiar "he who is not with me is against me" theme, declaring that when the statesman "does not actively advocate truth, he advocates error. Those who are not for truth are against it. There is here no neutrality."[99]

However, Wilson moderated this rigorous, idealistic view of the statesman with a plea for tolerance in politics. With perhaps an eye on what he saw as the excesses of Reconstruction, Wilson insisted that a statesman "should have a becoming sense of his own weakness and liability to err, and, while supporting with the utmost vigor what he considers to be the truth, he should treat his opponents with due forbearance, and should avoid all personal attacks, . . . which will only engender useless and unchristian enmity." He concluded by advocating that the statesman should have a faith in Jesus Christ, a truth based on "the Bible's standard, and let his whole conversation and life be such as becomes a Christian, and, therefore, a gentleman."[100]

From the point of view of his religious development, Wilson at this time saw the relationship of the Christian faith to political life as primarily one of relating morals to actions, principles to deeds; ignorant of the nature of actual political life, he showed no appreciation of the moral ambiguity inherent in most political decisions, indeed in most areas of life. For Wilson, the problem of being a Christian was not being able to do good or even determining what was good. Rather, confident of the truth revealed in "the Bible's standard," assured of his own duty and ability to obey that standard, Wilson maintained that the Christian life, in or outside of politics, was essentially the disciplined and faithful performance of one's duty. In Wilson's view as a young student, the wrong was always clear even if the outcome of the battle was at times ambiguous, and one could always be sure of doing right by opposing what was wrong. Any conflict was a battle over princi-

---

[97] Diary, Sept. 15, 1876, *ibid.*, p. 193.
[98] Sermon on I Timothy 4:12, April 10, 1898 (WP, DLC).
[99] "The Christian Statesman," Sept. 1, 1876, *PWW*, I, 188.
[100] *Ibid.*, p. 189.

ples, not personalities, which meant that personal attacks ought not to play any role in political affairs. While elevating political discourse to the realm of issues and principles, this attitude simultaneously encouraged a denial or suppression of ego-involvement in any contest for power.

Finally, these essays from the summer of 1876 are significant in their demonstration of the clarity of Wilson's religious ideas. It is unlikely that Wilson's father would have prevailed upon his son to write them if he had been the spiritually confused youth which he was at Davidson. His faith was, of course, immature in its stern legalism and rigorous moralism, and yet this faith represented the beginning of an articulate, critical, religious view of the world, and for Wilson it would be a source of strength and a standard of values during his years as a student.

Wilson's new spiritual confidence and clearly defined religious views coincided with his intellectual awakening during his sophomore year in college. According to Baker, this year was "among the most important in his whole life: a turning point,"[101] and there is little doubt that Wilson discovered his own intellectual abilities during that year. This discovery seems to have taken place almost exclusively outside the classroom. Although Wilson continued to do reasonably well in his studies, except in science, his class ranking steadily dropped throughout his four years at Princeton. His intellectual excitement came from his own reading and extracurricular activities. As Wilson later wrote of Edmund Burke, "His four years at college were years of wide and eager reading, but not years of systematic and disciplinary study. With singular, if not exemplary, self-confidence, he took his education into his own hands."[102]

Following his father's emphasis, Wilson's chief extracurricular activity involved debating, oratory, and writing. Within weeks after his entry into Princeton, Wilson joined the American Whig Society, one of the two literary and debating societies on the campus, and its activities preoccupied him during his first two years. His first presentation to the Society was an essay on "Rome was not built in a day," and he regularly declaimed on a variety of subjects before his peers. He naturally defended the negative in a debate over whether "a man should be judged by his efforts rather than by his success," and Southerner that he was, he represented the negative position in a debate over whether it was unwise to abolish the protective tariff.[103] These debates were no

---

[101] *WWLL*, I, 86.

[102] "Edmund Burke: The Man and His Times," *c*. Aug. 31, 1893, *PWW*, VIII, 321.

[103] Minutes of the American Whig Society, Sept. 24 and Oct. 29, 1875, March 2, 1877 and Nov. 12, 1878, *ibid.*, I, 75, 76, 78, 251, 434-35.

mere exercises for Wilson. In his senior year, he was selected by the Whig Society as one of the debaters in the competition with Clio Hall but refused to participate because he would have been forced to defend the right of universal suffrage, something he had described as the root of "every evil in this country."[104]

Wilson also took a great interest in the organizational affairs of the Whig Society, serving on committees to study various problems, helping to resolve points of procedure and constitutional order, and leading the Society as its Speaker of the House.[105] But one literary and debating organization was not enough for Wilson, and during his sophomore year, he organized the Liberal Debating Club. With his affection for British political life, Wilson constructed the club's constitution in patent imitation of the British parliamentary system. The control of the club's proceedings resided in a Secretary of State who proposed questions for discussion and whose tenure in office was dependent upon the majority of the club agreeing with his views. Subjects of discussion were brought up in the form of bills and were decided by majority vote.

The constitution once again reveals Wilson's interest in constructing orderly processes for every organization in which he became involved. It also "clearly forecast the structure that Wilson would soon advocate in essays and books for the American government." Furthermore, the constitution reflects Wilson's often repeated conviction that government must operate by debate and discussion, and that students should be engaged with pressing contemporary issues, not irrelevant or abstract questions.[106]

Wilson's reverence for constitutional order appears in his first political speech at Princeton. In discussing "The Union," Wilson ascribed its primary genius to "the Constitution, the main-spring of the Union, [which] has been the love and theme of our greatest statesmen in their youth, their guide and word in their old age."[107] And yet, throughout Wilson's years at Princeton, his interest in constitutional questions was overshadowed by a more pressing and overriding concern—the qualities of leadership. "We hope some day to become statesmen," he told the Whig Society in an oration on "The Ideal Statesman," "and I may say that no worthier ambition could influence us." Echoing his father's own admonitions, Wilson repeatedly emphasized that the key to success in politics was the pursuit of perfection through hard work and the

---

[104] See Editorial Note, Wilson's Refusal to Enter the Lynde Competition, *ibid.*, pp. 480-81; Diary, June 19, 1876, *ibid.*, p. 143.

[105] See, for example, Minutes of the American Whig Society, Sept. 28 and Nov. 16, 1877 and Feb. 1, 1878, *ibid.*, pp. 293, 319, 355.

[106] Constitution for the Liberal Debating Club, *c.* Feb. 1-*c.* March 15, 1877, *ibid.*, pp. 245-49. See also Editorial Note, The Liberal Debating Club, *ibid.*, p. 245.

[107] "The Union," Nov. 15, 1876, *ibid.*, p. 226.

fulfillment of ideals. Wilson linked work's inherent moral goodness to religion itself, for he concluded his oration with an espousal of the Protestant ethic that was chilling in its intensity. "Let me again remind you," he declared, "that it is only by working with an energy which is almost superhuman and which looks to uninterested spectators like insanity that we can accomplish anything worth the achievement. Work is the keystone of a perfect life. Work and trust in God."[108]

Wilson's perfect leader was a man of personal integrity and principle, who, through the commanding influence of his ideas and personality, could win the allegiance of others and guide nations. His chief characteristic was "independent conviction," which would not bend to political expediency. At a time of weak Presidents and the domination of American politics by Congress, Wilson ascribed "the present disorderly and chaotic condition of society" to "lack of independent conviction."[109] He praised Thomas Carlyle for being "a grim knight-errant meeting . . . fraud in all its forms and under whatever disguise";[110] he commended Bismarck's "keenness of insight, clearness of judgment, and promptness of decision."[111] Daniel Webster was "America's greatest statesman" whose "very independence made it impossible to strictly identify him with any particular party."[112] In William Pitt he lauded "the concentrating power of strong convictions" which harmonized his weaknesses and strengths and his "unhesitating, almost boundless confidence in himself, in the wisdom of his own aims."[113] Wilson's celebration of strong leaders did not blind him to their abuses of power, but he excused them and softened his criticism by praising the ends they sought. Slowly emerging in Wilson's political thought was a profound tension between the powerful leader realizing principles against all opposition and the need for government to proceed by debate and discussion and through constitutional means.

Wilson's interest in leadership was not confined to a theoretical level, and he actively sought opportunities to exercise his own powers as a student leader. In addition to filling various offices in the Whig Society and the Liberal Debating Club, he became involved with the student newspaper, *The Princetonian*. In the fall of his junior year, he was chosen to fill in temporarily for the managing editor who had resigned, and later in the year he was elected nearly unanimously by his class to serve as editor.[114] He used the columns of *The Princetonian* as a forum for his views on drama, music, history, politics, and various

---

[108] "The Ideal Statesman," Jan. 30, 1877, *ibid.*, pp. 242, 244-45.

[109] Notes for a speech, "Independent Conviction," *c.* July 16, 1877, *ibid.*, p. 279.

[110] Notes for a speech, "Thomas Carlyle," *c.* July 16, 1877, *ibid.*, p. 281.

[111] "Prince Bismarck," Nov. 1877, *ibid.*, pp. 311-12.

[112] "Daniel Webster and William Pitt," *c.* Aug. 10, 1878, *ibid.*, pp. 396, 397.

[113] "William Earl Chatham," Oct. 1878, *ibid.*, pp. 408, 412.

[114] Bragdon, *Wilson: The Academic Years*, pp. 34-35.

aspects of student life. His editorials were predominantly devoted to the social and extracurricular activities of the students. When he touched upon religious life on campus, it was only to commend visiting ministers for the power and eloquence, not content, of their sermons. When he treated academic affairs, he merely urged more study of English literature and applauded the new offering of Anglo-Saxon in the curriculum.[115] The place of debate and oratory in campus life was one of his constant concerns, and he repeatedly encouraged his fellow students to take advantage of the literary halls as a means of acquiring "social culture." Oratory, he advised, was a means to power. "Its object is persuasion and conviction—the control of other minds by a strange personal influence and power."[116]

Despite his regular surveys of student literary and debating activities, Wilson's chief concern was Princeton athletics. He urged students to support the Princeton teams and even served as secretary of the Football Association and briefly as president of the Base Ball Association. As secretary of the Football Association, he raised money to support the team, and even though he charged a controversial high admission, the Association brought in a profit which Wilson arranged to be applied against the deficit run up by the baseball team. In his editorials Wilson reiterated the need for a disciplined football team and criticized the players when they rejected the captain's leadership. "Until they learn to obey," he warned, "they will never learn to play with effect." His advice and his help in coaching the team paid off. Princeton went undefeated during the 1878 season and was scored on only once.[117]

Sports appealed to the competitive and combative strain in Wilson's personality, and of all the sports, he seemed to prefer football, perhaps because of its roots in English rugby but also because it emphasized physical struggle toward a definite goal. He could not excel in it personally, and so his energies were turned to organizing Princeton's football team and enlisting support for it. But in his defense of football and sports, a slight tone of priggishness emerged. Football, he insisted, was not as violent as it seemed, for at Princeton it was played with a "gentlemanly spirit." He criticized the "immodest attire" some students wore while exercising in the gymnasium; although acknowledging that sleeveless shirts were permissible, be maintained that the arm holes should be smaller to conceal more of the body. "Their natural

---

[115] Editorials in *The Princetonian*, Feb. 7, 1878, Jan. 30, 1879, and Oct. 10, 1878, *PWW*, I, 356-57, 450-51, 415.

[116] Editorials in *The Princetonian*, Feb. 6, 1879 and June 7, 1877, *ibid.*, pp. 454-55, 274-75.

[117] Editorial in *The Princetonian*, Nov. 7, 1878, *ibid.*, p. 431; Bragdon, *Wilson: The Academic Years*, pp. 39-41.

beauties, when unadorned," he complained, "are not so pleasing (are even disgusting) to us, however much they themselves may admire them."[118]

Wilson came to the end of his senior year at Princeton known as a leader of his class, a skilled debater and orator, and a lucid writer. He held nearly every student office to which he could have been elected, but during the latter part of his senior year there apparently was some reaction against the leadership exercised by him and his friends.[119] In any event, Wilson spent part of his senior year preparing his first major article, "Cabinet Government in the United States," which was accepted for publication by Henry Cabot Lodge and printed in the August 1879 issue of the *International Review*. It has been widely noted that there was little in Wilson's article that was new or profound, for he used Walter Bagehot's famous study, *The English Constitution* (1867 and 1872), as the basis for his critique of Congress and his suggested remedies. Bagehot's criticisms of the American presidential-congressional system had been given considerable publicity by Gamaliel Bradford in the New York *Nation*, and in other journals as well, and Wilson was deeply indebted to Bagehot, whom he used even to the point of imitating his style.[120]

In "Cabinet Government," Wilson combined his concern with leadership and constitutional order, as well as his admiration for British political institutions, into a strongly stated argument for reform of American political life. He deplored the decay of the two major parties in the United States and insisted that they were dying "for want of unifying and vitalizing principles." The nation was dominated by a Congress composed of "scheming, incompetent, political tradesmen whose aims and ambitions were merely personal." They conducted the business of the nation in closed committee meetings, and policy was determined in secret and without debate. "Debate," Wilson argued, "is the essential function of a popular representative body." In addition, Wilson regretted the dearth of dynamic leaders who would lead the political parties in a clash of contending principles and debate over policies; only in such discussion and interaction could wise and effective governmental action be pursued. "Eight words contain the sum of the present degradation of our political parties: *No leaders, no principles; no principles, no parties*." Wilson's solution was to make the Cabinet into a body of ministers directly responsible to Congress. This

[118] Editorials in *The Princetonian*, Sept. 26, 1878 and March 27, 1879, *ibid*., pp. 405-406, 467.

[119] Bragdon, *Wilson: The Academic Years*, p. 41.

[120] *Ibid*., pp. 56-62; Editorial Note, "Cabinet Government in the United States," *PWW*, I, 492-93; Arthur S. Link, *Wilson: Road to the White House* (Princeton, 1947), pp. 17-19.

would attract more qualified men to Congress, he insisted, and it would make skill in debate and personal qualities of leadership the characteristics of congressional proceedings.[121] Wilson, as Bragdon has suggested, "was in effect demanding that the entire American political system be radically altered so that he might realize his aspirations for public office and public service."[122]

Wilson's aspirations and ambitions when he finished college are dramatically illustrated by an agreement which he concluded with his classmate, Charles A. Talcott. He called the pact "a solemn covenant," and even though he did not mention God as a party to the agreement, the impact of his covenant theological heritage is clear. In a letter to his fiancée, Wilson recalled the event:

> I had then, as I have still, a very earnest political creed and very pronounced political ambitions. I remember forming with Charlie Talcott (a class-mate and very intimate friend of mine) a solemn covenant that we would school all our powers and passions for the work of establishing the principles we held in common; that we would acquire knowledge that we might have power; and that we would drill ourselves in all the arts of persuasion, but especially in oratory (for he was a born orator if any man ever was), that we might have facility in leading others into our ways of thinking and enlisting them in our purposes. And we didn't do this in merely boyish enthusiasm, though we were blinded by a very boyish assurance with regard to the future and our ability to mould the world as our hands might please. It was not so long ago but that I can still feel the glow and the pulsations of the hopes and the purposes of that moment—nay, it was not so long ago but that I still retain some of the faith that then prompted me.[123]

This was essentially Wilson's covenant for his entire life, pledging himself to a career in politics in which his principles would be realized.

Basically moral in character and preoccupied with power, the covenant represents Wilson's attempt during his senior year to establish a structure for his life, a goal for his ceaseless work, a duty which he must fulfill. From his Presbyterian father, Wilson had learned that God's relationship to people and to all of creation was a contractual, covenanted order, ruled by a moral law contained in the Bible. In that order God reserved total power but made individuals agents of divine will, giving them power and responsibilities for the accomplish-

---

[121] "Cabinet Government in the United States," Aug. 1879, *PWW*, I, 493-510.

[122] Bragdon, *Wilson: The Academic Years*, p. 62.

[123] WW to ELA, Oct. 30, 1883, *PWW*, II, 499-500.

on the wrong track. I had then, as I
have still, a very earnest political creed
and very pronounced political ambition.
I remember forming with Charlie Talcott (a class-mate and very intimate
friend of mine) a solemn covenant that
we would school all our powers and
passions for the work of establishing the
principles we held in common; that we
would acquire knowledge that we might
have power; and that we would drill
ourselves in the arts of persuasion, but
especially in oratory (for he was a born
orator if any man ever was) that we might
have facility in leading others into our
ways of thinking and enlisting them in
our purpose. And we didn't do this in
any mere, boyish enthusiasm, though we
were kindled by a very boyish assurances
with regard to the futures and our ability
to mould the world as our hands might
please. It was not so long ago but that

I can still feel the glow and the pul-
sations of the hopes and the purpose
of that moment—nay, it was not so
long ago but that I still retain some
of the faith that then prompted me. But
a man has to know the world before he
can work in it to any purpose. He has
to know the forces with which he must
coöperate and those with which he
must contend; must know how and
where he can make himself felt, not
reckoning according to the conditions and
possibilities of past times but according to
full knowledge of the conditions of the
present and possibilities of the immediate
future. He must know the times into
which he has been born; and this I
did not know when I left college and
chose my profession, as I proved by my
choice. The profession I chose was politics; the profession I entered was the
law. I entered the one because I thought

Wilson's description of his "solemn covenant." *Princeton University Library*

ment of God's work. In his agreement with Talcott, Wilson once again used this covenant theological view of the world and individualized it for himself. He placed himself, like all of creation, in a relationship to God with definite responsibilities and clear-cut goals. The order of the covenant once again became the young man's response to the uncertainty and confusion of his future professional life.

III

Graduate Student, 1879-1885

Wilson left Princeton with his covenanted future determined, but the means of establishing the principles he held in common with Talcott were not quite so clear. Law was the obvious route to fulfillment of such ambitions. "The profession I chose was politics; the profession I entered was the law. I entered the one because I thought it would lead to the other."[1] But even within a few months after his graduation, Wilson realized that membership in the legal profession was no guarantee that he would fulfill his covenant. "I have not yet hit upon any definite *plans* for the work we promise ourselves," he wrote Talcott during the summer of 1879. Until the opportunity presented itself, Wilson resolved to develop his talents, remain true to his principles, and resist the temptation to lower his ambitions. By staying clear of "the prejudices" and "foolish inaccuracies" of most lawyers, Wilson told Talcott, the two friends would be "strong for the struggle which, it is to be hoped, will raise us above the *pettiness* of our profession."[2] Each success, moreover, was interpreted as a step toward the fulfillment of the covenant. Congratulating Wilson on the publication of "Cabinet Government," Talcott wrote, "I know that it is but the beginning of exertions, which will win honor for yourself and influence the politics of our Country."[3]

Separation from Princeton and friends there was painful. "Since leaving Priceton I have not been in the brightest of moods," he wrote Talcott. "The parting after Commencement went harder than I had feared even. It most emphatically and literally *struck in*." He especially missed his friends and realized in his absence from them how aloof he often appeared to be. "When I am with any one in whom I am specially and sincerely interested, the hardest subject for me to broach is just that which is nearest my heart,"[4] he confessed. To another college friend he confided, "I, perhaps, am colder and more reserved than most of those who are fortunate enough to have been born in our beloved South; but my affection is none the less real because less de-

[1] WW to ELA, Oct. 30, 1883, *PWW*, II, 500.

[2] WW to C. A. Talcott, July 7, 1879, *ibid.*, I, 488.

[3] C. A. Talcott to WW, Oct. 1, 1879, *ibid.*, p. 575. See also C. A. Talcott to WW, Nov. 19, 1879, *ibid.*, p. 584.

[4] WW to C. A. Talcott, July 7, 1879, *ibid.*, pp. 487-88.

monstrative."[5] And yet in his letters, Wilson could be demonstrative enough, exclaiming to Robert Bridges, "You don't know how *longingly* I've been waiting for a letter from you," and signing himself "With much love, Your devoted friend."[6]

Wilson spent the summer after his graduation vacationing with his mother and brother in the Blue Ridge Mountains of North Carolina and South Carolina, occupying his time with the preparation of an essay, "Self-Government in France," a long, rambling assessment of the prospects of French democracy nearly a century after the French Revolution. Wilson contended that "the most important of all political facts in France" was "the thorough-going and minutely-complete *centralization* which has always, through her history, focused whatever powers of despotism her governments have possessed." The legacy of the Revolution had not disturbed this tradition of centralization, he insisted; rather, because the Revolution exalted "freedom gone mad and rioting in the garb of license," the history of France in the nineteenth century had become "little more than a record of the alternation of centralized democracy with centralized monarchy, or imperialism—in all cases a virtual despotism."

Wilson noted that the social impact of the Revolution had been greater than the political, destroying the nobility and weakening the hold of the church. However, he criticized the rising bourgeoisie and their lack of civic consciousness and castigated the church for its refusal to support a general educational system. Without education, France would not produce an enlightened citizenry, he contended, and ignorance only perpetuated the opposite tendencies toward license and despotism. In short, Wilson's conclusion was that the French people had failed to learn self-government, "the liberty of self-imposed obedience," which had to be cultivated by free institutions and calm, temperate administration.

His essay is significant in its awareness of French history and current political affairs, but even more striking is the patent Anglophilism that underlies his somewhat gloomy analysis of French politics. For example, in a direct comparison, Wilson argued that in England law and peaceful debate prevailed while in France force was supreme until governments fell "amid carnage and fierce convulsions."[7] Wilson spent nearly a year attempting to get this essay published, trying unsuccessfully the *International Review* and the *North American Review* and finally putting it away "in all the decency of burial."[8]

Shortly after his enrollment as a law student at the University of Vir-

[5] WW to Francis Champion Garmany, April 2, 1879, *ibid.*, p. 473.

[6] WW to R. Bridges, July 30, 1879, *ibid.*, pp. 489-90.

[7] "Self-Government in France," *c.* Sept. 4, 1879, *ibid.*, pp. 515-39.

[8] WW to R. Bridges, Sept. 18, 1880, *ibid.*, p. 677.

ginia in the autumn of 1879, Wilson picked up a copy of Albert Stickney's *A True Republic* (1879), whose call for permanent tenure during good behavior for all public officials gave Wilson another handle on which to hang his argument for cabinet government. His response to Stickney was "Congressional Government," a warmed-over version of his arguments in "Cabinet Government in the United States," with one significant exception. This later essay carried Wilson one step further in his emulation of British political institutions. He agreed with Stickney that a President ought to serve for life, subject only to good behavior. He should have the sole responsibility of choosing his Cabinet, but in contrast to "Cabinet Government," Wilson maintained that the Cabinet officers ought to be selected from Congress itself. A politically antagonistic President and Congress were not obstacles to good government; rather, the President would be compelled to choose members of Congress and devise a legislative program that would win the support of the majority party.

In his advocacy of reform for American political life, Wilson followed to the logical conclusion his imitation of British political institutions—an elected king, a cabinet of "responsible" ministers, and a legislative body proceeding by debate—"the cardinal feature of representative government."[9]

But Wilson's essay is notable for another reason besides the analytical dead end that he had reached. In a brief introductory passage on the Constitution, Wilson revealed his awareness that law must be adapted and altered for new social and political conditions. The provisions of the Constitution, in their "simplicity" and "limited scope," served as the principles of legislation, providing continuity in institutions and ideas, but not necessarily in details. This attitude predicted political development in Wilson, for despite his passion for constitutional order, he viewed that order not as rigid or permanent but as adaptable and flexible to social change.

Legal education at the University of Virginia was dominated by the imposing figure of John Barbee Minor. Tall and somewhat stout, Minor had served as Professor of Common and Statute Law at the University of Virginia since 1845 and had established a national reputation as one of the greatest legal scholars of the time. At the heart of his scholarship was a deep reverence and affection for the traditions of the common law, which he defended against virtually any alteration. His scholarly brilliance and legal philosophy, summed up in a massive, 5,000-page, four-volume *Institutes of Common and Statute Law* (1876-1879), was matched by his ardent piety. Each Sunday morning he led a Bible class in his lecture room for law students, and one of his former students explained that Minor "considered an acquaintance

---

[9] "Congressional Government," *c.* Oct. 1, 1879, *ibid.*, pp. 548-74.

with the Bible essential to every lawyer, looking with special favor and interest upon those in his department of like opinion—who earnestly attended and studied these Scriptural lectures."[10]

Wilson was undoubtedly one of those of like opinion; within weeks after his first encounter with Minor, he declared him "a *perfect* teacher" and said he could not conceive of a better one.[11] Throughout his life, Wilson considered Minor his greatest teacher next to his father, and Wilson's brother-in-law, Stockton Axson, believed that Minor did more to shape Wilson's views on the law than any one else.[12] Minor's extremely rigorous academic standards established the University of Virginia's reputation, and his pedagogical approach reinforced the educational philosophy Wilson had received from his father. "Thought is requisite as well as reading," Minor insisted; "for the purpose of thought, there must be time to *Digest*, as well as the *Industry* to acquire." "One cannot expect to gorge himself with law as a Boa Constrictor does with masses of food, and then digest it afterwards; the process of assimilation must go on, if it is to proceed healthfully and beneficially, at the same time with the reception of knowledge."[13] Wilson was entranced by Minor's eloquent lectures and plodded his way through his professor's tomes of legal knowledge, carefully annotating points in the margin.[14] Complementing Minor was Stephen O. Southall, who handled the courses in constitutional and international law, and while the former was clearly Wilson's primary field of interest, he apparently did not think highly of Southall as a professor.[15]

The University of Virginia was a natural place for Wilson to obtain the legal education that he hoped to use as the springboard into politics. It offered excellent training and was situated in a state that had given birth to many statesmen. While he was at Princeton, Wilson carefully wrote out cards identifying himself as "Thomas Woodrow Wilson   Senator from Virginia,"[16] and he clearly intended to use, if not Virginia, at least his native South as a means of securing the role of

[10] David M. R. Culbreth, *The University of Virginia* (New York and Washington, 1908), p. 432; Theodore S. Cox, "John Barbee Minor," *Dictionary of American Biography*. 24 vols. (New York, 1928-74), XIII, 26-27; WW to Robert Bridges, Nov. 7, 1879, *PWW*, I, 583, n. 1.

[11] WW to Robert Bridges, Nov. 7, 1879, *ibid.*, p. 581.

[12] *WWLL*, I, 112; R. S. Baker memorandum of an interview with Stockton Axson, Feb. 8, 10, and 11, 1925 (R. S. Baker Coll., DLC).

[13] Quoted in *WWLL*, I, 113.

[14] Some of these marginal notes are printed in *PWW*, I, 583-84.

[15] Wilson did retain his notebooks from Southall's lectures on constitutional and international law but never mentioned him in his correspondence. See the description of WW's notebook, *ibid.*, pp. 576, 602, and WW's notes on Southall's lectures on international law, *c.* Jan. 17, 1880, *ibid.*, pp. 594-96, and on constitutional law, March 9, 1880, *ibid.*, pp. 621-23.

[16] *WWLL*, I, 104.

leadership he wanted. But the reality of legal education was something less than Wilson had expected, and he quickly became discouraged.

"Law is indeed a hard task-master," he complained to Charles Talcott. He went on:

> I am struggling, hopefully but not with *over*-much courage, through its intricacies, and am swallowing the vast mass of its technicalities with as good a grace and as straight a face as an offended palate will allow. I have, of course no idea of abandoning this study because of its few unpleasant features. Any one would prove himself a fool, to be sincerely pitied by all wise men, who should expect to find any work that is worth doing easily done, accomplished without pain or worry; who should turn away from hard study to pursue disappointment in some other direction. . . . To relieve my feelings, therefore, I wish now to record the confession that I am most terribly bored by the noble study of Law sometimes, though in the main I am thoroughly satisfied with my choice of a profession. I think that it is the want of *variety*, principally, that disgusts me. . . . This excellent thing, the Law, gets as monotonous as that other immortal article of food, *Hash*, when served with such endless frequency.[17]

Lonely for his Princeton friends, he regretted that the University of Virginia did not have the same "opportunities for *moral* growth and intellectual invigoration such as we used to gain in our intercourse with the dear boys who were accustomed to meet after prayer meeting in No. 9 East Witherspoon." Despite the excellent instruction in law, he told Talcott, the possibilities for moral and intellectual stimulation "are fewer and further between than the proverbial angel's visits." It was, he concluded, "a splendid place for the education of the *mind*, but no sort of place for the education of the *man*."[18]

Some of Wilson's classmates remember him as slightly aloof and condescending in his attitude toward them and the university, and Wilson's father warned him not to be egotistical or arrogant. "Your descriptions of yr companions are admirably touched—but are they not just a bit acid?" he inquired. "Indeed you seem to feel this yourself. What we sometimes call 'sham' may be mere affectation—the difference between these being suggested by that between hypocrisy and self-deception."[19] As the year wore on, Wilson gradually made more friends, especially with Richard Heath Dabney, the son of one of Dr.

---

[17] WW to C. A. Talcott, Dec. 31, 1879, *PWW*, I, 591.

[18] *Ibid.*, pp. 591-92.

[19] Bragdon, *Wilson: The Academic Years*, pp. 70-71; JRW to WW, Nov. 19, 1879, *PWW*, I, 585-86.

Wilson's southern Presbyterian comrades, and they spent many hours talking, and, to relieve the tension of their studies, playing like school-boys. Dabney gave Wilson the nickname of "illimitable idiot" and Wilson responded in kind, calling Dabney "thou very ass."[20] The friendship lasted long after law school, and after Dabney returned to the University of Virginia as a member of the faculty, he tried to persuade Wilson to come back as president of the institution.

As at Princeton, Wilson's extracurricular activities became the core of his education. He was on the campus for less than a month before he joined one of the two campus literary and debating clubs, the Jefferson Society, and was soon elected secretary.[21] In the debates, he characteristically defended the limitation of suffrage and purportedly shocked some members when he proposed at one meeting that the United States Senate be abolished and Congress be made a unicameral legislature.[22]

Unanimously chosen the society's orator for March 1880, Wilson seized the opportunity to eulogize one of his heroes—John Bright—and to proclaim his vision of politics and the ideal leader. With scarcely a change from his earlier essay on "Christ's Army," Wilson declared that while tolerance was a worthy virtue, it had no place in political life. "Politics is a war of *causes*: a joust of principles," he argued. "In this grand contestation of warring principles he who doubts is a laggard and an impotent. . . . Absolute identity with one's cause is the first and great condition of successful leadership."[23] Always looking to history for moral lessons, Wilson maintained that the life of John Bright taught people that

> duty lies wheresoever truth directs us; that statesmanship consists, not in the cultivation and practice of the arts of intrigue, nor in the pursuit of all the crooked intricacies of the paths of party management, but in the lifelong endeavor to lead first the attention and then the will of the people to the acceptance of truth in its applications to the problems of government; that not the adornments of rhetoric, but an absorbing love for justice and truth and a consuming, passionate devotion to principle are the body and soul of eloquence: that complete identification with some worthy cause is the first and great prerequisite of abiding success.[24]

Principles and the successful leader—the two were indivisible in Wil-

[20] *WWLL*, I, 128.

[21] Minutes of the Jefferson Society, Oct. 18 and Nov. 22, 1879, *PWW*, I, 576, 587.

[22] *Ibid.*, Feb. 6, 1880, *ibid.*, p. 602; Bragdon, *Wilson: The Academic Years*, p. 76.

[23] Minutes of the Jefferson Society, Jan. 31 and March 6, 1880, *PWW*, I, 597-98, 608; "John Bright," March 6, 1880, *ibid.*, p. 617.

[24] *Ibid.*, p. 620.

son's mind. Yet within this framework, Wilson showed little aware-ness of the difference between the enlightened leader and the inspired demagogue, both of whom could be utterly committed to principles.

Wilson pursued many of the same themes in an essay for the univer-sity magazine on his boyhood model, Gladstone, whom he lauded for the "warrior qualities" of his mind. Obviously reflecting his own ideals, Wilson described Gladstone as "habitually militant, and all that he has written and said . . . has been written and said not so much as to communicate thoughts as to urge arguments and impart purposes." As in his essay on Bismarck, Wilson ignored Gladstone's religious faith and chose to talk instead of his principles and his ability to lead. This ability stemmed from Gladstone's "keen poetical sensibility," which allowed him "to throw himself, as if by instinct, on that side of every public question which, in the face of present doubts, is in the long run to prove the side of wisdom and of clearsighted policy."[25]

Each new biographical essay raised the leader to greater heights of influence and importance in Wilson's mind and simultaneously charged his imagination and resolve to become a leader himself. But the Gladstone essay also conveys another characteristic of the ideal leader that Wilson would find particularly valuable in interpreting his own life. He found at the heart of Gladstone's career an ability to change, develop, and grow. Inconsistencies inevitably arose, but Wil-son defended Gladstone against this charge, insisting that "few men stand in their old age where they stood in their youth." Consistency meant a refusal to acknowledge new truth when it was discovered and a resistence to change and progress.[26]

The principled, though imperious, leader dominated Wilson's think-ing about politics, and the uncomfortable questions of how principles could be judged were kept at bay by his basic faith in the "attention and will of the people." In a famous debate at the University of Vir-ginia with William Cabell Bruce on the threat of Roman Catholicism to democratic institutions, Wilson declared that the Catholic Church was not a threat to Americans because the democratic traditions "peculiar to our race" would resist the encroachment of Rome's authority. "The unassailable defense of *self-government*," strengthened by the Ameri-can public school system, had "forearmed" the people and assured the victory of democracy.[27] Constitutions, furthermore, guarded the will of the people through the principle of representation and guaranteed a government in which policy was formed by debate, not an individual's dictates.

[25] "William Gladstone," April 1880, *ibid.*, pp. 635, 628.

[26] *Ibid.*, pp. 632-34.

[27] News report of a debate, April 1880, *ibid.*, pp. 643-46.

Significantly, when Wilson drafted constitutions himself, it was this fundamental belief in the popular ratification of policies and a strong legislative body, not a powerful executive, that predominated. During his second year at Virginia, when he served as president of the Jefferson Society, he engineered a complete revamping of the club's constitution, serving as chairman of the drafting committee. He even managed its fate in the society's proceedings by arranging for the organization to form a committee of the whole, which enabled him to speak more effectively to the issue. Among the provisions of the new constitution were an elaborate but systematic order of government, diffusion of executive power, strong emphasis upon popular house ratification of executive rulings, and explicit provisions for the value and necessity of debate.[28] Clearly, when it came to formulating exactly how power ought to be shared, Wilson's glorification of the leader was moderated by a concern for constitutional order and a desire to diffuse power as broadly as possible. The covenant or contractual view of society and all human relations prevailed over emphasis on individualistic virtue and charismatic leadership.

In both his academic work and his independent study of writing and speaking, Wilson's father remained his chief teacher and critic. Always emphasizing clarity, Dr. Wilson told his son that the sentences of a speech "ought to resemble *bullets*—i.e. be compact and rapid, & prepared to make clean holes." He praised Wilson's decision to take elocution lessons at the University of Virginia, as well as his practicing singing to improve his speaking.[29] Wilson sent his father drafts of essays and speeches, which his father pored over, changing the structure of paragraphs, smoothing out his son's strained literary style, and sending them back with praise and encouragement. In returning Wilson's essay, "Congressional Government," his father declared, "It is capital, and increases, if anything could do so, my respect for my precious boy."[30] They conferred over where Wilson should send his articles for publication, compared notes over the state of the oratorical art, and shared their opinions about current affairs.[31]

---

[28] Jefferson Society Constitution, *c.* Dec. 4, 1880, *ibid.*, pp. 689-99; Editorial Note, The Constitution of the Jefferson Society, *ibid.*, pp. 688-89; see also WW's notes on Stephen Southall's lectures on constitutional law, March 9, 1880, *ibid.*, pp. 621-23.

[29] JRW to WW, Nov. 5, 1877, April 17 and Nov. 19, 1880, *ibid.*, pp. 315, 650-51, 687.

[30] JRW to WW, *c.* Dec. 13, 1879, *ibid.*, pp. 588-89. For other examples of JRW's advice to his son about writing, see especially the passage from one of JRW's letters that Wilson copied into a notebook, Jan. 14, 1878, *ibid.*, pp. 340-41, and JRW to WW, Feb. 25, 1879, *ibid.*, pp. 459-60.

[31] JRW to WW, Dec. 22, 1879, April 2 and 17 and May 6, 1880, *ibid.*, pp. 589-90, 646-47, 650-51, 654.

But even Dr. Wilson grew alarmed by Wilson's distaste for his legal studies, and when his son began to dream of a literary career for himself until political doors would open, his father cautioned, "That you will be known by-and-by, in literary circles [,] I have very little doubt: if you desire to be. I hesitate though, my precious one, to advise a mere literary career such as you seem to dream about now and then. At any rate, *far*, *far* better conquer the law."[32] Partially because of his own low spirits in Wilmington, his father also fretted about Wilson's feelings of depression and discouragement and repeatedly urged his son not to let his thoughts focus on himself and his difficulties. "Let the future care for itself is both the dictate of Scripture and of good sense," he assured Wilson and reminded him that his faith would help him in difficult times because "you can afford to trust in God, and He has so fitted His providence to your case that you can afford also to trust yourself."[33]

Contributing to Wilson's depression was his ill-fated love affair with his first cousin, Harriet ("Hattie") Woodrow who was studying at the nearby Augusta Female Seminary in Staunton. Wilson made several trips to visit her, often at the expense of his studies. He spent the Christmas holidays in 1879 with his uncle James W. Bones in Staunton, who dutifully reported to Wilson's parents that "Hattie spent the week with us & she & Jessie & Tommie had nice times together."[34] By the end of his first year, Wilson was in trouble with the faculty for missing too many classes. When he reported the trouble to his parents, his mother reassured him but his father admonished, "Your head went agog. Let it lead you to mistrust it."[35]

For more than a year and a half, Wilson ardently pursued Hattie, writing several long, affectionate letters and continuing to visit when he could. "My sweet Rosalind," "My precious Cousin," "Dearest Hattie," and "My sweetest Cousin" he called her, but he mistook her reserve for coyness. She was embarrassed by his visits and considered marriage between first cousins improper.[36] Finally, during the summer of 1881, Wilson proposed to her but she rejected him. Her denial was a blow, and he wrote to her immediately asking that she reconsider her

---

[32] JRW to WW, Dec. 22, 1879, *ibid.*, p. 589.

[33] JRW to WW, Oct. 5, 1880, *ibid.*, p. 682.

[34] James W. Bones to JWW, Jan. 13, 1880, *WWLL*, I, 130.

[35] JWW to WW, June 5 and 18, 1880, *PWW*, I, 659, 661; JRW to WW, June 5 and June 7, 1880, *ibid.*, pp. 658, 659-60.

[36] WW to Harriet Augusta Woodrow, *c.* April 14 and Oct. 5, 1880, *ibid.*, pp. 647-50, 678-82; Jan. 15 and 19 and May 10, 1881, *ibid.*, II, 12-17, 63-66; WW to R. Bridges, March 15, 1882, *ibid.*, pp. 106-108. See also Helen Welles Thackwell, "Woodrow Wilson and My Mother," *Princeton University Chronicle,* XII (1950), 6-18.

"dismissal." "I cannot sleep to-night—so give me the consolation of thinking, while waiting for the morning, that there is still one faint hope left to save me from the terror of despair."[37]

She remained firm, and Wilson responded to the defeat as his father had taught him—by fighting on. "My darling . . .," he wrote upon his return home, "[I] realize that my love for you has taken such a hold on me as to have become almost a part of myself, which no influences I can imagine can ever destroy or weaken." Hattie gave up; she refused to answer any more letters.[38] Six months later, Wilson found he was still "unable to speak of it without such a rush a feeling as makes clear expression next to impossible."[39]

The thwarted romance, dissatisfaction with the study of law, and frustration over his future in politics combined with the pressures of law school to undermine Wilson's health. He left the University of Virginia at the end of his first year in ill health but recovered sufficiently to reenter in the autumn of 1880. His mother worried constantly about his physical difficulties, and finally in December both parents demanded that Wilson return to Wilmington.[40] His father's motivation was mixed, for although he worried about his son, he also longed to have him back at home. As early as April 1880, he suggested that Wilson study law at home and exclaimed, "Think of what a joy it would be to me, and to all of us!"[41] Wilson conceded, withdrew from the university in December, and returned home; there a doctor found his digestive system seriously disturbed and warned him that he was on the verge of chronic dyspepsia.[42]

Undoubtedly, Wilson's illness was at least in part psychosomatic. His driving ambition and relentless intensity probably only aggravated a tendency toward ill health, and during his long stay at home of more than a year and a half, he wondered, "How can a man with a weak body ever arrive anywhere?"[43] And yet, his covenanted future was certain and his resolve undiminished. "My path is a very plain one—and the only question is whether I will have the strength to breast the hill and reach the heights to which it leads," he wrote to Robert Bridges. "My *end* is a commanding influence in the councils (and counsels) of my country—and *means* to be employed are writing and speaking. Hence my desire to perfect myself in both."[44] During his convalescence in Wilmington, Wilson worked hard at perfecting his writing and

[37] WW to H. A. Woodrow, Sept. 25, 1881, *PWW*, II, 83.

[38] WW to H.A. Woodrow, Oct. 3, 1881, *ibid.*, p. 89.

[39] WW to R. Bridges, March 15, 1882, *ibid.*, p. 107.

[40] JWW and JRW to WW, Dec. 14, 1880, *ibid.*, I, 701.

[41] JRW to WW, April 2, 1880, *ibid.*, p. 646.

[42] WW to Richard Heath Dabney, Feb. 1, 1881, *ibid.*, II, 17.

[43] Quoted in *WWLL*, I, 130.   [44] WW to R. Bridges, Jan. 1, 1881, *PWW*, II, 10.

speaking, delivering orations on political subjects to the empty pews of his father's church, composing essays on various subjects, and even making a clumsy attempt at poetry.[45]

His writings focused primarily on current political problems, and several indicate Wilson's development from a defender of the Confederacy to an ardent proponent of the New South. In "Stray Thoughts from the South" and "New Southern Industries," both published in the New York *Evening Post*, Wilson hailed the growth of industry in the South and painted a glowing picture of the region's commercial and economic future. He looked forward with anticipation to the influx of northern capital into the South to expand the textile industry and create new industries, and he predicted that the South would acquire its share of foreign immigrants to supplement the ready supply of cheap labor.[46] But, as Wilson realized, the uncertain future of the South involved "principally the things social and political, not the things commercial and industrial,"[47] and these revolved around the "problem" of the Negro. The South, Wilson insisted, would always be "solid" and Democratic because it refused to allow the domination of its political and social life by Republicans allied with "ignorant" southern Negroes.

In his essays, Wilson insisted that it was because black people were uneducated and thus unfit to govern that the South resisted and prevented their participation in political life,[48] but in his private notes he described Negroes as not only ignorant people but also as an "inferior" race.[49] Despite this blatant, though publicly veiled, racism, Wilson thought that the "key to the South's propen[sity] to homicide" was slavery. The presence of black slaves had bred in the culture an attitude encouraging the acquisition of power through violence rather than persuasion. He also believed that Memorial Day celebrations in honor of the Confederate dead only served to prolong the antagonism bred by the Civil War.[50]

In other essays, Wilson espoused the growing concern for reform of the civil service system, calling it "an issue of life and death" and

[45] WW to R. Bridges, May 24, 1881, *ibid.*, p. 70; "A River's Course," Dec. 1, 1881, *ibid.*, pp. 91-94; "A Song," Dec. 8, 1881, *ibid.*, p. 94.

[46] "Stray Thoughts from the South," Feb. 12, 1881, *ibid.*, pp. 19-25; "New Southern Industries," April 20, 1882, *ibid.*, pp. 119-25. See also WW's description of himself as a progressive Southerner in WW to the Editor of the *International Review, c.* April 30, 1881, *ibid.*, p. 48.

[47] "Stray Thoughts from the South," Feb. 12, 1881, *ibid.*, p. 20.

[48] "Stray Thoughts from the South," unpublished version, *c.* Feb. 22, 1881, *ibid.*, pp. 26-31; "The Politics and Industries of the New South," *c.* April 30, 1881, *ibid.*, pp. 49-55.

[49] Marginal note to A.H.H. Stuart's letter to the Editor of the Philadelphia *American, c.* Feb. 5, 1881, *ibid.*, p. 19.

[50] Marginal note to Alexis de Tocqueville, *Democracy in America*, Jan. 19, 1883, *ibid.*, pp. 294-95; WW to H. A. Woodrow, May 10, 1881, *ibid.*, p. 64.

labeling the system's "degradation" as "the gigantic evil beside which all the other dangers that threaten our republican union are dwarfed." Like the battle against the devil, the cause of reform was transformed by Wilson into a "crusade," and, dreaming of the role he might play, he insisted that young men and organization were absolute necessities. "There must be a great, combined, aggressive, constitutional agitation of opinion," he proclaimed, "and its organization, its leadership, and its impulse must be supplied by the strength, the purpose, and the ardor of the young." In preparation for the fight, he advised, education was the chief task of youth. "To study, then, to study is the imperious necessity which rests upon all young men of ambition."[51] As an unemployed young man of twenty-five, Wilson was clearly attempting both to justify his own independent study and create a world of politics which demanded his particular interests and skills, and throughout his later career he would often seek to define problems in terms that only his solutions would satisfy.

Wilson sent many of these essays to his friend Robert Bridges in New York, who served as a kind of literary agent for him, but many of the pieces never were published. Wilson was discouraged by these rebuffs but found a more encouraging response from the editor of the Wilmington *North Carolina Presbyterian*, who published three letters by Wilson signed "Anti-Sham." In them Wilson attacked the editor of the Wilmington *Morning Star* for praising some speeches by Archbishop James Gibbons of Baltimore and Bishop Joseph Keane of Richmond who had come to Raleigh to install a new bishop. Wilson accused the editor of encouraging "the aggressive advances of an organization whose cardinal tenets are openly antagonistic to the principles of free government" and charged that "education seems to be the chosen gate of Romish invasion in this country." Wilson's attack prompted an angry response from Catholics in Wilmington, but he considered it all good fun—"an amusing passage at arms"—and "a good chance to exercise myself in satire and ridicule."[52] Like his father, Wilson could occasionally use his verbal gifts as a sword.

Wilson's long stay at home was not a happy one, and he remained restless, driven by his ambition to fulfill his "solemn covenant." "The fact is, I rather envy you," he wrote Robert Bridges. "I am older than you are—I begin to feel very sedate under the burden of my twenty-five years—and yet you have already gotten a long start of me. I am not even licensed yet—I am not even entered for the race. But I'm very

---

[51] "What Can Be Done for Constitutional Liberty," *c.* March 21, 1881, *ibid.*, pp. 33-40.

[52] Anti-Sham Letters, Jan. 25, Feb. 15, and March 22, 1882, *ibid.*, pp. 97-99, 99-103, especially n. 1, pp. 113-17; WW to R. Bridges, March 15, 1882, *ibid.*, p. 108.

eager to get to work and shall run hard when I'm once fairly on the course."[53] After flirting with a career in journalism in the North,[54] Wilson resigned himself to trying to make a living at the law. After long thought and consultation with his father, Wilson settled on Atlanta because it was the center of life in the New South, and "some centre of activity" was what he eagerly sought. "Besides there is much gained in growing up with the section of country in which one's home is situate, and the South has really just begun to grow industrially. After standing still, under slavery, for half a century, she is now becoming roused to a new work and waking to a new life."[55]

Wilson arranged for a partnership with Edward I. Renick, who had received his law degree from the University of Virginia in 1881 but whom Wilson had never met. The two set up an office in August 1882, dividing the work so that Renick handled much of the research and office work and Wilson handled court appearances.[56] His diligent study at the University of Virginia and independent work in Wilmington paid off, and in October 1882 he was admitted to the Georgia bar after a performance at the examination which, according to the judge, was "not short of brilliant."[57]

Baker has suggested that Wilson's law practice was a rather obvious failure since he "never had a case of his own"; however, there were a few exceptions, one being the settlement of his mother's inheritance.[58] The publication of the Wilson papers has revealed that although the firm of Wilson and Renick started out slowly, it did begin to attract some business. The primary problem seemed to be that Wilson's heart was not in the practice of law, and he spent most of his time studying and writing. He later confessed, "Whoever thinks, as I thought, that he can practice law successfully and study history and politics at the same time is wofully mistaken. If he is to make a living at the bar he must be a lawyer *and nothing else*."[59] Impoverished by his lack of interest in practicing law, Wilson fell back on his father, who sent him a monthly allowance of $50.[60]

Wilson's law practice in Atlanta did have one constructive result, apart from his realization that he did not want to be a lawyer. The death of his mother's brother, William Woodrow, brought the settlement of

[53] *Ibid.*, p. 109.

[54] WW to R. Bridges, Aug. 25, 1882, *ibid.*, p. 137.

[55] WW to R. Bridges, Aug. 22, 1881, *ibid.*, p. 76; WW to C. A. Talcott, Sept. 22, 1881, *ibid.*, p. 82.

[56] WW to R. Bridges, Aug. 25, 1882, *ibid.*, pp. 137-38.

[57] *WWLL*, I, 148-49.   [58] *Ibid.*, p. 151.

[59] WW to ELA, Oct. 30, 1883, *PWW*, II, 501.

[60] Editorial Note, Wilson's Practice of Law, *ibid.*, pp. 144-45.

the estate to Wilson's attention, and in conjunction with this business, he visited his uncle James W. Bones in Rome, Georgia, in April 1883. Wilson went to church with the Bones family, and there he saw Ellen Louise Axson, the young woman he would marry. Wilson later recalled the occasion in a letter to her: "I remember thinking 'what a bright, pretty face; what splendid, mischievous, laughing eyes! I'll lay a wager that this demure little lady has lots of life and fun in her!' "[61] She was the daughter of the local pastor, the Rev. Samuel E. Axson, and Wilson quickly arranged to call on him at the manse to bring his father's greetings. After an uncomfortable but comical period in which her father failed to divine the real purpose of Wilson's visit, his daughter came in and was introduced. Wilson developed a new interest in the settlement of the Woodrow estate, and his visits to Rome increased. Within months he had decided he would marry her,[62] and although he hinted strongly to her concerning his intentions, he could not bring himself to propose openly.

By this time Wilson had dropped his first name Thomas and was known to his fellow lawyers as Woodrow Wilson. As early as 1879, he had started signing himself as T. Woodrow Wilson, and explained to Robert Bridges that the change was prompted by his mother's "special request, because this signature embodies *all* my family name."[63] Eventually he dropped even the first initial, but it seems clear that he did so in part to find a more distinguished and alliterative name than his boyhood label of "Tommy."[64]

And so it was Woodrow Wilson who made his political debut in Atlanta in testimony before the Tariff Commission appointed by President Arthur to study rates and policies. Wilson was persuaded to testify by Walter Hines Page, a friend of Renick's and a correspondent covering the commission's hearings for the New York *World*. Wilson's argument was brief but cogent, maintaining that a protective tariff was the mother of monopolies and destructive of the welfare of the United States, both domestically and in its relations with other countries.[65] He had few illusions about the effect of his remarks on a commission packed with protectionists ("this much ridiculed body of incompetencies," he called them) but hoped his remarks might make an impact on someone in Congress.[66]

[61] WW to ELA, Oct. 11, 1883, *ibid.*, p. 468.

[62] JWW to WW, June 21, 1883, *ibid.*, pp. 370-71.

[63] WW to R. Bridges, Nov. 7, 1879, *ibid.*, I, 583.

[64] JWW to WW, Aug. 23, 1880, *ibid.*, p. 674.

[65] Notes for the testimony, *c.* Sept. 23, 1882, *ibid.*, II, 139; transcript of the testimony, Sept. 23, 1882, *ibid.*, pp. 140-43.

[66] WW to R. H. Dabney, Jan. 11, 1883, *ibid.*, pp. 285-86; see also WW to R. Bridges, Oct. 28, 1882, *ibid.*, pp. 147-49.

Wilson's abundant spare time was spent reading in history and political science and writing. He completed a book-length manuscript, "Government by Debate," a long, repetitive reworking of his favorite theme—the adaptation of the cabinet system to American uses. It consisted of five chapters, each one making the same basic point: responsible government is characterized by debate over policies and issues; the means of guaranteeing that debate, rather than secretive committee action, was to have Cabinet members selected from Congress and responsible to that body. Wilson did add some new historical depth and analysis of contemporary politics to his argument, but essentially the book was a compendium of his previous work. Above all, it was "a tract for the times," a call for reform from an unknown political writer whose style veered frequently into verbosity and exaggeration.[67] Wilson and his "agent" Bridges tried valiantly but vainly to get it published.[68]

With shorter pieces, Wilson had better luck. A well-written and well-argued article on the convict-lease system in Georgia was published by the New York *Evening Post*. In it Wilson criticized the "gross abuses" involved in leasing convicts to work for private industry. The practice failed to generate sufficient revenues, Wilson objected, and it violated his belief that the state should not supply advantages for private gain. Wilson did not seem to be moved by primarily humanitarian considerations, for by his racist standards the convict-lease system did not even satisfy the objective of punishment. "The majority of the convicts," he wrote, "are of the lower class of negroes, who are accustomed to the severest and meanest kinds of manual work, and who are neither punished nor humiliated by being compelled to drudge in chains."[69] Another essay, which cast a condescending glance at the cultural and educational provincialism of the South, was rejected by the *Evening Post*, but Wilson was not crushed. "It is of no consequence, even in my eyes," he concluded.[70]

By February 1883, after a four-month try at the practice of law, Wilson had decided to make teaching and writing his profession. "My natural, and therefore predominant, tastes every day allure me from my law books; I throw away law reports for histories, and my mind runs after the solution of political, rather than of legal, problems, as if

[67] "Government by Debate," *c*. Dec. 4, 1882, *ibid.*, pp. 159-275; Editorial Note, "Government by Debate," *ibid.*, pp. 152-57.

[68] WW to Harper and Brothers, Dec. 4, 1882, *ibid.*, pp. 157-58; WW to R. Bridges, Jan. 4, Feb. 5, May 13, and Sept. 12, 1883, *ibid.*, pp. 280-81, 298-300, 354, 424-25; R. Bridges to WW, Jan. 7, July 30, and Aug. 15 and 30, 1883, *ibid.*, pp. 281-83, 395, 413.

[69] "Convict Labor in Georgia," *c*. Feb. 24, 1883, *ibid.*, pp. 306-11.

[70] "Culture and Education in the South," March 29, 1883, *ibid.*, pp. 326-32; WW to R. Bridges, May 13, 1883, *ibid.*, p. 354.

its keenest scent drew it after them by an unalterable instinct," he told Bridges. The goal remained the same, only redefined. "I want to make myself an *outside force in politics.*" His father had reservations about his decision, wondering whether his son's professional uncertainty was not becoming endemic. "Are you certain, *can* you be certain, that this enemy will not attack you again?" he asked Wilson, but then reassured him, "With your education, and gifts, and character, and opportunity, you may kick the world before you—*God* helping you as He will for the honest asking."[71] For his own part, Wilson felt that he had to escape from the "hum-drum life down here in slow, ignorant, uninteresting Georgia" and the depressing "atmosphere of broken promises, of wrecked estates, of neglected trusts, of unperformed duties, of crimes and of quarrels."[72]

Wilson's decision to abandon the law and enter The Johns Hopkins University came after the realization that his ambition could not be fulfilled at the bar. A professorship was the only feasible place for him, and "the only place that would afford leisure for reading and for original work, the only strictly literary berth with an income attached." This did not mean that he was sacrificing his goal of involvement in politics, but it did mean reconciling himself to being "an *outside* force in politics . . . through literary and non-partisan agencies." As he explained to his fiancée:

> . . . My predilections, ever since I had any that were definite, have always turned very strongly towards a literary life, notwithstanding my decided taste for oratory, which is supposed to be the peculiar providence of public men. With manhood came to me an unquenchable desire to excel in two distinct and almost opposite kinds of writing: political and *imaginative.* I want to contribute to our literature what no American has ever contributed, studies in the philosophy of our institutions, not the abstract and occult, but the practical and suggestive, philosophy which is at the core of our governmental methods; their use, their meaning, "the spirit that makes them workable." I want to divest them of the theory that obscures them and present their weakness and their strength without disguise, and with such skill and such plentitude of proof that it shall be seen that I have succeeded and that I have added something to the resources of knowledge upon which statecraft must depend.[73]

[71] WW to R. Bridges, April 29 and May 13, 1883, *ibid.*, pp. 343-44, 354-58; JRW to WW, Feb. 13, 1883, *ibid.*, p. 304, n. 1.

[72] WW to R. H. Dabney, May 11, 1883, *ibid.*, p. 350; WW to R. Bridges, April 29, 1883, *ibid.*, p. 343.

[73] WW to ELA, Oct. 30, 1883, *ibid.*, pp. 501-502.

With these goals in mind, Wilson enrolled at Johns Hopkins University in September 1883, and for the next two years he studied under Herbert Baxter Adams and Richard T. Ely, drove himself almost to the point of collapse at times, and relaxed in long, passionate love letters to his own "Eileen."

Dr. Wilson strongly supported his son's decision to study at Johns Hopkins, despite its reputation for caring little about religious orthodoxy (Thomas Huxley was the principal speaker at the opening exercises). Wilson's father hailed the institution upon its founding in 1876 as the only one in America which could "with strict propriety be called a *University*." Johns Hopkins was also strongly recommended by Wilson's uncle, James Woodrow, who suggested that Wilson apply for a graduate fellowship.[74] The fellowship application was denied, and Wilson's father once again underwrote his studies.

When Wilson entered Johns Hopkins, the university was in the initial stages of one of the most creative and exciting periods in its history. Under Adams' guidance, a generation of historians emerged from Hopkins and left a profound impression on the landscape of American historiography. In addition to Wilson, the doctoral students over the next two decades included John Franklin Jameson, John Spencer Bassett, William Peterfield Trent, Charles Homer Haskins, Frederick Jackson Turner, and Charles McLean Andrews. As Jameson later recalled, Johns Hopkins "was like the opening of the Pacific before the eyes of Balboa and his men. Here were no dated classes, no campus, no sports, no dormitories, no gulf between teacher and student where all were students, no compulsion toward work where all were eager."[75] One recent historian has concluded that in the field of American history, "after the Hopkins interlude, and with the exception of Frederick Jackson Turner, no single individual and no specific school exerted an influence comparable to the Johns Hopkins of the Adams era."[76]

Almost immediately Wilson encountered problems with his course of study in Baltimore, for he was frustrated in his pursuit of his first love—the study of constitutional development and theory. He was further annoyed by the reverence for the German scientific historical methods which had found a warm reception at Johns Hopkins, and he hated the tedium of researching minutiae. He complained bitterly that Adams' chief interest was "in the accurate details of history—in the

---

[74] Wilmington *North Carolina Presbyterian*, Aug. 2, 1876; James Woodrow to JWW, March 14, 1883, *PWW*, ii, 317-18; J. Woodrow to JRW, April 11, 1883, *ibid.*, pp. 335-36.

[75] Cited in Michael Kraus, *History of American History* (New York, 1937), p. 312.

[76] Bert James Loewenberg, *American History in American Thought: Christopher Columbus to Henry Adams* (New York, 1972), p. 366.

precise day of the month on which Cicero cut his eye-teeth—in past society for its own sake," and rebelled when Adams put him to work on one of his pet projects—tracing the history of contemporary American political institutions to earlier local governments in England and the American colonies. He found "very tiresome" the digging "into the dusty records of old settlements and colonial cities," particularly since it seemed totally unrelated to the purpose of his own historical inquiry. "My chief interest," he declared, "is in politics, in history as it furnishes object-lessons for the present."[77] After little more than a month of chafing under Adams' direction, Wilson went to him, "made a clean breast of it," explained what he wanted to do, and Adams turned him loose.[78]

Wilson attacked his work with diligence and intensity. He brashly resolved "to become an invigorating and enlightening power in the world of political thought and a master in some of the less serious branches of literary art." Realizing that such a goal might be pretentious and claiming no illusions about his own intellectual ability, he relied upon "hard work and a capacity for being taught." "I am by no means confident of reaching the heights to which I aspire," he told Ellen Axson, "but I *am* sure of being able to climb *some* distance; and I shall never be embittered by finding myself unable to get to the top."[79] For Wilson, life continued to be a journey toward the realization of ideals, and half the joy lay in the struggle. "There is always satisfaction in hard, conscientious work," he maintained, "in the earnest pursuit of a clearly-seen, however distant, ideal. . . . We admire and strive after virtue none the less because we know we *have* it not."[80]

Wilson pushed himself relentlessly, and his absence from Ellen Axson increased his tension. In his letters to her he confessed that his "strong passions" often threatened to get the best of him; "the only whip with which I can subdue them is the whip of hard study and that lascerates *me* as often as it conquers my crooked dispositions." He longed for her presence, but in her absence he used work as his "best recreation" and "only complete diversion." "It wears me out less than the passionate impatience at separation from you which must come with ease or idleness." Wilson adopted his father's solution for depression and introspection—work and the turning outward to the realization of a distant ideal. And yet the far-off ideals and his own immediate desires and needs continued to produce conflict. "I have the uncom-

---

[77] WW to ELA, Nov. 13, 1884, *PWW*, III, 430; Oct. 16, 1883, *ibid.*, II, 479-80.

[78] WW to ELA, Oct. 16, 1883, *ibid.*, p. 480.

[79] WW to ELA, Oct. 30, 1883, *ibid.*, pp. 503-504.

[80] WW to ELA, Jan. 8, 1884, *ibid.*, p. 654.

fortable feeling that I am carrying a volcano about with me," he confessed to Ellen. "My salvation is in being loved."[81]

During his first few months at Johns Hopkins, Wilson finished pasting together some sections of "Government by Debate," which by this time he had despaired of publishing as a book. The shortened version appeared as "Committee or Cabinet Government?" in the January 1884 issue of the *Overland Monthly*, and in it Wilson performed his familiar dissection of the ills of American politics and advocated the British parliamentary model as a means of reform.

The process of legislation through committees distinguished "our House of Representatives from the other great legislative bodies of the world," Wilson argued. The committees, in turn, were dominated by political bosses, whose power derived not from the wisdom of their views or their skill in debate but their ability to strike secret political bargains. "Such parties as we have, parties with worn-out principles and without definite policies, are unmitigated nuisances," he complained. "They are savory with decay, and rank with rottenness. They are ready for no service, but to be served." The solution was to create a system of cabinet government, which had "in it everything to recommend it." The government of cabinet officials would stand or fall on its ability to command support for its policies; "ugly beast caucus" would be destroyed through the open deliberations of a legislative body dependent upon debate; civil service reform would be assured because improper practices could be exposed by the legislators.

At its heart, Wilson insisted, cabinet government represented a way of linking the interests of the executive and legislative branches in the joint enterprise of providing responsible, efficient government. "First or last, Congress must be organized in conformity with what is now the prevailing legislative practice of the world," he concluded. "English precedent and the world's fashion must be followed in the institution of Cabinet Government in the United States."[82]

"Committee or Cabinet Government" was a way station on the road to Wilson's first book, *Congressional Government*. Obsessed with reform, the article was long on advocacy and short on careful, critical analysis. Its strength was the well-turned, if occasionally overwrought, phrase, and its weakness was a casual disregard for the difficulties of actually implementing the parliamentary system in the United States. *Congressional Government* possessed several of these same deficiencies, but in muting the call for reform, Wilson presented in this book a more carefully reasoned analysis of the functioning of American gov-

[81] WW to ELA, Dec. 7 and Aug. 23, 1884, *ibid.*, III, 522, 301.

[82] "Committee or Cabinet Government," *c*. Jan. 1, 1884, *ibid.*, II, 617, 625, 629, 632, 639, 640.

ernment and its defects. In the process, he exhibited a more than superficial understanding of national politics during the post-Civil War period of congressional supremacy.

Stylistically, *Congressional Government* was uneven. As in all things, Wilson set an ideal for his style, an ideal formed through his father's instruction and his own admiration for the magisterial writing of his British idols—Bagehot, Burke, Macaulay, and others. As he began work on *Congressional Government,* he described his hopes for his writing in a letter to Ellen Axson:

> I have imagined a style clear, bold, fresh, and facile; a style flexible but always strong, capable of light touches or of heavy blows; a style that could be driven at high speed—a brilliant, dashing, coursing speed—or constrained to the slow and stately progress of grave argument, as the case required; a style full of life, of colour and vivacity, of soul and energy, of inexhaustible power—of a thousand qualities of beauty and grace and strength that would make it immortal.—is it any wonder that I am disgusted with the stiff, dry, mechanical, monotonous sentences in which my meagre thoughts are compelled to masquerade, as in garments which are too mean even for *them*![83]

At its best, Wilson's style in *Congressional Government* fulfilled his dreams of strength and beauty. In speaking of committees in the House of Representatives, he could write:

> They have about them none of the searching, critical, illuminating character of the higher order of parliamentary debate, in which men are pitted against each other as equals, and urged to sharp contest and masterful strife by the inspiration of political principle and personal ambition, through the rivalry of parties and the competition of policies. They represent a joust between antagonistic interests, not a contest of principles. They could scarcely either inform or elevate public opinion, even if they were to obtain its heed.[84]

Flashes of wit occasionally brighten an otherwise dull treatment of the machinery of American government. In dealing with the Vice-President, Wilson noted that "the chief embarrassment in discussing his office is, that in explaining how little there is to be said about it one has evidently said all there is to say." And in comparing the President to the British Prime Minister, Wilson observed that the President's "usefulness is measured, not by efficiency, but by calendar months. It

---

[83] WW to ELA, Jan. 8, 1884, *ibid.*, pp. 654-55.

[84] *Congressional Government* in *ibid.*, IV, 55-56. All further references to *Congressional Government* will be cited as *CG* and page numbers will refer to the text as printed in *PWW*, IV.

is reckoned that if he be good at all he will be good for four years. A Prime Minister must keep himself in favor with the majority, a President need only keep alive."[85]

At its worst, Wilson's style was a jarring combination of alliteration, slang, and Anglicisms. The procedures of congressional committees were "palpably pernicious"; bills submitted to committees crossed "a parliamentary bridge of sighs to dim dungeons of silence."[86] He repeatedly used "but" instead of "only," and in search of his bold and fresh style, he occasionally mixed American slang with a tone of British propriety. Dealing with the cessation of criticism that followed approval of the Constitution, Wilson wrote: "Admiration of that one-time so much traversed body became suddenly all the vogue, and criticism was estopped."[87] His verbosity further obscured some of his central points, and his single-sentence explanations at times clarified nothing:

> In saying that our committee government has, germinally, some of the features of the British system, in which the ministers of the crown, the cabinet, are chosen from amongst the leaders of the parliamentary majority, and act not only as advisers of the sovereign but also as the great standing committee or "legislative commission" of the House of Commons, guiding its business and digesting its graver matters of legislation, I mean, of course, only that both systems represent the common necessity of setting apart some small body, or bodies, of legislative guides through whom a "big meeting" may get laws made.[88]

As his father advised him later, "You are not stingy enough, in your acts of creation."[89]

The question of Wilson's style is directly related to the validity of his argument in *Congressional Government*. Given the paucity of original research, his failure even to visit Congress while preparing the book, and his fondness for glib generalizations, the book suffers from the substitution of rhetoric for facts. His preeminent source, as it had been since Princeton, was Walter Bagehot's *English Constitution*, and Wilson proposed to follow Bagehot by analyzing Congress as it functioned, not as it was described in the Constitution. In this, Wilson considered his effort unique; ". . . we of the present generation are in the first season of free, outspoken, unrestrained constitutional criticism."[90] Such criticism, Wilson maintained, was essential because the original separation of coequal powers in the Constitution had given

---

[85] *Ibid.*, pp. 134, 138.
[87] *Ibid.*, p. 15.
[89] JRW to WW, Sept. 12, 1887, *PWW*, v, 588.
[86] *Ibid.*, pp. 69, 48.
[88] *Ibid.*, p. 71.
[90] *CG*, p. 16.

way to the supremacy of Congress and an augmentation of federal power. "The balances of the Constitution are for the most part only ideal," Wilson argued. "For all practical purposes the national government is supreme over the state governments, and Congress predominant over its so-called coördinate branches."[91]

Although Wilson relied heavily upon Bagehot and measured Congress against the ideal of the British Parliament, his analysis reveals two underlying assumptions that were at least reinforced by his Presbyterian heritage. At the heart of his father's preaching and the covenant theological tradition was a concern for a coherent order and structure for all human affairs, and in *Congressional Government* Wilson gave scant attention to the actual processes of legislation and focused instead on what he considered the chaotic structure of Congress, its committees of "little legislatures," and the absence of effective leadership.[92] Both houses, he wrote, "conduct their business by what may figuratively, but not inaccurately, be called an odd device of *disintegration*." Diffusing power may prevent its despotic use, Wilson conceded, but "the more power is divided the more irresponsible it becomes."[93]

By concentrating power in an individual and a political party, power and accountability were fused. Wilson's religious tradition had resolved the ambiguities of God's salvation by giving God and human beings complementary degrees of power and responsibility. In the same way, government should have a definite structure which made those who ruled publicly accountable for their policies. With more than a note of the Calvinist God who judges the people, Wilson described the best rulers as "those to whom great power is intrusted in such a manner as to make them feel that they will surely be abundantly honored and recompensed for a just and patriotic use of it, and to make them know that nothing can shield them from full retribution for every abuse of it."[94]

Wilson's second assumption in *Congressional Government* was that wise legislation was not produced by the contending interests of a representative body but through the efficacy of debate in shaping ideas and determining majority votes. In arguing this, his most immediate model was once again the practice of the British Parliament, and his affection for debate was in large measure derived from his father. And yet, in its system of presbyteries, synods, and a General Assembly, Presbyterian polity operated under the fundamental assumption that God's will for

[91] *Ibid.*, p. 40.

[92] *Ibid.*, p. 70; see also Roland Young, "Woodrow Wilson's *Congressional Government* Reconsidered," in *The Philosophy and Policies of Woodrow Wilson*, Earl Latham, ed. (Chicago, 1958), pp. 202-208.

[93] *CG*, pp. 46, 60.   [94] *Ibid.*, p. 155.

the church was determined by the church's representatives through discussion, debate, and majority votes, guided by the Holy Spirit. As a result, skill in oratory and debate was linked directly to the effective performance of God's will for the church.

Wilson repeatedly insisted that "representative government is government by advocacy, by discussion, by persuasion." When Cabinet officers were made directly responsible to Congress, he wrote, the result would be "government by discussion," and leaders would emerge who would win support through their oratorical power to convince and persuade. "It is natural that orators should be the leaders of a self-governing people," Wilson thought, but they could not be orators "without that force of character, that readiness of resource, that clearness of vision, that grasp of intellect, that courage of conviction, that earnestness of purpose, and that instinct and capacity for leadership which are the eight horses that draw the triumphal chariot of every leader and ruler of free men."[95]

A coherent structure of government, a faith in the power of debate and oratory to forge effective public policy, a concern to institutionalize positions of leadership within government—these were the notes Wilson consistently sounded throughout *Congressional Government*. Ironically, his celebration of congressional supremacy appeared in 1885, the first year of Grover Cleveland's presidency and the beginning of the decline of congressional power. The initial response to Wilson's book was overwhelmingly favorable. Gamaliel Bradford in the New York *Nation* predictably hailed it as "one of the most important books, dealing with political subjects, which have ever issued from the American press"; Wilson's friend, Albert Shaw, thought that he deserved "the credit of having inaugurated the concrete and scientific study of our political system"; but the *New York Times* reviewer found Wilson's argument and style "involved and clumsy."[96] Recent critics such as Arthur S. Link have faulted the book for its "amazing neglect or ignorance of economic factors in political life," and Roland Young has attributed its chief value to its partial analysis of Congress during the nineteenth century and its revelations about Wilson's early political thought, not its enduring contribution to American political science.[97]

Upon publication, Wilson immediately sent one copy to his fiancée

---

[95] *Ibid.*, pp. 117, 164, 118.

[96] Review of *Congressional Government* by Gamaliel Bradford in the New York *Nation*, Feb. 13, 1885, *PWW*, IV, 236; review by Albert Shaw in the Chicago *Dial*, March 1885, *ibid.*, p. 315; review in the *New York Times*, March 15, 1885, *ibid.*, p. 374. For an extended discussion of the contemporaneous reaction to *Congressional Government*, see Bragdon, *Wilson: The Academic Years*, pp. 135-40.

[97] Link, *Wilson: Road to the White House*, p. 15; Young, "*Congressional Government* Reconsidered," pp. 201-13. For a more positive assessment of *Congressional Government*, see Loewenberg, *American History in American Thought*, pp. 410-12.

and another to his father, to whom the book was dedicated. His father was overcome: "I wept and sobbed in the stir of the glad pain," he wrote his son. "God bless you, my noble child, for such a token of your affection."[98] His mother rejoiced and asked, *"Do you take it in, that you have made yourself famous?"*[99]

But Wilson was not elated, and his reaction to the first news of Houghton Mifflin's acceptance of his manuscript reveals how his ideals served to drive him on, his conception of life as a journey or a struggle toward the fulfillment of his covenant, and his anxiety over what should be his next goal. "It *was* unreasonable, I confess, to be low-spirited so soon after hearing of Houghton and Mifflin's decision about my *mss*," he told Ellen Axson,

> but then you must remember that I am constituted as regards such things, on a very peculiar pattern. Success does not flush or elate me, except for the moment. I could almost wish it did. I *need* a large infusion of the devil-me-care element. The acceptance of my book has of course given me the deepest satisfaction and has cleared away a whole storm of anxieties: it is an immense gain in every way. But it has sobered me a good deal too. The question is, what next? I must be prompt to follow up the advantage gained: and I must follow it up in the direction in which I have been preparing to do effectual political service. I feel as I suppose a general does who has gained a first foothold in the enemy's country. I must push on: to linger would be fatal. There is now a responsibility resting upon me where before there was none. My rejoicing, therefore, has in it a great deal that is stern and sober, like that of the strong man to run a race.[100]

Wilson's ceaseless work and driving ambition had brought him temporary success, but it was only "a first foothold in the enemy's country," and like a member of Christ's army, he resolved to remain "stern and sober" to achieve his primary goal—"effectual political service."

His only opportunity at Johns Hopkins to exercise his political aspirations was within his customary forum—the University's Literary Society. In Atlanta, he had composed a constitution for a Georgia House of Commons, which never materialized,[101] but at the Hopkins he transformed the Literary Society into the Hopkins House of Commons and

[98] JRW to WW, Jan. 30, 1885, printed as an Enclosure with WW to ELA, Feb. 1, 1885, *PWW*, IV, 208.

[99] JWW to WW, March 23, 1885, *ibid.*, p. 399.

[100] WW to ELA, Dec. 2, 1884, *ibid.*, III, 506-507.

[101] Draft of a Constitution for the Georgia House of Commons, *c.* Jan. 11, 1883, *ibid.*, II, 288-91.

drafted the constitution along the lines of the Liberal Debating Club at Princeton and the Georgia House of Commons. The constitution provided for a speaker, prime minister, and foreign and home secretaries. Bills were introduced, debated, and finally voted upon. If the ministers were not supported by the house, the speaker appointed a new prime minister.[102] Wilson's alteration of the Literary Society into the Hopkins House of Commons once again suggests that for him debate and oratory in themselves were not sufficient; they had to take place within the structure of a constitutionally ordered framework which resembled his favorite political institution as closely as possible.

Aside from his political studies and experience, Wilson's training at Johns Hopkins broadened his thought in one crucial area—economic theory. His mentor was Richard T. Ely, who, fresh from his doctoral training at the University of Heidelberg, was spreading the new theories of German economists with evangelical zeal. Wilson had absorbed the classical economic views of Lyman H. Atwater at Princeton, and other than a predisposition to view society in terms of its operation rather than theory, there is little evidence to suggest that prior to Johns Hopkins he had rejected his early training in Manchester liberalism. Under Ely's lectures on political economy, Wilson recorded the observation that the principle of the classical school of economics was "self interest without restraint."[103] In preparing his first academic lecture which dealt with Adam Smith, Wilson read *The Wealth of Nations* and numerous secondary works. He observed in his notes that Smith's principles countenanced the regulation of monopolies in order to preserve competition, but in the fragmentary draft of his lecture, he avoided detailed discussion of Smith's theories, describing him instead as having "the true instinct of an orator and teacher."[104]

The primary key to Wilson's developing economic views is his essay on nineteenth-century economists, which he prepared for Ely's projected "History of Political Economy in the United States." Ely had solicited the assistance of Wilson and another graduate student, Davis R. Dewey, in writing the book, but it appears that only Wilson produced his share of the manuscript. Wilson's assignment was to cover American political economists from Henry C. Carey to the pres-

[102] WW to ELA, Dec. 15, 1884, *ibid.*, III, 543, n. 3.

[103] Notes on Ely's Minor Course in Political Economy, Oct. 31, 1883, *ibid.*, II, 506. For an excellent study of Ely's economic views while a professor at Johns Hopkins, see Benjamin G. Rader, *The Academic Mind and Reform: The Influence of Richard T. Ely in American Life* (Lexington, Ky., 1966), pp. 16-129.

[104] Editorial Note, Wilson's Lecture on Adam Smith, *PWW*, II, 537-42; fragmentary draft of a lecture on Adam Smith, *c.* Nov. 20, 1883, *ibid.*, p. 544.

ent, and he presented a report on his findings to the Historical Seminary in March 1885. In his presentation, Wilson noted that American
economists tended to reject "the darker tenets of the British school of
writers," especially Malthus, and had not been predisposed toward
theory. He also found them proceeding by inductive methods rather
than the deductive methods of earlier economists who were "ministers
of the Gospel who taught p[olitical] e[conomy] along with the moral
sciences, or something of that sort."[105] In his manuscript for Ely's
book, Wilson further criticized Francis Wayland for his "constant
tendency to call all seemingly established principles of the science
laws of Divine Providence" and assigned him a place in the history of
economic thought "of no very great prominence."[106] Wilson saved his
most favorable remarks for Francis Amasa Walker, whom he praised
for taking the best of the classical school but being willing to accept
some of the findings of the newer historical school. Walker, wrote Wilson, was "essentially modern" in his realization that there was an "*art*
of political economy*," involving the careful balancing of private economic welfare with considerations of state policy.[107]

William Diamond found little of Wilson himself in this manuscript
for Ely's book and called it "a colorless . . . description,"[108] and in
fact the essay is little more than Wilson's compendium of the views of
various economists. However, it does indicate that Wilson had not
only read widely in nineteenth-century economic thought but also had
been dislodged by Ely from whatever adherence to classical economics
he had had. His actual economic views remained somewhat inchoate,
and even throughout his academic career, Wilson demonstrated an
abiding distaste for economic theory *per se*. He was fond of Adam
Smith, but as in his political studies, Wilson was primarily concerned
with how society functioned, economically and politically. Ely's influence on Wilson was due in large measure to Wilson's own desire to
view society in historical terms, to see how institutions adapted to
changing social conditions. In this respect Wilson was as "latitudinar-
ian" as the economists he described.[109]

Ely also prompted Wilson into at least a momentary predisposition
toward socialism. After reading Ely's *The Labor Movement in
America* (1886), Wilson drafted an essay on "Socialism and Democ-

---

[105] Draft of a report to the Historical Seminary, *c.* March 27, 1885, *ibid.*, IV, 422-24.

[106] Wilson's section for "A History of Political Economy in the United States," *c.* May 25,
1885, *ibid.*, p. 633.

[107] *Ibid.*, pp. 653, 663.

[108] William Diamond, *The Economic Thought of Woodrow Wilson* (Baltimore, 1943), pp.
30-32.

[109] Draft of a report to the Historical Seminary, *c.* March 27, 1885, *PWW*, IV, 424.

racy," in which he argued that socialism in a democratic state was merely radical and not revolutionary. "It is only a[n] acceptance of the extremest logical conclusions deducible from democratic principles long ago received as respectable," Wilson wrote. "For it is very clear that in fundamental theory socialism and democracy are almost if not quite one and the same." Wilson further accepted Ely's contention that political struggles were no longer ones between the individual and government; rather, Wilson said, the contest was "between government and dangerous combinations and individuals." The question of socialism at its roots was not essentially a political question, according to Wilson. It was one of policy and administration.[110] Though Wilson would later move away from such an easy acceptance of socialism as compatible with democracy during the turbulent 1890's, Ely's influence continued to shape his theory of administration and his approval of positive state action in many areas.

In one important area, Ely left no discernible imprint on Wilson's thought. Despite Ely's involvement in the social gospel movement, Wilson demonstrated little receptivity to the program or theology of this late-nineteenth-century attempt to apply Christianity to contemporary social problems.

During the fall of 1884, Wilson decided that two years of graduate work at the Hopkins were sufficient for his purposes. His father advised against trying to secure the doctorate; Wilson himself was passionately eager to get married, and he needed a source of income. He knew "that a degree would render me a little more *marketable*" but feared that his "mental and physical health . . . would be jeoparded by a forced march through fourteen thousand pages of dry reading." His fiancée concurred, and he left Johns Hopkins for a post at Bryn Mawr College. However, at Adams' urging he returned the next year to take special exams and submitted *Congressional Government* as his dissertation. The degree was awarded in May 1886, and Wilson exulted to Ellen, "I won the degree for *you*. . . . My spur in the struggle of preparation I have just been through was to please *you*, and to make *you* more comfortable. . . . If there's any triumph, it is yours."[111]

[110] "Socialism and Democracy," *c.* Aug. 22, 1887, *ibid.*, v, 559-63. The essay was never published.

[111] JRW to WW, Oct. 29, 1884, *ibid.*, III, 385; WW to ELA, Nov. 8, 1884, *ibid.*, p. 415; ELA to WW, Nov. 10, 1884, *ibid.*, p. 423; WW to EAW, May 30, 1886, *ibid.*, v, 269.

IV

Marriage and Early Professional Career

In the fall of 1885, Wilson began a seventeen-year career as a professor and scholar by joining the faculty of the newly established Bryn Mawr College. He arrived on the campus with his wife, Ellen Louise Axson, whom he had married on June 24, 1885, in Savannah, Georgia.[1] The significance of Wilson's relationship with his wife can hardly be exaggerated. "It was in many ways the most important experience of Woodrow Wilson's life," Ray Stannard Baker has written. "It was not until he met Ellen Axson, as he himself said, that he became 'fully himself.'. . . It was an attachment such as the youth himself had never dreamed of, such a 'new realization' as he could not have imagined."[2]

During his years at Johns Hopkins and later after they were married, Wilson found her love and affection absolutely essential for his physical and psychological well-being. When separated they wrote each other daily, sometimes twice a day. Wilson hated the times when they were apart and poured out his love in his letter. "I don't know," he wrote her from Baltimore in February 1884,

> how a fellow whose whole heart is wrapped up in a little sweet-heart of winsomest charms manages to live five or six hundred miles from her—at least I don't know how *this* fellow manages to do it without being overcome by discontent. I am sure that there never was a chap who suffered more than I do because of separation from the chief objects of his love.[3]

He told her how he despised "this dreary, lonly bachelorhood" and insisted, ". . . Marriage [is] . . . the *only* thing that stands in the way of my complete happiness."[4] The possibility of a broken engagement made him despondent, and he opened his heart to her. "It's a matter of life and death with me," he declared.

> If I am not to have my darling, I can have neither love nor hope to aid me in my work and it would grind me to death. . . . It is too late

---

[1] News item, June 25, 1885, *PWW*, IV, 735. His father and her grandfather, Isaac Stockton Keith Axson, performed the service.

[2] *WWLL*, I, 164-65; cf. *ibid.*, p. 241.

[3] WW to ELA, Feb. 24, 1884, *PWW*, III, 45.

[4] WW to ELA, Jan. 4, 1884, *ibid.*, II, 645, 646.

now to think of drawing apart, if she still loves me. She has become the most essential part of my life—my heart is given her in marriage already, and it must die if we are to separate now. . . . How I wish I knew how to *cry* that I might *spend* these feelings somehow. . . . I don't care a rap for myself, but I do care everything for you.[5]

The hundreds of letters which they exchanged are extremely enlightening in portraying their relationship and reflecting Wilson's personality. He confessed to her that he became "morbid" without companionship; that when he failed to write regularly, his feelings accumulated and sported "themselves beyond all bounds of moderation when finally they are let out"; that he was "a queer compound of love and selfishness"; and that he was "a man of a sensitive, restless, over-wrought disposition."[6]

Ellen responded to Wilson's love with an equally passionate espousal of her devotion to him. "I love *love love* you darling, oh *how* I love you," she exclaimed. "How I wish I could tell you the depth & strength & passion of my love!" "I love you more, a thousand times more than life; there is no standard great enough to measure my love." Just before their marriage, she promised Wilson, "You shall never want for wifely love and faith and sympathy, my darling, or for anything that love can give," and until her death in 1914, she never broke that promise. Her love for Wilson included a near-worship of his abilities and a subordination of herself to his plans and ambitions. She called him the South's "*greatest* son in this generation" and told him that he would be "my head—my *king*, not only because *I* will it but because *God* wills it, because He made you so to be."[7]

Her unflagging devotion and constant affection were a source of immeasurable strength to Wilson throughout their marriage, encouraging him during times of confusion and sustaining him during periods of conflict and difficulty. She gave him emotional stability, for as he told her, "Until you loved me, I used to be tormented with 'uneasy questionings' about *everything* in my future: *now* I am *uneasy* about *nothing* in that future."[8]

Like Wilson, Ellen Axson was the child of a southern Presbyterian manse. Her father and grandfather were distinguished ministers in the southern Presbyterian Church, and Wilson knew he was not marrying beneath his station. "She belongs to that class which has contributed so

[5] WW to ELA, April 15, 1885, *ibid.*, IV, 488-89.

[6] WW to ELA, Dec. 4, 1883, *ibid.*, II, 565; Aug. 23 and March 23, 1884, *ibid.*, III, 305, 96; Feb. 17, 1885, *ibid.*, IV, 263.

[7] ELA to WW, Feb. 11, 1889, *ibid.*, VI, 84; Jan. 4, 1885, *ibid.*, III, 582; June 17, 1885, *ibid.*, IV, 723; May 22, 1886, *ibid.*, V, 251; June 20, 1885, *ibid.*, IV, 730.

[8] WW to ELA in *WWLL*, I, 243.

much both to the literature and to the pleasures of social life,"[9] he bragged to Robert Bridges. Her tastes were indeed aesthetic, her love of art prompting a period of training at the Art Students' League in New York during 1884-1885, and she demonstrated a fair ability with oils. She broadened Wilson's tastes in art, architecture, and literature, and Wilson suggested that her reading would keep his mind "from dry rot by exposing it to an atmosphere of fact and entertainment and imaginative suggestion."[10]

The oldest in a family of two boys and two girls, she was born on May 15, 1860, and she bore a special responsibility for her sister and brothers because of family tragedy. In 1881, her mother died giving birth to her sister Margaret, and in 1884 during her engagement to Wilson, her father was committed to a mental hospital, apparently after becoming violent, and died there a few months later.[11] The ordeal shook her deeply and caused her moments of religious doubt, which she tried to resolve by reminding herself of God's goodness. "I *am sure* that the God, whose love is as infinite as His wisdom, has ordered it all for His own great and good purposes," she thought, "and I want to be not merely *submissive* to his will, but gladly acquiescent."[12] Wilson, too, reminded her of his "idea of *how* all things work together for good—through the careful performance of our duty."[13] Throughout her life, she was always quieter and more reserved than Wilson, who opened up in the context of his family. Later, when religious doubts again assailed her, she tried reading Hegel to resolve her questions.

Wilson's courtship and marriage produced a profound change in his relationship with his parents. Initially his mother was "greatly taken by surprise" and "felt distressed that you should be involved in any way just yet." If the relationship worked out, she warned, "there will needs be a weary waiting." Wilson sensed that his mother was torn because of his love for Ellen, and despite the growing intensity of his courtship, his mother still hoped he would return home to live with them.[14] Eventually, she resigned herself to the inevitable. "I am *sure* you will be happy in each other," she wrote her son. "She is very lovely, I think—so intelligent & every way attractive."[15]

Wilson's father also had some reservations about a precipitate mar-

[9] WW to Robert Bridges, July 26, 1883, *PWW*, II, 393.

[10] WW to ELA, Jan. 23, 1885, *ibid.*, III, 634.

[11] Charles Howard Shinn to WW, Jan. 21, 1884, *ibid.*, II, 661-62, n. 3; WW to ELA, June 1, 1884, *ibid.*, III, 200-201, n. 1.

[12] ELA to WW, Feb. 4, 1884, *ibid.*, p. 7; cf. ELA to WW, June 2, 1884, *ibid.*, pp. 201-202.

[13] WW to ELA, May 25, 1884, *ibid.*, p. 192.

[14] JWW to WW, June 7 and Oct. 3, 1883, *ibid.*, II, 365, 453; c. Nov. 24, 1884, *ibid.*, III, 482.

[15] JWW to WW, Oct. 11, 1884, *ibid.*, p. 348.

riage, but in general he took the marriage of his son much better than Wilson's mother did, and spoke of Ellen as the one "whom we both paternally & maternally love—big."[16] After the publication of *Congressional Government* and his marriage in 1885, Wilson moved perceptibly away from dependence on his father, who in turn became aware that his son had reached intellectual maturity and scholarly recognition, as well as emotional independence in establishing his own home and family. Discouraged by his unpleasant pastorate in Wilmington and onerous teaching duties at Southwestern University, Wilson's father gradually identified himself with his son and his escalating career. "You are my alter ego," he wrote Wilson in 1886. "What pleases you equally pleases me." Feeling that he had not achieved the success and prominence he craved, his father confessed, "You are assuredly my second edition, 'revised and improved,' as to contents, and with a far superior letter-press and binding. How I bless God that it is even so, and that no law of His forbids the pride your father takes in his larger son."[17]

After the birth of Wilson's three daughters and the death of his mother, Wilson's father relied even more on his son. "There is one thing always sure . . .," he told Wilson in a revealing letter during 1889,

> and this is that you are hour by hour in my thoughts and upon my heart: —and what is just as certain is, that you deserve the place which you occupy within the house of my soul, and even a bigger place were it a bigger soul. How, in my solitude, have I longed for the presence of that dear son in whose large love I trust so implicitly and in the wealth of whose gem-furnished mind I take such delight: him in whom my affections centre as my child, and my confidences as my friend. . . . You are preaching a gospel of order, and thus of safety in the department of political morals and conduct, such as has not heretofore been heralded, and success is therefore a personal gratification whilst it is also a public benefit. I feel *very* proud of you when I think of what you are doing and doing so well.[18]

The dominance of father over son had been reversed, and Dr. Wilson consoled himself that while his son was not a minister, he preached "a gospel of order" and did so successfully.

Wilson's marriage further reveals the enduring impact of his Presbyterian heritage and his appropriation of the covenant theology to understand his life. A constitutionalist in all things, Wilson picked up the

[16] JRW to WW, May 17 and Oct. 9, 1884, *ibid.*, pp. 183-84, 343.

[17] JRW to WW, Nov. 15, 1886, and March 12, 1887, *ibid.*, v, 391, 467.

[18] JRW to WW, March 6, 1889, *ibid.*, vi, 137.

term "compact" and used this liturgical synonym for "covenant" to describe the intimate relationship he shared with Ellen. "I long to be made your master—only, however, on the very fair and equal terms that, in exchange for the authority over yourself which you relinquish, you shall be constituted supreme mistress of me," he told her. "That seems to be a fair compact. Besides, having studied constitutions of various sorts, I have not failed to observe that the constitution of the great and ancient State of Matrimony is *Love*."[19] He jokingly suggested that during their separation, they should establish "an inter-State Love League (of two members only, in order that it may be of manageable size)" and of course he would draw up the constitution.[20]

But Wilson was deeply serious about their "compact" of marriage, and its terms were absolute honesty about their thoughts and feelings. "You can find no better or surer way of making me happy;—and you could invent no surer or swifter way of making me miserable," he told Ellen, "than by with-holding your *whole* confidence from a mistaken desire to save me pain or anxiety. You know it's a compact, that henceforth we are to be one in hopes and plans and anxieties and sorrows and joys: . . . I'm bent upon keeping you in mind of the fact because I know from experience how hard, well-nigh impossible, it is to throw off the habit of trying to bear all burdens, small and great, *alone*, with what seems a sort of unselfish devotion."[21] During their married life, each reminded the other that their "compact" required a full report of each other's health and well-being,[22] and there is little doubt that both saw their relationship as more profound and even sacred because of their covenant. They often referred to the fact that Providence brought them together, and Wilson repeatedly expressed his gratitude to "God for his infinite goodness to me in giving me *such* a wife for my strength and delight."[23]

Wilson's covenant with his wife is especially significant in its explicit recognition of God as the witness or even the initiator of the compact, and in this regard his covenant with Ellen differs from the one concluded with Charles A. Talcott, which had only an implicit reference to God in its stress on the importance of adhering to principles. In the pact with Talcott, Wilson used the idea of a covenant to give meaning and order to his goals in life; in his compact with Ellen he utilized it once again to describe the structure of his emotional life with his wife. In short, the covenant provided Wilson an inclusive concept which embraced society, his purpose in life, and his own inner life. For

[19] WW to ELA, Feb. 21, 1884, *ibid.*, III, 38.
[20] WW to ELA, July 15, 1884, *ibid.*, p. 248.
[21] WW to ELA, Feb. 2, 1884, *ibid.*, pp. 3-4.
[22] WW to EAW, Feb. 10, 1898, *ibid.*, X, 387.
[23] WW to EAW, June 24, 1892, *ibid.*, VIII, 18-19.

this intense, highly sensitive young man, the covenant represented a way of making life orderly and predictable, even as it imposed new responsibilities in turning him outward beyond himself. "A man who lives only for himself," Wilson later observed, "has not begun to live—has yet to learn his use, and his real pleasure too, in the world." The bachelor was "an amateur in life."[24]

Wilson went to Bryn Mawr with reservations about the wisdom of accepting an appointment to what Ellen called "a female college." He haggled with the college authorities over his rank and salary, holding out for $2,000 and an Associate Professorship, but finally settling for $1,500 and the title of Associate. His father called his faculty rank "certainly absurd, but not necessarily humiliating," and urged him to take the job anyway. "Commence at once your climb even though your ladder seem so short," Dr. Wilson advised, "and it will lengthen as you ascend."[25] The president of this Quaker college, James E. Rhoads, had some reservations of his own and wanted to make certain that Wilson's philosophy of history would supplement and augment the religious and moral emphasis of the institution. After an interview, Rhoads was reassured and told Wilson, "From our conversation and from the testimony [of] others, I feel assured that the moral and religious lessons of History will in thy hands be used to fortify a wide and comprehensive yet well-defined faith in Christianity."[26]

For three years, from 1885 to 1888, Wilson was the sole professor of history at Bryn Mawr, but as Ellen had suspected, he found the education of women something less than stimulating. He had retained many of his southern attitudes toward women and confided to Ellen, "I have all my life long sought to cherish that chivalrous, almost worshipful, regard for woman which seems to me the truest badge of nobility in man."[27] Although Wilson believed in the value of college education for women and later sent his three daughters to college, he apparently felt that men and women should be educated differently and separately. When he heard in 1894 that the University of Virginia had started admitting women to classes there, he wrote to a friend that he considered the development "most demoralizing" and "gratuitous folly." "I do not mean that it leads to vice; though occasionally it does; but it *vulgarizes* the whole relationship of men and women," he said. ". . . The generalization is a *fact* itself, and of my own observation."[28]

Wilson repeatedly vented his dissatisfaction with the academic at-

---

[24] News report of a speech in Plymouth, Mass., July 14, 1894, *ibid.*, p. 611; "When a Man Comes to Himself," Nov. 1, 1899, *ibid.*, xi, 265.

[25] ELA to WW, Nov. 28, 1884, *ibid.*, iii, 495; JRW to WW, Jan. 15, 1885, *ibid.*, pp. 612-13.

[26] James E. Rhoads to WW, Dec. 1, 1884, *ibid.*, p. 502.

[27] WW to ELA, April 24, 1884, *ibid.*, p. 146.

[28] WW to Charles William Kent, May 29, 1894, *ibid.*, viii, 583-84.

mosphere at Bryn Mawr, lamenting that "here I have no associates who are more than mildly interested in the topics I care most for," and finding that his writing on "governmental topics" was divorced from his actual teaching duties.[29] He was annoyed at what he considered his low salary, and by the fall of 1887, he was thoroughly discouraged. "Lecturing to young women of the present generation on the history and principles of politics is about as appropriate and profitable as would be lecturing to stone-masons on the evolution of fashion in dress," he exploded to his journal. "Passing through a vacuum, your speech generates no heat."[30] To Robert Bridges he complained, "I find that teaching women relaxes my mental muscle."[31]

Wilson's discontent was aggravated by his having to work under M. Carey Thomas, the dean of the college and the woman who inspired Bryn Mawr's early growth and development. Since Wilson was the only member of the faculty who had received his graduate training from an American institution and who did not have his doctorate, she prodded him into returning to Johns Hopkins for his degree. There were grounds on both sides for tension in the relationship; she exhibited a distaste for Wilson's field of study, and he undoubtedly communicated his condescending attitude toward women. She later found Tennyson's line, "Put thy sweet hand in mine and trust in me," an apt summary of Wilson's chauvinism.[32]

Wilson offered different courses each year of his teaching at Bryn Mawr. During 1885-1886, he taught a course in Greek and Roman history; in the first semester of the 1886-1887 academic year, he covered English history and taught a course dealing with special topics in American history, and during the second semester he surveyed French history and the Italian Renaissance and the German Reformation. In his last year, Wilson provided instruction in political economy and politics, with special attention to American political development. Like most new professors, Wilson conducted his classes almost exclusively by lecture, including his meetings with the one graduate student assigned to him each year.[33] He defended this pedagogical method and insisted, "Some of the subtlest and most lasting effects of genuine

[29] WW to Walter Hines Page, Oct. 30, 1885, *ibid.*, v, 38; WW to R. Bridges, Dec. 20, 1885, *ibid.*, p. 95.

[30] WW to EAW, Oct. 8, 1887, *ibid.*, pp. 612-13; Confidential Journal, Oct. 20, 1887, *ibid.*, p. 619.

[31] WW to R. Bridges, Dec. 30, 1887, in Bragdon, *Wilson: The Academic Years*, p. 151.

[32] *Ibid.*, pp. 145, 159-61.

[33] See the Editorial Notes, Wilson's Teaching at Bryn Mawr, 1885-86; Wilson's Teaching at Bryn Mawr, 1886-87; Wilson's Teaching at Bryn Mawr and the Johns Hopkins, 1887-88, *PWW*, v, 16-17, 349-50, 600-602; see also Wilson's descriptions of his courses, *ibid.*, pp. 104-106, 441-44, 659-63.

oratory have gone forth from secluded lecture-desks into the hearts of quiet groups of students; and it would seem to be good policy to endure much indifferent lecturing . . . for the sake of leaving places open for the men who have in them the inestimable force of chastened eloquence."[34] His own efforts at lectern eloquence were apparently appreciated by the Bryn Mawr students. One recalled, "His lectures were fascinating and held me spellbound," and another considered Wilson "the most interesting and inspiring college lecturer" she ever heard.[35]

In Wilson's teaching of history and politics, he sought to impress upon the students the influence of leaders in history and emphasized the development of constitutional law and political institutions. As Wilson stated in his review of his first year of courses, the instruction was "illustrative of important epochs or of political principles," and "the attention of students was directed to the influence of leading historical characters upon contemporary events."[36] The purpose of studying history in Wilson's view was preeminently moral. It was not enough merely to learn history; one should learn from it.[37] Wilson made certain that his students did not overlook history's lessons. Machiavelli's political theory recognized "no morality but a sham morality meant for deceit"; the progress of humanity was linked to cooperation between groups of individuals; "discussion has been the mother and nurse of all free governments."[38]

But Wilson's lectures were not all moral aphorisms, and they demonstrated a tremendous amount of preparation. In fact, Wilson's lecture on Greco-Roman history formed the basis for some of his chapters in his textbook, *The State*, and he was capable of offering what were at that time new historical interpretations. For example, he suggested that the social, rather than the political, causes of the American Civil War were decisive and that political rhetoric only masked the underlying social and economic differences between the two sections.[39] He also insisted that his students see the connection between historical events and current affairs, and he even taught the history of England backwards to make the point.[40]

[34] "An Old Master," c. Feb. 1, 1887, *ibid.*, p. 445.

[35] Helen A. Scribner to R. S. Baker, March 13, 1926, and Mary Tremain to R. S. Baker, Jan. 21, 1926 (R. S. Baker Coll., DLC).

[36] Wilson's review of his course work at Bryn Mawr, c. June 1, 1886, *PWW*, v, 274.

[37] Notes for a lecture, "The Preliminary Age," c. Sept. 24, 1885, *ibid.*, p. 20.

[38] Notes for a lecture on Machiavelli, c. Feb. 8, 1887, *ibid.*, p. 459; notes for a lecture, "The Preliminary Age," c. Sept. 24, 1885, *ibid.*, p. 18; notes for a lecture, "The Value of Discussion," c. Sept. 29, 1885, *ibid.*, p. 22.

[39] Editorial Note, Wilson's Teaching at Bryn Mawr, 1885-86, *ibid.*, p. 17; notes for two lectures on the Civil War, c. Oct. 18 and 20, 1886, *ibid.*, pp. 352-56.

[40] Wilson's review of his course work at Bryn Mawr, c. June 1, 1887, *ibid.*, pp. 512-13.

His lectures also reflect his indebtedness to his religious heritage, particularly the Calvinist tradition. Two of the "leading historical characters" on whom Wilson focused were Luther and Calvin. "As a monk," Wilson told his students, "Luther thoroughly detested the doctrine of works," and "he discovered in Paul and Augustine the doctrine that gave him peace and hope, the doctrine of justification by faith."[41] But Wilson's real enthusiasm was saved for Calvin. Although Calvin was "inferior to [Luther] in sympathetic genius, he was superior to him in power of logical analysis, and superior to all predecessors and successors as an organizer of reform." Calvin's chief contribution, Wilson declared, was "that remarkable polity which was profoundly to affect Scotland, England, and France and which constitutes, even more than his doctrine, his claim to greatness and revolutionary influence." In obvious admiration, the aspiring politician observed, "[Calvin] may be called the great reforming Christian *statesman*—and Providence put him in the best possible field for the exercise of his supreme gifts." In describing the politically active French Huguenots, Wilson further revealed something of his own predisposition for political life. "Their participation in politics," he stated, "was an almost necessary outcome of their adherence to the faith of the great Christian statesman of Geneva: their work promised to be a reconstruction of the society as his had been."[42]

In his own religious practice, Wilson remained steadfastly loyal to the religious tradition of his youth, and he and Ellen joined the Presbyterian Church of Bryn Mawr. Both appreciated the sermons and ministry of William H. Miller, who then occupied that church's pulpit. "How profoundly thankful we ought to be that we have Mr. Miller!" Wilson exclaimed to his wife. When a minister substituted for the regular pastor and delivered a sermon on "the authenticity of the Mosaic authorship," Wilson abruptly left in the middle of the service. "He prayed flippantly," Wilson complained to Ellen. "Not a word, I feel sure, went to Heaven—every word made me cold and sick—for I longed to hear a prayer: I am sure I should have recognized one had I heard it." In a revealing statement of himself and the strength he received from worship and his faith, Wilson asked Ellen: "What is one who is above all things else sensitive to spiritual influences . . . to do when thrown into the congregation of a fellow like this one of this morning, as we are upon any move either of ours or of Mr. Miller's likely (or at least liable) to be! My Sabbath's would be seasons of mortification and torture. I fear I should take refuge in the Episcopal service, to escape preaching."[43]

[41] Notes for a lecture on Luther and Zwingli, *c.* April 12, 1887, *ibid.*, p. 487.
[42] Lecture on "Calvin—Geneva, France," *c.* April 14, 1887, *ibid.*, pp. 488, 490.
[43] WW to EAW, Oct. 9, 1887, *ibid.*, p. 614.

During these troubled years at Bryn Mawr, Wilson also suffered the loss of his mother; her death in April 1888 was a source of great grief to him. Traveling to her funeral, he wrote to Ellen, "The pain is so recent that *I cannot write* about it at all." "As the first shock and acute pain of the great, the irreparable blow passes off," he told her later, "my heart is filling up with tenderest memories of my sweet mother, memories that seem to hallow my whole life—which seem to explain to me how it came about that I was given the sweetest, most satisfying of wives for my daily companion." "If I had not lived with such a mother," he added, "I could not have won and seemed to deserve—in part, perhaps, deserved, through transmitted virtues—such a wife—the strength, the support, the human source of my life."[44] In times of sorrow and distress Wilson found comfort and strength in Ellen's love and declared, "Oh, my sweet, my matchless little wife, how *everything*—whether sorrow or joy, trial or triumph—seems to conspire to draw me *to you*."[45] Supremely happy, he flatly concluded, "Marriage has been the *making* of me both intellectually and morally."[46]

Behind Wilson's dissatisfaction at Bryn Mawr was the gnawing sense that he was not fulfilling the terms of his covenant with Talcott for "effectual public service." In 1885, even before he had entered his teaching career, he confided to Ellen,

Yes, darling, there is, and has long been, in my mind a "lurking sense of disappointment and *loss*, as if I had missed from my life something upon which both my gifts and inclinations gave me a claim"; I do feel a very real regret that I have been shut out from my heart's *first*—primary—ambition and purpose, which was, to take an active, if possible a leading, part in public life, and strike out for myself, if I had the ability, a *statesman's* career. That is my heart's—or, rather, my *mind's* deepest secret, little lady.[47]

In opting for an academic and literary life, Wilson recognized the challenges and opportunities, as well as his own abilities to influence political life through his writings. Nevertheless, he told her,

my feeling has been that such literary talents as I have are *secondary* to my equipment for other things: that my power to write was meant to be a handmaiden to my power to speak and to organize action. Of course, it is quite possible that I have been all along entirely misled in this view: I am ready to accept the providential ordering of my life as conclusive on that point.[48]

[44] WW to EAW, April 18 and 19, 1888, *ibid.*, pp. 718, 719, 720.
[45] WW to EAW, April 20, 1888, *ibid.*, p. 720.
[46] WW to Richard Heath Dabney, May 31, 1888, *ibid.*, p. 731.
[47] WW to ELA, Feb. 24, 1885, *ibid.*, IV, 287.
[48] *Ibid.*, pp. 287-88.

Temporarily satisfied with his profession, Wilson kept his ideals in force, his goals in sight, and his covenant faithfully intact. In 1886, he told Talcott that "the old compact between us is . . . *ipso facto* renewed," and suggested that they could fulfill their covenant "by substituting a common cause, a common purpose of public service." And yet, he admitted, "I constantly feel the disadvantages of the *closet*. I want to keep close to the *practical* and *practicable* in politics; my ambition is to add something to the *statesmanship* of the country, if that something be only thought, and not the old achievement of which I used to dream when I hoped that I might enter practical politics."[49]

The thought that Wilson wished to contribute to the statesmanship of the country took a significant new turn during his years at Bryn Mawr. Rather than continuing to advocate the reform of Congress along the lines of the British Parliament and to pursue his constitutional studies, Wilson struck out on a new and far more ambitious project. His purpose was nothing less than to describe and interpret the origins, development, and problems of the modern democratic state.

In 1889, Wilson surveyed his work and described it as a task of interpretation, not origination. His investigation was no mere scholarly inquiry, for Wilson brashly believed that by interpreting his age he would also interpret himself and thereby account for his political creed. "It was in keeping with my whole mental make-up," he reflected,

> . . . and in obedience to a true instinct, that I chose to put forth my chief strength in the history and interpretation of institutions, and chose as my chief ambition the historical explanation of the modern democratic state as a basis for the discussion of political progress, political expediency, political morality, political prejudice, practical politics, &c.—an analysis of the thought in which our age stands, if it examine itself.[50]

The task, as Wilson envisaged it, was not another attempt to study how political institutions operated but to probe deeper into the principles upon which government rested. Striving to fuse a philosophical and functional view of politics, Wilson maintained that "Aristotle studied politics so; but did not get further than the outward differences of institutions—did not press on beyond logical distinctions to discover the spiritual oneness of government, the life that lives *within* it. The ideal thing to do would be to penetrate to its *essential character* by way of a thorough knowledge of all its outward manifestations of character."[51]

[49] WW to Charles Andrew Talcott, Nov. 14, 1886, *ibid.*, v, 389.

[50] Confidential Journal, Dec. 28, 1889, *ibid.*, vi, 463.

[51] WW to Horace Elisha Scudder, July 10, 1886, *ibid.*, v, 304.

Wilson's work was indeed characteristic of his whole make-up, for in focusing on the ideological bases of political institutions, Wilson intended to integrate morality into the affairs of government. In classic Calvinist terms, Wilson believed it was necessary to recognize "politics as a sphere of moral action." "God is not the head of the state," he wrote, "but he is the Lord of the individual and the individual cannot be moral who is immoral in *public* conduct."[52]

Wilson's first attempt to chart the boundaries of his study was "The Modern Democratic State," which he wrote sometime during December 1885. The method he chose was largely a result of his training under Adams and Ely at Johns Hopkins and his reading of Bagehot, Herbert Spencer, Sir Henry Maine, and other writers.[53] It emphasized the study of political institutions in historical, not theoretical terms, or as Wilson put it, "The true philosophy of government can be extracted only from the true history of government."[54] "The historical view of government is in any case the only fully instructive view," Wilson insisted. ". . . It is the only view not utterly barren. Only history can explain modern democracy either to itself or to those who would imitate it."[55]

With such a method, it was natural for Wilson to view the history of political institutions in evolutionary terms, and he saw democracy as the apex of the long process. "The present trend of all political development the world over towards democracy is no mere episode in history," he said. "It is the natural resultant of now permanent forces which have long been gathering, which brought modern lights out of mediaeval shades, and which have made the life of the most advanced nations of our day the wide, various, vigorous, complex, expanding thing that it is." Wilson repeatedly likened democracy to the stage of adulthood in human growth and argued that it came only to societies which had achieved "the maturity of freedom and self-control."[56]

The basis of democracy is morality; "its only stable foundation is character." The people "must have acquired adult self-reliance, self-knowledge, and self-control, adult soberness and deliberateness of judgment and sagacity in self-government, adult vigilance of thought and quickness of insight."[57] The crucial problem confronting democratic governments, Wilson believed, was that no one had exposed the principles on which the system rested and achieved a synthesis of its many parts. "For lack of proper synthesis [democracy] limps and is threatened with incapacity for the great social undertakings of our

[52] Memoranda for "The Modern Democratic State," *c.* Dec. 1-20, 1885, *ibid.*, p. 59.

[53] Editorial Note, Wilson's First Treatise on Democratic Government, *ibid.*, p. 55.

[54] WW to H. E. Scudder, July 10, 1886, *ibid.*, p. 304.

[55] "The Modern Democratic State," *c.* Dec. 1-20, 1885, *ibid.*, p. 65

[56] *Ibid.*, pp. 70, 63.   [57] *Ibid.*, pp. 63, 71.

modern time," he wrote. "Its synthesis includes more than its *organization*. . . . A synthesis of principle must precede a synthesis of form and function."[58]

Wilson, in short, was proposing to synthesize the basis of democratic government with moral principles, which he confidently expected to read out of the history of political institutions. Wilson's moral synthesis, however, was considerably confused and contradictory. It reveals many of the tensions which not only were inherent in his earlier political thought but also plagued his later thinking about politics. For example, Wilson insisted that the nature of the synthesis must be an organic conception of society. "Society is an organism which does not develop by any cunning leadership of a single member, but with slow maturing and all-round adjustment," he declared, but this inevitably undermined his faith in the effectiveness of the charismatic leader. Consequently, he insisted that society's organic development was "led at last into self-consciousness and self-command by those who best divine the laws of its growth." Society was both organic and personal—organic because it was bound by common allegiance to certain moral principles; personal because leadership was necessary to make those principles concrete in the affairs of state and to permit self-expression.[59]

Once again, the problem of the demagogue, whose undemocratic principles won the allegiance of the people, loomed before Wilson, and he characteristically brushed it aside as unthinkable. "Institutions which favour strong statesmanship under representative forms of govt. inevitably make the statesman stronger than the charlatan," he announced. "He rallies about himself, not mobs, but parties. He binds men to himself not by a vague community of sentiment but by a definite and decisive oneness of purpose." Still frustrated by his life in the "closet" of academia, Wilson argued that positions of leadership should go to those who could win the support of the people. "No man high in the confidence of the people in political matters should be suffered to go long without the harness of office."[60]

Wilson published this essay in revised form as "Character of Democracy in the United States" in 1889, and it served as his first attempt at what he set as the *magnum opus* of his scholarly career, his "Philosophy of Politics." This work was never completed, partly because Wilson became distracted by other, more lucrative writing projects; partly because he increasingly sensed the magnitude of the work he

---

[58] Memoranda for "The Modern Democratic State," *c*. Dec. 1-20, 1885, *ibid.*, p. 59.

[59] "The Modern Democratic State," *c*. Dec. 1-20, 1885, *ibid.*, pp. 65-66, and Memoranda for "The Modern Democratic State," *c*. Dec. 1-20, 1885, *ibid.*, pp. 60-61.

[60] "The Modern Democratic State," *c*. Dec. 1- 20, 1885, *ibid.*, p. 87.

had set before him; partly because his thinking changed under the social upheaval of the 1890's; and partly, one suspects, because Wilson believed that finally the moral synthesis of democracy could not be achieved in theoretical terms but only through action, especially through the leadership of a gifted, eloquent man. Many of the themes of "The Modern Democratic State" endured throughout his later writing: the insistence upon the organic character of society balanced against the need for individual self-expression, especially in political leaders; the emphasis upon the moral basis of democracy—its "principles"; democracy as the fullest expression of political life; and a faith in the progressive evolution of societies to democratic forms of government.

These themes were scarcely unique to Wilson, for they were widely advanced in late-nineteenth-century American society as a way of re-knitting the social fabric rent by the Civil War. Wilson's formulation was naïve in its almost total disregard for the way in which industrialization, urbanization, and immigration were transforming the homogeneity and common moral values on which society rested. On the other hand, his emphasis upon the organic nature of society would later serve as a powerful new basis for his own progressive credo in politics—a call for reform to tame the disintegrating forces in American society and restructure it along moral principles.

"The Modern Democratic State" is also illustrative of how some of the basic assumptions in the covenant theological tradition had deeply influenced Wilson's thinking. The covenant theology walked the same narrow line between a severe individualism (God's election of the individual to salvation) and an emphasis on the corporate character of all human affairs (God's covenant with his people, the church). Wilson's view of society as an organism was reinforced by the covenant theology's own inclusive, comprehensive way of seeing the world. Even in his rejection of the formal constitutional conception of society, he moved away from the narrow contractualism of the covenant tradition only to embrace it more fully by stressing the idea of society as bound by common allegiance to certain values.

Wilson's other writings during his years at Bryn Mawr provided some relief from the abstractions of political philosophy. He blasted the Blair bill for federal aid to education because he considered education a responsibility of the states;[61] penned his first book reviews;[62]

---

[61] WW to R. Bridges, Feb. 17 and March 2, 1886, *ibid*., pp. 126-28, especially p. 128, n.2.

[62] Review of the Greville Memoirs in the Chicago *Dial*, printed at Feb. 1, 1886, in *ibid*., pp. 100-104, and a review of von Holst's *The Constitutional Law of the United States of America* in the Philadelphia *Press*, printed at April 17, 1887, in *ibid*., pp. 490-99. Actually, Wilson's very first book review appeared in the *Daily Princetonian* and analyzed John Richard Green's *A Short History of the English People* (London, 1874). It is printed at May 2, 1878, *ibid*., I, 373-75.

called for a new political party formed with "a new, genuine and really meant purpose held by a few strong men of principle and boldness";[63] and criticized the gulf between tariff taxation and appropriation of public monies.[64] Wilson also decided to try his hand at literary criticism, a move at least initially greeted with conspicuous failure. He told his wife in 1887, "I have devoted myself to a literary life,"[65] but his devotion was hardly met by acclaim in the literary world. His first effort, "The Eclipse of Individuality," was rejected and his second, "The Author Himself," was written in 1887 but not published until 1891. He chose a *nom de plume*, "Axson Mayte," for the former because he was worried that some people would think him frivolous and insufficiently interested in academic work.[66]

The purpose of Wilson's literary criticism was primarily moral, an insistence that writers deal with the important and constructive values of human life. Too much reading obscures a writer's vision, he believed, and, reflecting his own educational experience, he advised: "The Rule for each man is, Not to depend on the education which others organize or prepare for him; but to strive to see things as they are and *to be himself as he is*. Defeat lies in self-surrender."[67] Wilson even tried his hand at original literary work, dashing off under the name of Edward Coppleston a short story about a frustrated lawyer who forsook law for the literary life;[68] starting another story, "Margaret";[69] and outlining a novel, "The Life and Letters of John Briton."[70] Wilson's failure to get these works published was no loss to American letters, but they are indicative of the extraordinary range of his creative energies.

Wilson's frustrations at Bryn Mawr mounted steadily. Bound by his contract, he was compelled in 1887 to turn down an attractive offer from the University of Michigan.[71] He dreamed of returning to Princeton, and to advance his candidacy he accepted an invitation to

[63] "Wanted,—A Party," *c*. Sept. 1, 1886, *ibid.*, VI, 342-46; originally published in the *Boston Times*, Sept. 26, 1886.

[64] "Taxation and Appropriation," *c*. Jan. 12, 1888, *ibid.*, pp. 653-56; originally published in Albert Shaw (ed.), *The National Revenues* (Chicago, 1888), pp. 106-11.

[65] WW to EAW, Oct. 8, 1887, *PWW*, V, 613; see also Wilson's Confidential Journal, Oct. 20, 1887, *ibid.*, p. 619.

[66] WW to R. Bridges, April 7, 1887, *ibid.*, p. 475.

[67] "The Eclipse of Individuality," *c*. April 7, 1887, *ibid.*, pp. 476-83; "The Author Himself," *c*. Dec. 7, 1887, *ibid.*, pp. 635-45.

[68] "The World and John Hart," *c*. Sept. 1, 1887, *ibid.*, pp. 567-84.

[69] This is described in Bragdon, *Wilson: The Academic Years*, p. 437, n. 27.

[70] Editorial Note, Wilson's Desire for a Literary Life, *PWW*, V, 474-75.

[71] James Burrill Angell to WW, April 9, 1887, *ibid.*, pp. 485-86; WW to J. B. Angell, *c*. April 12, 1887, *ibid.*, p. 486; WW to the President and Trustees of Bryn Mawr College, June 29, 1888, *ibid.*, pp. 743-47.

address the Princeton alumni of New York. The speech, "The Scholar in Politics," was a disaster. His serious, pedagogical style thoroughly bored the audience; some got up and walked out; and a subsequent speaker made fun of Wilson's grave demeanor. Wilson still managed to get some mileage out of the effort. The speech was eventually published as an essay, "Of the Study of Politics," in the *New Princeton Review*, and in it Wilson urged that the man of the world and the man of books "be merged in each other in the student of politics."[72] Clearly, this was Wilson's hope for his own career, and he naïvely attempted to secure the post of Assistant Secretary of State, with neither experience nor influence but with the expectation of combining his study of politics with practical implementation.[73]

By 1888, Wilson felt that President Rhoads had not lived up to the terms of his contract in failing to provide him with a teaching assistant "as soon as was practicable." He also found it difficult to live on his salary of $2,000 per year. In June, Wilson was approached about the possibility of accepting the Hedding professorship at Wesleyan University in Middletown, Connecticut. Despite the fact that the school year at Bryn Mawr had ended and despite Wilson's contractual commitment to stay at Bryn Mawr for two more years, he began negotiations with both Wesleyan and Bryn Mawr. He secured an offer from Wesleyan of a lighter teaching schedule and a salary of $2,500. He also told Dr. Rhoads that he did not feel bound by the terms of his contract but that he would stay if his salary was increased to $3,000 and if he could leave whenever a more attractive post opened up. The trustees refused to accept Wilson's interpretation of the agreement, nor would they bargain for his services. Wilson broke the contract and resigned on June 29, 1888, leaving considerable ill-will in his wake.[74]

His motivation for going to Wesleyan was in part financial and a product of his desire to advance his professional career at a more established institution. In addition, as he confided to Robert Bridges, "I have for a long time been hungry for a class of *men*."[75] Wilson found

[72] Editorial Note, Wilson's "First Failure" at Public Speaking, *ibid.*, pp. 134-37; an address to the Princeton alumni of New York, *c.* March 23, 1886, *ibid.*, pp. 137-41; "Of the Study of Politics," *ibid.*, pp. 395-406.

[73] WW to J. B. Angell, Nov. 7 and 15, 1887, *ibid.*, pp. 625-26, 629-30; J. B. Angell to WW, Nov. 12, 1887, *ibid.*, pp. 628-29.

[74] John Monroe Van Vleck to WW, June 6, 16, 21, and 29, 1888, *ibid.*, pp. 734-35, 737, 738, 747-48; WW to J. M. Van Vleck, June 7, 1888, *ibid.*, pp. 735-36; Minutes of the Executive Committee of the Bryn Mawr Board of Trustees, June 27, 1888, *ibid.*, pp. 739-40; J. E. Rhoads to WW, June 27 and July 6, 1888, *ibid.*, pp. 741-42, 749; WW to the President and Trustees of Bryn Mawr College, June 29, 1888, *ibid.*, pp. 743-47; J. E. Rhoads to Martha Carey Thomas, June 30, 1888, *ibid.*, p. 748.

[75] WW to R. Bridges, Aug. 26, 1888, *ibid.*, p. 764.

Wesleyan a far more pleasant place to teach and pursue his research and writing, and except for his repressed political ambitions, he enjoyed his two years of great activity and work there. His teaching load included courses in western European and American history, the history of political institutions, American constitutional history, and political economy.[76] His lectures were extremely popular with the students. As Wilson said of Adam Smith as a lecturer, "He bestowed the most painstaking care . . . not only upon what he was to say, but also upon the way he was to say it."[77] In his lectures Wilson conveyed in clear and compelling fashion not only knowledge but a contagious interest in his subject. Occasional light moments kept the students interested: "Business is business, which is just another way of saying that it is not Christianity." Or, referring to an insane king of England, "When he came to years of discretion, he was found to have no discretion."[78]

Wilson threw himself into the extracurricular life of the campus, and during his second year, he was elected "by acclamation" as one of the directors of the Football Association. Wilson helped to coach the team, designed some of its plays, and, brandishing an umbrella, walked the sidelines shouting encouragement. The Wesleyan eleven's fortunes picked up markedly after Wilson aided them, and their record for 1889 was one of the best compiled by a Wesleyan football team up to that time.[79]

Wilson also moved to establish his favorite organization—a debating society modeled after the British House of Commons—and in 1889 the Wesleyan House of Commons was founded, with the constitution of course written by Wilson. In commending this structure to the Wesleyan students, Wilson pointed out its success at Johns Hopkins and emphasized the valuable training in oratory and debate which it would provide. He also observed that "to imitate the House of Representatives would be patriotic, but not interesting." The British model would make the debates more dramatic, he believed, because the ministry would stand or fall on the basis of skill in debate.[80] But the Wesleyan House of Commons did not prosper. Attendance was erratic, and to Wilson's annoyance, members thought it great sport to vote the ministry out of office on a whim. Not surprisingly, the organization died when Wilson left for Princeton in 1890.[81]

[76] Wilson's Copy for the Wesleyan Catalogue for 1888-1889, c. Dec. 1, 1888, *ibid.*, VI, 26-27; Wilson's Copy for the Wesleyan Catalogue for 1889-1890, c. Dec. 1, 1889, *ibid.*, pp. 431-32.

[77] "An Old Master," c. Feb. 1, 1887, *ibid.*, V, 452.

[78] Bragdon, *Wilson: The Academic Years*, p. 168.

[79] News items, Oct. 26 and Dec. 9, 1889, *PWW*, VI, 408, 451-52; Bragdon, *Wilson: The Academic Years*, pp. 172-73.

[80] Constitution for the Wesleyan House of Commons, c. Jan. 5, 1889, *PWW*, VI, 39-44; news items, c. Jan. 8, 1889, *ibid.*, pp. 45-46.

[81] Editorial in the *Wesleyan Argus*, Oct. 9, 1889, *ibid.*, pp. 401-402; WW to John Franklin Jameson, March 20, 1890, *ibid.*, p. 556, n. 3.

Wilson's relatively light teaching load at Wesleyan gave him time to finish his textbook on government, *The State*. In this book he surveyed and compared the development of political institutions in the West. Link has described it as "probably Wilson's greatest scholarly achievement,"[82] and measured against his poorly researched *Congressional Government* and his "popular" books of the 1890's, this verdict is in part accurate. Wilson culled substantially from German political and administrative historians, particularly the impressive series entitled *Handbuch des Oeffentlichen Rechts der Gegenwart* which was edited by Heinrich Marquardsen of the University of Erlangen. His indebtedness to the Marquardsen volumes even extended to rather thinly veiled plagiarism. *The State* contains striking similarities in textual matter to the Marquardsen series as well as some noticeable gaps. For example, when Wilson wrote *The State*, Marquardsen's *Handbuch* did not yet include the volumes on Italy and Russia, and so Wilson skipped over these two countries in his own book. However, *The State* did assemble in one place a great deal of useful information on the political and institutional history of the West, and it became a standard textbook, going through several editions and revisions and eventually being translated into Japanese, French, Russian, Italian, Spanish, and German.[83]

The virtues of *The State* were also its defects, because for all of Wilson's research, the information was basically unsynthesized, and the only truly analytical chapters were the last four dealing with the nature, functions, and objects of government and law. Valuable as an outline of Wilson's political philosophy, these chapters are similar to his earlier theoretical statement in "The Modern Democratic State." He stressed the progressive evolution of political institutions and foresaw the triumph of democratic forms of government as inevitable. He also viewed society as organic and integrated by both the force of common beliefs and values and the individual's commitment to self-realization and the progress of society. Law differed from one society to another, Wilson argued, but its base was tradition and custom, as well as a higher law containing "certain common moral judgments, a certain evidence of unity of thought regarding the greater principles of equity." "There is," Wilson believed, "a common legal conscience in mankind."[84] The purpose of government was consequently the realization of society's goals. "The rule of governmental action is necessary cooperation; the method of political development is conservative adaptation, shaping old habits into new ones, modifying old means to accomplish new ends."[85]

The influence of the covenant theological tradition, interacting with

---

[82] Link, *Road to the White House*, p. 21.

[83] Editorial Note, Wilson's "The State," *PWW*, VI, 244-52.

[84] *The State, c.* June 3, 1889, *ibid.*, p. 278.   [85] *Ibid.*, p. 311.

Wilson's study of the common law under John B. Minor at the University of Virginia and his historical studies at Johns Hopkins, is clearly evident in Wilson's desire to see society as an organism, progressively evolving through common traditions to the formation of democratic political institutions. Wilson repeatedly argued that individuals are bound by governments which arise out of the "compact" of society itself—out of "the common habit, an evolution of experience, an interlaced growth of tenacious relationships, a compact, living, organic, whole, structural, not mechanical."[86] He further paid tribute to the political contribution of the Christian tradition, claiming that Christianity encouraged the idea of individual rights by giving "each man a magistracy over himself by insisting upon his personal, individual responsibility to God."[87]

The sources of Wilson's political thought are so complex and intertwined that it is an impossible, indeed fruitless, task to sort them out or claim an exclusive influence for his Presbyterian heritage. Nevertheless, it is important to note how easily this tradition combined with Wilson's own educational experience and predispositions. For example, Wilson's faith in progress and his description of the evolution of political institutions were obviously influenced by Herbert Spencer and Walter Bagehot, who shared a common belief in evolutionary theory as applied to society. Wilson had been enamored with Bagehot since his undergraduate days at Princeton, and he read Spencer and listened to lectures on his social theory at Johns Hopkins.[88]

[86] *Ibid.*, p. 256. Despite the great influence of the covenant theological tradition on Wilson's political thought, he specifically rejected Locke's contention that a social compact was formed in a state of nature. As early as 1883, he called Locke's social compact an "unnecessary fiction," and in 1886 while preparing *The State*, Wilson wrote, "Just as most economists have, until very lately, deduced their whole science from certain hypothetical states of fact and an analysis of certain fictitious kinds of men, so most writers on politics have—like Hobbes, Locke, Rousseau, *et id omne genus*—evolved government out of a primitive condition of mankind for the actual existence of which they could adduce no sort of evidence." Wilson claimed his approach would be different, developing political theory out of the study of the history of government, or, as he put it, "The true philosophy of government can be extracted only from the true history of government." The only concession which Wilson was willing to make to Locke's social compact formed in a state of nature characteristically involved an historical analogy. Since the writers of the first state constitutions in the American colonies made a distinct choice of one form of government as opposed to another, this might be "a case in point for Locke or Rousseau, a case of *contract*, of the debated selection by bodies of free men of the particular sort of government that suited them." Yet Wilson consistently viewed government and constitutions in historical terms, "*not*," as he said, "*a la Rousseau, Locke, et al.*" See WW's marginal note to Theodore D. Woolsey, *Political Science or the State*, c. May 8, 1883, *ibid.*, II, 345; WW to Horace Elisha Scudder, July 10, 1886, *ibid.*, V, 303-304; "The Modern Democratic State," c. Dec. 1-20, 1885, *ibid.*, p. 67; WW to R. H. Dabney, Nov. 7, 1886, *ibid.*, p. 384.

[87] *The State*, c. June 3, 1889, *ibid.*, VI, 263.

[88] Notes on lectures by Professor George Sylvester Morris on Herbert Spencer, Nov. 12 and 19, 1884, *ibid.*, III, 426-28, 457-58.

Wilson was even favorably disposed to Charles Darwin himself, for when his uncle James Woodrow became involved in a controversy over evolution at Columbia Theological Seminary during the early 1880's, Wilson vehemently sided with his uncle. If his uncle lost his fight, Wilson said, then "Dr. McCosh ought to be driven out of the church, and all private members like myself ought to withdraw without waiting for the expulsion which should follow belief in evolution." When James Woodrow's opponents were successful in driving him from his chair at Columbia, Wilson was enraged, declaring that his thoughts were "too harsh" for the pages of a letter and concluding that "our dear church . . . has indeed fallen upon evil times of ignorance and folly!"[89]

Wilson's defense of his uncle, at least to some degree, undoubtedly was simply family loyalty, but his appropriation of Darwin, Spencer, Bagehot, and others in no way compromised his own Calvinist creed. The idea of the survival of the fittest merely reinforced what Wilson's father had taught him and what he himself believed—that the world was an alien arena in which contesting principles vied for supremacy; that hard work guaranteed success; that defeat should evoke greater exertion; that a person of diligence and ability could achieve greater things than those who went before him. Social Darwinism and the Protestant ethic went hand in hand to sanction Wilson's driving ambitions and approve his ceaseless activity.

And yet it can also be argued that by the time Wilson wrote *The State*, his covenant theological heritage had undermined one critical assumption in Social Darwinist ideology. Wilson rebelled against the strict application of the laws of nature to the laws of society because he believed that this eliminated the aspect of human choice. Just as his covenanter predecessors had taken the capriciousness of predestination out of God's hands and shared salvation between God and humanity, so Wilson also wanted to preserve a degree of individual freedom in political affairs.

"Human choice enters into the laws of the state, whereas from natural laws that choice is altogether excluded: they are dominated by fixed necessity," Wilson maintained. "Human choice, indeed, enters every part of political law to modify it. It is the element of change; and it has given to the growth of law a variety, a variability, and an irregularity which no other power could have imparted."[90] As a result, Wilson could not countenance the radical laissez-faire state that the Social Darwinists proposed, for this masked the choices of individuals with the veil of immutable laws. Wilson also believed that it turned over to

---

[89] WW to ELA, June 26, 1884 and Jan. 11, 1885, *ibid.*, pp. 217-18, 598.

[90] *The State*, c. June 3, 1889, *ibid.*, VI, 283; see also Wilson's critique of Bagehot's *Physics and Politics*, c. July 20, 1889, *ibid.*, p. 335.

the individual responsibilities which only the state could discharge equitably.

Wilson's philosophy of the state was, in fact, striking in its provisions for positive state action in a variety of areas. He differentiated between what he called the state's constituent functions (those it was obligated to provide, such as law enforcement) and its ministrant functions (those which were optional and based on political feasibility, such as regulation of trade, aid to education, etc.). In the disputed area of government regulation of corporations, Wilson was vague but saw it as merely "one side of the modern regulation of the industrial system, and is a function added to the antique list of governmental tasks."[91] "One may justly conclude," wrote Wilson, "not indeed that the restraints which modern states put upon themselves are of little consequence, or that altered political conceptions are not of the greatest moment in determining important questions of government and even the whole advance of the race; but that it is rather by gaining practical wisdom, rather by long processes of historical experience, that states modify their practices; new theories are subsequent to new experiences."[92] Striking an obscure balance somewhere between laissez-faire and socialism, Wilson fundamentally relied on the demands and needs of society, interpreted by the "practical wisdom" of its leaders, to determine the proper course of political action.

Despite the interrelationship between Wilson's religious tradition and his political thought, profound tensions remained between them. The principles which Wilson sought to read out of the history of institutions still had to be realized in modern political life; the "common legal conscience in mankind" was contradicted by the changing nature of law in different times and cultures; the man of thought seemed to be frustrated in realizing his ideals and becoming the man of action. Wilson recognized these tensions developing within him, for as he declared in a lecture on Bagehot, "It is necessary to stand . . . in the midst of thought and also in the midst of affairs, if you would really comprehend those great *wholes* of history and of character which are the vital substance of Politics."[93]

He further saw the dichotomy building up in his spiritual life, and in a remarkable self-revelation to his confidential journal, he noted:

> I used to wonder vaguely why I did not have the same deep-reaching spiritual difficulties that I read of other young men having. I *saw* the intellectual difficulties but I was not *troubled* by them: they seem to have no connection with my faith in the essentials of the religion I

[91] *The State, c.* June 3, 1889, *ibid.*, p. 300.   [92] *Ibid.*, p. 301.
[93] "A Literary Politician," July 20, 1889, *ibid.*, p. 354.

had been taught. Unorthodox in my reading of the standards of the faith, I am nevertheless orthodox in my faith. I am capable, it would seem, of being satisfied spiritually without being satisfied intellectually.[94]

When it came to a direct application of ethical principles to governmental policy, Wilson drove the wedge still deeper. He argued that the province of law is "not distinctively ethical" and neatly assigned ethics, religion, and law to their separate places. "Ethics concerns the development of character; religion, the development of man's relations with God; law, the development of men's relations to each other in society."[95]

This graphically demonstrates the separation and compartmentalization of Wilson's thinking. Satisfied spiritually while dissatisfied intellectually, he apparently felt that he could maintain the division between the implications of his religious and political thought and keep them from impinging on one another. This division was hardly unique in the history of the Christian tradition, but Wilson, in a certain sense, had absorbed and adopted an element inherent in his covenant theological heritage, namely the separation of the sphere of grace from the sphere of nature. This dichotomy encouraged a divorce between the absolute commands of God for the individual and the more relative laws by which society governed itself. Wilson could thus stand aloof from many of the intellectual controversies of the late nineteenth and early twentieth centuries, simultaneously retaining his political relativism and his deep and profound religious convictions. Intellectually he had protected his religion from the attacks from other spheres of knowledge in order to preserve the emotional stability and security which his faith provided him.

Wilson's faith matured during his years at Wesleyan, and some of the division between his religious and political thought began to break down. This development was due in part to the influence of Azel W. Hazen, the pastor of the First Congregational Church in Middletown. Wilson had been asked to teach Sunday School in the Second Congregational Church, but in November 1888 he and his wife chose to join Hazen's church instead.[96] Wilson enjoyed a lifelong friendship with Dr. Hazen, and his influence, as well as the more mature integration of Wilson's political and religious thought, is dramatically shown in one of Wilson's favorite popular lectures, "Leaders of Men."

First delivered in June 1890 and several times thereafter during the

---

[94] Confidential Journal, Dec. 28, 1889, ibid., p. 462.

[95] The State, c. June 3, 1889, ibid., p. 280.

[96] Stockton Axson to EAW, c. Oct. 19, 1888, ibid., p. 15, n. 2; WWLL, I, 300.

1890's, this address is remarkable for Wilson's serene confidence in political progress throughout history. Wilson also utilized more fully the language of the King James Version of the Bible and emphasized that the Christian law of love was the foundation of unity in all societies and the only proper inspiration for political leaders. He quoted with approval the words of John Bright:

> May I ask you, then, to believe, as I do most devoutly believe, that the moral law was not written for men alone in their individual character, but that it was written as well for nations great as this of which we are citizens. If nations reject and deride that moral law, there is a penalty which will inevitably follow. It may not come at once, it may not come in our lifetime; but, rely upon it. . . .[97]

Wilson declared that religious leaders, whose "leadership of rebuke" gave them special moral authority, had a special sympathy for those who followed them. "In Calvin . . . love is the sanction of justice." Only by revering the will of the people and by adhering to Christ's law of love could a statesman be a "deeply human man, quick to know and to do the things that the hour and his people need."[98]

While this emphasis upon the Christian law of love was not foreign to Wilson's thought, in "Leaders of Men" it appeared much more explicitly and with much greater importance. Wilson had moderated his earlier rigorous idealism and absolute identification with principles as the criteria for the leader. He acknowledged the danger of a demagogue appearing with adherence to certain principles but argued that the leader is distinguished from the demagogue by his desire to use power to serve others rather than to aggrandize his own authority and to substitute persuasion for coercion. He acknowledged his indebtedness to Dr. Hazen's preaching by quoting from one of his sermons: " 'You are poor fishers of men,' it has been said of a certain class of preachers; 'you do not go fishing with a rod and a line, and with the patient sagacity of the true sportsman. You use a telegraph pole and a cable: with these you savagely beat the water, and bid men bite or be damned. And you expect they will be caught!' "[99] Under Dr. Hazen's influence and as a result of his deepening love for his wife, Wilson had softened his harsh views of political responsibility. No longer was politics simply a matter of rigid adherence to just principles; it had become the realization of those principles in acts mitigated and enlightened by Christian love.

Another possible influence on Wilson's maturing religious thought

---

[97] "Leaders of Men," June 17, 1890, *PWW*, vi, 655; Editorial Note, "Leaders of Men," *ibid.*, pp. 644-46.

[98] *Ibid.*, pp. 666, 671.   [99] *Ibid.*, pp. 661, 669.

was the visit to Middletown of the evangelist Dwight L. Moody. Wilson was affected by Moody's preaching, for as late as 1914 he recalled the experience of being in a barber shop with Moody and feeling as if he had been at an evangelistic service. The barbers became very quiet and knew, according to Wilson, "that something had elevated their thought. And I felt that I left that place as I should have left a place of worship."[100] Wilson apparently shared the platform with Moody at one of the university chapel services, and one student remembered the effect of Moody's sermon on Wilson. Normally, Wilson used the morning prayers found in *The Book of Common Prayer*, Morris B. Crawford recollected, but

> one morning, while Mr. Moody was conducting a series of meetings in Middletown, Mr. Wilson, who evidently had been touched, as we all had been, by the intense earnestness of the great evangelist, voiced his prayer for us in his own words, which, by their earnestness, their originality and beauty of expression, their precise adaptation to the demands of the moment, were far more effective than any possible prescribed form of prayer could have been. Nobody who heard that prayer could doubt that Woodrow Wilson was a man of profound faith in God.[101]

The quickening of his religious life coincided with a realization of his own developing maturity. "Have I told you that latterly—since I have been here," he wrote Ellen from Baltimore,

> a distinct *feeling* of maturity—or rather maturing—has come over me? The *boyish* feeling that I have so long had and cherished is giving place, consciously, to another feeling—the feeling that I am no longer young (though not old quite!) and that I need no longer hesitate (as I have so long and sensitively done) to assert myself and my opinions in the presence of and against the selves and opinions of old men, "my elders." It may be all imagination, but these are the facts of consciousness at the present moment in one Woodrow Wilson—always a slow fellow in mental development—long a child, longer a difident youth, now at last, perhaps, becoming a self-confident (mayhap a self-assertive) man. I find I look older, my former (Princeton) college friends here being the witnesses.[102]

At Wesleyan, the introspective, uncertain Wilson "came to himself," to use his phrase, and found a new self-confidence and assertiveness

---

[100] *The Congregationalist*, Nov. 12, 1914, quoted in *WWLL*, I, 315-16.

[101] Morris B. Crawford, "Some Reminiscences of Woodrow Wilson," *Wesleyan University Alumnus* (March 1924), p. 10.

[102] WW to EAW, March 9, 1889, *PWW*, VI, 139.

which his father had tried to give him. The author of two books, a successful teacher admired by his students, secure in the love of his wife, the father of three children, Wilson exhibited a new sense of assurance during his two years in Middletown, en route to a Princeton professorship. He resigned himself to academic life and temporarily shelved his political dreams. He was less intense and less demanding after earning a degree of success and looked with openness, tolerance, and anticipation to the future and its possibilities.

Completely isolated from and unaware of the tensions in American society which would produce the social and political turmoil of the 1890's, Wilson wrote in his journal: "I find myself exceedingly tolerant of all institutions, past and present, by reason of a keen appreciation of their reason for being—*most* tolerant, so to say, of the institutions of my own day which seem to me, in an historical sense, intensely and essentially reasonable, though of course in no sense *final*." And, standing on the eve of his appointment to Princeton, he asked a question startling for both its arrogance and its prophetic quality: "Why may not the present age write, through me, its political *autobiography*?"[103]

[103] Confidential Journal, Dec. 28, 1889, *ibid.*, VI, 463.

V

Professor at Princeton–
THE PHILOSOPHER OF LAW

Wilson's appointment to the faculty of Princeton in 1890 was a partial realization of his academic ambitions. To miss the opportunity to teach at his alma mater, he wrote to a friend, would dash all his cherished hopes, but he added that he remained "suspicious of good fortune" till he actually obtained the position.[1] A number of Wilson's classmates from Princeton, especially Robert Bridges, conspired to arrange his election, but even after he had received the news he desired to hear, he responded as he did when he learned that *Congressional Government* had been accepted for publication. "I find that everybody regards my election to P. as a sort of crowning success," he wrote to his father. "Congratulations pour in from all sides: evidently I am 'writ down' in the category of 'successful men.' I suppose I ought to feel an immense accession of personal satisfaction,—of pride; but somehow I can't manage it."[2]

Despite his immediate reaction, Wilson was extremely happy to teach at Princeton, and although his twelve years as a professor were hardly idyllic or restful, they were among the happiest of his life. One of his chief sources of pleasure was his wife and three daughters—Margaret, Jessie Woodrow, and Eleanor Randolph—who arrived in rapid succession, in 1886, 1887, and 1889 respectively. According to Bliss Perry, a fellow faculty member, the Wilson family life "was singularly happy,"[3] but it was blighted in one respect. The Wilsons desperately wanted a son. "Ah, how I hope that dream may be realized!" Wilson exclaimed to Ellen in 1889 before Eleanor's birth, but he tried to prepare her, and himself, for another daughter. "When I think of our precious, our delightful little daughters, I can't help being as glad at [the] thought of having another little girl—almost—as at the thought of having a boy. . . . They are lights to the house—treasures of amusement, as well as everything that ought to make a parent's heart glad,—charming in nothing more than in their individuality."[4] When

---

[1] WW to R. Bridges, Aug. 9, 1889, *PWW*, VI, 364.

[2] WW to JRW, March 20, 1890, *ibid.*, p. 554.

[3] Bliss Perry, *And Gladly Teach* (Boston and New York, 1935), p. 153.

[4] WW to EAW, Feb. 24, 1889, *PWW*, VI, 110.

the doctor told Ellen that her third child was a girl, she burst into tears. Wilson assured her that "no child of ours shall be unwelcome," but old grandfather Wilson was disappointed too. "Oh, it's just another of Woodrow's little annuals," he grumbled but told his son, "Somehow I had—unreasoningly of course—hoped for a boy—but the divine Father who has events in His own hand, moulds all things for the best."[5]

Wilson did not slight his daughters, and he showered affection on them and devoted a great deal of time to his three "little chicks." Like his father, he played word games with them and entertained them with impersonations: the supercilious, monocled Englishman, the dour Scotsman, the riotous Irishman, and the girls' favorite—the staggering, incoherent drunk. He used his hands to imitate the sound of galloping horses or the flight of birds and created castles out of their blocks.[6] Ellen supervised the girls' education, and every weekday morning they had lessons in the three R's, geography, and history. She introduced them to literature—Homer, Dryden, Shakespeare, the Romantic poets, and English novelists, and believed that even when the children did not understand the meaning, they could appreciate the beauty of the words.[7] The Wilsons did not ignore religious education, and their home was permeated by what Wilson once called "the atmospheric pressure of Christianity." All the children were required to memorize the Westminster Shorter Catechism and bound to strict observance of the Sabbath. They attended church regularly, but Mrs. Wilson refused to send the children to Sunday School and taught the girls the stories of the Bible herself.[8]

The Wilsons were dissatisfied with both the First and Second Presbyterian Churches during the early years of their residence in Princeton, partially because the two churches experienced a rather rapid turnover of ministers. It was not until 1897 that the Second Presbyterian Church's pulpit was held by a man who met Wilson's demanding standards, and in May the family joined the church.[9] Part of the reluctance of the Wilsons to transfer their membership to Princeton was their affection for their former pastor, Dr. Hazen, in Middletown. "It has been a solace to us to feel that we were still members of your church, even if we could not see or hear you,—and the churches here have for long been in such a condition of would-be change that we have had no very ill conscience in the matter," Wilson wrote to Hazen. "But now we have settled conditions at last, and a clear duty in the

---

[5] Eleanor Wilson McAdoo (ed.), *The Priceless Gift: The Love Letters of Woodrow Wilson and Ellen Axson Wilson* (New York, 1962), p. 171; JRW to WW, Oct. 30, 1889, *PWW*, vi, 408.

[6] McAdoo, *The Priceless Gift*, pp. 181-82, 209-10.

[7] *Ibid.*, p. 186.   [8] *WWLL*, ii, 49.

[9] Azel Washburn Hazen to WW, April 1, 1897, *PWW*, x, 210-11, n. 1.

matter:— we *must* ask for a letter."[10] Dr. Hazen released his members, and his letter reveals the kind of devotion which the Wilsons gave to the church. "You were *ideal* parishioners while here . . . ," he wrote them. "I can never forget your reverent, worshipful bearing in our services, nor your *patient* attention to my too barren words, while your many utterances of regard for myself will long be cherished as a comfort and an inspiration."[11]

In joining the Second Presbyterian Church, the Wilsons associated with the socially less prominent Presbyterian Church in Princeton, and within weeks after they became members, Wilson was elected an elder. Despite a schedule crowded with teaching, lecturing, and writing responsibilities, Wilson gave time and energy to the work of the church, serving on presbytery as well as session committees, and even speaking for a Christian Endeavor Day held at the Second Presbyterian Church.[12] In 1905, Wilson and his friend, John Grier Hibben, led an effort to unite the First and Second Presbyterian Churches, which stood virtually across the street from each other, but social divisions between the two congregations resulted in Second Church's rejection of the merger. Wilson was disgusted and joined a large group from the Second Church in transferring their memberships to the First Church.[13]

During his absences from home, Wilson dutifully reported on the sermons he heard and the churches he visited, and Ellen kept him informed about the services in Princeton.[14] On a trip to the South, he went to church and felt at home. "I have just come from church,— where I heard a really excellent old-fashioned sermon,—and feel . . . as if I had fallen once again into the slow paced southern life which seems to me the most natural of all."[15] But Wilson could be sharply critical of sermons he disliked. One minister preached "like a Methodist rather than like a Presbyterian"—"in the manner of a big bass drum," he declared. After it was over he told the pastor he was glad to have heard the sermon, but he meant that "I *am* glad that it's *over*."[16] Never one to depreciate the value and power of oratory, Wilson nevertheless was repelled by demonstrations of rhetorical excesses

[10] WW to A. W. Hazen, March 29, 1897, *ibid.*, p. 201.

[11] A. W. Hazen to WW, April 1, 1897, *ibid.*, p. 211.

[12] News items, May 22, 1897, *ibid.*, p. 242; Oct. 28, 1899, and Jan. 13 and Feb. 10, 1900, *ibid.*, xi, 263, 370, 401.

[13] News item, Nov. 11, 1905, *ibid.*, xvi, 218-19, ns. 1, 2, 3; Minutes of the Session of the Second Presbyterian Church, Nov. 25, 1905, *ibid.*, pp. 234-35, n. 1.

[14] EAW to WW, Feb. 5, 1898, *ibid.*, x, 376. For examples of Ellen's reactions to sermons she heard while away from Princeton, see EAW to WW, Nov. 19, 1899 and Feb. 11, 1900, *ibid.*, xi, 279, 402.

[15] WW to Edith Gittings Reid, Feb. 27, 1898, *ibid.*, x, 462; cf. WW to EAW, Feb. 27, 1898, *ibid.*, p. 461.

[16] WW to EAW, June 19, 1898, *ibid.*, p. 565.

from the pulpit. He liked his preachers to be direct and humble and preferred that their sermons convey "simplicity and obviousness."[17]

The church and his home—these were two basic sources of Wilson's emotional stability, and at the center of his life was his wife. When he was separated from her, they exchanged letters daily, and his departures from her almost immediately brought forth his passionate professions of longing for her and the comfort of her arms. "Two more letters besides this one," he wrote to her in 1895,

> and then I come myself, to claim you, to take possession of you,—
> of all the time and love you can give me: to take you in my arms and
> hold you till I have made sure, by feeling your heart beat against
> mine and by seeing once more the very depths of your eyes, that I
> am really at home once more, with the woman who has made me
> and kept me what I am. I tremble with a deep excitement when I
> think of it. I verily believe I never quivered so before with eager
> impatience and anticipation. I know that I was not half so much ex-
> cited on the eve of our marriage.[18]

Wilson was hardly the austere, aloof person that so many people observed in public, and his letters to his wife reveal the sexual passion and intensity of their relationship. He called himself Ellen's "intemperate lover," and shortly before he was about to return home, he asked her, "Are you prepared for the storm of love making with which you will be assailed?"[19]

The repeated professions of ardor and affection, as strong in the 1890's and 1900's as during their courtship and early marriage, tempt one to conclude that the love passages became a stylistic mannerism. However, there can be little doubt that Wilson's separation from his home was a serious disruption of his emotional life. "Every time I am separated from you, my own Eileen," he wrote her, "I seem to see one more element of my dependence upon you—of my devotion to you. This time I am afraid that it is a *selfish* element I see. . . . The feeling is not *wholly* selfish: it is *you* I miss."[20]

Wilson expressed not only his loneliness in being away from Ellen but also his coronation of her as "a queen" and his dependence upon her for strength. He praised "her power to bless and purify and idealize life for those who love her," for "it is this that makes her my queen!"[21] He declared that he was nothing without her and said, "Ah, darling, I

---

[17] WW to EAW, Aug. 27, 1906, *ibid.*, XVI, 441.

[18] WW to EAW, Feb. 25, 1895, *ibid.*, IX, 225.

[19] WW to EAW, Feb. 6, 1894, *ibid.*, VIII, 460.

[20] WW to EAW, June 19, 1892, *ibid.*, p. 8.

[21] WW to EAW, Feb. 4, 1894, *ibid.*, p. 455.

trust it is not wrong to worship you as I do. You are the presiding genius of both my mind and heart."[22]

Ellen, in turn, believed that her mission in life was to give Wilson faith in himself and confidence in his own powers,[23] and her view of him was no less exalted than his estimation of her. Groping for enough superlatives, she wrote to him, "The combination of qualities found in you is the rarest, finest, noblest, grandest of which human nature is capable." She sensed his ambitions for political life and considered him exceptionally qualified because he had

> such strength and nobility of character combined with such ineffable tenderness, such unselfishness and thoughtfulness in things great and small, & a nature so exquisitely gifted in power of sympathy, —of understanding others . . . and the orator's gift,—the "personal magnetism" and *all* those gifts which go to make a born leader of men, combined with powers of thought of such a kind that he must undoubtedly rank as a *genius*, no less than Burke himself; and added to all this a strength of purpose and of will and powers of application which result in achievements so great that while yet in his early manhood his rank is among the foremost thinkers of his age![24]

While constantly inflating Wilson's self-esteem, Ellen also assured her husband of the love which he needed and demanded. "Woodrow, my own, my love," she professed, "I am sure that I am the happiest woman in the world—that *no* other is so blessed."[25]

In return, Wilson occasionally relaxed that self-control which he praised in his essays on democracy and set as the style of his own life. "All my passions are upon so terrible a scale of power," he confessed to her, and after receiving one of her letters, he reported that "it not only brought a flood of tender gratefulness into my heart, but it brought a burst of tears into my eyes."[26]

Wilson and Ellen shared a common religious faith that bound them together and appeared most explicitly in times of illness or death. When his brother-in-law Stockton Axson recovered from an attack of appendicitis, Wilson declared, "I thank God with all my heart for his wonderfully merciful providence in the whole matter from first to last. He has been singularly gracious to us."[27] When the daughter of some

[22] WW to EAW, Jan. 30, 1894, *ibid.*, p. 443.

[23] WW to EAW, June 23, 1892, *ibid.*, pp. 17-18.

[24] EAW to WW, April 3, 1892, *ibid.*, VII, 542.

[25] EAW to WW, July 26, 1893, *ibid.*, VIII, 293.

[26] WW to EAW, Feb. 11 and 13, 1894, *ibid.*, pp. 472, 480. See also WW to EAW, Aug. 20, 1899, *ibid.*, XI, 235-36.

[27] WW to EAW, Feb. 14, 1900, *ibid.*, p. 411. See also EAW to WW, Feb. 12,1900 and WW to EAW, Feb. 15, 1900, *ibid.*, pp. 405-406, 413.

friends died, Wilson was deeply moved and admired their "Christian fortitude" during the tragedy. "I wish," he wrote Ellen, "I could hope for half their fortitude and faith under like circumstances! My own Christianity seems of so mild and pale a type alongside minds of such a quality as theirs."[28] Wilson's faith remained unshaken, perhaps even unaffected, by death, although it is clear that he personally felt it deeply.[29]

Tragedy affected Ellen's faith more drastically, and Wilson quickly assured her to "accept the infinite blessing God in his mercy has brought us and be *glad*, not anxious, because of it."[30] Always emphasizing the ultimate benevolence of God's will, Wilson wrote on another occasion, "The only relief I have had has been derived from thought of [God] and submission to his Providence. It must be for the best. God grant we may see it soon, before this blackening of the future cuts us too near the quick."[31] During the many attacks of ill health that plagued her husband, Ellen included with nearly every letter a short prayer for his health and safety: "Oh may God in His mercy bless and keep you, and bring you back to me safe and *well*."[32] Wilson also prayed for his wife during her illnesses[33] and reflected his awareness of God's care over him in his constant use of "God willing" or "Providence permitting."[34]

The most frequent cause of Wilson's agonizing absences from home was his six-week series of lectures on administration at The Johns Hopkins University. Wilson began these lectures in 1888 and delivered them each winter until 1897, and they represent one of the most significant but little-noticed aspects of his professional academic career. The appointment to the lectureship at Johns Hopkins came after Wilson presented a paper, "The Study of Administration," to the Cornell Historical and Political Science Association in early November 1886.[35] Wilson's motivation in accepting this position was partially academic recognition, but the $500 stipend was a persuasive incentive. "It will be a sadly dreary business being separated so long from Ellie and the

[28] WW to EAW, Feb. 22, 1900, *ibid.*, p. 434; see also WW to EAW, June 18 and 21, 1892, *ibid.*, VIII, 5-6, 12.

[29] WW to EAW, June 18, 1892, *ibid.*, pp. 5-6; WW to Annie Wilson Howe, April 21, 1895, *ibid.*, IX, 247-48.

[30] WW to EAW, Feb. 15, 1900, *ibid.*, XI, 413.

[31] WW to EAW, Jan. 27, 1895, *ibid.*, IX, 133.

[32] EAW to WW, June 18, 1896, *ibid.*, p. 521. Cf. EAW to WW, June 1 and 4, Aug. 13 and 17, 1896, *ibid.*, pp. 508-509, 510-11, 568-69, 573.

[33] WW to EAW, Feb. 8, 1898, *ibid.*, X, 381.

[34] See, for example, WW to EAW, Feb. 27, 1895 and Feb. 6, 1896, *ibid.*, IX, 233, 409, and Feb. 16 and 27, 1898, *ibid.*, X, 397, 461.

[35] Editorial Note, Wilson's "The Study of Administration," *ibid.*, V, 357-59; Herbert Baxter Adams to WW, Nov. 25, 1886, *ibid.*, pp. 393-94.

babies," he told his father, "but Ellie and the babies must be supported—so, [therefore] must the separation."[36]

Wilson's interest in administration had first been stimulated by Richard T. Ely at Johns Hopkins during 1884-1885, and Wilson set his initial thoughts on paper in a short, unpublished essay, "The Art of Governing," which he wrote during November 1885. Since there were virtually no American authorities working on the problem of administration at that time, Wilson once again relied heavily on German authorities—Johann C. Bluntschli, Heinrich Rudolf von Gneist, as well as the volumes in Marquardsen's *Handbuch des Oeffentlichen Rechts der Gegenwart*.[37]

Wilson recognized that his basic problem involved taking the work of German political scientists, attuned to the needs of a highly centralized government, and appropriating it for an American context. Administrative theory, he argued, "must be adapted, not to a simple and compact, but to a complex and multiform state, and made to fit highly decentralized forms of government. If we would employ it, we must Americanize it, and that not formally, in language merely, but radically, in thought, principle, and aim as well." Wilson insisted that administrative theory was necessary to adjust democracy to the new conditions produced by industrialization and the concentration of economic power; and in defining the field of inquiry, he gave it his own characteristic moral purpose: "The object of administrative study is to rescue executive methods from the confusion and costliness of empirical experiment and set them upon foundations laid deep in stable principle." Order based on principles—this was Wilson's essential thrust in studying administration, and he maintained that it was "closely connected with the study of the proper distribution of constitutional authority."[38]

[36] WW to JRW, Jan. 13, 1889, *ibid.*, VI, 49. Wilson's annual trip to Baltimore proved to be such a strain that Ellen secretly attempted to secure a lectureship for him at Columbia University, rather than Johns Hopkins. Writing to John Bates Clark in 1897, Ellen described her husband as "being singularly dependent upon his home life" and his absence as "a great and increasing trial to him." "Of course," she added, "a man,—or woman,—of the world would think us a pair of silly children to make a tragedy of a five weeks separation. But his temperament,—his way of putting his *whole self* into every lecture, and every written page, really makes it rather important for his physical and mental well-being that I should be constantly at hand, to 'rest' him, as he says." Wilson gave up his Hopkins lectures in 1898, after a group of Princeton friends had augmented his salary in order to free him from the financial necessity. EAW to John Bates Clark, June 3, 1897, *ibid.*, X, 260.

[37] Arthur S. Link, "Woodrow Wilson and the Study of Administration," in *The Higher Realism of Woodrow Wilson*, pp. 38-42.

[38] "The Study of Administration," *c.* Nov. 1, 1886, *PWW*, V, 363-64, 377, 370, 373. This essay was eventually published in the *Political Science Quarterly* in July 1887. For an analysis of interpretations of Wilson's "Study of Administration," which also demonstrates the ambiguities and limitations of Wilson's argument, see Richard J. Stillman, II, "Woodrow Wilson and the

In his early thought on administration, Wilson followed Bluntschli and others in making a sharp distinction between political and administrative considerations. In 1886 he believed that the separation was "too obvious to need further discussion" and that the crucial relationship was between administrative practice and constitutional principles of liberty and self-realization.[39] Accordingly, Wilson's lectures prior to 1890 focused on the practical side of administration, but almost immediately his neat division began to break down. He realized that the state was essentially political and that there could be no easy application of the business principles of efficiency to the political order. "Between money-making and political liberty there are radical differences," Wilson declared in 1888. ". . . Business-*like* the administration of govt. may and should be—but it is not business. It is organic *social life*."[40] Apparently aware of the chaotic analytical framework he had established for his study of administration, Wilson restricted himself to a descriptive treatment of the origins and development of administration throughout history. He emphasized that theory ought to emerge from the history of administration, that the study ought to be comparative in nature, and significantly, that administrative theory was particularly needed for municipal reform. American cities, he stated, had "a general *scheme of law* but no *organic integration*."[41]

By 1890, Wilson recognized that administrative questions were essentially political ones, and this idea was reinforced by his reading of Karl von Gareis' *Allegemeines Staatsrecht*, Otto von Sarwey's *Allegemeines Verwaltungsrecht*, and Georg Jellinek's *Gesetz und Verordnung*.[42] The difference was immediately apparent. Wilson announced to the Hopkins students that after two years of lectures he still found himself *"in the region of description,"* and he proposed to move on to a more analytical treatment of administration. The subject, he now argued, was *"by nature, a subject in Public Law."* It stood at the heart of some of the most pressing social and political questions of the day, and he wanted it understood that administration was a question of *"organization, of effective means,"* a task of adjusting the machinery of government "to historical conditions, to liberty."[43]

Study of Administration: A New Look at an Old Essay," *American Political Science Review,* LXVII (1973), 582-88.

[39] "The Study of Administration," *c.* Nov. 1, 1886, *PWW*, v, 371.

[40] Lecture notes, "The Functions of Government," *c.* Feb. 18, 1888, *ibid.*, p. 690.

[41] Lecture notes, "Systems of Municipal Organization," March 2, 1888, *ibid.*, p. 704. See also Wilson's lecture notes for 1889 in *ibid.*, vi, 86-87, 90-92, and Wilson's review of his lectures at Johns Hopkins in 1889, *ibid.*, p. 327.

[42] Link, "The Study of Administration," p. 42; Editorial Note, Wilson's Lectures on Administration at the Johns Hopkins, 1890, *PWW*, vi, 482-84.

[43] Notes for Lectures on Administration, Feb. 3-March 10, 1898, *ibid.*, p. 485.

After 1890, Wilson's lectures increasingly focused on the interrelationship between law, politics, and administration. As Link has observed, Wilson became "one of the first scholars to realize . . . the truth of the generalization that is now commonplace—that all government was destined to be administration."[44] Wilson rejected the idea that government was divided into legislative, executive, and judicial bodies which provided checks and balances upon each other; rather, adopting a purely functional interpretation, Wilson noted that all branches of government in practice exercised the three responsibilities which were theoretically separated. Administrative problems united government at all levels, and the crucial issue was relating constitutional principles and administrative action. Such an administrative view of government would *"give us administrative elasticity and discretion,"* as well as "free us from the idea that checks and balances are to be carried down through all stages of organization."[45]

In fact, at the foundation of Wilson's theory of administration was an attempt to destroy the idea of government as a necessary evil whose power must be controlled by law and structural balance. The organic character of the state, Wilson believed, made it the highest expression of individual life in society.

> *The State*, therefore, *is an abiding natural relationship*; neither a mere convenience nor a mere necessity; neither a mere voluntary association nor a mere corporation; nor any other artificial thing created for a special purpose, but *the eternal, natural embodiment and expression of a higher form of life than the individual*, namely, that common life which gives leave to individual life, and opportunity for completeness,—makes individual life possible and makes it full and complete.[46]

In effect, Wilson was making theological claims for the state, extending to the political sphere what his Calvinist forbears had traditionally claimed for the church. The state's existence was natural, eternal, even spiritual, unaffected by laws which created "neither State nor Govt."[47]

In such a glorified view of the state, the inevitable stumbling block was individual rights, and on this issue Wilson clumsily tried to strike some sort of balance between the collectivism of the state and individualism. He insisted that individual rights in the abstract did not "constitute an absolute check on administrative action" but that legislation separated "those invasions of individual right by executive power which are necessary to the order and energy of the State from those

---

[44] Link, "The Study of Administration," p. 43.
[45] Notes for Lectures on Administration, *c.* Jan. 26, 1891-Feb. 27, 1894, *PWW*, vii, 121-22.
[46] *Ibid.*, p. 124.   [47] *Ibid.*, p. 128.

which are unnecessary, arbitrary, and tyrannical." He continued to
maintain that there was no final tension between the individual and the
state because the state was an organism, binding all people together
under a constitution guaranteeing political liberty. That liberty, he argued, was "*not the negation of order, but the perfection of it,*—the
equable and cooperative play of elements, the harmonious correlation
of forces. *It is action within the best order.* Like health, it depends
upon a nice balance of functions[.]"[48]

Wilson was so convinced of the importance of guaranteeing the in-
violability of the state that he rejected the democratic idea that
sovereignty remained with the people. Instead, he asserted that
sovereignty was relinquished by the people to their elected representatives and that "to possess any substance or virility, [sovereignty must]
be conceived of as the daily operative force of Gov't., and not simply
the ultimate consent of the governed."[49]

This increasing rigidity in Wilson's political thought and the emphasis upon order and social stability were probably reactions to the economic and political upheavals of the late 1880's and 1890's. Even
more striking is Wilson's realization that his administrative theory
ought to be applied primarily to the problems of American cities. In
1895 he delivered a speech at Johns Hopkins and roughly outlined
what later became known as the commission form of city government.[50] By 1896 his Hopkins lectures attracted so much attention that
they were regularly reported in the local press.

Like many urban reformers of the day, Wilson compared American
cities to their European counterparts and found them wanting. They
were inefficiently managed; the "better classes" were politically inactive; political power was divided between municipalities and states and
even within municipalities. He bemoaned "the general disintegration
of the system" and considered "the idea of checks and balances . . .
wholly out of place in administration."[51] Wilson proposed that the
governments of cities be seen as "chiefly, if not exclusively, administrative in character"; that their governments ought to be integrated; and
that administration ought to be centralized "to get rid of the present
pernicious system of legislative interference."[52]

The 1896 lectures coincided with an outbreak of reform sentiment in
Baltimore, and when Wilson finished his series at the Hopkins, he was

[48] *Ibid.*, pp. 153, 158.

[49] Notes for Lectures on Administration, *c.* Feb. 1, 1892-Feb. 27, 1895, *ibid.*, p. 432.

[50] News report, Feb. 26, 1895, *ibid.*, IX, 228-31; see also the news report of March 3, 1896,
ibid., pp. 477-80.

[51] News report, Feb. 28, 1896, *ibid.*, p. 464.

[52] *Ibid.*; news report, March 4, 1896, *ibid.*, pp. 482-83.

invited, along with Theodore Roosevelt and others, to address a rally sponsored by the local Reform League. The meeting was called to protest the Baltimore Council's obstruction of the mayor's reform policies, and Wilson took the platform to urge the citizens not to lose heart in their fight. He asked them "whether this will be a display of spasmodic strength on your part, or whether you will go forth and put your shoulder to the wheel of good government. . . . I am a believer in the long processes of reform. Everything will come as you mean it if you only continue to mean it."[53]

This plea for steadfastness of purpose and Wilson's ability to switch from classroom lecturing to political stumping was thoroughly characteristic. His Hopkins lecture notes were for the most part dry, scholarly definitions and expositions of administrative and political theory, but his students remembered him differently. "Dr. Wilson is here," Frederick Jackson Turner reported. "Homely, solemn, young, glum, but with that fire in his face and eye that means that its possessor is not of the common crowd."[54] Charles McLean Andrews recalled, "No course we took gave us such a sense of the power of a single individual to shed light on the most difficult problems. We all felt it."[55] Similarly, Frederic C. Howe saw that Wilson the professor blended easily into Wilson the preacher. "Listening to him, I got hints of impressions received at home, when preachers lamented our lukewarmness to Christian ideals, our neglect of responsibility to the church," Howe recalled. ". . . Great men had departed from Capitol Hill; the Senate no longer reverberated to the high morality of earlier days. Democracy was not concerned over issues of great constitutional import. Politics had become the struggle of vulgar interest, of ignoble motive, of untrained men."[56]

But Wilson did not have to restrict the expression of his moral and religious principles to the classroom, for one of the striking characteristics of his activity during the 1890's is the large number of religious addresses, chapel talks, and meditations which he delivered. He had been trained in the homiletical art by his eloquent father, and students and friends repeatedly testified to the power of his religious speaking. After one of Wilson's chapel talks at Princeton, one student wrote a letter home noting that "there was no stretching or lounging in seats while he was talking."[57]

[53] *Ibid.*, pp. 485-86.

[54] Frederick Jackson Turner to Caroline Mae Sherwood, Feb. 13, 1889, *ibid.*, vi, 88.

[55] Bragdon, *Wilson: The Academic Years*, p. 192.

[56] Frederic C. Howe, *Confessions of a Reformer* (New York, 1926), pp. 6-7.

[57] Anonymous letter, March 10, 1902, in the *Pittsburgh Leader*, Sept. 22, 1902, quoted in Bragdon, *Wilson: The Academic Years,* p. 208.

Attendance at chapel services, held five times a week, was required of all Princeton students, and they were somewhat less than enthusiastic about the ordinance. But when Wilson spoke, "he brought with him an atmosphere of reverence and sincerity which subdued even the students of Nassau Hall of my boisterous generation," a Princeton alumnus recollected. "He had a magnificent, resonant voice, and I can still recall his incomparable reading of the Scriptures."[58] His prayers were especially powerful, and a minister stated that Wilson "prayed like a man who knew God not only as a fact in history or a doctrine in theology or an ideal in ethics, but as an experience in his own soul."[59] His prayers were also somewhat moralistic in character, for they generally expressed "the hope that we young men might be worthy and effective tools in the hands of an omnipotent will."[60]

There is little doubt that both as a professor and later as president of the university, Wilson was one of the students' favorite speakers. He regularly led the meetings of the Philadelphian Society (the campus religious organization) and the Laymen's Conference, as well as the services in Marquand Chapel and at the University Place (Cumberland) Presbyterian Church. Despite what appeared to be a deepening and maturing of Wilson's religious thought at Wesleyan and a greater awareness of God's grace, his religious talks during the early years at Princeton were once more moralistic and legalistic in character.

In notes for a talk in October 1890, Wilson emphasized that the students should "be sensitive regarding [God's] judgments—have a moral regard for him, and [therefore] keep his commandments, *because* this is 'the whole of man.' " Reaffirming his faith in an unchanging moral law, Wilson declared, "What is politic seems to vary—what is righteous stands fast."[61] Later in the same academic year he spoke at a chapel service, telling the students that college life was "artificial, full of temptations to disingenuousness," but the person who had "*genuineness*," the combination of good motives and "just, upright, truthful" actions, would be blessed by God.[62]

This moralistic theme appeared frequently in most of Wilson's religious speeches, and it is almost as if he consciously recalled many of his earlier religious emphases as a student at Princeton. In May 1893 the *Daily Princetonian* reported that Wilson had emphasized that "the righteous man should not be long-faced or morose, but joyful, diligent, fervent in spirit." "We are to-day living in the light and we should

---

[58] Raymond B. Fosdick, "Personal Recollections of Woodrow Wilson," *The Philosophy and Policies of Woodrow Wilson*, p. 29.

[59] The Rev. John J. McDowell to R. S. Baker, quoted in *WWLL*, I, 71.

[60] Fosdick, "Personal Recollections," p. 30.

[61] Notes for a talk before the Philadelphian Society, *c.* Oct. 30, 1890, *PWW*, VII, 58.

[62] Notes for a chapel talk, April 5, 1891, *ibid.*, pp. 187-88.

seize every opportunity for doing our whole duty," Wilson declared and warned soberly, "Above all, let us not be frivolous, but serious in the proper sense, as on that depends our future success."[63] In a chapel talk, Wilson the legalist defined the Christian life in simple terms: "sin is the transgression of the *law*." The solution to the problem of a spiritual life became merely obedience to the law—a discipline exerted upon the self. Just as Wilson refused to accept an inherent conflict between individual liberty and the demands of society, so also he ignored the possibility that the requirements of the moral law might also be a form of bondage. Rather, as he put it, *"the highest freedom* [is] rightly conceived to be *self-government*, self-direction, a self-originated rectitude, a self-sustained order."[64]

Wilson was eager to make the moral law more than a matter of mere principle and sought to see that the students learned to rely on a firm moral code. This internalization of discipline is clearly seen in Wilson's espousal of the honor code at Princeton. Wilson was not the founder of this historic system, and in fact the initiative came from the members of the Class of 1893. The dean of the faculty, James Ormsbee Murray, introduced the resolution, which was adopted unanimously.[65] But the honor code was the occasion for an early confrontation between Wilson and President Francis Landey Patton, and Bliss Perry remembered the fight. In sardonic terms, Patton ridiculed the idea that a student would pledge his honor "as a gentleman" not to give or receive aid during examinations. He claimed that a "gentleman's honor" permitted a man the latitude to seduce women or kill another man in a duel but forbade cheating at cards.

Wilson, according to Perry, "grew white and very quiet, and it was then he was most dangerous." He considered Patton's remarks an affront to southern chivalry as well as to the character of American students. Without insulting Patton, Wilson conveyed the impression that he understood the undergraduates better than the Bermudian Patton, and he did so "with unmistakable clearness and with a passion that swept the faculty off their feet."[66] The *Daily Princetonian* pronounced the system an *"unqualified* success" in the two upper classes, and when the faculty was forced to discipline some offenders in the lower classes, Wilson was grateful that the younger faculty members banded together in support of the system and "saved the college from irreparable disgrace."[67]

The moralistic emphases of Wilson's religious talks spilled over into

[63] News report of a talk before the Philadelphian Society, May 5, 1893, *ibid.*, VIII, 207.

[64] Notes for a chapel talk, May 7, 1893, *ibid.*, p. 208.

[65] Minutes of the Princeton University Faculty, Jan. 18, 1893, *ibid.*, p. 79, n. 1.

[66] Perry, *And Gladly Teach*, pp. 130-31.

[67] WW to Winthrop More Daniels, Feb. 27, 1893, *PWW*, VIII, 139-40, n. 1.

his classroom lectures and his public addresses as well. He made sure that his students left his courses with a proper understanding of politics, economics, and law. "State and criticise the theoretical basis of Socialism," he asked them in a final examination.[68] A student might well have mistaken Wilson's lectures on law for ones in religion, for Wilson described law as "a *Body of Principles*, a body of Doctrine."[69] In the midst of the social unrest of the 1890's, Wilson admonished an audience in Springfield, Massachusetts, that when authority was diminished, "the cohesive principle of society"—obedience—was weakened. Obedience to the law, he reminded them, was "the perfect freedom."[70]

Wilson's preoccupation with obedience and authority characterized his early years as a professor at Princeton. This was in part his initial reaction to the rise of populism, labor strikes, and the devastating financial panic which began in 1893. In his youth, Wilson had turned to covenant modes of thinking to structure his own life during periods of personal disorder, and when confronted with disorder on a national scale, the covenant tradition once more appeared with greater urgency in his lectures. Law, he told the Princeton undergraduates, was *"an organic product,* the result of the association of men with each other and the consequent institution of certain definite relationships between them."[71] Always stressing the contractual nature of social relations, Wilson described the various sources of public law but insisted that they were "reduced to *one*, viz., *Compact*."[72] He believed that constitutions were essential for the stability of society and gave them a sanctified status, especially the American constitution. It "should be reverenced as *the solemn Covenant of a People*,"[73] he said.

Wilson gave even more explicit testimony to the force of his Scottish covenanter inheritance in his own thought, for he was fond of describing the covenanter movement in Scotland in 1638. "To Wilson it was one of the outstanding events in the long struggle for liberty," a former student recalled. "It was here that freedom of conscience took root; this was a steppingstone by which the past made its way into a future of wider justice. We who had the privilege of listening to him when he was in this kind of mood always came away feeling that we had been in

[68] Examination in the History of Political Economy, Jan. 23, 1891, *ibid.*, VII, 108.

[69] Notes for a lecture, "Law: Its Character," Oct. 20, 1891, *ibid.*, p. 312.

[70] News report of a speech in Springfield, Mass., Nov. 25, 1890, *ibid.*, p. 81.

[71] Notes for a lecture, "Place of Law in the General Theory of Society," Sept. 26, 1891, *ibid.*, p. 304.

[72] Lecture notes on Public Law, "Written Constitutions," *c.* Sept. 22, 1894-Jan. 20, 1895, *ibid.*, IX, 23.

[73] Lecture notes on American Constitutional Law, "The Constitution as an Administrative Instrument," March 9, 1894, *ibid.*, VIII, 520.

the presence of someone upon whom had fallen the mantle of the old prophets of liberty."[74] Indeed, Wilson's interpretation of history was decidedly Whiggish. "The history of politics has been the history of liberty; that is, the history of the enlargement of the sphere of independent individual action at the expense of the sphere of dictatorial authority."[75]

The greatest advantage of Wilson's reliance on a contractual view of society was that it provided a means of striking a balance, sometimes delicate and uneasy, between the conflicting claims of order and freedom. Constitutions restricted both the arbitrary exercise of power by the state and the untrammeled use of freedom by the individual, and they made these sanctions explicit in *"a definite set of imperative rules . . . recognized and maintained in the adjustment of the powers of the government to the life of the Community* and the free activity of the individual."[76]

Nowhere is this tension more evident than in Wilson's discussion of sovereignty, for he insisted it was limited and divided between the people and the governments they constituted. The unique characteristic of modern constitutional, democratic governments was that the people had made this divided sovereignty recognizable and definite. They "have sought to give certainty and permanence to those relations, defining, either by means of stubborn practice or solemn covenants contained in written documents, the extent and the conditions of their subordination."[77]

The idea of limited and divided sovereignty and a contractual view of society provided Wilson with a "gospel of order" to preach to a turbulent American society. His sermon is revealed in one of his most popular and famous addresses, "Democracy," which he first delivered in December 1891 and many times thereafter during the 1890's. It revealed that Wilson retained many of the conservative theories of democratic government which he had held since an undergraduate. It further reflected his distrust of what he considered the radical democratic tendencies of the populists and other reformers.

He was confident that "those who framed our federal government had planned no *revolution*." They sought to establish a government for

[74] Fosdick, "Personal Recollections of Woodrow Wilson," p. 33.

[75] "Political Sovereignty," Nov. 9, 1891, *PWW*, VII, 335.

[76] Notes on American Constitutional Law, "Individual Liberty," May 4, 1894, *ibid.*, VIII, 553.

[77] "Political Sovereignty," *ibid.*, VII, 336. Wilson delivered this paper for the first time before the Faculty Philosophical Club at President McCosh's home. According to Ray Stannard Baker, when Wilson finished his presentation, McCosh grunted, "Umph! I have always held that sovereignty rests with God." Wilson replied, "So it does, Dr. McCosh, but I did not go quite so far back in my discussion" (*WWLL*, II, 18-19).

the people, "but they thought also that it ought to be *guarded* against the heats and the hastes, the passions and the thoughtless impulses of *the people*, no less than against selfish *dynasties* and hurtful *class intrigues*." Although affirming that the people were the "*source* of authority," Wilson insisted that they were not "*authority itself*." American government is democratic, according to Wilson, only insofar as it is representative, only in the sense "*that it draws all the governing material from the people*,—from such *part* of the people as will fit themselves for the function."

Leadership was essential for such a democracy, and, continually structuring political life to fit his own aspirations, Wilson declared that society ought to encourage "*self-selection* for leadership and influence." "*Self-preparation* is the stimulating law of success for every man," he asserted. While he labored in the obscurity of academic life, he consoled himself with the work ethic of his father. "Even though it [self-preparation] conduct through ways of struggle and sacrifice, where one must scorn delight and live labourious days,—even though it cost nights racked with every aching pain of study, *it must be accomplished*."[78]

Despite all the emphasis on order and the organic nature of society, Wilson was confronted with the fact that late-nineteenth-century American society was becoming increasingly fragmented and divided. Corporations vied with labor unions; western and southern farmers could find no community of interests with eastern manufacturers; new immigrants fought for economic and political recognition in an alien society; and cities contended with states and the national government for political control. Wilson could blithely preach that at the heart of "the true American spirit" was the "fundamental doctrine [of] the right of every man to choose his own principles and his own life,"[79] but the turmoil of the 1890's contradicted him. As early as 1891 he conceded to his Princeton students that "laws must now be made for groups and occupations, and the habits or practices in which they are rooted proceed from such groups and occupations." Yet Wilson still needed "a principle"—a means of formulating laws amidst the contending interests of different groups. He tried to fall back on "the guiding direction of the *human conscience*, the god-given sense of righteousness and holiness,"[80] but human consciences too clearly contradicted each other.

The breakthrough came in the tumultuous year of 1893 when Wilson

[78] "Democracy," Dec. 5, 1891, *PWW*, vii, 350, 352, 356, 357.

[79] "The True American Spirit," Oct. 27, 1892, *ibid.*, viii, 37.

[80] Notes for a lecture, "Place of Law in the General Theory of Society," Sept. 26, 1891, *ibid.*, vii, 305.

abandoned his political mentor, Walter Bagehot, to become a follower of Edmund Burke. As late as March 1891, Wilson had retained his indebtedness to Bagehot and wrote, "For me [Bagehot] has a great and enduring fascination," and a friend described Bagehot as Wilson's "ideal and master." However, by 1893, Wilson stated flatly, "If I should claim any man as my master, that man would be Edmund Burke."[81]

This shift, stimulated by domestic political developments and Wilson's struggle to find a new organizing principle for American politics, indicates Wilson's recognition of the necessity of reform short of revolution in American society. Sharing Burke's distrust of the dangerous possibilities inherent in a majoritarian democracy, Wilson wanted to be certain that reform was accompanied by order and constructive change. These themes are brilliantly illuminated in Wilson's essay, "Edmund Burke: The Man and His Times," which he finished in August 1893. Hailing Burke as "the apostle of the great English gospel of Expediency," Wilson proclaimed the pressing urgency of reform to meet contemporary problems and insisted with Burke that "it is both better and easier to reform than to tear down and reconstruct."[82]

During the same summer of 1893, Wilson noted "the grave social and economic problems now thrusting themselves forward," and stated, "Under such circumstances, some measure of legislative reform is clearly indispensable. . . . We must look and plan ahead. We must have legislation which has been definitely forecast in party programmes and explicitly sanctioned by the public voice."[83] But he cautioned that "reform must come piecemeal, and by example; not all at once and by authority."[84] People must remember that the object of government was not liberty but justice, "not the advantage of one class, even though that class constitute the majority, but right equity in the adjustment of the interests of all classes."[85]

Wilson's new devotion to Burke and espousal of the "gospel of expediency" brought new tensions and contradictions to his religious and political thought. In a series of lectures in July 1894 before the School of Applied Ethics, sponsored by the Ethical Culture Society at Plymouth, Massachusetts, Wilson declared that political morality "*has*

[81] WW to Charles Fisk Beach, Jr., March 3, 1891, *ibid.*, p. 173; Caleb Thomas Winchester to WW, Oct. 24, 1891, *ibid.*, p. 315; WW to C. T. Winchester, May 13, 1893, *ibid.*, VIII, 211. Cf. WW to C. T. Winchester, May 29, 1893, *ibid.*, p. 219.

[82] "Edmund Burke: The Man and His Times," Aug. 31, 1893, *ibid.*, pp. 342, 343. See also the Editorial Note to this essay, *ibid.*, pp. 313-18.

[83] "Government Under the Constitution," *c.* June 26, 1893, *ibid.*, p. 270.

[84] "Should an Antecedent Liberal Education Be Required of Students in Law, Medicine, and Theology?" July 26, 1893, *ibid.*, p. 290.

[85] "Edmund Burke," *ibid.*, p. 341.

no other standard than that of Expediency." However, in a statement
that reveals the growing dichotomy between his religious convictions
and his political theory, he argued, "*The individual Ethic* is *absolute*,
but *the social Ethic* is utilitarian. '*Sin is the trangression of the law*,' of
the law, that is, of *political progress.*"[86] Similarly, Wilson equated
justice and expediency and maintained that "*only that is expedient
which tallies with prevalent standards of judgment* as to conduct and
its responsibilities. Justice and expediency, consequently, have shifting boundaries,—shifting with ethical conceptions and social developments." Therefore, Wilson concluded, "*the standard cannot be the
same for the State as for the individual*; for they are not similarly made
up. *The State is a complex* of individual forces. *It must depend upon
average judgments and follow a utilitarian Ethic.*"[87]

Wilson still retained a function for religion within this view of society and the state, but its place suggests that the influences which altered
his political thought did not affect his religious convictions. Wilson
was still the consummate legalist in religion, for in defining the "vehicles" of progress in history, he discerned "*Struggle*, with its discipline; *Religion*, with its ideals of duty; *Education*, with its enlightenment, and its instruction in means."[88] The primary function of religion
was the inculcation of ideals of duty which would motivate people to
realize the moral law through political action. Wilson showed no
awareness of the possibility that the demands of duty and the moral law
might conflict with the dictates of expediency, or of the potential in-
compatibility of his individual ethic and social ethic.

Wilson had adopted a more flexible, relativistic, and reformist political theory, but he continued to stress absolutes and ideals in his religious talks. At a meeting of the Philadelphian Society in the spring of
1895, he delivered a typical homily on Psalm 1:2 ("His delight is the
law of the Lord; and in his law does he *meditate* day and night"). He
described the law of the Lord as "simply the perfect way of life—
*spiritual enlightenment and insight. A fixed and certain, yet broad and
universal standard.*"[89] But a few months earlier Wilson had jotted in
his notebook:

Political Sin is the transgression of the law of political progress
(rightly understood)[.] The act which is politically sinful in one

[86] Notes for a lecture, "Political Liberty, Political Expediency, and Political Morality in the
Democratic State," July 10, 1894, *ibid.*, p. 607.

[87] Notes for a lecture, "The Nature of the State and Its Relation to Progress," July 2, 1894,
ibid., p. 600.

[88] *Ibid.*, p. 599.

[89] Notes for a religious talk, April 4, 1895, *ibid.*, IX, 243; see also the news report in the *Daily
Princetonian*, April 5, 1895, *ibid.*, p. 244.

generation, consequently, is not so in another generation; for the law of political progress, though in one sense always the same, does not utter the same particular commands from generation to generation. It is unchangeable only in being uniform.

Parallel: The Laws of Ethics, as developed independently of Revelation.[90]

Wilson gradually began to sense the contradiction between the "fixed and certain, yet broad and universal standard" on which he urged his students to meditate and the utilitarian ethic that he also wanted applied to political life, but he was content to see the two separated.

" 'Shall I live here on terms of utility' I ask myself," he inquired in a speech in Washington in February 1895. "What about the other and spiritual world? But society does not know any other world. It must save itself in this world. Therefore, I believe that the social ethic is a utilitarian ethic, not an absolute one; that it is what you may accomplish by agreement, not by an abstract process of right and wrong; that it is so much of the right as you can get the prevalent majority to observe and respect."[91]

Despite the ways in which Wilson's covenant tradition had shaped his fundamental assumptions about politics and society, he refused to integrate fully his political and religious thought. He argued, "My individual morality is my relationship to God, my social morality is my relationship to my fellowmen."[92] Unwilling or unable to draw the implications of his reformist political theory with its relativistic utilitarian ethic for his belief in an eternal and unchanging moral law, Wilson simply insisted that the two areas were not the same. The absolute ethic was for a relationship to God, and the relative ethic was for relationships with others. One was solely individualistic, the other primarily social.

By the middle of 1895, Wilson had responded to the pressures and tensions in American society, and while increasingly conservative in his Burkean emphasis on order, he also avoided becoming reactionary by stressing the need for political institutions to adapt creatively to social change.[93] But his political thought had far outpaced his religious thought, and when confronted by the differences between the uncompromising absolutes of his Christian faith and the easy flexibility of his

---

[90] An outline and memorandum for "The Philosophy of Politics," c. Jan. 26, 1895, *ibid.*, p. 129.

[91] News report, Feb.22, 1895, *ibid.*, p. 217.

[92] *Ibid.*, pp. 217-18. See also the notes on WW's course in Jurisprudence, taken by Andrew Clerk Imbrie, quoted in Bragdon, *Wilson: The Academic Years*, p. 262.

[93] See his address, "The Legal Education of Undergraduates," c. Aug. 23, 1894, *PWW*, VIII, 647-57.

belief in expediency, Wilson drove a wedge between them. He ignored the question of how the state should act when expediency and justice were contradictory. But for a man who abhorred disintegration, who demanded a moral foundation for everything he attempted, and whose mind constantly strove for a synthesis of all problems, this dichotomy would not long endure.

VI

Professor at Princeton–
THE LITERARY HISTORIAN

By the mid-1890's Wilson enjoyed a sense of self-assurance and achievement. It was stimulated by his popularity as a teacher, fame as an author, acknowledged eloquence as a speaker, and the unflagging affection of his wife and daughters. "I seem myself to have become in so many ways another fellow," he wrote Ellen from Johns Hopkins, "more confident, steady, serene, though not less susceptible to all sorts of influences wh[ich] experience might have been expected to render me indifferent to: enjoying in a certain degree a sense of power,—as if I had gotten some way upon the road I used so to burn to travel, and yet restless and impatient with ambition, as of old—a boy and yet a man."[1] But Wilson's ambition, although tempered by new confidence and serenity, drove him to the brink of physical collapse during the crucial academic year of 1895-1896. In October he was stricken with another of his frequent intestinal attacks, and by the spring he was overworked and exhausted. Sometime during May 1896 he suffered what was apparently a small stroke which rendered his right arm and hand virtually useless.[2]

The stroke was a crisis for a man only thirty-nine years old, and Wilson knew he needed a rest. He spent the summer in the British Isles, relaxing and recovering, but his letters indicate that he reacted to his physical breakdown as he did to all adversity—by resisting it. He quickly taught himself to write with his left hand, and when he grumbled about his condition, he complained of "this useless left hand," not his incapacitated right hand.[3] Ellen was very concerned and worried about his actual condition. "Tell *me* the *truth*," she pleaded, "the whole truth, whatever it is; anything is better than this awful suspense."[4] Wilson's father was equally alarmed and declared, "I am afraid Woodrow is going to die."[5]

---

[1] WW to EAW, Jan. 24, 1895, *PWW*, IX, 124.

[2] Edwin A. Weinstein, "Woodrow Wilson's Neurological Illness," *Journal of American History*, LVII (1970), 333; WW to Harper and Brothers, May 27, 1896, *PWW*, IX, 506-507, n. 2.

[3] See for example WW to EAW, June 9 and 14, 1896, *ibid.*, pp. 513, 515.

[4] EAW to WW, June 18, 1896, *ibid.*, p. 520.

[5] R. S. Baker memorandum of interviews with Stockton Axson, Feb. 8, 10, 11, 1925 (R. S. Baker Coll., DLC).

His condition was diagnosed as "neuritis," and Wilson himself dismissed it as "writer's cramp."[6] He enjoyed his trip to England immensely, but the effects of the partial paralysis persisted throughout the next academic year. He typed most of his correspondence, confessing to a friend, "This disabling of my right hand (I am picking this labouriously out with my left) has made an enormous difference in my life: for I cannot afford a secretary."[7] In March 1897 he told his old friend Dr. Hazen, "I am a great deal better now; but it is still unwise to write more than a few lines."[8]

Although Wilson characteristically tried to ignore the effects of his stroke, it produced subtle yet profound changes in his thought and personality. According to his brother-in-law Stockton Axson, who visited frequently and for long periods, Wilson returned from England a different man. Before the stroke Wilson had time to "loaf and invite his soul," and the two brothers-in-law often took long bicycle rides. They enjoyed relaxed conversations with the elderly Dr. Wilson, but after 1896 Axson talked with Dr. Wilson alone. Wilson's physical collapse "freshened his sense of mission in the world," Axson believed. It was as if he had decided, "I must be about my father's business."[9]

The crisis in Wilson's health also drove him to recover his emphasis on the Christian law of love which he had previously enunciated in his 1890 speech, "Leaders of Men." The old notes of duty and moral principles did not disappear from his religious thought, but Wilson gave them a new basis. Faced with the disintegration of his health, he began to stress that an individual must be recreated from within, and the imagery of his language increasingly focused on love as a source of wholeness and power.

Speaking to the Philadelphian Society in May 1896, Wilson declared that the Christian was the person whose motives had been purged, whose inner, spiritual life had been transformed by "the expulsive power of a new affection." Perhaps feeling that his poor health was a sign of personal unworthiness or the outward sign of inner disease, Wilson told the students, "If we wish to get a bad thing out of our souls, we must get a good thing in. True virtue consists in having a purpose which will dislodge the inclination and tendencies to vice." He assured them, "Love is the one thing which can displace, by the expulsiveness of its nature, the very evils of the soul. And inasmuch as

[6] Weinstein, "Wilson's Neurological Illness," p. 333.

[7] WW to John Franklin Jameson, Jan. 8, 1897, *PWW*, x, 99.

[8] WW to A. W. Hazen, March 29, 1897, *ibid.*, p. 201.

[9] R. S. Baker memorandum of interviews with Stockton Axson, Feb. 8, 10, 11, and 24, 1925 (R. S. Baker Coll., DLC).

the love of God is the greatest and most perfect form of love, it is not only our duty but our privilege to allow this affection to fill our whole life and soul."[10]

Individuals were still the active agents in Wilson's world; it was their duty and privilege to open themselves to God's love. But Wilson's agonizingly slow recovery from his stroke prompted further modification of his religious thought. No longer willing to talk in terms of obedience to the law as the highest expression of Christian faith, Wilson began to emphasize that only God's grace and forgiveness made human activity meaningful and worthwhile. Using the last clause of Romans 7:6 as his text, Wilson, in November 1896, delivered a homily to the Princeton students on the theme, "We should serve in newness of spirit, and not in the oldness of the letter." We are "not disobedient to the law," he told the students, *but disburdened* of it: free of all law by [a] change of attitude toward it." Obviously referring to the honor code, Wilson stated, "The change [is] *illustrated in our own college life*, where the things of truth and honesty are becoming not so much matters of law as of spirit." Still pained by the stiffness in his right hand and reflecting on the difficulties of his illness, Wilson concluded, *"Things seen in the fine revealing light of faith are the real verities of life."*[11]

This recovery of an element of grace and love in Wilson's religious thought was undoubtedly forged out of the emotional crucible produced by his stroke. Unable to work and to strive toward his ideals as he had in the past, Wilson rediscovered and gave new importance to an element in his father's preaching and the historic proclamation of his church—that people are not saved by fidelity to ideals or obedience to a moral law but through God's love.

Wilson's illness is scarely surprising in the light of his schedule. He came to Princeton in 1890 under the impression that a school of law would be established there and that he would be responsible for its planning and development. When President Patton's expressions of support for Wilson's plans turned out to be mere talk, Wilson resolved to try to raise the money himself. From 1891 to 1893, he took to the alumni circuit, explaining his vision of a law school at Princeton and trying to drum up support. "We need money," he candidly told the Maryland alumni. "One of the things I am most anxious to see at Princeton is a law school. I want it to be better than any other law school in the country. I want a distinctive Princeton school."[12] He told

[10] News report, May 15, 1896, *PWW*, IX, 502-503.
[11] Notes for a chapel talk, Nov. 8, 1896, *ibid.*, X, 42.
[12] News report, Feb. 3, 1893, *ibid.*, VIII, 121.

his friend Heath Dabney that the law school was his "dearest scheme" but complained that "everything is ready for its realization, except the money!"[13] He tried to solicit the help of his classmate, Cyrus McCormick,[14] who did encourage him but failed to provide the needed funds.

Wilson's vision for a school of law dated back to 1888 when President Daniel Coit Gilman asked him to outline the structure for such a school at Johns Hopkins. The project stalled, but Wilson saw a chance to give it new life when he came to Princeton. Wilson basically envisaged a school which would train men in the broad principles of law and equip them to be administrators, judges, and politicians, as well as practicing attorneys. The emphasis would not be practical, but theoretical, focusing on the history and development of law, its nature, function, and relationship to the state. Wilson's course offerings at Princeton during the early 1890's were designed to offer a basic undergraduate introduction to this kind of training, and he defended it as the only viable legal education for students in a rapidly changing society.[15]

"We devote our instruction to the preparation of attorneys, who direct the *business* of the law and must be technical experts, and neglect to provide ourselves, in any systematic way, with barristers, who handle the *principles* of the law in argument, and who must possess a knowledge of legal reasoning at once comprehensive and flexible," he told the American Bar Association. The practical aspects of law, Wilson believed, could always be learned through apprenticeship and legal practice. What students needed was a philosophical base—"a clear idea how [law] is in fact generated in society and adapted from age to age to its immediate needs and uses."[16] A law school based on such a philosophy, he confidently predicted to the Princeton alumni of Delaware, would be "the hit of the generation."[17] However, Wilson's optimism was exhausted by 1893, and he dropped the plan, only to revive it again when he became Princeton's president in 1902.[18]

The shattered dream of a law school at Princeton was the first of several developments that made Wilson frustrated with President Patton's lack of leadership. He allied himself with a cabal of young faculty members who sought to make the academic standards of the uni-

[13] WW to R. H. Dabney, July 1, 1891, *ibid.*, VII, 234.

[14] Cyrus Hall McCormick to WW, Jan. 28, 1892, *ibid.*, p. 379, n. 1; WW to EAW, May 5, 1892, *ibid.*, pp. 618-19.

[15] A Plan for a School of Public Law, *c.* May 22, 1888, *ibid.*, V, 729; WW to Daniel Coit Gilman, May 22, 1888, *ibid.*, p. 730; Editorial Note, Wilson's Plans for a School of Law at Princeton, *ibid.*, VII, 63-68.

[16] "Legal Education of Undergraduates," *c.* Aug. 23, 1894, *ibid.*, VIII, 655, 650. Cf. Wilson's address to the World's Columbian Exposition, "Should an Antecedent Liberal Education Be Required of All Students in Law, Medicine, and Theology?" July 26, 1893, *ibid.*, pp. 285-92.

[17] News report, Dec. 17, 1892, *ibid.*, p. 58.

[18] Editorial Note, Wilson's Plans for a School of Law at Princeton, *ibid.*, VII, 63-68.

versity more rigorous and provide a measure of direction during Patton's indolent administration. Wilson had his own powerful friends on the Board of Trustees and among the alumni, and when he was asked to become the president of the University of Illinois at a salary of $6,000, Wilson promptly parlayed the offer to his own advantage. With his wife's prodding, he secured an assistant to relieve him of the instruction in political economy and a raise in his salary to $3,500, making him the highest paid member of the Princeton faculty and second only to Patton himself.[19]

Wilson's irritation with Patton was further aggravated by his attempt in 1896-1897 to bring Frederick Jackson Turner to Princeton as professor of history. Patton opposed Turner in part because he was a Unitarian,[20] and Wilson was furious. As faithful a Presbyterian as any Princetonian, Wilson could not understand such sectarian considerations when a man of Turner's ability was available. "I am probably at this writing the most chagrined and mortified fellow on this continent!" he exclaimed to Turner and told his wife he might resign.[21]

Besides becoming involved in major administrative matters, Wilson devoted long hours to committee work, serving extensive terms as Senior Class Officer and member of the Discipline Committee and the Committee on Special and Delinquent Students, as well as shorter terms on the committees on outdoor sports, the graduate school, and the library. He was also chosen on several occasions as one of the faculty representatives to communicate faculty concerns to the Board of Trustees. He avidly supported student extracurricular activities, serving as coach of the debate team and arbiter of a treaty between Whig and Clio Halls regulating the solicitation of members, and he defended the students' right to make up annual songs poking fun at the faculty.[22] As in his Princeton student days, Wilson became a vocal football fan and predictably defended the game because it developed "more moral qualities" than any other sport. "Ordinary athletics produce valuable qualities—precision, decision, presence of mind and endurance." But "this game produces two other qualities not common to all athletics, that of co-operation, or action with others, and self-subordination."[23]

The students packed his classes; as early as 1891 he had 160 students; and while they played the customary pranks on him like forcing him to eject the town drunk from one of his classes, the students re-

[19] WW to EAW, April 27 and 30, 1892, *ibid.*, pp. 598, 602; EAW to WW, April 30 and May 3 and 8, 1892, *ibid.*, pp. 604, 609, 625-26; WW to Francis M. McKay, May 12, 1892, *ibid.*, pp. 632-33.

[20] WW to EAW, Feb. 16, 1897, *ibid.*, x, 164.

[21] WW to F. J. Turner, March 31, 1897, *ibid.*, p. 201; WW to EAW, Jan. 29, 1897, *ibid.*, p. 123.

[22] Bragdon, *Wilson: The Academic Years*, pp. 213-14, 208.

[23] News report of a speech in Philadelphia, Feb. 14, 1894, *PWW*, VIII, 482-83.

spected and revered him. From 1896 to 1903, Wilson was chosen seven times as the favorite professor by the senior class,[24] and the rapport he established with the students was vivid in Booth Tarkington's memory. "I think we felt that Wilson understood us and understood us more favorably than any other man on the faculty," he recalled. "We had a feeling that we were being comprehended in a friendly way, that he'd be for us and that he'd be straight with us."[25]

Wilson's academic responsibilities at Princeton occupied only one part of his life. In addition to his course in administration at Johns Hopkins, Wilson became a favorite lecturer on law and politics at other institutions. From 1892 to 1897, he lectured on constitutional law at the New York Law School; [26] in 1893 on constitutional government at the Brooklyn Institute of Arts and Sciences;[27] in 1895 on politics and law at the Columbian University in Washington, D. C.;[28] in 1895 and 1901 on "Great Leaders of Political Thought" for the American Society for the Extension of University Teaching;[29] in 1898 on Bagehot, Burke, and Sir Henry Maine at Johns Hopkins;[30] in 1898 on constitutional government at Richmond College;[31] and in 1898 on municipal government at the Brooklyn Institute of Arts and Sciences.[32] He was also the "prime mover" at the Madison Conference on History, Civil Government, and Political Economy of 1892, and the report made a substantial impact on the teaching of history and politics in secondary schools for the next fifteen years.[33] These activities significantly extended Wilson's influence and reputation in academic circles and substantially increased his income.

During the 1890's Wilson also established a reputation as an engaging, entertaining after-dinner speaker. His apprenticeship was spent at

[24] WW to R. H. Dabney, July 1, 1891, *ibid.*, vii, 233; news item, April 23, 1904, *ibid.*, xv, 272-73; Bragdon, *Wilson: The Academic Years*, pp. 205, 213.

[25] Quoted in *ibid.*, p. 209.

[26] See the Editorial Note, Wilson's Lectures at the New York Law School, *PWW*, vii, 470-72, and the two reports of the lectures printed at March 11 and 25, 1892, *ibid.*, pp. 472-79, 512-19.

[27] See notes for the lectures, *c.* Nov. 15-Dec. 27, 1893, *ibid.*, viii, 405-14; Editorial Note, Wilson's Lectures at the Brooklyn Institute of Arts and Sciences, *ibid.*, pp. 404-405.

[28] News reports, Feb. 21 and 22, 1895, *ibid.*, ix, 211-13, 216-18.

[29] See the Editorial Note, Wilson's Lectures on Great Leaders of Political Thought, *ibid.*, pp. 326-27; news item, Jan. 12, 1901, *ibid.*, xii, 71.

[30] "Edmund Burke: A Lecture," Feb. 23, 1898, *ibid.*, x, 408-23; "Walter Bagehot: A Lecture," Feb. 24, 1898, *ibid.*, pp. 423-42; "A Lawyer With a Style," Feb. 25, 1898, *ibid.*, pp. 443-61. These lectures were all underwritten by the Donovan Foundation.

[31] News reports, Oct. 28 and 29, Nov. 1, 2, 4, and 17, 1898, *ibid.*, xi, 44-47, 49-52, 57-62, 62-66, 67-71, 73-74.

[32] Lecture notes, Nov. 18-Dec. 15, 1898, *ibid.*, pp. 74-84; news reports, Nov. 19 and Dec. 17, *ibid.*, pp. 85-86, 90-91.

[33] Editorial Note, The Madison Conference on History, Civil Government, and Political Economy, *ibid.*, viii, 61-63; Minutes of the Conference, Dec. 28-30, 1892, *ibid.*, pp. 63-73.

dinners of the Princeton alumni, and after his initial disastrous speech before the New York alumni in 1886, Wilson kept his lecture style from stifling the convivial spirit of the alumni dinners. Throughout the 1890's, Princeton alumni were beginning to organize local alumni associations, and Wilson's speeches encouraged fidelity to alma mater. He sprinkled his talks with a liberal dose of anecdotes, dividing his notes into two equal columns—the points he wanted to make and the stories he wanted to tell.[34] Several of his jokes involved ridiculing Negroes, and one alumnus called Wilson "the best narrator of darky stories that I ever heard in my life."[35]

For the most part, Wilson's after-dinner speeches consisted of superficial moralisms and nothing that would be too provocative. "When a man has gone out from Princeton," he observed, "he stands for all that means business and nothing which means foolishness." Or, he needlessly urged the Society of Colonial Wars to perpetuate the memory of those conflicts because they were part of a nationalizing process which unified the country. He defended collegiate athletics for developing "manly qualities" and "wanted to see the fighting spirit kept alive, not to engage in senseless and wrongful wars, but to combat injustice and to fight when there was something worth while to fight for." Occasionally he would outline the political plight of the country and consciously or unconsciously offer himself as a solution. "Princeton must come to the aid of the country with a trained hand and a mind equal to the occasion," he told the Chicago alumni.[36] These vacuous remarks were just what the audiences demanded; as the *Washington Post* reported after one address, Wilson's "speech was very witty, abounding in good humor."[37]

Ever since his covenant with Charles Talcott in which he resolved to master the art of oratory so as to enlist others in his purposes and lead them into his way of thinking, Wilson had been determined to use public speaking as a means of extending his influence in public life. His after-dinner speeches were a pleasant diversion, but they rarely permitted him the opportunity to speak out on the issues of the day and infrequently brought him monetary rewards. Consequently, Wilson turned to the public lecture platform to achieve his goals and secure an additional source of income.

[34] See, for example, his notes for a talk to the Baltimore alumni, Feb. 2, 1893, *ibid.*, p. 119.

[35] See WW's notes for a speech to the Pittsburgh alumni, March 21, 1895, *ibid.*, ix, 239-40, and speech to the New England Society of New York, Dec. 22, 1900, *ibid.*, xii, 56; R. B. Fosdick to R. S. Baker, June 23, 1926 (R. S. Baker Coll., DLC).

[36] News report of a speech to the Baltimore alumni, Feb. 19, 1892, *PWW*, vii, 443; notes for a speech to the Society of Colonial Wars, May 19, 1899, *ibid.*, xi, 120; news report of a speech in St. Louis, Dec. 30, 1897, *ibid.*, x, 359; news report of a speech to Chicago alumni, Jan. 14, 1899, *ibid.*, xi, 94.

[37] News report, Feb. 10, 1898, *ibid.*, x, 387.

During the 1890's he delivered a staggering number of public lectures and addresses. Not counting his regular course lectures at Princeton and Johns Hopkins or his Princeton chapel talks or his alumni speeches, Wilson delivered more than 100 addresses in various cities across the country between 1890 and 1902. He used the same speeches again and again—"Leaders of Men," "Democracy," "Patriotism," "Religion and Patriotism," "Liberty," "Burke," Bagehot," etc. Charles D. Atkins of the Society for the Extension of University Teaching called Wilson "one of the immortals of the American lecture platform," and John Bach McMaster remembered him as "a man who could talk about potatoes and make it sound like Holy Writ."[38]

His theme throughout the 1890's was, as his father had described it, the "gospel of order," and Wilson combined his practiced eloquence with a homiletical urgency. One observer's reaction reveals the power of Wilson's delivery and the appeal he would have as a politician. "I heard Woodrow Wilson the other night," he stated. "He is putting truth and Christianity in politics. It was a great talk. His subject—it doesn't matter which it was; he would give the same message under any subject."[39] He seldom passed up an opportunity to give a speech, and occasionally he even consented to speak without an honorarium. "I can't imagine why I consent to do this sort of thing," he grumbled to Ellen, ". . . but such is your husband—hungry—*too* hungry—for reputation and influence."[40]

All these academic appearances absorbed a great deal of Wilson's time and sapped his energy, but he still found time to write. He spent his mornings in his study, with Ellen guarding the door to prevent any interruptions, and steadily picked out on his typewriter numerous reviews, essays, and books. His concentration was intense. Bliss Perry remembered telling Wilson that he got up from his desk and smoked his pipe when he was unable to find the right word. "You lose your concentration," Wilson replied. "Now I force myself to sit with my fingers on the keys and *make* the right word come."[41]

Wilson's literary production during the 1890's was almost completely divorced from his main academic interest—the study of politics. At Wesleyan and Bryn Mawr, Wilson's teaching responsibilities included primarily history courses, with some courses in political economy and law, but he wrote mainly on political subjects. At Princeton, he taught politics and jurisprudence, but he wrote as an his-

---

[38] Quoted in Bragdon, *Wilson: The Academic Years*, p. 230.

[39] Burton Alva Konkle to R. S. Baker, passage taken from Konkle's diary during one of WW's speaking tours during the years between 1896 and 1899; quoted in *WWLL*, ii, 73.

[40] WW to EAW, July 30, 1894, *PWW*, viii, 634.

[41] Perry, *And Gladly Teach*, pp. 156-57.

torian and literary critic. This division of labor testifies to the extraordinary range of Wilson's interests and his refusal to narrow his energies to one field. At the same time, it also suggests his consuming desire to affect American life in whatever way he could. No avenue of prominence was to be avoided; no opportunity for influence was to be rejected.

Wilson's interest in history can be traced to his home and particularly the influence of his father, whose own intellectual concerns ranged broadly across literature, history, and current affairs. The religious atmosphere of Wilson's home included an emphasis on the individual and the responsibility to obey God's law. As early as his youthful historical essays on Gladstone and Bismarck, Wilson sought to highlight the importance of individuals in history—the force of personality, the power of a visionary leader, the courage of the solitary figure. Wilson's particular covenant heritage also encouraged him to see individuals in terms of their contractual relationships in society, formed by habit, experience, and law.

And so when Wilson approached the study of history, he came predisposed to see the significance of great people but also how society was bound together. He also came as an amateur; what little training he had, he largely rejected. At Johns Hopkins, Herbert Baxter Adams encouraged the scientific study of history—reverence for facts above all and diligence in archival research, but Wilson saw the field quite differently. "My chief interest," he declared, "is in politics, in history as it furnishes object-lessons for the present."[42] Wilson insisted that the historian had a responsibility to make judgments about his material, for "there are moral facts as well as material, and the one sort must be as plainly told as the other." But Wilson saw his purpose as not only moral but literary as well. The historian's task was "to give a true impression of his theme as a whole—to show it, not lying upon his page in an open and dispersed analysis, but set close in intimate synthesis, every line, every stroke, every bulk even, omitted which does not enter of very necessity into a single and unified image of the truth." Telling the truth was only one half of the effort, according to Wilson. The historian must also exercise his imagination and communicate the object lessons of history in compelling fashion. "Histories are written in order that the bulk of men may read and realize; and it is as bad to bungle the telling of the story as to lie, as fatal to lack a vocabulary as to lack knowledge."[43]

With such a vision of his craft, Wilson tended to be a popular histo-

---

[42] WW to EAW, Nov. 13, 1884, *PWW*, III, 430.

[43] "On the Writing of History," *c.* June 17, 1895, *ibid.*, IX, 297, 298, 305.

rian, writing history that others might "read and realize." He paid his respects to the traditional shibboleths like research ("The writing of history must be based upon original research and authentic record")[44] and the value of local history ("The history of a nation is only the history of its villages written large").[45] But there is little evidence that he obeyed his own admonitions. Archives were unknown territory to him, and in writing he relied heavily on the monographs of others. He considered his own calling more exalted and more difficult—"to give hint of great forces and of movements blown upon by all the airs of the wide continent." In short, the historian must become "a sort of prophet," providing "knowledge of our character, alike in its strength and its weakness: and it is so we get our standards for endeavor,—our warnings and our gleams of hope. It is thus we learn what manner of nation we are of, and divine what manner of people we should be."[46]

Wilson's first major historical work was *Division and Reunion, 1829-1889*, a volume in the Epochs of American History series which was edited by Albert Bushnell Hart. Wilson was invited to undertake this assignment in 1889 and the book was published in 1893. Hart's request was a distinct honor but also a surprise since Wilson had published no important historical work.[47] After initially hesitating, Wilson agreed to the project, but the attraction was not financial since he was promised only $500 upon publication of the book.[48] He proved to be an editor's headache. His deadline was extended; he haggled over using English instead of American spellings; his manuscript was much too long and had to be shortened; he disputed Hart's suggestions for additions to the bibliography.[49] But Hart persevered with the novice historian, and the result was unquestionably Wilson's best historical writing.

In contrast to much of his later historical work which is more popular in character, *Division and Reunion* is marked by careful research in printed original sources, judicious use of secondary works, and flashes of historical insight. Wilson's overriding themes were the influence of sectionalism in American history and the impact of the Civil War in creating a unified nation. Even before Frederick Jackson Turner had developed his understanding of the importance of the West in American history, Wilson formulated this thesis in terms of the South in *Division and Reunion*, and it is possible that Wilson's conversations with

[44] *Ibid.*, p. 298.

[45] "The Course of American History," May 16, 1895, *ibid.*, p. 257.

[46] *Ibid.*, pp. 258, 257.

[47] Bragdon, *Wilson: The Academic Years*, p. 233.

[48] Albert Bushnell Hart to WW, April 23, 1889, *PWW*, VI, 174-75.

[49] See the Editorial Note, Wilson's *Division and Reunion*, *ibid.*, VIII, 141-48.

Turner at Johns Hopkins influenced Turner considerably.[50] Wilson believed that slavery as an economic and social institution shaped the
South, while manufacturing and railroads molded the North. "A sharp
and almost immediate divergence between them, both in interest and
opinion, was inevitable," he wrote.[51] His descriptions of the Old South
would have moved any devotee of the Lost Cause. The South had an
aristocracy, but it was democratic, "not of blood, but of influence, and
of influence exercised among equals." "There were abounding hospi-
tality and generous intercourse; but the intercourse was free, unstudied
in its manners, straight-forward, hearty, unconstrained, and full of a
truly democratic instinct and sentiment of equality."[52] But Wilson had
few illusions about its permanence. The 1830's brought "a great national democracy . . . into the presence of the slavery controversy,"
and despite slavery's sanctions in habit and law, it lacked "a single
stable foundation,—the acquiescence of national opinion."[53]

Wilson chose to make few judgments about slavery as such. He
reached the conclusion, then safe and now verified by innumerable
studies, that "scarely any generalization that could be formed would be
true for the whole South, or even for all periods alike in any one section of it."[54] He found its "most demoralizing feature" to be "its effect
upon the marriage relation" among Negroes, but his work-ethic conscience was also horrified by slavery's effect on the " 'poor whites' "
—"one of the most singular non-productive classes that any country
has ever seen."[55]

The Civil War came, Wilson contended, because the South was
forced by the economic and political power of slavery to defend an
outdated conception of the nation as a confederation. "Constitutions
are not mere legal documents," Wilson added; "they are the skeleton
frame of a living organism; and in this case the course of events had
nationalized the government once deemed confederate." He wrote of
the war as a tragedy—the lives lost, the property destroyed, the money
expended. Reconstruction was a period of constitutional strain and distortion, and when its "excesses" had passed, "normal conditions of
government and of economic and intellectual life were at length restored." He bade farewell to the bloody shirt, arguing that the postwar
prosperity of the country had dissolved sectional allegiances. "Northern interests became identified with southern interests, and the days of
inevitable strife and permanent difference came to seem strangely re-

[50] WW to F. J. Turner, Aug. 23, 1889, *ibid.*, VI, 368-71.

[51] *Division and Reunion, 1829-1889* (New York and London, 1893), p. 40.

[52] *Ibid.*, pp. 106, 107.   [53] *Ibid.*, p. 119.

[54] *Ibid.*, p. 125.   [55] *Ibid.*, pp. 127, 128.

mote." New problems loomed before the nation, but the first century of the nation's constitution "closed with a sense of preparation, a new seriousness, and a new hope."[56]

Considering Wilson's origins in the South, his view of the historian as moral critic, and the sectional antagonisms which still prevailed, *Division and Reunion* is remarkable for its balanced, measured treatment of the Civil War period. Hermann von Holst hailed Wilson's "unimpeachable honesty and undeviating singleness of purpose," but Frederic Bancroft disputed Wilson's contention that the South's view of the constitution as a confederation had not changed since 1789. Bancroft also suspected that Wilson wrote "with a view to brilliancy in style and arrangement rather than to a complete mastery and sober presentation of all the facts."[57] Even Wilson's father managed to join the chorus, writing an anonymous, fulsome review which praised Wilson as "a rare scholar, a ripe thinker and an accomplished writer. . . . Never was there a more impartial estimate of men and of men's conduct."[58] More recent critics have concurred in this judgment, and one has concluded that prior to Wilson "no southern historian produced a more balanced treatment of the sectional conflict."[59]

Upon completing *Division and Reunion*, Wilson's historical writing turned more toward biography and broad, synthetic surveys of the nation's past. He continued to argue for a moralized version of history, maintaining that America's past "has taught us how to become strong, and will teach us, if we heed its moral, how to become wise, also, and single-minded."[60] Scorning the idea of objectivity, he wrote that the historian "distributes flavor to his taste, reconceives the story, recasts it, colors it to his own eye."[61] And yet, when the moral judgments of one author did not agree with his own, he fumed, "Are we writing homilies or are we writing history?"[62]

The answer, in terms of Wilson's work, was both. His purpose was to reconstruct the past in terms that would inspire loyalty and affection for the nation and unify it around national, not provincial, ideals. He

[56] *Ibid.*, pp. 211, 273, 298, 299.

[57] Von Holst's review in the New York *Educational Review* (June 1893), in *PWW*, VIII, 222; Bancroft's review in the *Political Science Quarterly* (Sept. 1893), in *ibid.*, p. 345.

[58] Review in the New York *Church Union*, April 15, 1893, in *ibid.*, p. 191.

[59] Charles E. Cauthen and Lewis P. Jones, "The Coming of the Civil War," *Writing Southern History: Essays in Honor of Fletcher M. Green*, Arthur S. Link and Rembert W. Patrick, eds. (Baton Rouge, La., 1965), p. 231; see also Louis Martin Sears, "Woodrow Wilson," *The Marcus W. Jernegan Essays in American Historiography* (Chicago, 1937), pp. 108-10, 119; and Loewenberg, *American History in American Thought*, pp. 416-18.

[60] "The Making of the Nation," *c.* April 15, 1897, *PWW*, X, 222.

[61] "Anti-Slavery History and Biography," Aug. 1893, *ibid.*, VIII, 299.

[62] Review of Goldwin Smith, *The United States: An Outline of Political History, 1492-1871,* *c.* Sept. 5, 1893, in *ibid.*, p. 350.

constructed "A Calendar of Great Americans," which sought to discern "a distinctively American standard and type of greatness." The American spirit, he said, is the bold, resolute, individualistic spirit which tamed a continent. "It is . . . a hopeful and confident spirit. It is progressive, optimistically progressive, and ambitious of objects of national scope and advantage." Only Lincoln qualified as "the supreme American of our history"; John Adams was "an eminent Puritan statesman" but he "had none of the national optimism"; Jefferson "was not a thorough American because of the strain of French philosophy that permeated and weakened all his thought."[63]

Wilson fed the fires of nationalistic spirit, encouraging his readers to see the United States as exceptional and blessed by God. "Unquestionably we believe in a guardian destiny!" he exclaimed. "No other race could have accomplished so much with such a system [of constitutional government]; no other race would have dared risk such an experiment." The true problem was perpetuating the progress of the country, for "the history of the United States has been one continuous story of rapid, stupendous growth, and all its great questions have been questions of growth."[64]

This was not the scientific history of which Herbert Baxter Adams had dreamed, but it was the type of history the American public wanted to read—to justify their past and to sanction the imperialistic thrust of the late 1890's. It was also historical writing that sold magazines and books, and Wilson was constantly besieged by editors for more material. He began a short history of the United States, but in 1895 when *Harper's Magazine* offered him $1,800 for six essays on George Wahington, Wilson dropped the project in favor of the more lucrative endeavor.[65] He needed the money for the new house that he and Ellen were building in Princeton, and he quickly dashed off the essays.

The strain of the magazine deadlines and supervising the construction of the house contributed to Wilson's physical collapse and stroke in May 1896, and the essays, later published in book form as *George Washington*, bear all the marks of haste and carelessness. As Marcus Cunliffe has noted, "Throughout the work there is an excess of general narrative, a dearth of genuine biography."[66] Wilson used all of his stylistic mannerisms, especially the Anglicisms, to an extreme, and the result was a flowery, inflated narrative. He often began his sentences with " 'Twas," " 'Tis," or " 'Twould," and substituted "but" for "only" and "ere" for "before." Wilson's affected aristocratic style

---

[63] "A Calendar of Great Americans," *c*. Sept. 15, 1893, *ibid.*, pp. 369, 374, 378, 372, 373.

[64] "The Making of the Nation," *c*. April 15, 1897, *ibid.*, x, 235, 228.

[65] Henry Mills Alden to WW, June 28, 1895, *ibid.*, ix, 311.

[66] "Introduction" to Wilson's *George Washington* (New York, 1969), p. vii.

permeated the entire book; for example, in describing Washington's visit to Governor Shirley in Boston, he wrote:

> He went very bravely dight in proper uniform of buff and blue, a white-and-scarlet cloak upon his shoulders, the sword at his side knotted with red and gold, his horse's fittings engraved with the Washington arms, and trimmed in the best style of the London saddlers. With him rode two aides in their uniforms, and two servants in their white-and-scarlet livery. Curious folk who looked upon the celebrated young officer upon the road saw him fare upon his way with all the pride of a Virginian gentleman, a handsome man, and an admirable horseman—a very gallant figure, no one could deny.[67]

George Washington was nothing more than a potboiler, designed for rapid public acquisition and Wilson's material gain. As his father told him, "I'm glad you let Washington do his own dying."[68]

George Washington marks the fusion of Wilson's dual attempt to be both historian and literary stylist. He found the traditional limits of historical and political writing extremely confining, and he complained to a friend that "the tribe I professionally belong to (historians, economists, jurists,—what not!) are desperately dull fellows. They have no more *literature* in them than an ass has of beauty. . . . I am not only not a scholar, but I don't want to be one."[69]

He saw himself as an English man of letters, masterfully surveying the culture and its values. His medium was the essay, and Wilson often made these short pieces serve two or even three purposes—as a lecture, as a magazine article, and as a chapter in a collection of essays. The first of these volumes was *An Old Master and Other Political Essays*, published in 1893. It consisted of his earlier articles on Adam Smith, sovereignty, the character of democracy in the United States, and American constitutional government. In 1896, he pasted together some of his literary and historical pieces and published *Mere Literature*. In the title essay, he delivered a frontal attack on "this scientific and positivist spirit of the age" and frankly contended that there was "a natural antagonism . . . between the standards of scholarship and the standards of literature." The article is characteristically Wilsonian in its demands that literature embody moral values and the author reflect spiritual principles. "Scholarship is material; it is not life," he asserted. "It becomes immortal only when it is worked upon by convic-

---

[67] *Ibid.*, pp. 92-93.

[68] R. S. Baker memorandum of interviews with Stockton Axson, Feb. 8, 10, and 11, 1925 (R. S. Baker Coll., DLC).

[69] WW to C. T. Winchester, May 29, 1892, *PWW*, VIII, p. 220.

tion, by schooled and chastened imagination, by thought that runs alive out of the inner fountains of individual insight and purpose."[70]

Wilson's careers as philosopher of law, historian, and literary critic reveal the basic unity of his entire thought, particularly as influenced by his covenant religious heritage. In all these areas, he attempted to see life in terms of its wholeness—the diverse forces which affected people, the power of the individual imagination to mold opinions, and most of all the fundamental values which unified human activity and gave it meaning. He exalted literature for its ability to evoke those values and rebelled against science because he thought that it divided life and made it subject to mechanistic laws. In this respect, his literary and historical work is a more accurate gauge of the dynamics of his thought during the early 1890's, for his political thought had temporarily created a dichotomy between individual and social morality, expediency and justice.

Wilson's stroke in 1896 aided in transforming his thinking and resolving the growing chasm between his religious and political thought. The change became evident as soon as he returned from England, when he delivered one of his most famous speeches, "Princeton in the Nation's Service." The occasion was Princeton's sesquicentennial celebration, and President Patton chose Wilson as the principal speaker. The address became famous for Wilson's defense of a liberal education and his criticisms of science. "I am much mistaken if the scientific spirit of the age is not doing us a great disservice, working in us a certain great degeneracy," he declared. "Science has bred in us a spirit of experiment and a contempt for the past. It has made us credulous of quick improvement, hopeful of discovering panaceas, confident of success in every new thing."[71]

Equally important, however, this speech marked the beginning of a greater degree of integration of his political and religious thought. Wilson stated, "It is noteworthy how often God-fearing men have been forward in those revolutions which have vindicated rights, and how seldom in those which have wrought a work of destruction." The influence of John Witherspoon on the graduates of Princeton was profound, he argued, for "there was a spirit of practical piety in the revolutionary doctrines which Dr. Witherspoon taught. No man, particularly no young man, who heard him could doubt his cause a righteous cause or deem religion aught but a prompter in it. Revolution was not to be distinguished from duty in Princeton."[72]

Religion, Wilson said, ought always to have the effect of driving

---

[70] "Mere Literature," c. June 17, 1893, *ibid.*, pp. 240, 249.

[71] "Princeton in the Nation's Service," Oct. 21, 1896, *ibid.*, x, 29.

[72] *Ibid.*, pp. 21-22.

people toward social service, toward the political expression of their spiritual beliefs. "We can easily hold the service of mankind at arms length while we read and make scholars of ourselves, but we shall be very uneasy, the while, if the right mandates of religion are let in upon us and made part of our thought." Characterizing Princeton in good Calvinist terms as "a school of duty," Wilson concluded with a plea for the place of religion in an academic curriculum designed to produce people who would serve society. If education gave students "no vision of the true God," he believed, "it has given them no certain motive to practise the wise lessons they have learned."[73]

The speech was an overwhelming success. It marked Wilson as the leader of the faculty and the most logical successor to Patton. Ellen Wilson called the celebration "the grandest thing of the sort . . . that America has ever seen," and she was overwhelmed by the reaction to Wilson's address.

> It was the most brilliant, *dazzling*, success from first to last. And *such* an ovation as Woodrow received! I never imagined anything like it. And think of *so* delighting *such* an audience, the most distinguished, everyone says, that has ever been assembled in America;—famous men from all parts of Europe. They declared there had been "nothing to equal it since Burke"; with scores of other compliments equally great. . . . As for the Princeton men some of them simply fell on his neck and wept for joy. They say that those who could not get at Woodrow were shaking each others hands and congratulating each other in a perfect frenzy of delight that Princeton had so covered herself with glory before the visitors.[74]

Wilson's speech did retain a large measure of Burkean conservatism, and this continued to characterize many of his speeches and political writings during the late 1890's. But his weakened physical condition and the increasing emphasis in his religious thought on God's love and grace gradually encouraged a subtle shift in his political thought. No longer quite so preoccupied with social order and stability, Wilson began stressing the individualistic side of the covenant heritage. Liberty and freedom in a democratic society became a pressing concern, and the sense of mission which his stroke had imparted found expression in his exaltation of leadership in making constructive reforms.

In 1894, Wilson had told his wife he found political liberty "*very* difficult to handle and illustrate, and I could not speak as directly and simply upon it as I can upon the other topics of the course."[75] But after his stroke of 1896, Wilson repeatedly turned to the subject of liberty

[73] *Ibid.*, pp. 21, 20.

[74] EAW to Mary Eloise Hoyt, Oct. 27, 1896, *ibid.*, p. 37.

[75] WW to EAW, July 26, 1894, *ibid.*, VIII, 627.

and gave his favorite subjects a new twist. "By a 'constitutional' government we do not mean simply a government with a constitution," he declared. ". . . We mean a government in which there is a constitution of liberty."[76] This was not a return to the laissez-faire individualism of his youth, for Wilson still retained a concern for social stability. The object of law was *"the creation, modification, or clearer definition of some right or duty of the individual,"* and the strength of society was "the perfect and easy adjustment of each man to his fellows."[77]

Wilson's new concern with liberty was part of his resistance to the effects of his stroke—his inability to use his right arm—but it was also encouraged by his rediscovery of God's love and grace. Consequently, he became less preoccupied with the feeling that he had to justify himself by his deeds. And yet, Wilson for the most part did not transfer his religious sense of freedom into his political thought but made it spiritual and individualistic. Emphasizing again "the expulsive power of a new affection," Wilson told the Laymen's Conference in Princeton that "only love transforms" and that "individual salvation *is* national salvation."[78] Similarly, he told the black students of Hampton Institute that "we are free, when . . . the spirit is at the helm and we have the perfect use and control of all of our faculties. . . . It is the spirit's knowledge as well as intention that sets a man free."[79] When a person is released from bondage to the law, Wilson believed, he is liberated to serve others in society, and by his personal example of a Christian life he "sheds abroad light and directs others to Christ."[80]

As Wilson recovered from his stroke, even the idea of spiritual liberty began to be moralized again and replaced by the idea that an individual had the capacity to free himself. In one of his literary essays, "On Being Human," published in September 1897, Wilson described a type of Aristotelian individual adhering to a golden mean of virtue. He also raised the perplexing question of how someone could arrive at such a state of moral moderation. "By what means is this self-liberation to be effected,—this emancipation from affectation and the bondage of being like other people? Is it open to us to choose to be genuine? I see nothing insuperable in the way," he assured the magazine's readers, "except for those who are hopelessly lacking in a sense of humor. . . . If you live in a large world, you will see that standards are innumerable . . . and that a choice must be made amongst them."[81]

---

[76] "Liberty," Jan. 31, 1897, *ibid.*, X, 131.

[77] "The City 'Executive,' " Dec. 2, 1898, *ibid.*, XI, 79; "Liberty," Jan. 31, 1897, *ibid.*, X, 130.

[78] Notes, March 28, 1897, *ibid.*, p. 198.

[79] "Liberty," Jan. 31, 1897, *ibid.*, p. 129.

[80] News report of a speech to the Philadelphian Society, April 2, 1897, *ibid.*, p. 211.

[81] "On Being Human," June 2, 1897, *ibid.*, pp. 251-52.

This reassertion of Wilsonian moralism facilitated Wilson's identification of religion and patriotism during the period leading up to the Spanish-American War. In January 1898, Wilson argued that patriotism was the duty of religious people, and that political involvement meant *"translating principle into social action."*[82] "Socialize your religious motives in working for your country; then patriotism will not have to be hastened by speeches," he admonished his audience.[83] But Wilson realized that the problems posed by the war were not solved by simply identifying devotion to God with devotion to one's country. *"What ought we to do?"* Wilson asked himself. "It is not simply a matter of expediency: the question of expediency is itself infinitely hard to settle. It is a question also of moral obligation. What *ought* we to do?"[84]

His answer was political service, and throughout the late 1890's, Wilson's chafing at the restraints of academic life prompted him to concentrate on the duty of enlightened, moral individuals to enter politics and use their gifts in behalf of others. As he told the Princeton students in March 1898, "Self-development, character, prowess,— these cannot be ends in themselves. They are by-products; [they] arise out of self-forgetful endeavour; [they] are the children of love and high devotion."[85] Later that spring, he picked up the familiar theme of the Christian soldier from his earlier religious essays and focused on life as a struggle to remain true to principles. "No man reaches an end without travelling a hard path, for every endeavor carries with it hardness," he declared, but "our Christian religion is the most independent and robust of all religions, because it puts every man upon his own initiative and responsibility." The duty of a Christian was "to carry the war into the enemy's country," he said. "The men who are thinking of their country and their God are the best fighters."[86] But, he warned, anyone who enters politics "should be careful of his conduct when in office and be ready to sacrifice himself for principle, if need be."[87]

Just as Wilson became increasingly moralistic and legalistic as the immediacy of his stroke dimmed, so also he returned to his work with increased zeal. He accepted even more speaking engagements and continued to push himself to the limits of physical endurance. By the end of the academic year in 1899, Ellen thought "he seemed worn out" and persuaded him to spend the summer abroad.[88] He departed for

---

[82] Notes for a speech, "Religion and Patriotism," Jan. 16, 1898, *ibid.*, pp. 365-66.

[83] News report, Jan. 17, 1898, *ibid.*, p. 366.

[84] Memorandum, "What Ought We to Do?" *c.* Aug. 1, 1898, *ibid.*, p. 576.

[85] Notes for a chapel talk, March 13, 1898, *ibid.*, p. 477.

[86] News report of a speech to the Philadelphian Society, May 20, 1898, *ibid.*, p. 533.

[87] News report of a speech to the Philadelphian Society, May 19, 1899, *ibid.*, XI, 119.

[88] McAdoo (ed.), *The Priceless Gift*, p. 210.

England to recuperate, this time with Stockton Axson, and the two men walked and bicycled throughout the British Isles.

This physical setback reaffirmed and strengthened Wilson's awareness of God's grace in his spiritual life, and in November 1899 after his return to Princeton, he wrote what is perhaps his most complete and eloquent statement of his religious faith, "When a Man Comes to Himself." Accepted immediately but not published until 1901 by the *Century Magazine*, the article is clearly autobiographical, and in utilizing the biblical parable of the prodigal son, Wilson revealed his gradual realization of his own spiritual maturity.

He recalled his early youth filled with ambitious dreams and stated that a man came to himself "after experiences of which he alone may be aware: when he has left off being wholly preoccupied with his own powers and interests and with every petty plan that centers in himself; when he has cleared his eyes to see the world as it is, and his own true place and function in it." He believed that the process was one of "disillusionment, but it disheartens no soundly made man."[89]

In the development of maturity, in the process of coming to oneself, Wilson declared that the Christian faith is essential for self-realization. Explicitly rejecting the moralistic and legalistic themes of his youth, Wilson enunciated a clearer understanding of God's grace, the power of love, and the relationship of religious faith to moral action. "Christianity has liberated the world," he wrote,

> not as a system of ethics, not as a philosophy of altruism, but by its revelation of the power of pure and unselfish love. Its vital principle is not its code, but its motive. Love, clear-sighted, loyal, personal, is its breath and immortality. Christ came, not to save himself, assuredly, but to save the world. His motive, his example, are every man's key to his own gifts and happiness. The ethical code he taught may be no doubt be matched, here a piece and there a piece, out of other religions, other teachings and philosophies. Every thoughtful man born with a conscience must know a code of right and of pity to which he ought to conform; but without the motive of Christianity, without love, he may be the purest altruist and yet be as sad and as unsatisfied as Marcus Aurelius.
>
> Christianity gave us, in the fullness of time, the perfect image of right living, the secret of social and of individual well-being; for the two are not separable, and the man who receives and verifies that secret in his own living has discovered not only the best and only way to serve the world, but also the one happy way to satisfy himself. Then, indeed, he has come to himself.[90]

[89] "When a Man Comes to Himself," *c*. Nov. 1, 1899, *PWW*, xi, 263-64.
[90] *Ibid*., p. 272.

This statement, coming after his stroke of 1896 and weakened physical condition, was Wilson's declaration of his spiritual coming of age—his own religious maturity. Although elements of the dichotomy between his religious faith and his political thought were hidden beneath the surface, he had even achieved a partial integration of these two important parts of his life. Christianity is "the secret of social and of individual well-being," and "a man *is* the part he plays among his fellows. He is not isolated; he cannot be. His life is made up of the relations he bears to others. . . . It is by these that he gets his spiritual growth."[91]

Even in his "spiritual maturity," Wilson's primary connection between his religious faith and political thought still remained at the individual and personal level. The chief influence of religion, in Wilson's view, was to drive the individual toward the altruistic service of others. Yet he insisted simultaneously that this service should result in influence and prominence. Men loved power and greatness, he declared, because it afforded them "so pleasurable an expansion of faculty, so large a run for their minds, an exercise of spirit so various and refreshing; they have the freedom of so wide a tract of the world of affairs." But, Wilson cautioned, "if they use power only for their own ends, if there be no unselfish service in it, if its object be only their personal aggrandizement, their love to see other men tools in their hands, they go out of the world small, disquieted, beggared, no enlargement of soul vouchsafed them, no usury of satisfaction."[92]

The Wilsonian synthesis of personal religion and political power was complete. The Christian faith drove people toward serving others. To accomplish that goal, a person must be a leader and possess power. The only limit and justification for such power was its use in behalf of others. On the one hand, Wilson's formulation of personal religion was merely a simple paraphrase of the historic Christian affirmation that self-fulfillment was achieved through self-denial and sacrifical service. On the other hand, Wilson seemed unaware of how even altruistic efforts could be motivated and twisted by selfish considerations. Particularly in the realm of politics, there remained no means for evaluating the policies of a leader who claimed to be serving the people while aggrandizing his own power.

Wilson returned repeatedly to this theme of unselfish service, describing the noble individual as the one who "has . . . a margin, a surplus, a free capital of character, which he can expend in undertakings which are for the general welfare as well as in undertakings for himself." True nobility was the "fine exercise of one's quality outside

---

[91] *Ibid.*, p. 264.

[92] *Ibid.*, p. 266. See also his Philadelphian Society talk using the theme of "When a Man Comes to Himself"; notes, Nov. 2, 1899, *ibid.*, p. 273; news report, Nov. 3, 1899, *ibid.*, pp. 274-75.

of the narrow circle of self-interest."[93] But in proclaiming the gospel of service, Wilson moderated his exaltation of the individual by stressing again the corporate, organic character of society. Personal liberty, he insisted, was not untrammeled and without restraint, for liberty was "a social question and not an individual question." Freedom was always cooperative and involved "the best adjustment between governmental power and individual initiative." The economic structure of American society, Wilson believed, was unjust precisely because it did not strike this adjustment and balance. Some people and corporations received advantages which discouraged and suppressed the opportunity of others. But Wilson was confident that new means could be found to create "a fair field" of equal opportunity. "That is the essence of equality," he said. "It is the equality of chance, of opportunity, and not the equality of results, for we should have a dead uniformity and the absence of growth if there were equality in result."[94]

This concern with adjustment and balance was characteristic of Wilson's entire approach to the study of politics and society and indicative of the pervasive influence of the covenant theological tradition. The essence of that heritage was an attempt to mediate between God's power and human will, divine authority and human freedom. Wilson remained a Burkean conservative in advocating orderly change, but during the late 1890's he gradually became impressed by the way that individual freedom was being unfairly limited by the structure of American society. This concern with liberty was partially Wilson's reaction to and denial of his own physical disabilities, his new awareness of love and grace which gave him a greater sense of personal freedom, and his perception of economic inequality in American society.

But in one important respect he refused to countenance a more complete involvement of religion in political affairs. Perhaps as a result of the traditional separation of church and state in his southern Presbyterian background, he resisted the new political activism in the churches produced by the social gospel movement. As early as 1895 he had bemoaned the fact that "our novels have become sociological studies, our poems vehicles of criticism, our sermons political manifestos." In 1900 he argued that *the object of the church as an organization* [is] the *salvation of souls,*—only indirectly *the purification of Society. That it must effect indirectly, by example*, not by organizing vs. particular vices but by kindling a light in which no vice can live."[95]

That did not stop Wilson from speaking out himself on how society

[93] "Spurious Versus Real Patriotism in Education," Oct. 13, 1899, *ibid.*, p. 245.

[94] *Ibid.*, pp. 254-59.

[95] "On an Author's Choice of Company," Nov. 10, 1895, *ibid.*, IX, 343; notes for a religious address, Jan. 17, 1900, *ibid.*, XI, 376.

ought to be saved and purified, and his speeches began to reflect a more pressing concern for solutions to the political and social problems of American society at the turn of the century. Despite his initial reservations about America's imperialistic adventure in the Spanish-American War, Wilson was convinced that the victory was not only inevitable but right. It prevented Germany and Russia from acquiring the land, and Wilson believed that if anyone should hold territory, it ought to be the United States, "inasmuch as hers was the light of day, while theirs was the light of darkness."[96]

In his speeches around the country, Wilson popularized Frederick Jackson Turner's frontier thesis and applied it to American expansion overseas. Since America's domestic frontier was closed, "the law of expansion into new territory" had been checked. In a typical fusion of moralism and nationalistic zeal, Wilson proclaimed that "our interests must march forward, altruists though we are; other nations must see to it that they stand off, and do not seek to stay us. It is only just now . . . that we have awakened to our real relationship to the rest of mankind."[97]

He further defended American democratic government as unique in the moral basis on which it rested. "It is for this that we love democracy: for the emphasis it puts on character; for its tendency to exalt the purpose of the average man to some high level of endeavor; for its just principle of common assent in matters in which all are concerned; for its ideals of duty and its sense of brotherhood." The righteousness of democracy was also linked to the need to preserve it as a moral example to the world. "All mankind deem us the representatives of the moderate and sensible discipline which makes free men good citizens, of enlightened systems of law and a temperate justice, of the best experience in the reasonable methods and principles of self-government, of public force made consistent with individual liberty."[98]

But America as moral example to the world merged easily into America as the moralizer of the world, the evangelist of democracy. "We shall not realize these ideals at home," Wilson argued, "if we suffer them to be hopelessly discredited amongst the people who have yet to see liberty and the peaceable days of order and comfortable progress." To moralize both the nation and the world, Wilson realized, required power and leadership, and he sought to see them unified. "We shall see now more clearly than ever before that we lack in our domestic arrangements, above all things else, concentration, both in political leadership and in administrative organization," he said, and despite

---

[96] News report, Nov. 2, 1898, *ibid.*, p. 66.
[97] "Democracy and Efficiency," *c.* Oct. 1, 1900, *ibid.*, XII, 11, 13.
[98] *Ibid.*, pp. 8, 10.

this contradiction between espousing both democracy and concentrated power, Wilson looked to the future with a kind of millennial hope. The world would be changed, he felt, "according to an ordering of Providence hardly so much as foreshadowed until it came."[99]

As the twentieth century loomed before him, Wilson looked back on America's past, and in its history he found encouragement for the country. Turning again to historical themes in both his speaking and writing, Wilson considered a century to be "our dramatic unit." The first century was one of colonization, the second one of war and independence, the third one of nation-making, and the fourth one of perfecting government. The United States had come "to full maturity with this new century of our national existence and to full self-consciousness as a nation."[100] Nevertheless, Wilson argued that "the history of the United States has a unity which belongs to that of no other modern nation," and its unity was principally moral—the lesson "that Wisdom and Right are of old, and do not alter with environment."[101]

Wilson used this basic framework and approach in writing his *History of the American People*, part of which was first serialized in *Harper's Magazine*. The complete text was later published in 1902 in a five-volume, profusely illustrated edition. It was another of Wilson's efforts at popular history, and in this sense it succeeded admirably, bringing him $12,000 for the magazine installments and $40,000 in royalties by 1910.[102] Wilson produced the text with extreme haste, attempting to keep up with the magazine's deadlines and the publisher's demand for copy for the book. The result was a style which resembled some of the excesses of *George Washington* and a some-time casual disregard for facts. When errors were pointed out to him, Wilson merely replied, "I am not an historian: I am only a writer of history, and these little faults must be overlooked in a fellow who merely tries to tell the story, and is not infallible on dates."[103]

In covering the period since the Civil War, Wilson shed some of the restraint which had characterized *Division and Reunion* and let his opinions show openly. He was alarmed by Reconstruction, the carpetbaggers who "swarmed out of the North to cozen, beguile, and use" the liberated slaves, whose "ignorance and credulity made them easy dupes." He contrasted the immigration from northern and western Europe ("the sturdy stocks") with "the multitudes of men of the lowest class" who came from southern and eastern Europe after the Civil

---

[99] *Ibid.*, pp. 10-11, 17, 18.
[100] "The Ideals of America," Dec. 26, 1901, *ibid.*, p. 226.
[101] "Editor's Study," Jan. 1901, *ibid.*, p. 62; notes for a speech, Dec. 6, 1900, *ibid.*, p. 42.
[102] Bragdon, *Wilson: The Academic Years*, p. 251.
[103] WW to Richard Watson Gilder, Jan. 28, 1901, *PWW*, XII, 84.

War. In words which would later haunt him during his political career, he wrote, "They came in numbers which increased from year to year, as if the countries of the south of Europe were disburdèning themselves of the more sordid and hapless elements of their population." He described the labor and agrarian unrest of the 1890's more dispassionately but was clearly disturbed by the "process of revolution" being wrought by combinations of capital, labor, and agriculture. The statesman's task was plain—to alleviate the social discontent "and make law the instrument, not of justice merely, but also of social progress."[104]

Reviewers quickly spotted the book's strengths and weaknesses. Wilson's former student, Charles McLean Andrews, considered it not really a history of the American people but a description of changes in political theory and practice. But he praised Wilson's tone—"full of optimism, life, and courage, like the people of whom it treats, patient to bear, eager to preserve."[105] Frederick Jackson Turner gave the book a friendly reception but pointed out numerous factual mistakes and Wilson's barely restrained affection for both the South and the Democratic party.[106] But it was George Louis Beer who exposed Wilson's near-total reliance upon monographic literature. He called the book a "slipshod, mechanical, uncritical work," found nothing "new in view-point or in ideas for which we are indebted to Wilson," and acerbicly praised Wilson's style. "Its very vagueness, its tendency toward general rather than specific statements, and the consequent absence of detail make Wilson's work pre-eminently comprehensible and readable."[107]

Indeed, the superficiality of Wilson's popular historical writing makes him susceptible to the judgment of one of his mentors, Walter Bagehot, who while criticizing another author, might have been writing about Wilson instead. "He was a man of elegant gifts, of easy fluency, capable of embellishing anything, with a nice wit, gliding swiftly over the most delicate topics; passing from topic to topic like the *raconteur* of the dinner table, touching easily on them all, letting them go as easily; confusing you as to whether he knows nothing, or knows everything."[108]

---

[104] *A History of the American People*, 5 vols. (New York and London, 1902), v, 46, 212-13, 264, 300.

[105] Review printed in *The Independent*, Dec. 11, 1902, *PWW*, xiv, 280-83.

[106] Review in the *American Historical Review* (July 1903), *ibid.*, pp. 516-19.

[107] Review in the New York *Critic* (Feb. 1903), *ibid.*, pp. 338-46.

[108] Quoted by Wilson in a review of Goldwin Smith, *The United States: An Outline of Political History, 1492-1871*, in *ibid.*, viii, 356-57. For other analyses of Wilson's historical work see Sears, "Woodrow Wilson," pp. 102-21; Marjorie L. Daniel, "Woodrow Wilson—Historian," *Mississippi Valley Historical Review*, xxi (1934), 361-74; Bragdon, *Wilson: The Academic Years*, pp. 246-54; and Loewenberg, *American History in American Thought*, pp. 409-21.

One historical work (aside from *Division and Reunion*) which redeemed Wilson's academic reputation as an historian was an incisive chapter on state rights for the *Cambridge Modern History*. Completed in 1899, Wilson's essay recapitulated his argument in *Division and Reunion* that the South had clung to the outmoded political theory of confederation. This principle, Wilson wrote, "meant standstill in the midst of change; it was conservative, not creative; it was against drift and destiny; it protected an impossible institution and a belated order of society; it withstood a creative and imperial idea, the idea of a united people and a single law of freedom."[109] This essay showed Wilson at his best—the careful historian, capable of broad, synthetic treatments of major themes and developments.

Wilson's historical study had led him to conclude that "the problem of every government is leadership: the choice and control of statesmen and the scope that shall be given to their originative part in affairs; and for democracy it is a problem of peculiar difficulty."[110] In 1899 Wilson jotted in his notebook that "the most helpful service to the world . . . awaiting the fulfillment of its visions would be an elucidation, a real elucidation, of the laws of leadership,"[111] and in his remaining years as a professor, Wilson became obsessed with the nature of leadership. The subject would form the core of his "Philosophy of Politics," and Wilson had planned to spend the academic year 1901-1902 in Europe working on the book, but his father's illness kept him at home. Still the theme of leadership consistently permeated his speaking and writing. He urged Princeton men to preserve their ideals as they entered careers in journalism.[112] He held up Gladstone as "the type of what a man may make of himself when fired by high ambition and resolve."[113] He contrasted reformers with true leaders who did not merely convince people but helped them find practical ways of correcting wrongs.[114] And he prodded the members of the Philadelphian Society "*to realize Christ in the world*," especially in "the *field of public life*."[115]

Wilson was convinced that the nation needed leaders more than it needed changes in its constitution. In a thinly veiled plea to be elevated from academic life, he proclaimed, "Let us put our leading characters at the front; let us pray that vision may come with power; let us ponder our duties like men of conscience and temper our ambitions like men who seek to serve, not to subdue, the world; let us lift our thoughts to

[109] "State Rights (1850-1860)," *c*. Dec. 20, 1899, *PWW*, xi, 345; see also Wilson's essay, "Politics (1857-1907)," *c*. July 31, 1907, *ibid.*, xvii, 309-25.

[110] "The Real Idea of Democracy," *c*. Aug. 31, 1902, *ibid.*, xii, 178.

[111] Memoranda for the "Philosophy of Politics," *c*. Sept. 10, 1899, *ibid.*, xi, 239.

[112] Notes for a speech to the Princeton University Press Club, April 30, 1901, *ibid.*, xii, 139.

[113] News report of a talk to the Philadelphian Society, May 3, 1901, *ibid.*, p. 140.

[114] Introduction to *The Autobiography of Benjamin Franklin*, July 18, 1901, *ibid.*, p. 169.

[115] Notes for a talk, Feb. 20, 1902, *ibid.*, p. 273.

the level of the great tasks that await us, and bring a great age in with the coming of our day of strength."[116]

Wilson's desire to fill that role could scarcely be contained. His increasing national reputation brought him repeated offers of educational leadership, and at various times during the 1890's he considered and rejected the presidencies of the University of Illinois, the University of Virginia, the University of Alabama, Washington and Lee University, the University of Nebraska, and the University of Minnesota. The frequency of these offers and Wilson's restless ambition prompted some friends on the Princeton Board of Trustees to band together in 1898 to supplement his income and keep him at Princeton. Wilson received an extra $2,500 per year and promised to give up his Johns Hopkins appointment and not to leave Princeton for five years.[117]

To his students he outwardly seemed a man at peace with himself. "I saw in him only an agreeable, supremely intelligent human being—wise—kind—but a fellow human being," Booth Tarkington remembered. "He *looked happy*. His eyes were bright. As I picture him in the memory of undergraduate years, I see gaiety in his eyes. He seemed to be a person getting what he wanted out of life."[118] But he was not getting what he wanted. He needed a position of leadership, for by May of 1902 he had concluded that leadership eluded analysis; instead what was needed was "the *sensitive*, the *conceiving*, the interpreting, the *initiative* mind *with the addition of will power* or of such subtle persistency as will put strong wills at the disposal of the managing intellect."[119]

He did not have to wait much longer. The faculty and younger members of the Princeton Board of Trustees finally became aroused about the crisis developing because of President Patton's incompetent leadership. Initially the insurgent faculty and trustees proposed an executive committee composed of representatives from the Board and the faculty that would discharge the duties of the president, and Wilson became deeply involved in the behind-the-scenes maneuvering to divest Patton of his power. The chief complaint was that Patton had allowed the academic standards of the university to decline and that he had lost the confidence of the faculty. After delicate negotiations between Patton and members of the Board, Patton realized that his situation was no longer tenable and agreed to a premature retirement. When he told the trustees he had planned to retire after five more years in any case, a group of trustees offered him $31,500, plus assurances of the

---

[116] "The Ideals of America," Dec. 26, 1901, *ibid.*, p. 227.

[117] Cornelius Cuyler Cuyler to WW, with Enclosure, May 16, 1898, *ibid.*, x, 529-30, n. 1.

[118] Quoted in Bragdon, *Wilson: The Academic Years*, p. 209.

[119] Memorandum on Leadership, May 5, 1902, *PWW*, xii, 365.

promotion of his son to professor of philosophy. Patton submitted his resignation as president of the university at the June meeting of the Board.[120] Shortly thereafter he moved across the street to become the first man to hold the title of president of Princeton Theological Seminary (even though he still held his professorship at the university until his retirement).

Within hours, Wilson was elected president. The action could hardly have been as surprising as he suggested. "This thing has come to me as a thunderbolt out of a clear sky," he told the alumni.[121] Wilson's election as president, in fact, marked the triumph of alumni influence in university affairs, as opposed to the earlier domination by Presbyterian ministers. His policy as president built upon this new base of support, and his early stunning achievements were in great measure due to his ability to persuade the alumni to underwrite his vision for Princeton. Ironically, it was also opposition from the alumni that proved to be Wilson's undoing during the latter years of his presidency, leaving future presidents to struggle with how great a role the alumni should play in determining university goals and policy.

But the bitterness of these later developments did not even loom on the horizon in June 1902. Faculty, students, and alumni agreed that Wilson was the man to arrest Princeton's decline under Patton and to bring the university into the twentieth century. As Ellen Wilson reported to a friend, "It is enough to frighten a man to death to have people love & believe in him so and *expect* so much. Yet on the other hand it is like going in with the tide; he is only the leader of the Princeton forces and all this enthusiasm will surely be a strong power impelling the University forward."[122]

Wilson himself was undaunted, seeing himself as the disinterested leader whom he had praised so often. "The objects we seek in a university are not selfish objects," declared the man who went from president of Princeton to Governor of New Jersey and President of the United States. "There is here no interest served which is a personal interest. We are here to serve our country and mankind, and we know that we can put selfishness behind us."[123]

---

[120] The entire story of the negotiations leading up to Patton's resignation is meticulously detailed in the correspondence during the spring of 1902 printed in *ibid*. See also the Editorial Note, The Crisis in Presidential Leadership at Princeton, *ibid*., pp. 289-93.

[121] News report of an alumni speech, June 14, 1902, *ibid*., p. 420.

[122] EAW to Florence Stevens Hoyt, June 28, 1902, *ibid*., p. 464.

[123] News report of an alumni speech, June 14, 1902, *ibid*., p. 421.

Wilson's class picture in 1879

Janet Woodrow Wilson about 1874
Joseph Ruggles Wilson about 1874

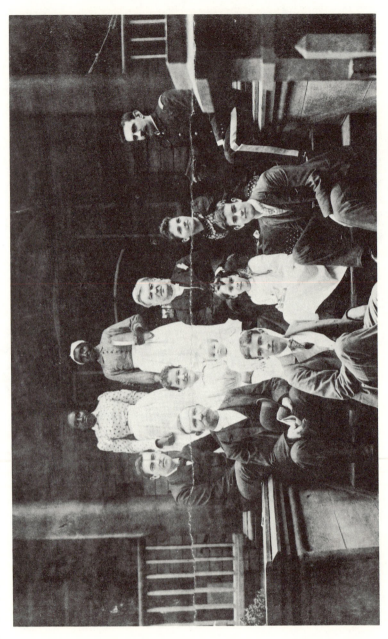

The Wilson family in Columbia, South Carolina, in 1892. *First row:* Wilson Howe, George Howe, Jr. *Second row:* Dr. George Howe, Jessie Kennedy (daughter of Marion Wilson Kennedy, Wilson's sister). *Third row:* Woodrow Wilson, Annie Wilson Howe (Wilson's sister and wife of Dr. George Howe) and her daughter Annie, Joseph Ruggles Wilson, Kate (Mrs. Joseph R.) Wilson, and Joseph R. Wilson. *Fourth row:* Nannie and Minnie, family servants

Woodrow Wilson as a young lawyer in Atlanta

Ellen Louise Axson about the time of her engagement

The Woodrow Wilson family:
Eleanor, Woodrow Wilson, Ellen Axson Wilson, Margaret, and Jessie

Wilson as Princeton's Sesquicentennial Orator

Wilson at the time of his election to Princeton

Wilson in 1908

Cleveland Hoadley Dodge

Andrew Fleming West

John Grier Hibben

Moses Taylor Pyne

Mary Allen Hulbert Peck at approximately
the time she and Wilson met

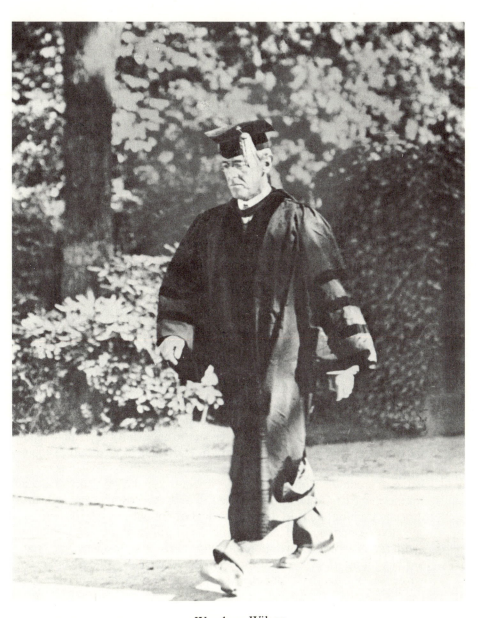

Woodrow Wilson

VII

Educational Statesman, 1902–1906

Wilson's election to the presidency of Princeton University gave him the position of leadership which he had sought for his entire life, and it quieted his spirits. "I find, now that I get a certain remove, that my election to the presidency has done a very helpful thing for me," he told Ellen. "It has settled the future for me and given me a sense of *position* and of definite, tangible tasks which take the *flutter* and restlessness from my spirits."[1] He considered his new post as a religious vocation and described it as "a sort of laying on of hands" and "a call of duty."[2] He regretted not being able to finish his "Philosophy of Politics," "the task for which, by means of my historical writing, I have all these years been in training." But he realized that the project was "too problematical and distant to be handled now,"[3] and he was confident that he had made the right decision. "When I can tell you the circumstances I am sure that you will say that it was my duty to accept," he wrote to a friend. "It was a singularly plain, a *blessedly* plain, case."[4]

Congratulations poured in from friends and admirers, and newspapers were struck by the dramatic suddenness of Wilson's election and Princeton's departure from past precedent in choosing a layman to lead the university. Southern newspapers in particular were proud of their native son and saw the move as a sign that sectional divisions were being overcome.[5] Robert Bridges' glowing sketch of Wilson's career for the *Review of Reviews*, concluded, "With this cosmopolitan education and training, he is to-day the product of no section,—he is a representative American."[6] Henry Fairfield Osborn, a Princeton alumnus and famous zoologist, was confident that Wilson's presidency marked the beginning of "the Augustan age" for Princeton, and Bliss Perry wrote to Wilson that "nobody, surely, ever entered upon such an

[1] WW to EAW, Aug. 10, 1902, *PWW*, xiv, 70.

[2] WW to Jabez Lamar Monroe Curry, July 15, 1902, *ibid.*, p. 15; WW to Harry Augustus Garfield, July 16, 1907, *ibid.*, xvii, 284.

[3] WW to F. J. Turner, Jan. 21, 1902, *ibid.*, xii, 240; WW to Richard Watson Gilder, Oct. 31, 1902, *ibid.*, xiv, 190.

[4] WW to Edith Gittings Reid, July 12, 1902, *ibid.*, p. 3.

[5] Link, *Road to the White House*, p. 37, n. 3.

[6] "President Woodrow Wilson," July 1902, *PWW*, xii, 468.

office as yours with so general and sincere a chorus of praise and good wishes."[7]

Amidst all the adulation, Wilson was aware of the enormous responsibilities which he had assumed and may have even sensed the friction and ill-feeling which would mark his later years as president. "The rewards of my presidency seem to be coming to me now (lest they should lack at the end?)," he commented and added, "Hereafter come hard work, the deep waters of responsibility, for Princeton is to be handled at a crisis in her development."[8] David Benton Jones, a prominent trustee and one of Wilson's strongest supporters, emphasized to Wilson the critical situation which the university faced. "You are not greatly to be congratulated upon the change that has come to you," he wrote. "The task is burdensome even if it were entirely clear just what should be done. It is always a matter of great perplexity to be made responsible for any large undertaking during a period of uncertainty or of transition."[9] Wilson agreed but did not feel that the presidency was a burden. "There is a vast deal to be done and it is impossible yet to plan it wisely all the way through. It will be wisest to make our general purpose distinct to ourselves, and the outline of the means by which we mean to seek its attainment, and then attack the details one at a time."[10]

Wilson's first attempt to make his purpose distinct was his inaugural address, which he titled "Princeton for the Nation's Service," echoing the title of his famous sesquicentennial oration of 1896. He turned what he called his "old hack mind" to the assignment of spelling out his educational credo—the "ideas wherewith to clothe my ideals."[11] He seemed delighted with the challenge and confessed to Ellen, "I never worked out the argument on liberal studies, which is the theme of my inaugural, before, never before having treated myself as a professional 'educator,' and so the matter is not stale but fresh and interesting. . . . I feel like a new prime minister getting ready to address his constitutents."[12]

In contrast to the 1896 oration, Wilson had a few kind words to say for science. He believed that "the thought of the modern time is based on science" and argued that "it is as necessary that the lad

---

[7] Henry Fairfield Osborn to WW, Aug. 2, 1902, printed as an Enclosure with EAW to WW, Aug. 5, 1902, *ibid.*, xiv, 54; Bliss Perry to WW, July 20, 1902, *ibid.*, p. 35.

[8] WW to Thomas Raynesford Lounsbury, July 16, 1902, *ibid.*, p. 20.

[9] David Benton Jones to WW, Aug. 7, 1902, *ibid.*, p. 64.

[10] WW to D. B. Jones, Aug. 11, 1902, *ibid.*, p. 75.

[11] WW to EAW, July 14 and 18, 1902, *ibid.*, pp. 9, 24.

[12] WW to EAW, July 19, 1902, *ibid.*, p. 27.

should be inducted into the thinking of the modern time as it is that he should be carefully grounded in the old, accepted thought which has stood test from age to age." The problem confronting American education, Wilson insisted, was one of specialization and disintegration. Academic disciplines were narrowly conceived and competed for the intellectual allegiance of the students. Colleges produced narrow graduates, able to accomplish specific tasks but without the broad, humanistic perspective Wilson perceived as necessary for a rapidly changing world. "We have too ignorantly served the spirit of the age,—have made no bold and sanguine attempt to instruct and lead it," he lamented. "Its call is for efficiency, but not narrow, purblind efficiency."[13]

Princeton's mission, he declared, was to offer a general education infused with moral ideals and imperatives. "I do not see how any university can afford such an outlook if its teachings not be informed with the spirit of religion, and that the religion of Christ, and with the energy of a positive faith," Princeton's first lay president assured his audience.

> The argument for efficiency in education can have no permanent validity if the efficiency sought be not moral as well as intellectual. The ages of strong and definite moral impulse have been the ages of achievement; and the moral impulses which have lifted highest have come from Christian peoples,—the moving history of our own nation were proof enough of that. Moral efficiency is, in the last analysis, the fundamental argument for liberal culture.[14]

This evangelical plea for the virtues of general, moral education is indicative of the pervasive influence of Wilson's Presbyterian heritage. It had long insisted that responsible members of the covenant could discharge their duties only through reading the Scriptures and the education of the young. It was a tradition which had made education an ethical endeavor, linking the development of the mind to moral assertion in the world, and Wilson retained that Calvinist emphasis. "We are here not merely to release the faculties of men for their own use, but also to quicken their social understanding, instruct their consciences, and give them the catholic vision of those who know their just relations to their fellow men." Giving the gospel of service his characteristic American formulation, he declared, "Here in America . . . social service is the high law of duty, and every American university must square its standards by that law or lack of its national title. . . . We are not put into this world to sit still and know; we are put into it to act."[15]

[13] "Princeton for the Nation's Service," Oct. 25, 1902, *ibid.*, pp. 180, 183.
[14] *Ibid.*, p. 184.   [15] *Ibid.*, pp. 183-84.

Wilson's covenant style of thinking molded his educational credo in more subtle ways as well. The thrust of the covenant theological tradition was an inclusive vision of a world in which everything had its place, and Wilson complained that the diversification of knowledge had encouraged an incoherent view of human behavior. Knowledge, like God's sovereignty, was complete and unified. "Learning is not divided. Its kingdom and government are centred, unitary, single." The role of the university thus became an imperial one, and Wilson's use of geographical imagery reveals how clearly he was attempting to reduce the world to his stipulated structure and order. "The university," he believed, "must stand in the midst, where the roads of thought and knowledge interlace and cross, and, building upon some coign of vantage, command them all. . . . In planning for Princeton, . . . we are planning for the country."[16]

Princeton's education was also not a training to be offered to everyone but only to an elect who would carry its broad vision into the world. "It is for the minority who plan, who conceive, who superintend, who mediate between group and group and must see the wide stage as a whole." Wilson refused to accept this idea of education as undemocratic. "The college is no less democratic because it is for those who play a special part."[17]

The address was well received by democrats and aristocrats alike, and the guests ranged across the spectrum—Booker T. Washington, Mark Twain, William Dean Howells, Robert T. Lincoln, J. P. Morgan. The *Princeton Alumni Weekly* accurately summed up Wilson's address as "an academic profession of faith," and Wilson's brother-in-law, Stockton Axson, termed it entirely appropriate. "In a masterly address, most impressively delivered, you had struck exactly the right note," he observed.[18]

Wilson's inaugural address represents his attempt to spell out the basis of the policies he would pursue as president. He believed that the most important thing in the beginning of an undertaking was "to establish ideals," adding, "If a man does not do so, he is like a wanderer and always astray."[19] Despite all its idealism, the speech was also remarkably vague about how Wilson intended to arrest the university's academic decline and its financial deterioration. After the tensions which had led to Patton's early retirement, Wilson wisely decided to move slowly, to win the support of the faculty and alumni, and to phrase his plans in only the broadest possible terms. As he told the

[16] *Ibid.*, pp. 175, 174, 170.   [17] *Ibid.*, p. 176.

[18] News report, Nov. 1, 1902, *ibid.*, pp. 191-95; Stockton Axson to WW, Oct. 27, 1902, *ibid.*, p. 187.

[19] News report of a talk to the Philadelphian Society, Sept. 29, 1904, *ibid.*, xv, 495.

Washington alumni during the spring of 1903, "Generalities are good things to stick to, particularly in matters of education."[20]

This was Wilson's public approach; privately he had already worked out the needs of the university and his plans for its development. At his first meeting as president with the Board of Trustees, he analyzed Princeton's problems and presented his solutions. The university was "insufficiently capitalized for its business"; the faculty was overworked and underpaid; scientific equipment was badly needed; the curriculum required reorganization to prevent duplication and chaotic development. "But what we need more than mere reorganization is in many things a radical change of method." He proposed hiring fifty tutors who would offer instruction in subjects rather than test the content of lectures or books. "Ordinary class-room and lecture work cannot accomplish the purpose at all," Wilson said. "This one thing is our central and immediate need." He also said that four things were essential for the university's growth—a graduate college, a school of jurisprudence, a school of electrical engineering, and a museum of natural history. In financial terms, Wilson's plans were staggering. The four buildings alone required $6.65 million; endowment for the fifty tutors involved $2.25 million; and increases in staff salaries and other improvements meant a total of $12.5 million to implement Wilson's program for Princeton.[21]

Former President Grover Cleveland moved that the Board approve Wilson's plans and authorize him to approach people who might be able to provide the needed funds, and the Board agreed. Wilson's authority was further strengthened by a Cleveland resolution giving Wilson the power to reorganize "the teaching force to create such vacancies . . . as he may deem for the best interest of the University."[22] Wilson used this extraordinary power to remove faculty members only once. In 1904-1905 he tried to force the resignation of Arnold Guyot Cameron, a professor of French who delighted his classes with an abundance of witty stories and a minimum of instruction. After pressure from Cameron's friends on the Board and among the alumni, Wilson relented and agreed to extend Cameron's contract but only for another year.[23] The animosity generated during the Cameron affair must have made Wilson chary of using his authority in the future, for with the exception of the delicately encouraged retirement of chemist

[20] News report, March 28, 1903, *ibid.*, XIV, 401.

[21] WW to the Board of Trustees of Princeton University, Oct. 21, 1902, *ibid.*, pp. 150-61. Hereinafter the Board of Trustees of Princeton University will be referred to as Trustees.

[22] Two resolutions by Grover Cleveland, Oct. 21, 1902, *ibid.*, p. 162, n. 1.

[23] A complete description of Cameron's firing is contained in n. 1 to WW to Arnold Guyot Cameron, Nov. 18, 1903, *ibid.*, XV, 52-54.

Henry Bedinger Cornwall in 1910,[24] there is no other evidence that he tried to remove faculty members of professorial rank.

Wilson immediately took his plans for Princeton to his constituents, first to the Chicago alumni, next to New York. In early December 1902, he told the New Yorkers that it would cost $2.25 million to obtain the new tutorial plan. The alumni whistled in astonishment, and Wilson replied, "I hope you will get your whistling over, because you will have to get used to this, and you may thank your stars I did not say four millions and a quarter, because we are going to get it (applause). I suspect that there are gentlemen in this room who are going to give me two millions and a quarter to get rid of me." He outlined the total fund-raising program of $12.5 million and declared, "There is not another university in the world that could transmute twelve millions and a half into so much red blood."[25] He told the Baltimore alumni that he was confident that the entire amount could be raised, and at the end of his first year as president he said that he was pleased by the enthusiasm of the alumni and their desire to participate in serious discussion of Princeton's plans and ideals.[26]

Wilson knew that mere discussion was no substitute for money, and to a meeting of New York bankers he quipped that he was well-qualified to discuss the currency because he never saw any.[27] He set to work at once to raise the sums that were needed for his vision of Princeton. He appealed to his classmate, Cyrus McCormick, and sent Andrew Carnegie a plea which attempted to capitalize on their common Scotch heritage. "The Scots blood that is in me makes me wish to renew the traditions of John Witherspoon's day in the old place," Wilson wrote. Later he outlined his complete development plan, calling Carnegie's attention especially to the school of law—"the centre of my most interesting hopes for Princeton."[28] Carnegie was not moved; instead he decided to give the university a lake, and Wilson later grumbled, "We needed bread and you gave us cake."[29]

Wilson detested the job of raising money, calling himself "the offi-

[24] Wilson made very attractive arrangements for Cornwall's pension and retirement benefits. WW to Henry Bedinger Cornwall, May 4 and June 4, 1910, *ibid.*, xx, 409-10, 499-500; H. B. Cornwall to WW, May 7 and June 6, 1910, *ibid.*, pp. 422, 505.

[25] For the Chicago speech, see WW's notes, Nov. 26, 1902, *ibid.*, xiv, 223, and news reports, Nov. 28 and 29, *ibid.*, pp. 225-27. For the New York address, see the text printed at Dec. 9, 1902, *ibid.*, pp. 268-76.

[26] News report of a speech to the Baltimore alumni, Feb. 14, 1903, *ibid.*, pp. 358-59; interview with WW, May 16, 1903, *ibid.*, p. 459.

[27] News report, Dec. 19, 1902, *ibid.*, p. 298.

[28] WW to C. H. McCormick, Dec. 14, 1902, *ibid.*, pp. 291-92; WW to Andrew Carnegie, Dec. 27, 1902 and April 17, 1903, *ibid.*, pp. 306-307, 411-15.

[29] *WWLL*, ii, 156.

cial beggar of the University." He confessed to a member of the Board, "I could be very happy in administering the affairs of the University if only I did not have to beg for money. The necessity to do that lies, I must say, like a burden on my spirits. But I knew when I took office that I should have to do it and I try not to wince too much."[30] At least one trustee, David B. Jones, sensed that Wilson's devotion to the financial affairs of the university was not complete or enthusiastic, and he soon became Wilson's primary financial adviser. In October 1903, he suggested to Wilson that they find ten men to donate $5,000 per year and twenty who would give $2,500. This would "capitalize" the university's deficit, and Wilson quickly adopted the idea. Within a year, the $100,000 was pledged, and the group was formalized as the Committee of Fifty.[31]

As a fund-raiser, Wilson's chief contribution to Princeton was attracting money for the material improvement of the campus. During his presidency, eight buildings were completed: the gymnasium (1903); Seventy-Nine Hall (1904), student dormitory and offices for Wilson; Patton Hall (1906), a dormitory; McCosh Hall (1907), a classroom building; Palmer Physical Laboratory (1908), the physics building; Guyot Hall (1909), the biology and geology building which included a museum of natural history; Campbell Hall (1909), a dormitory; and Holder Hall (1910), a dormitory. In addition, a gateway to the campus was erected in 1905 in honor of Nathaniel FitzRandolph, who donated the original land to the university; the faculty room in Nassau Hall was constructed in 1906; and British industrialist Sir William Mather in 1907 contributed a copy of the sun dial at Corpus Christi College, Oxford University. Substantial amounts of real estate were also acquired by the university, including the 221-acre Springdale golf links (1905) and Carnegie Lake (1906).

Tudor Gothic architecture had been stipulated as the style for new university buildings at the sesquicentennial celebration in 1896, and after complaints about the haphazard architectural development of the campus, Ralph Adams Cram, an expert in the English Gothic medium, was selected the university architect in 1907 and served in that capacity until 1930.[32] Wilson's ideals of educating American men for national

[30] WW to Alexander Van Rensselaer, Jan. 13, 1904, *PWW*, xv, 123; WW to Edward Wright Sheldon, *c.* March 30, 1904, *ibid.*, p. 219.

[31] D. B. Jones to WW, Oct. 24, 1903 and March 15 and July 5, 1904, *ibid.*, pp. 28-29, ns. 1 and 3, 191-93, 405-406, n. 3; WW to Robert Garrett, June 29, 1904, *ibid.*, p. 397; Trustees' Minutes, Dec. 8, 1904, *ibid.*, pp. 569-70.

[32] R. Garrett to Archibald Douglas Russell, Jan. 26, 1907, printed as an Enclosure with R. Garrett to WW, Jan. 26, 1907, *ibid.*, xvii, 19-21; WW to R. Garrett, Feb. 13, 1907, *ibid.*, pp. 35-36; WW to A. D. Russell, Feb. 13, 1907, *ibid.*, pp. 36-37; Trustees' Minutes, March 14, 1907, *ibid.*, pp. 71-72; Ralph Adams Cram to WW, March 28, 1907, *ibid.*, pp. 96-97.

service in the twentieth century clashed with buildings reflecting a late medieval ethos, but Wilson saw no incongruity. The house he built in 1896 was constructed as a Tudor manor house, and he saw Tudor Gothic as a means of linking Princeton with centuries of tradition. "We have declared and acknowledged our derivation and lineage," he maintained. "We have said, 'This is the spirit in which we have been bred'; and as the imagination, as the recollection of classes yet to be graduated from Princeton are affected by the suggestions of that architecture, we shall find the past of this country married with the past of the world and shall know with what destiny we have come into the forefront of the nations."[33]

Despite Wilson's success as a fund-raiser, he seemed remarkably unconcerned with the university's financial affairs. In the eight years of his presidency, Princeton's budget nearly tripled, jumping from about $225,000 to more than $700,000. The Committee of Fifty's contributions helped to offset these costs, but Wilson's pursuit of excellence at Princeton brought increasing expenditures and continuous deficits, which were quietly made up by wealthy trustees.[34] Wilson himself preferred the exalted role of Princeton's prime minister to the demeaning position of the university's penurious beggar, and his achievements in raising money were in large measure due to his ability to generate support from alumni who were stirred by his ideals for Princeton.

Like his political thought, Wilson's educational philosophy retained the same profound tension between individualism and organicism, and at different points during his presidency he emphasized one to the exclusion of the other or tried to strike some kind of accommodation between them. During his early years as president, Wilson realized that he was confronted with an unruly student body, lax academic standards, a chaotic curriculum, and a faculty grown relaxed under Patton's laissez-faire leadership. Just as he responded to the social turmoil of the 1890's, Wilson reacted by insisting on the need for recreating an organic community. Order, wholeness, coherence, direction, authority—these became the distinguishing characteristics of his first academic reforms at Princeton and the prevailing notes of his public addresses and alumni speeches.

In this respect, Wilson's election to the presidency prompted a sudden shift away from his emphases on individualism and freedom during the late 1890's. The man who had hailed the frontier spirit as the quintessence of Americanism dramatically reversed his field, arguing that the "gist" of the university was its goal of community life. "It is absolutely necessary that the American university should be a compact

[33] Address to the Princeton Alumni of New York, Dec. 9, 1902, *ibid.*, xiv, 269.

[34] Treasurer's Reports, 1902-1910 (University Archives, NjP).

and homogeneous community. The individualistic spirit is not American."[35] Repeatedly he stressed that the university was "a community of ideals" and that its function was "to make Idealists."[36]

Earlier Wilson had sought to understand the state as an organic community united by common beliefs and traditions, and he similarly viewed the university as bound by its shared values. The *Daily Princetonian* summarized these convictions which he expressed at the paper's annual banquet. "The real Princeton spirit," Wilson told the students, "is that which binds us together by agreement on the great principles to which our lives are devoted. The bond of union is that community of thought which comes from sharing a purpose in the things that are worth while, from concerted action in the things we believe in."[37]

Although Wilson was convinced that ideals unified Princeton from within and gave it its distinctive character, he was also aware that outside the university differing ideals clashed for supremacy. By temperament and conviction, he saw a college education as moral training, molding and disciplining the student for moral combat in the world. Throughout his speeches on education, athletic and military imagery predominated, and the college man appeared as a moral athlete or Christian soldier. He saw the university as "the pacemaker for the mind," showing it "the pace that it must strike at the outset if it would keep a winning gait throughout all process of endeavor."[38] A college, he believed, was really a mental gymnasium, exercising the mind. "Study of any kind disciplines the mental faculties and makes them supple and better fitted to tackle problems." He urged students to get their minds in shape because "the gymnastics of the mind fit it for all that the world needs done." "Beware of the man who has his mind in athletic shape," he solemnly warned.[39]

Such a man would be prepared to see the world as a whole and to fight the battle of ideals. With the same fervor that marked his youthful essay on "Christ's Army," Wilson declared, "We must know each other and form ourselves into armies of peace, armies of thought, ar-

---

[35] News report of a speech at the Brooklyn Institute of Arts and Sciences, Dec. 12, 1902, *PWW*, XIV, 283-84.

[36] News report of a speech, "The National and University Life," April 18, 1903, *ibid.*, p. 416; notes for a speech to the Schoolmasters Association of New York and Vicinity, Oct. 8, 1904, *ibid.*, XV, 506.

[37] News report, March 23, 1905, *ibid.*, XVI, 36.

[38] "The Relation of University Education to Commerce," Nov. 29, 1902, *ibid.*, XIV, 238.

[39] Interview in the New York *Herald*, June 11, 1905, *ibid.*, XVI, 117; news report of a speech at the Northeast Manual Training School in Philadelphia, Nov. 18, 1905, *ibid.*, p. 226; see also news reports of speeches in Kansas City, Missouri, and Youngstown, Ohio, May 12, 1905, and April 1906, *ibid.*, pp. 98-100, 354-55.

mies of ideals, that are ready to shed their life's blood toward its realization."[40] What was needed was leadership and statesmanship for an age of confusion and doubt.

> We are come upon a new thirteenth century, a new age of discovery, where the voyage is not by the old seas or across unknown continents in search of fabulous cities, but out upon the great shadowy main of the mind's life, where the battle is being fought for existence in the maintenance of ideals, for the deciphering of morals, for the clearing away of doubts and alarms; where, when the battle is over, a day of high anticipation shall dawn, and men shall see again the visions of belief, feel again the certitude of hope.[41]

College men could provide that leadership and statesmanship, for they were "the trustees of America's morals."[42]

As a leader of those trustees, Wilson set out promptly to tighten discipline at Princeton and raise academic standards. During his first year as president, he wrote to the secretaries of various classes asking them to curb the excessive drinking at commencement reunions. He also became concerned about the lax administration of entrance examinations.[43] The current dean of the faculty that first year was Samuel Ross Winans, a holdover from the Patton regime, so Wilson took the lead in enforcing academic requirements. During the first semester of 1902-1903, forty-six students were expelled from Princeton for academic reasons, and the *Alumni Weekly* observed, "The campus view of it seems to be that with the new administration a Draconian policy has come in." A campus humor magazine printed a cartoon showing Wilson sitting on the deserted steps of Nassau Hall and covered with cobwebs. The caption, parodying a popular whisky advertisement, read, "1910 That's All!"[44]

In 1903, Wilson's friend, Henry Burchard Fine, joined the administration as academic dean, and the tough new policy continued. In his first report to the Board, Fine dryly noted, "We have as fine and clean a body of undergraduates as any in the land and . . . to keep them clean, as orderly as is necessary, and properly attentive to their college duties, we do not need new and more stringent rules and regulations,

---

[40] News report of a speech to the Princeton Alumni in Washington, D. C., March 28, 1903, *ibid.*, XIV, 403.

[41] "The Statesmanship of Letters," Nov. 5, 1903, *ibid.*, XV, 36.

[42] News report of a speech to the Wesleyan University Club of New York, Dec. 9, 1905, *ibid.*, XVI, 244.

[43] WW to the secretaries of various classes of Princeton University, c. May 10, 1903, *ibid.*, XIV, 455-56; Lawrence Cameron Hull to WW, Dec. 11, 1902, *ibid.*, p. 278.

[44] News item, March 7, 1903, *ibid.*, p. 383; cartoon reprinted in *ibid.*, p. 384.

but the strict and fair enforcement of the rules we already have." When students refused to obey, Fine said, there was only one solution— dismissal.[45] After only one year Fine could report, "The strict enforcement of the rules of scholarship is lessening the number of men who fall below the passing mark."[46]

Wilson and the faculty also tightened up the honor system because, as he told the students, certain rules had "fallen too much in neglect."[47] Wilson did, however, relax one requirement that the students found particularly onerous. In 1905, the faculty approved a revision of the chapel regulation, making attendance mandatory on Sundays and twice a week at daily services.[48] Wilson even enforced moral discipline on the Board of Trustees. In 1905, the Equitable Life Assurance Society was implicated in a scandal involving the mismanagement and abuse of company funds. Two Princeton trustees, John J. McCook and Charles B. Alexander, served as directors and legal counsel to the company, and Wilson personally demanded and received their resignations from the Princeton Board.[49]

In the first years of his presidency, Wilson also succeeded in reforming the administrative structure of the university. In June 1903, he received authorization from the trustees to reorganize the faculty, and eleven departments were created with chairmen who reported annually to the president.[50] This was the first step in an even more far-reaching reform of the entire curriculum. In the autumn of 1903, Wilson requested each departmental chairman to formulate an ideal curriculum for their course of study,[51] and a faculty committee, headed by Wilson and Andrew Fleming West, presented its report in April 1904.[52] After a series of meetings, and some amendments, the new course of study was adopted.[53] "There was singularly little debate,—practically none at all, only informal canvassing of details," Wilson wrote to Ellen. "Everyone seemed to accept the *principle* of the report and all the main features of the scheme at once and without cavil; and the final adoption

[45] H. B. Fine to the Trustees' Committee on Morals and Discipline, Oct. 21, 1903, *ibid.*, xv, 20-21. In his first semester as dean, Fine expelled seventy-five students. See H. B. Fine to the Trustees' Committee on Morals and Discipline, March 10, 1904, *ibid.*, pp. 186-88.

[46] H. B. Fine to the Trustees' Committee on Morals and Discipline, Oct. 21, 1904, *ibid.*, pp. 523-24.

[47] WW to the Editor of the *Daily Princetonian*, c. Feb. 10, 1904, *ibid.*, p. 164.

[48] H. B. Fine to the Trustees' Committee on Morals and Discipline, Oct. 21, 1905, *ibid.*, xvi, 200-203.

[49] John James McCook to the Trustees, Feb. 5, 1906, *ibid.*, p. 303; Charles Beatty Alexander to the Trustees, Feb. 5, 1906, *ibid.*, p. 304, n. 1.

[50] Curriculum Committee to the Trustees, June 5, 1903, *ibid.*, xiv, 474; WW to the Trustees, Dec. 10, 1903, *ibid.*, xv, 73-74.

[51] See for example John Howell Westcott to WW, Oct. 19, 1903, *ibid.*, pp. 17-19, n. 1.

[52] Report of the Committee on the Course of Study, April 16, 1904, *ibid.*, pp. 252-63.

[53] Faculty Minutes, April 19, 21, 22, 25, 1904, *ibid.*, pp. 293-95.

was characterized by real cordiality. All of which makes me very happy. It is not, as it stands now, exactly the scheme I at the outset proposed, but it is much better."[54]

Princeton's new course of study stood in striking contrast to both its earlier curriculum and those of other institutions. Harvard, Cornell, Stanford, and other colleges offered students a virtually free elective system, and Columbia provided a three-year bachelor's degree program. Wilson rejected the abbreviated college course and considered free electives antithetical to a well-defined liberal education. The chief characteristics of the new Princeton program were its integration of all degree programs; a comprehensive series of required courses with limited freedom of selection during the last two years; concentrations in a particular field for juniors and seniors; and the creation of the new degree of Bachelor of Letters for students who lacked proficiency in Greek.[55]

Wilson's ideas for reforming the curriculum were hardly new, for he had warned the Board of the need for action in his first report in October 1902.[56] In its provisions for liberal, nonprofessional studies and carefully regulated course programs, the curriculum embodied Wilson's ideal of the university—the place where the unity of knowledge was conveyed and preserved, the source of a broad vision of human beings and society. In further reorganizing the university into departments with appointed chairmen, Wilson boldly clarified lines of authority and extended his own control over all phases of academic life. Taken together, these two actions represented Wilson's reaction against the chaotic administrative procedures of his predecessor and his characteristic desire for clearly defined order, structure, coherence, and authority. "It was high time that the various courses of the University should have some sort of co-ordination and sequence," Wilson told the alumni at the 1904 commencement. ". . . We believe that in study as in everything else there must be guidance by those who have had experience, and submission to guidance by those who have had none."[57] The plan was well received, Wilson told the Board, "even by that arch conservative the undergraduate himself."[58]

---

[54] WW to EAW, April 26, 1904, *ibid.*, p. 296. Wilson also told Ellen that Patton claimed to admire the plans but had *"some* cynical remarks." "Perhaps," he noted, "he does not foresee that they will involve a good deal more work for George," Patton's son and professor of philosophy. WW to EAW, May 6, 1904, *ibid.*, p. 312.

[55] Editorial Note, The New Princeton Course of Study, *ibid.*, pp. 277-92; for discussions of Wilson's educational policy, see Laurence R. Veysey, "The Academic Mind of Woodrow Wilson," *Mississippi Valley Historical Review*, XLIX (1963), 613-34, and Bragdon, *Wilson: The Academic Years*, pp. 287-311.

[56] WW to the Trustees, Oct. 21, 1902, *PWW*, XIV, 152.

[57] Speech at an alumni luncheon, June 14, 1904, *ibid.*, XV, 379.

[58] WW to the Trustees, Dec. 8, 1904, *ibid.*, p. 565.

The themes of order and authority which predominate in Wilson's reform of the curriculum reveal how thoroughly covenantal modes of thought had influenced his own basic assumptions. In formulating a philosophy of education which sought an inclusive conception of the world, Wilson was remaining true to a basic impulse in the covenant theological tradition. Drawing again on geographical imagery, he declared, "We must make for a student a sort of circle of knowledge, and when he goes around that circle he has boxed the compass."[59] Wilson had no doubts about who should provide the direction or define the circle of knowledge. Authority lay with the teacher, not the student. "It is the teacher's duty," he insisted, "to lay before the pupil the compass and chart and show him where men have explored and where the dark continents of thought lay."[60]

However, within the covenant tradition and Wilson's own thought, there was a tension between power and order on the one hand and freedom and shared authority on the other. In both his religious and political thought, Wilson vacillated between these two poles. When disorder threatened him personally or the organic nature of society, he responded by stressing the need for integration and power. When disorder subsided and power appeared to become coercive, he emphasized freedom and individualism.

Similarly, as Princeton's educational statesman, Wilson moved from his policies of rigorous curricular requirements and clear administrative control toward recovering an element of individuality and creativity in the educational process. Wilson realized, as he announced to the Board in 1904, that "the acquisition of information is, indeed, not education at all; that education is a training necessary in advance of information, a process of putting the mind in condition to assimilate information and know what to do with it when it is acquired: that ideas, principles, schemes of thought, and methods of investigation govern facts and determine their place and value."[61] The result was one of Wilson's most constructive innovations at Princeton—the preceptorial plan.

The model for Wilson's preceptors was obviously the tutorial system at Oxford and Cambridge. And yet, as in so many things, Wilson's concept of the preceptorial plan was largely a product of his own experience. In attempting to break down the barriers between student and teacher through preceptors who lived and worked with students, Wil-

[59] News report of a speech at the Northeast Manual Training School in Philadelphia, Nov. 18, 1905, *ibid.*, xvi, 226.

[60] News report of a speech at the Brooklyn Institute of Arts and Sciences, Dec. 12, 1902, *ibid.*, xiv, 285.

[61] WW to the Trustees, Dec. 8, 1904, *ibid.*, xv, 562.

son sought to recreate the intimate educational training he had received from his "greatest teacher"—his father. In addition, his undergraduate education at Princeton took place largely outside the classroom, prompting him to remark in 1903, "I have always believed that the best work of a college was done between the hours of 6 in the evening and 9 in the morning, when the men worked their effects upon each other."[62]

In spelling out his ideas, Wilson emphasized that preceptorial instruction represented "a radical change of method," not merely a supplement to professors' lectures. "The governing idea is to be that [students] are getting up *subjects*—getting them up with the assistance of lecturers, libraries, and a body of preceptors who are their guides, philosophers, and friends," Wilson explained. "The process is intended to be one of reading, comparing, reflecting; not cramming, but daily methodical study."[63]

He told the students that more written work would be required and that each would be assigned to a preceptor who would guide his reading. While making courses more demanding, Wilson insisted that the purpose of the plan was to create a partnership between faculty and students and free the student for creative academic work. The preceptor, he believed, would "bring out and strengthen the individual characteristics of each man." Wilson promised that students would make a major discovery. "It is really a pleasure to use your mind, if you have one, and many a man who now never dreams what fun it is to have ideas and to explore the world of thought, may be expected, in his intercourse with his preceptors, to find learning a rare form of enjoyment, the use of his faculties a new indulgence. He may even discover his soul, and find its spiritual relations to the world of men and affairs."[64]

Wilson forged ahead with the preceptorial plan, even though the estimated $2.5 million in endowment necessary for it had not been raised, and in the spring of 1905 he made his first appointments. In finding the candidates, Wilson sought men who were sociable and who would mix easily with the students. He clearly intended that they should have the background and social standing which would merge easily with the middle- and upper-class breeding of most Princeton students. They would be selected, he contended, "primarily upon their standing as gentlemen," and "if their qualities as gentlemen and as

[62] News report of a speech in Lowell, Mass., Jan. 3, 1903, *ibid.*, xiv, 316.

[63] WW to the Trustees, Oct. 21, 1902, *ibid.*, p. 153; "The Princeton Preceptorial System," *c.* June 1, 1905, *ibid.*, xvi, 108.

[64] "The Preceptors," April 28, 1905, *ibid.*, pp. 84-85; speech to the University Press Club banquet, April 17, 1905, *ibid.*, p. 62; "New Plans for Princeton," June 24, 1905, *ibid.*, p. 149.

scholars conflict, the former will win them the place." He also wanted preceptors who were committed to Princeton and loyal to its ideals, "who feel a certain love for the place, and who are in entire sympathy with its spirit, and understand the scope of the plan which is being developed."[65]

Fortunately, in many cases he found gentlemen who were also scholars, many of whom went on to distinguished careers at Princeton and other institutions. Wilson evoked from them a deep personal commitment; as one preceptor recalled his initial interview, "I had never before talked face to face with so compelling a person. Before the talk was over my loyalties were entirely committed to him. Had Woodrow Wilson asked me to go with him and work under him while he inaugurated a new university in Kamchatka or Senegambia I would have said 'yes' without further question."[66]

Wilson had the same ability to attract excellent teachers and scholars to the senior positions in the faculty. He invigorated the faculty in both the sciences and the humanities with several important appointments: Harry Augustus Garfield in politics; Frank Thilly in philosophy; James Hopwood Jeans in mathematics; Edwin Grant Conklin in biology; Frank Frost Abbott and Edward Capps in classics; Owen Willans Richardson in physics. These men accepted positions to a great degree because of Wilson's own appeal. When Capps arrived on the campus, he asked Conklin, "What brought you to Princeton?" Conklin replied, "Woodrow Wilson, and what brought you here?" "The same," Capps said.[67]

Wilson's method of making faculty appointments contrasted sharply with Patton's and signaled a decisive new development in the administration of Princeton University. Patton had assiduously obtained the approval of the trustees' Curriculum Committee before any professors were named, and he occasionally even offered two or three candidates for the committee's decision. However, beginning with the appointment of Harry Augustus Garfield as Professor of Politics in 1903, Wilson took control over all faculty hiring away from the Board. After consulting with departmental heads and other concerned faculty members, he made the appointments and simply submitted candidates to the Board for *pro forma* approval. On one occasion, he was tempted to

[65] Speech to the University Press Club banquet, April 17, 1905, *ibid.*, p. 62; see also WW to Hamilton Holt, June 7, 1905, *ibid.*, pp. 110-11; and H. B. Fine to WW, July 29 and Aug. 12, 1905, *ibid.*, pp. 163-65, 178-79.

[66] Robert K. Root, "Wilson and the Preceptors," *Woodrow Wilson: Some Princeton Memories,* William Starr Meyers, ed. (Princeton, 1946), p. 15.

[67] Edwin Grant Conklin, "As a Scientist Saw Him," *ibid.*, p. 59.

name his nephew George Howe to the faculty, but Ellen Wilson finally prevailed against it, fearing possible charges of nepotism.[68]

In light of Wilson's hostility to science prior to his election as president, perhaps his most surprising reform was the foundation that he built for Princeton's later achievements in scientific study. As his major faculty appointments reveal, Wilson saw that Princeton needed distinguished scientists to become a major American university. These additions to the faculty, as well as the funds provided for research, equipment, and buildings, represent one of Wilson's most enlightened and enduring contributions to Princeton's development. In this work, Wilson's policy was guided and spurred by Henry B. Fine, whom Wilson appointed as Dean of the Departments of Science in 1909. But the achievement is also a tribute to Wilson's capacity for change and his openness to scientific inquiry. In fact, as Wilson looked back on his presidency in 1910, he rated the improvements in scientific study as one of the distinguishing features of his administration.[69]

Wilson's early reforms, especially the preceptorial plan, were widely regarded as important innovations in American academic life. The campus view of the preceptorial system was enthusiastic, the *Nassau Literary Magazine* pronouncing it "generally even universally popular." The trustees' Curriculum Committee reported that faculty and students had "given it the hearty co-operation of work which it has demanded from their hands" and predicted that the new reforms were "likely to prove a reformation to University education in this country little less than revolution."[70]

The reforms raised Princeton to a position of new prominence in the estimation of many academics; in 1906 the principal of Phillips Academy Andover declared, "For over a year I have felt strongly that Princeton bade fair not only to equal the other institutions of her class, but possibly to wrest from them the leadership in scholarship and the best kind of college spirit. . . . If Princeton by her tutorial system is able to save the universities and large colleges from ignoring the individual and the deeds of the individual, she will have done a splendid thing for the higher American education."[71]

[68] David Ruddach Frazer to WW, Oct. 23, 1903, *PWW*, xv, 26, n. 2; EAW to WW, April 26, 1903, *ibid.*, xiv, 428-29; WW to EAW, April 29, 1903, *ibid.*, pp. 434-35.

[69] See for example Wilson's address to the Princeton Alumni Association of Maryland, March 11, 1910, *ibid.*, xx, 232-33.

[70] Bragdon, *Wilson: The Academic Years*, p. 307; Curriculum Committee to the Trustees, *c*. June 11, 1906 and *c*. June 12, 1905, *PWW*, xvi, 421, 128.

[71] Alfred Ernest Stearns to Charles Grosvenor Osgood, Nov. 15, 1906, *ibid.*, p. 486; see also Melancthon William Jacobus to WW, Dec. 20, 1905, *ibid.*, pp. 273-74.

Some people considered Wilson's preceptorial plan part of "the great *democratic* movement in modern American education and American University life,"[72] but despite his emphasis on recovering individualism in education, Wilson hardly transformed Princeton into a democratic institution available to students of all economic strata. Wilson himself admitted that Princeton was "in danger of becoming regarded, to her great detriment and discredit, as one of the most expensive places in the country at which a student can take up residence,"[73] but he did little to insure that the university broadened the composition of the student body. Princeton did make scholarship grants, but only in the form of loans, and while Wilson professed his admiration for those willing to work to pay for their education, he considered it "every man's duty to choose the sort of work which will maintain his self-respect and social standing."[74] Wilson intended that Princeton produce intellectual leaders—"a certain number of men to see life and its affairs with a comprehensive and comprehending view"[75]—but the economic facts of student life at Princeton meant that this intellectual aristocracy was a social aristocracy as well.

Wilson also preserved Princeton's reputation as the Ivy League college most congenial to Southerners. In 1904, Wilson declared, "I would say that, while there is nothing in the law of the University to prevent a negro's entering, the whole temper and tradition of the place are such that no negro has ever applied for admission, and it seems extremely unlikely that the question will ever assume a practical form." Wilson's confidence was substantiated by the evidence; no black student had enrolled at Princeton up to that time. But in 1909 Wilson had to face the issue directly. "I want so much to come to your school at Princeton," G. McArthur Sullivan wrote to Wilson. "I am a poor Southern colored man from South Carolina, but I believe I can make make [*sic*] my way if I am permitted to come. Please Sir, send me a catalog and information as to whether a colored man may enter there." Wilson drew the line sharply, advising Sullivan that it was "altogether inadvisable for a colored man to enter Princeton," and suggesting that he pursue his education in the South. The university secretary told Sullivan that if he was intent upon studying in the North, he might consider Harvard, Dartmouth, and especially Brown because it was "a Baptist Institution."[76]

[72] M. W. Jacobus to WW, March 26, 1909, *ibid.*, XIX, 122.

[73] WW to the Trustees, Oct. 21, 1902, *ibid.*, XIV, 160.

[74] Trustees' Minutes, Oct. 7, 1903, *ibid.*, XV, 14-15; WW to Morgan Poitiaux Robinson, Oct. 30, 1903, *ibid.*, p. 32.

[75] "Princeton's New Plan of Study," *c.* Aug. 29, 1904, *ibid.*, p. 455.

[76] WW to John Rogers Williams, Sept. 2, 1904, *ibid.*, p. 462, n. 2; G. McArthur Sullivan to WW, Nov. 20, 1909, *ibid.*, XIX, 529; WW draft letter to G. M. Sullivan, *c.* Dec. 3, 1909, *ibid.*,

Wilson's adherence to an old Princeton tradition was a reflection of even deeper racist feelings. He reacted strongly against President Theodore Roosevelt's appointment of Dr. William D. Crum as Collector of the Port of Charleston, S. C., and Mrs. Minnie M. Cox as postmistress of Indianola, Mississippi. In February 1903, Wilson told a group of amused Baltimore alumni that the ground hog had gone back into his hole that year because he was afraid the President would put a "coon" in. Privately, he told some friends that Crum's appointment was intolerable to white merchants—"too much for them to stand." He believed that individual Negroes were "splendid" but that they were exceptions. Social intercourse among whites and blacks, Wilson feared, would bring about intermarriage that "would degrade the white nations, for in Africa the blacks were the only race who did not rise."[77]

Wilson's revitalizing of Princeton's academic life obscures one important aspect of his educational philosophy. He was convinced that, while colleges could be restructured and reorganized, education remained the transmission of ideas which could not be institutionalized. In this regard, his educational and religious ideas were inextricably linked, for he believed that education was basically spiritual in character, recreating individuals and providing the values by which they could live. "The function of our universities," he told students at the University of Michigan, "is in essence, a vehicle of spirit to enable you to discover your souls and use them in the service of your fellowmen, to see your opportunities, and to know how wide they are in the pursuit of truth."[78]

Wilson's educational and religious speeches are virtually indistinguishable, for he repeatedly focused on the same two themes—the spirituality of education and the gospel of service. "In educating a man you are dealing with his spirit, and nothing but his spirit," he told the Princeton alumni in Tennessee, and "when you deal with a man's spirit you are dealing with his career." He fervently believed that "learning, pure learning," was "the salvation of the race," and called upon the alumni to become idealists because only ideals survived.[79]

He liked to describe universities as "the nurseries of the nation's ideals" and believed that a college education would recreate and transform the individual. "It is through the instrumentality of the University

p. 550; Charles Williston McAlpin to G. M. Sullivan, Dec. 6, 1909, *ibid.*, pp. 557-58. There were black students who had attended Princeton, but they were enrolled at Princeton Theological Seminary and took courses at the university.

[77] News report, Feb. 14, 1903, *ibid.*, XIV, 358; Diary of Mary Yates, July 31, 1908, *ibid.*, XVIII, 386.

[78] News report, April 1, 1905, *ibid.*, XVI, 45.

[79] News reports, Nov. 29, 1905, and Oct. 28, 1906, *ibid.*, pp. 237, 477.

that men are stripped of wrong impulses, and are brought to see true conditions and true standards of life by means of research and investigation," he told the Philadelphian Society. ". . . Thus a man who has sought out the mysteries of life, who sees the truth of things, who has heard many voices of counsel, will not be overcome by the voices of uproar in the day of adversity, but will be able to look beyond his immediate surroundings and see and know that an overruling Providence is above all things."[80]

Wilson considered religion an indispensable part of this spiritual education, particularly at Princeton, which he said had always been known as "a place of sound religion."[81] As president, Wilson performed many religious duties, from officiating at the Sunday worship services in Marquand Chapel to speaking at the daily services and before religious groups. He was also charged with the responsibility of recruiting and entertaining the Sunday preachers, a task made difficult by Wilson's critical standards of homiletical skill. "We have not been fortunate enough to find a great many preachers who can give our men the kind of sermons that seem the only kind worth while," he told Anson Phelps Stokes, Jr., secretary of Yale University. His choices were overwhelmingly from the Presbyterian Church, and his favorite was J. Sparhawk Jones of Baltimore. In evaluating preachers, Wilson looked with a discerning eye. Concerning W. Robson Notman of the Fourth Presbyterian Church of Chicago, Wilson wrote, "He is in no sense a master of the phrase. The details of his sermons do not satisfy one, but somehow in the bulk each sermon of his seems to lift you to a fine and impressive view, and I consider him an important element in our variety." His acerbic comments extended even to members of the Princeton faculty. "Henry van Dyke preached in chapel," he noted in his diary, "with his usual charm and superficiality."[82]

What Wilson demanded in preachers was a sense of spiritual authority and genuine conviction. "Much of the prevailing unbelief of the young people of today, I am firmly convinced, is due to the analytic and doubting preachers of our pulpits," he declared in 1904. ". . . Are you going to believe a doctrine which has a great question mark around it? . . . Youth respects authority. If you doubt what you say, those who listen to you will doubt, and if you disbelieve, those who listen to you

---

[80] Notes for a speech at Princeton, Nov. 2, 1906, *ibid.*, p. 479; news report, Nov. 7, 1902, *ibid.*, XIV, 201, 202.

[81] Notes for a speech welcoming the American Philosophical Association to its meeting in Princeton, Dec. 29, 1903, *ibid.*, XV, 111.

[82] WW to Daniel Moreau Barringer, Sept. 16, 1902, *ibid.*, XIV, 131-32, n. 1; WW to Anson Phelps Stokes, April 30 and May 3, 1907, *ibid.*, XVII, 125-26, 129-30; Diary, Jan. 17, 1904, *ibid.*, XV, 134.

will disbelieve."[83] Yet he had no patience with rigid dogmatism, believing instead that "between the ages of eighteen and twenty-two you create doubt by ramming dogma down the throat."[84]

Despite his deep Presbyterian heritage, Wilson was not a sectarian, maintaining that "the day of the battle of creeds" was over and that "it was spiritual amusement for us to split hairs." He took specific issue with Patton's description of Princeton as "a Presbyterian college" and candidly noted that it was Presbyterian only in the sense that "the Presbyterians of New Jersey were wise and progressive enough to found it." During his administration, Princeton was formally declared a nonsectarian institution, and the act was not mere rhetoric. Just as Wilson had defended his uncle James Woodrow's right to espouse Darwinian theories of evolution and fought to have the Unitarian Frederick Jackson Turner appointed to the faculty, he also tried to attract scholars to Princeton without regard for the religious beliefs. In 1904 he appointed the first Jew to Princeton's faculty, Horace Meyer Kallen, and in 1909, the Roman Catholic David A. McCabe joined the teaching staff.[85]

In one important area, Wilson took decisive steps to remove the aura of fundamentalism from Princeton. Patton had achieved prominence and notoriety within the Presbyterian Church by his involvement in the famous Swing heresy case and by his rigorous defense of conservative Presbyterianism.[86] Wilson apparently felt that Patton's approach to religious instruction was detrimental to academic freedom, and when he became president, he took immediate action. Before 1902, Patton had handled most of the biblical courses at Princeton, but after his resignation as president, all biblical instruction was temporarily eliminated. Patton and his son, George Stevenson Patton, were restricted to offering courses in ethics. Indeed, it was not until 1905 when Lucius Hop-

[83] News report of a speech to the Philadelphia Sabbath School Association, Feb. 27, 1905, *ibid.*, p. 179.

[84] *New York Tribune*, Dec. 2, 1902.

[85] *Ibid.*; news reports of speeches to the Presbyterian Unions of Baltimore and New York, Dec. 5 and 2, 1902, *PWW*, XIV, 261, 253; Trustees' Minutes, Oct. 20, 1906, *ibid.*, XVI, 468-69; WW to the Trustees, Jan. 1, 1910, *ibid.*, XIX, 678. Kallen, who later achieved prominence as a leading Zionist and a founder of the New School for Social Research, stayed at Princeton for only one year. His obituary in the *New York Times* suggested that he was dismissed from the faculty because he was an avowed unbeliever. There is no evidence in the Wilson papers that Wilson participated in a decision to dismiss Kallen or that he was fired because of his religious beliefs. See the *New York Times*, Feb. 17, 1974. Yet Wilson's ecumenism had its limits, for he felt very uncomfortable presiding at a service conducted by an Anglo-Catholic priest. WW to EAW, March 21, 1904, *PWW*, XV, 201, ns. 4, 5.

[86] See Lefferts A. Loetscher, *The Broadening Church* (Philadelphia, 1954), *passim*; William R. Hutchison, "Disapproval of Chicago: The Symbolic Trial of David Swing," *Journal of American History*, LIX (1972), 30-47.

kins Miller was appointed Assistant Professor of Biblical Instruction that courses in the Bible were again offered. However, even then, they were offered outside of the departmental structure of the curriculum.[87]

Although Wilson had little patience with the rigid dogmatism that Patton represented, his larger goal was religious instruction that was academic and scholarly. There may also have been a more practical motivation, for Wilson could not afford religious disputes at the university while he pursued his program of reform. But his attitude toward religion at Princeton was also deeper than merely expedient admistrative policy. He was convinced, as his father had said, that faith was "an affair of the heart" and that religion was not finally susceptible to academic analysis. "Religion cannot be handled like learning," he wrote in *The Handbook of Princeton*.

> It is a matter of individual conviction and its source is the heart. Its life and vigour must lie, not in official recognition or fosterage, but in the temper and character of the undergraduates themselves. That religion lies at the heart of Princeton's life is shown, not in the teachings of the class room and of the chapel pulpit, but in the widespread, spontaneous, unflagging religious activity of the undergraduates themselves. . . . Sound and liberal learning and equally sound and liberal religion lie together at the foundation of all that her sons most admire in the University.[88]

In his numerous religious speeches both at Princeton and throughout the nation, Wilson sought to create that spirit. One newspaper even labeled this Presbyterian elder the "Rev. Dr. Woodrow Wilson," and as Arthur Walworth has said, he became the "university pastor."[89]

Repeatedly Wilson sounded the themes of service and the power of spiritual ideals. There were only two motives in life—self-aggrandizement and service, he told the Trenton, New Jersey, YMCA. "The one motive for service is love. If you would know the true spirit of love, love something greater than yourself and catch its glory."[90] He sought to portray the Christian faith as a power which pervaded a person's thoughts, will, and actions. "Neither men nor society can be saved by opinions," he stated. "Nothing has power to prevail but the conviction which commands, not the mind merely, but the will and the whole spirit as well." He saw in John Wesley a figure who embodied the power of faith and used it to extend God's influence in the world.

---

[87] See the *Catalog of Princeton University* for the late 1890's through 1906; WW to Lucius Hopkins Miller, March 18, 1903, *PWW*, xiv, 396, n. 3.

[88] Introduction to *The Handbook of Princeton*, c. Aug. 1, 1904, *ibid.*, xv, 428-29.

[89] News report of a speech about the YMCA in Pittsburgh, Pa., Nov. 23, 1908, *ibid.*, xviii, 521; Walworth, *Woodrow Wilson*, p. 84.

[90] News report, Feb. 9, 1903, *ibid.*, xiv, 355.

Characteristically mixing political and religious terms, Wilson described Wesley as "a sort of spiritual statesman, a politician of God, speaking the policy of a kingdom unseen, but real and destined to prevail over all kingdoms else."[91]

On occasion, Wilson demonstrated how the trauma of 1896 had softened some of the harsh aspects of his religion of service and duty. Using Romans 7 as his text, he told the Philadelphian Society in 1903 that individuals ought to serve in newness of spirit, not in the oldness of the letter of the law. In a speech in 1906 at Hartford Theological Seminary, he stated that the tasks of the ministry were impossible to perform "except by the influence and power of the Holy Spirit." "The beauty of the Gospel," Wilson said, "is that it is a Gospel which leaves us, not the barren hope that in our own strength we can be useful, but the splendid, fruitful hope that there is One who if we but rely upon Him can inform us with these things and make our spirits to be the true spirits of God."[92]

Even some of the dichotomy between his political and religious thought began to disappear, for Wilson could not deny a role for the church in realizing ideals in the world. "The salvation of the individual is made largely dependent on the salvation of society, and this can only be done by co-operation and mutual helpfulness," he said in 1903. "[The Church] is called upon to keep alive the social instinct which is the instinct of unselfishness and co-operation. The sympathy of the Church with society is the highest expression of the Church's life, and the application of these principals of her spirit can save society from sordidness and greed."[93]

More common, however, were the familiar themes of the individual's duty to obey God's law, the call to unselfish service, and the need to remain true to ideals. Wilson solemnly admonished the graduates of 1903, "As you enter life's hard paths do not seek after success, but strive for honor, remembering that honorable success is the only real success. . . . You may not have wealth or great influence, but you have got the knowledge of Christ's power and love, so there is no excuse for not seeing what is your duty and doing what is right."[94] The senior class in 1904 asked Wilson to deliver the baccalaureate sermon; he accepted and preached at every baccalaureate service but one until his resignation in 1910.[95] He frequently used this "day of reckoning," as

[91] "John Wesley's Place in History," June 30, 1903, *ibid.*, pp. 514, 506-507.

[92] News report, Oct. 2, 1903, *ibid.*, xv, 10; "The Minister and the Community," March 30, 1906, *ibid.*, xvi, 351.

[93] News report of an address at the Second Presbyterian Church of Philadelphia, Dec. 14, 1903, *ibid.*, xv, 98-99.

[94] News report, June 10, 1903, *ibid.*, xiv, 484.

[95] News item, March 5, 1904, *ibid.*, xv, 182. Only illness prevented Wilson from fulfilling his obligation in 1906.

he called it, to impress once again upon the Princeton students the necessity of remaining true to moral ideals amidst the temptations of life.

His first sermon set the stage for the ones that followed, and his chosen text was apt: "And they shall fight against thee: but they shall not prevail against thee: for I am with thee, saith the Lord, to deliver thee" (Jeremiah 1:19). "It is our modern philosophy," Wilson declared,

> that virtue is not for the cloister and the convent but for the open field and the dusty road and every place of work and intercourse: for the cleansing of the world and the deliverance of those who toil in it. God is abroad, not shut up behind conventicle walls; and the college man ought to be the best man among the men of God, because by training and enlightenment a citizen of the world of good and evil. It is no doubt ordained that the world shall be saved, not only by the foolishness of preaching, but also by the courage of action and the satisfying nobility of unimpeachable conduct; and colleges cannot make serviceable men unless they make men of brains also men of principle.[96]

College had been their training ground, Wilson said, not a surcease from the world which they would enter upon graduation, and he wished them well in their struggle. "May God bless you and give you in perfect revelation as your lives advance a vision of the Christ and his perfect saving grace."[97]

Despite the influential impact of his Presbyterian heritage, Wilson's baccalaureate sermons, like most of his religious talks, are notable for the absence of specific theological ideas. Wilson himself admitted as much. "I am no theologian," he confessed, and he maintained that he preached nothing "not written on the face of life and of providence."[98] His religious concerns were preeminently moral, not theological, in character; the Christian life was merely the task of acting out God's certain commands in a world of good and evil. The contribution of his covenant theological heritage was primarily in giving him a way of understanding the world—a predisposition to see things in synthetic, wholistic terms and a tendency to make all issues reducible to well-defined moral categories.

By 1905, however, Wilson was clearly attempting to redefine his ethics and principles in order to deal with the crisis facing American society, a society torn by new economic, political, and social problems. In 1904, he had confidently asserted the immutability of Chris-

---

[96] Baccalaureate sermon, June 12, 1904, *ibid.*, pp. 372-74.
[97] *Ibid.*, p. 374.   [98] *Ibid.*, p. 369.

BACCALAUREATE ADDRESS, June 12, 1904.

"And they shall fight against thee: but they shall not prevail
against thee: for I am with thee, saith the Lord, to deliver
thee." Jer. I.,19.

YOUNG GENTLEMEN: Not all of your life is before you. Much of it is

passed: the part in which your motives find their most intricate root-

age, the part in which your strength has been formed and determined.

That is a shallow view of life which makes youth no essential part

of it and represents the years in which you must follow your callings

and earn your livelihood and obtain your final place of influence

in the world as the only period in which you really live and estab-

lish yourselves among men. You have already lived more than a third

of the time alloted you,—some of you have lived quite half, some

nearly all of it. Those of you who go the longest journey in the

world will find, ere the full tale of your years is told and the end

come, that the fountains you draw refreshment from are still the

fountains you drank of in your youth: that the things which stir you

are the same that stirred you in the long, dreaming days of expecta-

tion when you were boys. No one of you will ever shake off the per-

sonality he has now already made for himself or wholly lose the

naive impressions of the days in which he has come to maturity.

"I have no patience", says Ruskin, in one of those passages in

Wilson's baccalaureate address in 1904. *Library of Congress*

tian ethics, declaring that "the spirit of morality was changed and established once and for all by the coming of Christ into the world," and that this was "not the age for debate."[99]

His baccalaureate sermon of 1905 demonstrates that the awesome dimension of this task of reknitting the fabric of American society had made a deep impression upon him. "We seek to regulate our life and are baffled," he said. "Law will not come at our bidding or merely because of our need. No sufficient rule of guidance seems to be anywhere discoverable." One possible reaction, he admitted, was withdrawal from the world, but his Calvinist faith could not countenance such a response: "For us, alike by nature and by faith, such ways of life, such quiescences of thought are impossible. Our powers stir too imperiously within us, and our consciences tell us that we should use them: the quietude of inaction is not peace but imprisonment."[100]

But for Wilson, action was not effective unless it was rightly directed, and that was the heart of the question. "It is easy enough to talk of assessing moral values and of increasing the stock of good in the world, but what is good and what is evil, for us individually and for the world in which we live?" Wilson asked. "May we not determine that question by our experience, candidly interrogated and interpreted?" The students' experience at Princeton should have provided the answer, he believed. Drawing again on the comprehensive framework of the covenant tradition, Wilson told the graduates that the purpose of their education had been to enable them "to see life whole,—not as a thing of parts and patches, but as a thing entire, undivided, woven of spirit and of matter, governed by laws of thought as well as of material force, a thing to use for happiness and greatness as well as for gain and aggrandizement." The task was theirs, but they should realize that the Christian did not so much think God's thoughts after him as do his deeds with him. "You are of the same spirit with your maker," Wilson assured them, "not his slave, but, if you will, his partner."[101]

The gospel of duty and service made a powerful impact on students. One man who left Princeton to become a missionary in China wrote to Wilson in 1909, "Your words & principles were no small factor in helping me to decide to go, for my life work, to the hardest field I could fill; for the Lord is surely pleased to have us, for love to His Son, man the neediest places, unsurfeited with workers." Even fifty years later, another student remembered the indellible impression Wilson made on him. "For me Wilson lit a lamp which has never been put out.

[99] *Ibid.*, p. 368.

[100] Baccalaureate sermon, June 11, 1905, *ibid.*, xvi, 120, 121-22.

[101] *Ibid.*, pp. 126, 128, 124.

. . . [He] introduced us to the kingdom of the mind and held up before our eyes what Whitehead later called 'an habitual vision of greatness.' "[102]

Wilson demanded as much from himself as he did from his students, and during the first four years as president he drove himself relentlessly—presiding over academic reorganization at Princeton, delivering speeches throughout the country, and soliciting the support of the alumni. Although he reduced his course load, he never gave up teaching while he was president.[103] He found the details of his work extremely tedious, complaining to his diary in 1904 that he had been kept in his office "till quarter of 5 on business that might have been finished before 3 if academic men were only prompt in movement and brief in statement!"[104]

His family and friends provided the necessary relief from this pressure. "Deep perturbations are natural to me, deep disturbances of spirit," he told Ellen. "I could not make the impression I do, I could not be what I am, if I did not take such serene happiness from my union with you. You are my spring of content; and so long as I have you, and you are happy, nothing but good and power can come to me. Ah, my incomparable little wife, may God bless and keep you!"[105] When she was in Italy in the spring of 1904, he missed her terribly. "I prayed in chapel last Sunday for all who were on journeys, and my voice nearly betrayed me: a sudden convulsion gripped my throat,—I ought not to have risked it!"[106]

He realized that as he grew older, friendship seemed to be "the principal thing" in life,[107] but he realized that among many acquaintances he had very few friends. "Plenty of people offer me their friendship," he admitted,

but, partly because I am reserved and shy, and partly because I am fastidious and have a narrow, uncatholic taste in friends, I reject the offer in almost every case; and then am dismayed to look about and see how few persons in the world stand near me and know me as I am,—in such wise that they can give me sympathy and close support of heart. Perhaps it is because when I give at all I want to give my whole heart, and I feel that so few want it all, or would return measure for measure. Am I wrong, do you think, in that feeling? And can

[102] Charles Ernest Scott to WW, Feb. 22, 1909, *ibid.*, XIX, 65; Fosdick, "Personal Recollections of Woodrow Wilson," p. 35.

[103] WW to Edward Graham Elliott, July 15, 1902, *PWW*, XIV, 12-13, n. 2.

[104] Diary, Jan. 12, 1904, *ibid.*, XV, 121.

[105] WW to EAW, Aug. 9, 1902, *ibid.*, XIV, 68.

[106] WW to EAW, March 24, 1904, *ibid.*, XV, 207.

[107] WW to Robert Randolph Henderson, May 20, 1901, *ibid.*, XII, 144.

one as deeply covetous of friendship and close affection as I am afford to act upon such a feeling?[108]

The friends who satisfied Wilson's demands and needs most completely were John Grier and Jenny Hibben; and with Jack Hibben Wilson established perhaps the most intimate friendship of his life. Hibben was his confidant, adviser, and almost daily companion; but having established such a relationship, Wilson was torn by happiness and fear of losing the Hibbens as friends. "How profoundly grateful I am and thankful to God for your sweet and satisfying friendship," he wrote to them on Thanksgiving 1902. "Even if you should find me out and cease to love me, I at least have the precious possession of the years that have bound us together." When the Hibbens gave him a copy of *The Imitation of Christ* for his birthday, he was deeply moved and promised to try to be "worthy of such a gift." "It is a subtle evidence of your affection for me which will make me all the more anxious to *be* what you deem me."[109]

The demands of Wilson's career were made even more burdensome by a succession of family illnesses and deaths. One of the most crushing blows came when Wilson's father died in 1903. "It has quite taken the heart out of me to lose my life-long friend and companion," he told a friend. "I have told you what he was to me. And now he is gone and a great loneliness is in my heart. No generation ahead of me now! I am in the firing line. The more reason to be steady and attend to the fighting without repining." Wilson threw himself into his work to assuage his grief, but months later he still felt the effects of his father's death.[110]

Serious illness also struck the Wilson family with dismaying frequency. His daughters, Jessie and Nellie, underwent surgery for tubercular glands in April 1901 and December 1906, but the worst period was from April 1904 to April 1905. During that time, Jessie contracted diptheria while touring Italy with her mother in the spring of 1904; Margaret contracted malaria in Italy the following fall and subsequently had a nervous breakdown; and Stockton Axson suffered another nervous breakdown that incapacitated him for virtually the entire academic year.[111]

[108] WW to E. G. Reid, Feb. 16, 1902, *ibid.*, p. 272.

[109] WW to Jenny Davidson Hibben and John Grier Hibben, Nov. 27, 1902 and Dec. 23, 1903, *ibid.*, XIV, 224, and XV, 110. Hibben joined the Princeton faculty in 1891; he served as Stuart Professor of Logic (1897-1912), Stuart Professor of Philosophy (1912-32), and as President (1912-32).

[110] WW to E. G. Reid, Feb. 3, 1903, *ibid.*, XIV, 347-48; WW to James Woodrow, Jan. 30, 1903, *ibid.*, pp. 335-36; Diary, Jan. 21, 1904, *ibid.*, XV, 137.

[111] Stockton Axson to WW, April 2, 1901, *ibid.*, XII, 117-18, n. 1; EAW to WW, April 23, 1903, *ibid.*, XIV, 423-24; EAW to Anna Harris, March 11, 1905, *ibid.*, XVI, 28-29; J. G. Hibben to WW, July 14, 1905, *ibid.*, p. 155; EAW to Anna Harris, Feb. 12, 1907, *ibid.*, XVII, 33-34.

The deepest tragedy occurred in the spring of 1905. The Wilsons had always opened their home to relatives, and they raised Ellen's brother, Edward, who received his bachelor's degree from Princeton in 1897. For both Ellen and Woodrow, Edward Axson came very close to being the son they never had. In April 1905, Axson, his wife, and son were drowned in a freak accident when their carriage went off a ferry in northwestern Georgia.[112] Ellen was shattered by the loss of her "darling boy and his little family," and Wilson tried mightily to contain his grief. He told the Philadelphian Society shortly after the accident that a man's "voluntary thoughts" could discipline his life. "By them, we may, in the midst of labors rest ourselves, in the midst of excitement calm ourselves, and in the midst of sorrow be soothed."[113] This self-discipline was barely sufficient; a year later the mention of Axson's name brought tears to Wilson's eyes.[114]

Wilson's own health began to deteriorate under the strain of the presidency and his bereavement. In the spring of 1903, a prominent trustee warned him about doing too much and asked him to reduce his commitments. "You are too valuable to Princeton and to us to risk the work of the next twenty years for a single speech or journey."[115] Wilson vacationed in Europe with his wife during the summer of 1903, but a year later he had an operation for a hernia condition, which was further complicated by phlebitis in his right leg.[116] By the end of the academic year 1905-1906, Wilson was exhausted. On May 28 he woke up blind in one eye due to a blood vessel which had burst.

Ellen was shocked. "Of course we had a dreadful week," she reported to a friend. ". . . It is something wrong with the circulation due entirely to a general condition of overstrain. The doctors said he must stop *all* work at once, that it was impossible to exaggerate the critical nature of the situation. . . . He is of course *very* nervous." A few weeks later, Ellen was convinced Wilson was suffering from "hardening of the arteries, due to prolonged high pressure on brain and nerves." "He has lived too tensely. . . . Of course, it is an awful thing—a dying by inches, and incurable. But Woodrow's condition has been discovered in the very early stages and they think it has already been 'arrested.' "[117]

Actually, Wilson apparently had suffered a severe stroke, and although he recovered partial sight in his left eye, the vision was perma-

[112] WW to R. Bridges, April 28, 1905, *ibid.*, XVI, 86, n. 1.

[113] EAW to Anna Harris, Feb. 12, 1907, *ibid.*, XVII, 34; news report, May 5, 1905, *ibid.*, XVI, 91.

[114] Bragdon, *Wilson: The Academic Years,* p. 310.

[115] Moses Taylor Pyne to WW, March 5, 1903, *PWW*, XIV, 382.

[116] WW to R. Bridges, Dec. 9, 1904, *ibid.*, XV, 571, n. 1.

[117] EAW to Mary Eloise Hoyt, June 12, 1906, *ibid.*, XVI, 423; EAW to Florence Stevens Hoyt, June 27, 1906, *ibid.*, p. 430.

nently impaired.[118] Sensing that he might be near death, Wilson sent a
message to the graduating class of 1906 in place of his baccalaureate
sermon and wrote, "Our good-bye is not yet a final word of parting. It
is an affectionate greeting at a turning of the way. We shall ever be
comrades in all true things and all worthy aspirations, lifted by the
same spirit through all toils and all achievements."[119] Later, he reconsidered the message and eliminated the word "yet." He left for a
summer of recuperation in the lake country of England, and after three
months of rest he had made a near-total recovery. By the end of August
he was able to write rather than type his letters to Ellen, and a Scottish
doctor told him it would be better for a man of his temperament to go
back to work in moderation.[120] But when he returned in September, he
was a different man.

[118] WW to Jerome Davis Greene, May 30, 1906, *ibid.*, p. 412, n. 1; Weinstein, "Wilson's
Neurological Illness," pp. 334-37.

[119] Message to the graduating class of 1906, June 10, 1906, *PWW*, xvi, 420.

[120] WW to EAW, Sept. 2, 1906, *ibid.*, pp. 445-46.

VIII

Conflict and Turmoil, 1906–1910

"You know that if you be ill nothing will go well with you," Wilson declared in his baccalaureate sermon of 1905. "Good fortune will sit as uncomfortably upon you as bad; and, if bodily health be thus indispensable to you, is there no such thing as spiritual health? Will not distempers of the mind and spirit as easily mar your fortunes?" A year before his severe stroke, Wilson himself described the relationship between physical health and spiritual well-being, and in doing so suggested the impact which his physical collapse would have on his thought and personality. "You shall not find happiness without health," he told the graduates, and he held before them a vision of God's "saving health, which must be known among all nations before peace will come and life be widened in all its outlooks."[1] Returning from England in the autumn of 1906, Wilson resolved that as God's "partner," he must pursue the task of bringing saving health to Princeton with even greater vigor and determination.

Princeton had been dramatically revitalized during Wilson's first four years as president, the New York *Evening Post* observing that he had "ruined what was universally admitted to be the most agreeable and aristocratic country club in America by transforming it into an institution of learning."[2] Wilson's reforms represented a continuation of the policies of former president James McCosh, who had sought to make Princeton a major American university with wide influence and high academic standards. Like McCosh, Wilson relied on young faculty members to reinvigorate the faculty, and in creating the preceptorial plan, he secured a powerful base of young faculty support for his academic policies. In maintaining that Princeton should offer a broad, disciplined, liberal education, Wilson was sounding a characteristic theme of McCosh's educational philosophy and recalling Princeton to the days he had known as an undergraduate under his presidency. When Wilson sought to diminish the influence of the student eating clubs at Princeton, he was also following the initiative of McCosh, who had banned fraternities among the students.[3]

[1] Baccalaureate sermon, June 11, 1905, *PWW*, xvi, 122, 126.

[2] Quoted in EAW to Anna Harris, Feb. 12, 1907, *ibid.*, xvii, 35.

[3] Thomas Jefferson Wertenbaker, *Princeton, 1746-1896* (Princeton, 1946), pp. 290-343; Varnum Lansing Collins, *Princeton* (New York, 1914), pp. 221-50. See also Hardin Craig, *Woodrow Wilson at Princeton* (Norman, Okla., 1960), pp. 42-63. Craig goes to some lengths in at-

In response to the prohibition of fraternities and Princeton's failure to provide adequate dining facilities, undergraduate eating clubs sprang up during the late 1870's and 1880's. As a student, Wilson himself was a member of one of these clubs, the Alligators. During the 1890's, however, the composition of the student body began to change, thereby transforming the clubs. The industrial expansion and prosperity of the late nineteenth century brought an increasing number of students from wealthy families; simultaneously, the town of Princeton shed its image of a quiet college village and took on its appearance as a suburban haven for bankers, industrialists, and merchants of New York and Philadelphia. This change was accelerated when Grover Cleveland left the White House in 1897 to assume manorial housekeeping in Princeton. An atmosphere of wealth and a concern for social standing pervaded both the town and the university, and the eating clubs provided an undergraduate equivalent to the world of social respectability which students would presumably enter upon graduation. What had begun as an institution serving the utilitarian function of physical sustenance became a means of providing social recognition for the sons of both old and *nouveaux riches*.

With the support of young alumni, the clubs began in the 1890's to construct large, elegant houses adjacent to the campus. They were commanding residences, some reportedly costing as much as $100,000. In addition, since the clubs were restricted to upperclassmen, another group of clubs for lowerclassmen developed and served as "feeders" for the larger eating clubs. The intense interclub rivalries that plagued the recruitment of members were reduced only temporarily by various treaties between the clubs. New members endured a disruptive period of pledging and hazing, and for many sensitive young students, failure to win election to a club blighted their entire undergraduate education.[4]

One father reported to Wilson that when his oldest son did not make a club, "it was such an intense humiliation and it grieved him so that he was ashamed for a year to tell us about it and it was only in the privacy of a canoe trip that he told me that his heart had been broken over the matter." Another student's "spirit was absolutely crushed and

---

tempting to demonstrate McCosh's influence on Wilson's educational and philosophical beliefs. While Wilson did depend on McCosh's educational precedents at Princeton, the entire thrust of his religious, political, and educational thought was essentially antitheoretical. When Wilson spoke of philosophy, he meant a description of how things worked and how they ought to work—the underlying moral principles of individual and corporate life. He had little interest in McCosh's concern with the more abstract questions of epistemology and metaphysics. Indeed, as Wilson told Edward Graham Elliott, his mind was not philosophical, and when he felt he was leaving "the solid basis of fact," he "shied off." Elliott's memorandum of a conversation with Wilson, Jan. 5, 1903, *PWW*, xiv, 322-24.

[4] Bragdon, *Wilson: The Academic Years*, pp. 316-18.

broken. He felt that he had been branded with some personal disgrace.
. . . The mental anguish and misery of this boy can hardly be overestimated."[5]

Leon M. Levy, a young Jewish lawyer, told Wilson that Princeton was dominated by so much prejudice that as a student he had only four friends. Two were Jewish and two others were Gentiles, one of whom may have been Norman Thomas. Levy told Wilson that he was a Jew but "not of the worst type," and in moving terms he described his experiences at Princeton. "I was only at Princeton two years but in that brief period I suffered more social humiliation, and drained the dregs of more class prejudice than ever before or I am thankful to say ever since; and all sir, because of your abominable system of club life. The democracy of Princeton! Faugh! The essence of and acme of snobbishness, that's what I found." Harold Zeiss of the Class of 1907 confirmed Levy's indictment. He told Wilson that the upper class clubs were "the acme of snobbish[ness] and 'bootlicking' that results from a system of cliques." As a nonmember of a club, he testified that those who failed to be selected were "often miserable and [could] not become whole hearted Princeton men."[6]

Wilson's response to the human toll exacted by the club system was a restructuring and reordering of student life at Princeton—the quadrangle plan. In devising and defending this proposal, Wilson demonstrated how his stroke in 1906 had encouraged a dramatic change in his attitudes and thinking. His temporary blindness and partial paralysis were in fact a confrontation with death—"a dying by inches," as Ellen had described it. Wilson typically resolved to meet the effects of the stroke with resistance, and by resting regularly and curtailing his schedule he was able to conserve his meager energies. But his physical collapse also prompted him to use what he must have thought were his remaining years in realizing the principles which he held dear. He forged ahead with his plan for the restoration of Princeton.

The timing of Wilson's quadrangle plan reveals the new zeal and determination with which he attacked the problems of Princeton. In 1903, he had allowed to go unchallenged a sanguine report to the trustees on the club situation, and in 1904 he told an alumnus that "the commercial spirit of the age" had not had a deleterious effect at Princeton. "I do not think I am deceiving myself," Wilson said, "in believing that, while wealth and social distinctions are showing themselves in the University as elsewhere, the heart of the place has not been touched, and that its spirit is still wholesomely democratic."[7]

[5] James Albert Green to WW, June 17, 1910, *PWW*, xx, 536-38.

[6] Leon Michel Levy to WW, *c*. June 25, 1907, *ibid.*, xvii, 222-24; Harold Zeiss to WW, June 27, 1907, *ibid.*, pp. 233-34.

[7] A Report to the Board of Trustees of Princeton University on the Club Situation, *c*. June 8, 1903, *ibid.*, xiv, 479-84; WW to Zephaniah Charles Felt, Dec. 6, 1904, *ibid.*, xv, 552.

In a talk to alumni during November 1905, he hinted generally that the preceptorial plan might be followed by some attempt to reorganize the social life of the students. In February 1906, he prepared a memorandum and asked, "What is the future of the Upper Class Clubs? More and more expense and only social aims or University aims?"[8] But in September 1906 while he was recuperating in the lake country of England, Wilson sketched the location of the new quadrangles on the map of the Princeton campus and wrote to his close friend on the Board, Cleveland H. Dodge, "The summer has brought to maturity the plans for the University which have for years been in the back of my head but which never before got room enough to take their full growth."[9] In December he laid his plans before the trustees, and although he later admitted that he once thought it would take twenty-five years to institute the system of quadrangles,[10] he presented it to the Board as if it were immediately obtainable.

Wilson's "quad" plan was in the form of a supplement to his annual report to the trustees, delivered on December 13, 1906. He emphasized that though the proposal was "radical in character," it was "the fruit of very mature consideration" and had "been taking form" in his mind "for many years." The upperclass clubs, he charged, threatened "a kind of disintegration" of Princeton life, and he predicted that they would also produce "a deep demoralization." "No one who has watched this influence in recent years can doubt that the spirit of the place is less democratic than it used to be," he asserted.

> There is a sharp social competition going on, upon which a majority of the men stake their happiness. It seems to grow more and more intense and eager from year to year, and the men who fail in it seem more and more thrust out of the best and most enjoyable things which university life naturally offers—the best comradeships, the freest play of personal influence, the best chance of such social consideration as ought always to be won by natural gifts and force of character.

Wilson warned repeatedly in the report of "the slow, almost imperceptible and yet increasingly certain decline of the old democratic spirit of [Princeton] and the growth and multiplication of social divisions."[11]

As a remedy, he proposed that students be required to live together in colleges rather than clubs. He realized, he said, that these colleges

---

[8] Notes for a speech to the Princeton Alumni Association of the Oranges (New Jersey), Nov. 8, 1905, *ibid.*, XVI, 214, n. 3; news report, Nov. 10, 1905, *ibid.*, p. 218; Memorandum, Feb. 17, 1906, *ibid.*, pp. 314-15.

[9] The map is reprinted in *ibid.*, p. 447; WW to C. H. Dodge, Sept. 16, 1906, *ibid.*, p. 453.

[10] *WWLL*, II, 226-27.

[11] A Supplementary Report to the Trustees, *c.* Dec. 13, 1906, *PWW*, XVI, 519, 520, 523.

would divide the life of the university to a still greater degree but insisted that it would actually unite students on a deeper basis. "The disintegration is taking place, a disintegration into atoms too small to hold the fine spirit of college life," he noted. "We must substitute for disintegration a new organic process. The new body will have divisions, but all the parts will be organs of a common life. It is reintegration by more varied and more abundant organic life. This is the time to act, when the fluid mass trembles upon the verge of some sort of final crystallization."[12]

Wilson's vision of the quadrangles involved all four classes of students living and eating together, with some single faculty members residing in the colleges with the students. Like the preceptorial plan, this reorganization of student life took its inspiration from the English model of Oxford and Cambridge; Wilson had also known a similar arrangement at the University of Virginia. However, in emphasizing the way in which the "quad" plan would create an organic academic community, Wilson gave it his own characteristic stamp. His covenant heritage had encouraged him to see society as an organism bound by common principles and traditions, and education as the means of providing a comprehensive vision of the unity of knowledge. The university likewise became an organic community, and divisive and disintegrating influences had to be eliminated. But in linking his plea for an organic reconstruction of student life to his attack on the clubs as undemocratic, Wilson added a new note to his educational philosophy.

Princeton had long prided itself on being a democratic institution, however misguided that pride may have been, and Wilson may simply have been using the vague idea of democracy to advance his ideas. Yet by explicitly criticizing clubs for their social exclusiveness, Wilson was also attacking their undemocratic nature—the selection of men on the basis of wealth and social standing. Although he had previously been critical of social pretense, there is little in Wilson's earlier life to suggest his emergence as a defender of egalitarian democracy. His heroes—Burke and Bagehot—were political conservatives who had encouraged him to distrust some aspects of majoritarian democracy and the common people. But it was Wilson's stroke more than anything else that created the conditions for a profound alteration in his views on education and society. After his illness, he began to look with an increasingly critical eye at social divisions at Princeton and in American society as well. Like many others, he sensed that the disruptive forces of unrestrained industrialization and urbanization were creating a more rigidly stratified, undemocratic society.

However deeply Wilson's convictions might have run, his conver-

[12] *Ibid.*, p. 525.

sion was incomplete. In February 1907, only two months after his frontal assault on the clubs as undemocratic, he admitted to Cleveland H. Dodge, "It becomes clearer to me every day that I made the mistake, in reporting to the Board, of putting my own plans only on one and that not the most important ground of desirability to be considered." The Board had authorized a committee to consider the "quad" plan, and Wilson promised "to lay the matter before them in an entirely different light" at the next meeting.[13] Wilson's retreat on the issue of the clubs' social exclusiveness may have been due to his own partial commitment to democratic values, but it was also a strategem made necessary by the political situation that he faced on the Board of Trustees.

It would be wrong to describe the trustees merely as a collection of rich, unreconstructed, conservative businessmen and a handful of Presbyterian ministers. Several demonstrated considerable social concern and enlightened thinking that was uncharacteristic of their backgrounds. Yet the Board was dominated by wealth. Moses Taylor Pyne, the most powerful trustee, had inherited a vast estate based on railroad money and went into semiretirement in his thirties to devote himself to Princeton. Cyrus McCormick was in the process of assembling the International Harvester Company. Bayard Henry was a Philadelphia lawyer and a director of several corporations. Dodge enjoyed immense affluence from the family mining company. Robert Garrett and Cornelius C. Cuyler were prominent bankers. John L. Cadwalader was a well-connected Wall Street lawyer whose clients included some of the largest corporations in the nation. These were hardly men who would swallow an attack upon the detrimental influence of wealth *per se*; Wilson had temporarily forgotten his constituency on the Board.

Wilson also faced the problem of reconciling the potential conflict between his plan for the reorganization of undergraduate social life and the development of the graduate college. Soon after the December trustees' meeting, Dodge reported to Wilson that Grover Cleveland opposed the "quad" plan because he feared that it would interfere with the construction of the graduate college. Although Cleveland had supported Wilson's early reforms at Princeton, he was deeply committed to the graduate school and college, largely through the influence of its dean, Andrew F. West. It was West who had helped Cleveland settle in Princeton; in gratitude Cleveland had named his estate, "Westland." Dodge himself had reservations about the "quad" plan and questioned Wilson's haste. "I do not see how we can carry out your ideas immediately," he wrote. Wilson was unperturbed. "There need be no antagonism at all," he replied, "between the plans I suggested to the

<hr />

[13] WW to C. H. Dodge, Feb. 20, 1907, *ibid.*, XVII, 47.

Board and the plans we had already set our hearts upon."[14] Henry B. Thompson, another trustee, did not care for the idea of "quads," but confessed that after closer examination he might be persuaded. He suggested that instead of setting up new quadrangles, the present club system ought to be expanded so that every student could enjoy membership.[15] Wilson immediately rejected this idea as "clearly impracticable."[16]

Furthermore, Wilson made a fatal mistake in neglecting the faculty and alumni. In laying the groundwork for curricular reform and the preceptorial plan, he had assiduously curried the favor of the faculty, trustees, and alumni in numerous speeches, meetings, and conferences. In contrast, there is little evidence that Wilson consulted anyone before springing his "quad" plan on the Board in December 1906. Public discussion, he stated, would be "unwise."[17] His stroke had hardened his attitudes. He rested in Bermuda during January 1907 and returned as the imperious leader whom he had often praised, determined to institute the "quad" plan. In March he reported orally to the Board on the committee's progress in studying the plan. Simultaneously the club situation worsened, with more violations of the Inter-Club Treaty regulating the recruitment of members.[18]

A new treaty was drawn up, but Wilson saw it as only a temporary measure. "The remedies are not simple," he wrote George Corning Frazer, a trustee of the University Cottage Club. ". . . They must . . . be radical in character, and their aim must be to bring the clubs and the whole social life of the undergraduates into organic relations with the University itself." Meanwhile, he curtly informed Frazer, the remedies were being prepared, and the club men would be consulted when "the plans seem to us in a satisfactory shape to be submitted to conference."[19]

Wilson finally took a few faculty members into his confidence on April 15. He invited Harry A. Garfield, Paul van Dyke, and Dean Fine

[14] C. H. Dodge to WW, Dec. 19, 1906, *ibid.*, XVI, 535; WW to C. H. Dodge, Dec. 20, 1906, *ibid.*, p. 536.

[15] Henry Burling Thompson to C. H. Dodge, Feb. 18, 1907, *ibid.*, XVII, 41-43. Dodge sent this letter to Wilson.

[16] WW to C. H. Dodge, Feb. 20, 1907, *ibid.*, p. 47.

[17] Supplementary report, *c.* Dec. 13, 1906, *ibid.*, XVI, 519.

[18] Trustees' Minutes, March 14, 1907, *ibid.*, XVII, 72; George Corning Frazer to H. B. Fine, March 18, 1907, *ibid.*, pp. 83-85, n. 2. Wilson's state of mind is also reflected by his contradictory behavior. On Feb. 14, 1907, he told the Philadelphia alumni that a large gift to Princeton was imminent. Four days later, before the Baltimore alumni, he denied that he said any such thing and later told Pyne that the news reports were an "outrageous misrepresentation," "a deliberate lie out of the whole cloth." News reports, Feb. 15 and 19, 1907, *ibid.*, pp. 38-40, 43-45; WW to M. T. Pyne, Feb. 21, 1907, *ibid.*, p. 48.

[19] WW to G. C. Frazer, April 16, 1907, *ibid.*, pp. 110-11.

to his home, and despite the informality of the setting, Wilson rose to address the men. He spelled out his vision of the quadrangles for Princeton, but van Dyke was dubious, fearing a mortal blow to his own club, Ivy. Garfield was enthusiastic. Fine was described afterwards as having "all the zeal of a late convert."[20] David B. Jones promised his support at the trustees' meeting and warned that if the club situation continued, Princeton would suffer financially and academically. "The fact is, that for some time a considerable portion of the under graduate body has looked upon Princeton University as simply an academic and an artistic background for the club life," Jones declared.[21]

In late May, Wilson told the members of the trustees' committee considering the "quad" plan that he would have "a definite action to suggest" at the committee's meeting on June 6, and on June 3 he sent a memorandum to the presidents of all the clubs outlining his ideas. He told the club officers that the memorandum came from him as an individual and was submitted for their discussion at the clubs' annual commencement banquets.[22] Three days later, the trustees' committee met and unanimously approved the report which had been written entirely by Wilson. On June 10, the entire Board met to consider the committee's action.

Wilson, as chairman of the committee, made a lengthy presentation, defending the "quad" plan as an organic conception of the university. Both the "Report on the Social Coordination of the University" and Wilson's remarks focused on the need to fuse the intellectual and social life of the campus into a coherent whole. Nowhere did Wilson now explicitly attack the clubs as undemocratic, though he did argue that they divided students "into groups and cliques whose social ambitions give them separate and rival interests quite distinct from, plainly hostile to, the interests of the University as a whole."[23]

The primary purpose of a university, the report stated, was intellectual, and the clubs separated the social life of the students from their intellectual life. They also drove a wedge into the social life of the campus, which should be united by allegiance to the university and a student's academic class. The organization of the clubs was "entirely outside university action" and had "no organic connection whatever with anything academic." It produced "interests which absorbed the attention and the energy of the best undergraduates as of all others," and yet nowhere interpenetrated the associations which arose out of

[20] WW to H. A. Garfield, April 13, 1907, *ibid.*, p. 108. Bragdon, *Wilson: the Academic Years*, p. 319; D. B. Jones to WW, May 15, 1907, *PWW*, xvii, 147.

[21] D. B. Jones to WW, May 15, 1097, *ibid.*, pp. 147-48.

[22] WW to R. Garrett, May 27, 1907, *ibid.*, p. 159. Franklin Murphy, Jr., to WW, June 7, 1907, *ibid.*, p. 187, n. 2; the memorandum is part of the news release printed at June 10, 1907, *ibid.*, pp. 204-206.

[23] Report on the Social Coordination of the University, *c.* June 6, 1907, *ibid.*, p. 183.

study. It carried "no flavour with it which it might not as well have in any other town or in any other similar environment."[24] Just as he had clarified lines of authority and reorganized academic life, Wilson was now seeking to extend the ideal of organic unity to every aspect of campus life.

Wilson also presented the "quad" plan as the logical, inevitable supplement to the preceptorial plan. "Before the establishment of the preceptorial system, with its necessary corollary of the intimate association of teacher and pupil,—the coördination of the undergraduate life with the teaching of the university,—these things were not so near the heart of our plans and hopes for Princeton's intellectual development and academic revitalization," Wilson declared. "But now they are of the essence of everything we are striving for, whether on the undergraduate or on the graduate side of the University's work, and we are bound to consider the means by which to effect an immediate reintegration of our academic life."[25]

Wilson presented no figures on the cost of the plan. He suggested that the club houses might be absorbed by the university and administered by a group of trustees from the clubs, but the report and his presentation to the Board vacillated on the crucial issue of whether the clubs would be abolished. In the report, he candidly asserted, "The effect of this plan upon the upper-class clubs would be either their abolition or their absorption," but in his presentation he hedged the issue. "The clubs simply happen to stand in the way," he said, adding that they were not detrimental to the university and their spirit was "singularly fine."[26]

Wilson's arguments mesmerized the Board. Despite the insufficiently endowed preceptorial plan, despite the annual deficits, despite the unknown and unspecified expense of the "quad" plan, the Board authorized Wilson "to take such steps as may seem wisest for maturing" the proposal. The language was somewhat ambiguous, but as the news release put it, the effect of the action was clear. The Board had "adopted the essential idea and purpose of the plan."[27] Even Moses Taylor Pyne, who had written the favorable report of the clubs in 1903 and who enjoyed a charter membership in Ivy Club, supported the committee's action. Only one trustee, Joseph B. Shea, voted against the idea because he thought that Wilson was forcing the proposal through the Board with undue haste.[28]

Wilson repeatedly promised "common counsel among all con-

[24] *Ibid.*, p. 181.　　　　　　　　　　[25] *Ibid.*, p. 185.

[26] *Ibid.*, p. 186; news release, *c.* June 10, 1907, *ibid.*, pp. 199-200.

[27] Report on the Social Coordination of the University, *c.* June 6, 1907, *ibid.*, p. 186; Trustees' Minutes, June 10, 1907, *ibid.*, p. 198; news release, *c.* June 10, 1907, *ibid.*, p. 204.

[28] D. B. Jones to WW, June 12, 1907, *ibid.*, p. 210. Stockton Axson, "Memorandum of the Princeton Controversy" (R. S. Baker Coll., DLC).

cerned"[29] in developing the "quad" plan, but he clearly intended that the discussion should involve only its details and methods of realizing it. He had, in fact, presented the faculty, clubs, and alumni with a *fait accompli*. When Henry van Dyke inquired about the meaning of the Board's action, Wilson replied, "It was the understanding at the meeting of the Board in June that the essential idea and purpose of the plan for residential quads had been adopted, but that there was a very wide range of choice as to details and methods, and that there was to be the freest possible inquiry about how the idea might best be realized by common counsel." Van Dyke angrily responded that the faculty had not been consulted and that as far as he was concerned, the plan seemed "full of the gravest perils to the life and unity of Princeton." Wilson promised "to bring the matter in some suitable form to the attention of the faculty next year."[30]

Wilson did receive some support from older members of the faculty, and Theodore W. Hunt, who had taught Wilson as an undergraduate, wrote, "Even should you fail in this new departure, you would fall with your face toward the light."[31] The club men were predictably opposed, although one admitted, "We know something has to be done and we stand ready to help out in any place which will be for the good of the University."[32]

Initially Wilson rather naïvely predicted support for the "quad" plan, but by July a violent reaction had set in. He almost relished the controversy. "The fight for the quads is on very merrily," he reported, dismissing a good deal of the opposition as "wild talk."[33] His combative temperament aroused, he escalated the terms of the struggle. He considered it, he said, "not as a fight for the development, but as a fight for the restoration of Princeton." "My heart is in it more than it has been in anything else," he told Dodge, "because it is a scheme of salvation." Alarmed by Wilson's singleminded determination, Dodge pleaded with him to use evolutionary, not revolutionary, methods. Wilson replied that financial support would answer his opponents.

[29] Report on the Social Coordination of the University, *c*. June 6, 1907, *PWW*, xvii, 186; news release, *c*. June 10, 1907, *ibid.*, p. 203; notes for a speech to the alumni, June 11, 1907, *ibid.*, p. 209.

[30] Henry van Dyke to WW, July 3 and 5, 1907, *ibid.*, pp. 246, 260-61; WW to H. van Dyke, July 5 and 8, 1907, *ibid.*, pp. 260, 263.

[31] Theodore Whitefield Hunt to WW, June 26, 1907, *ibid.*, p. 231; see also William Berryman Scott to WW, June 26, 1907, *ibid.*, pp. 231-32.

[32] William Wirt Phillips, President of the Cap and Gown Club, to WW, June 25, 1907, *ibid.*, p. 221; for an example of the more prevalent club opinion, see Franklin Murphy, Jr., president of Tiger Inn, to WW, June 18, 1907, *ibid.*, pp. 216-17.

[33] WW to C. H. McCormick, June 14, 1907, *ibid.*, p. 212; WW to M. W. Jacobus, July 1, 1907, *ibid.*, p. 241.

"Money will lubricate the evolution as nothing else will."[34] He was eager to get in touch with Mrs. Russell Sage, widow of the railroad magnate, with a request for funds, but Dodge wisely counseled against "the advisability of approaching her during the hot weather."[35]

Actually Wilson had little time to consider how he would raise the money to finance the "quads," for he was overwhelmed by an intense and bitter opposition. He retreated to the Adirondacks, as he said, in hope of "restoring my self-possession and . . . steadying and clearing my judgment."[36] But there was no escape. West, seething over the "quad" plan's threat to his cherished dream of a graduate college, wrote Wilson an angry letter, accusing him of peremptory action and failure to consult with the faculty or "other persons properly interested and deeply concerned." "I feel bound to say that not only the thing that has been done, but the manner of doing it, are both wrong—not inexpedient merely—but morally wrong," West fumed. ". . . If the spirit of Princeton is to be killed, I have little interest in the details of the funeral."[37] Wilson retorted that West's remarks were "wholly gratuitous" and assured him that "common counsel" and "the freest possible discussion" would follow in the autumn.[38]

Even his friend Jack Hibben opposed him. The two had long talks, which became frank and somewhat heated. Hibben warned of "the dangers which attend this plan as regards the vital interests of Princeton" and implored Wilson to be more flexible. "I had hoped," he wrote Wilson, "that you would be willing, not necessarily to change your own point of view, but merely to allow the question to be reopened for more detailed investigation & discussion." Ellen told Hibben that her husband intended to insist upon the plan "without yielding in any respect whatsoever," but Wilson said that was a misunderstanding. He claimed that he was open to compromise and discussion, but he quickly narrowed the terms of the compromise and sounded the theme of his authority. "What I am . . . not able to yield is the principle of the whole thing, namely, that the club basis of our life (that is, the elective basis) must give place to an organization abso-

[34] WW to C. H. Dodge, July 1 and 3, 1907, *ibid.*, pp. 240-41, 245-46; C. H. Dodge to WW, July 2, 1907, *ibid.*, p. 243.

[35] C. H. Dodge to WW, July 9, 1907, *ibid.*, p. 265.

[36] WW to J. G. Hibben, July 16, 1907, *ibid.*, p. 284.

[37] Andrew Fleming West to WW, July 10, 1907, *ibid.*, pp. 270-71.

[38] WW to A. F. West, July 11, 1907, *ibid.*, p. 280. The alienation between the two men grew. Thompson reported to Pyne that West's attitude had become "almost vindictive." "It seems a pity to me that a man of his capacity should have such a silly streak of opposition in him toward the President..I do not know whether the President's attitude towards him is much better; but to an outsider the whole thing seems silly." H. B. Thompson to M. T. Pyne, July 30, 1907, *ibid.*, p. 309.

lutely controlled, not negatively, but constructively and administratively, by the university authorities." He admitted that the opposition was so strong that he might eventually stand "isolated and helpless," but he resolved to fight for his ideals. "Failure is bitter, how bitter it would be impossible to say, for a man convinced of duty as I am," he told Hibben, "but worse than either, infinitely worse, is it to shirk. To shirk would kill me; to fail need not."[39]

As the summer wore on and the opposition grew, Wilson became more obdurate, displaying all the tenacity of purpose he had described as a characteristic of the Christian soldier. Stockton Axson said that he never saw "Wilson more stiffly bent and insistent on a project," and thought that Wilson might resign if the plan was not quickly realized. Henry B. Thompson visited Wilson and found him "nervous and excitable." According to Thompson, Wilson interpreted the Board's action "as a *final endorsement of the idea*," was unwilling to compromise, and was obsessed with the "quads." "Wilson is somewhat inclined to make light of and override Alumni sentiment," he reported, "on the ground if we are right they must be wrong."[40] Wilson constantly raised the stakes involved in the "quad" plan and personalized it, calling it "nothing less than the most critical work of my whole administration"; he insisted that "the whole ultimate success of what we have recently attempted and achieved at Princeton [is] dependent on the execution either of this plan or of some other equivalent to it in object and effect."[41]

The more stubborn Wilson became, the more his support disintegrated. Thompson found the alumni in Philadelphia and Wilmington, Delaware, adamantly against the plan and admitted to Pyne that "Wilson's eloquence" had "overpersuaded" the trustees; Bayard Henry described the alumni opposition as "practically unanimous"; Dodge urged Wilson to go slow and build "for the long future"; and Pyne began to back off from his earlier support.[42] Harold G. Murray, the secretary of the Committee of Fifty, reported that an "overwhelming majority" of the alumni disapproved of the "quad" scheme, and he painted a bleak financial picture. "My cancellations run into the

[39] J. G. Hibben to WW, July 8, 1907, *ibid.*, pp. 263-64; WW to J. G. Hibben, July 10, 1907, *ibid.*, pp. 268-69.

[40] Winthrop More Daniels to J. G. Hibben, Aug. 9, 1907, *ibid.*, pp. 342-43; H. B. Thompson to C. H. Dodge, Sept. 10, 1907, *ibid.*, pp. 379-81.

[41] WW to C. H. Dodge, Aug. 4, 1907, *ibid.*, p. 335; WW to Bayard Henry, Aug. 6, 1907, *ibid.*, p. 338.

[42] H. B. Thompson to Harold Griffith Murray, July 16, 1907, *ibid.*, p. 285; H. B. Thompson to M. T. Pyne, July 30, 1907, *ibid.*, p. 308; B. Henry to WW, July 29, 1907, with Enclosures, B. Henry to H. B. Thompson, July 13, 1907 and M. T. Pyne to B. Henry, July 17, 1907, *ibid.*, pp. 301-307; C. H. Dodge to WW, Aug. 6, 1907, *ibid.*, p. 341.

thousands," he complained and noted that since the alumni had been drained "pretty nearly dry" by appeals for the preceptorial system, the university was financially dependent on only two men—Pyne and Dodge.[43] Another alumnus informed Wilson that he was greatly mistaken if he thought "any considerable body of the alumni" was behind him and estimated that three-fourths to nine-tenths were against the idea.[44] Actually, the opposition seemed to be located primarily in the East and among the younger alumni who had been members of clubs. At the same time, the eastern alumni were more numerous, and the younger men tended to be more active in alumni affairs and consequently more influential.

When the university reconvened in September, the campus was in turmoil. "Never before has any movement excited such interest," the *Daily Princetonian* commented.[45] Wilson immediately set out to secure a formal vote of support from the faculty, and his friend Winthrop More Daniels introduced a motion calling for concurrence with the "quad" plan at a faculty meeting on September 26. Henry van Dyke introduced a contrary resolution requesting that a committee of faculty, trustees, alumni, and students study the club situation. Hibben rose to second van Dyke's motion, and Wilson turned pale. "Do I understand that Professor Hibben seconds the motion?" he asked. "I do," Hibben replied.[46] The "quad" plan had separated Wilson from his closest friend, and Hibben became a leader of the opposition. Four days later, the van Dyke resolution came to a vote and was decisively defeated, 23 to 80, with more than 50 preceptors—nearly all of them—voting against the motion.[47]

At the next faculty meeting, on October 7, with the Daniels resolution still pending, Wilson took the floor to deliver what many remembered as one of the greatest speeches of his life. "We are called upon at this time to set the country an example of constructive worth," Princeton's prime minister declared. "It is not in our choice to stand still, because Princeton is the natural leader among all the Universities of America." The life of universities was disintegrating and needed a new principle of coherence. "The honormen are outside of clubs, the Faculty are outside of clubs, the University is outside of the clubs. The clubs therefore estopp any plan for organic reorganization." "Every

[43] H. G. Murray to Andrew Clerk Imbrie, Sept. 12, 1907, *ibid.*, pp. 381-83.

[44] Francis Speir, Jr., to WW, Sept. 20, 1907, *ibid.*, pp. 395-96.

[45] Editorial in the *Daily Princetonian*, Oct. 2, 1907, *ibid.*, p. 411.

[46] Faculty Minutes, Sept. 26, 1907, *ibid.*, pp. 402-403; Stockton Axson, "Memorandum of the Princeton Controversy" (R. S. Baker Coll., DLC).

[47] Faculty Minutes, Sept. 30, 1907, *PWW*, XVII, 407-408. After the vote, Wilson prepared a careful analysis of who voted on which side. See n. 1 to the Faculty Minutes, Sept. 30, 1907, *ibid.*, p. 408.

principle and practice of exclusiveness" had to be obliterated. Wilson artfully tried to draw both the defenders of the clubs and those supporting West's graduate college into his cause. He asked that club men join him "in a common undertaking" to realize essentially what West proposed for the graduate college—"its close dining hall, common room &c. adapted to the undergraduate life." He insisted that the details remained to be worked out but asked for commitment to his ideal. "I beg of you to follow me in this hazardous, but splendid adventure," he concluded.[48]

Events had moved beyond the control of the faculty. Several trustees had decided that some sort of compromise was necessary, but as Thompson discovered, Wilson was "absolutely obdurate." "I can see only one way out of this situation, with honor to the University, and that is, a manly withdrawal of the scheme by Wilson himself," Thompson told Dodge. He added despairingly, "I have stopped worrying about this. What is the use?"[49] Thompson's prediction was correct. At the trustees' meeting on October 17, Pyne introduced a motion calling on Wilson to withdraw the "quad" plan, and the Board approved. Dodge introduced an explanatory statement, also approved, which said that the Board recognized that Wilson's views had not changed and pledged not to hinder him in his efforts "to convince the members of the Board and Princeton men generally that this plan is the real solution to the problem of coordinating the social and intellectual life of the University."[50]

Despite this salve, Wilson was livid and started a letter of resignation after the meeting.[51] But a night's sleep changed his perspective. In an interview with the New York *Evening Sun* on the following day, he stated: "I do not consider that the trustees are opposed to the quad system on principle, but merely reversed their former decision on reconsidering the matter, as they thought that the university and alumni were not sufficiently informed or prepared for the new plan." He predicted "the ultimate acceptance of the system" and proposed to take his cause to the alumni during the winter and spring.[52]

Pyne was furious. "The Trustees," he wrote to a fellow trustee, "turned down the plan on its merits, or rather its demerits, as it was absolutely Utopian and could not be carried out under any considera-

[48] Abstract of WW's speech prepared by A. F. West, Oct. 7, 1907, *ibid.*, pp. 422-24. See also WW's notes, Oct. 7, 1907; Diary of William Starr Myers, Oct. 7, 1907; and Faculty Minutes, Oct. 7, 1907, *ibid.*, pp. 420-21, 424, 421-22.

[49] H. B. Thompson to C. H. Dodge, Oct. 15, 1907, *ibid.*, p. 435. After several more faculty meetings, Daniels' revised resolution was permanently tabled on Nov. 4, 1907. See Faculty Minutes, Nov. 4, 1907, *ibid.*, pp. 467-68.

[50] Trustees' Minutes, Oct. 17, 1907, *ibid.*, pp. 441-42.

[51] WW to the Trustees, Oct. 17, 1907, *ibid.*, pp. 443-44.

[52] Interview, Oct. 18, 1907, *ibid.*, pp. 444-45.

tion. . . . [It was] turned down finally and for good, and the only reason it was not turned down harder was to save the feelings of the President." Pyne even threatened to withdraw his support from the university if Wilson persevered.[53]

Privately, Wilson knew that Pyne's interpretation of the finality of the Board's action was correct. "I have got nothing out of the transaction except complete defeat and mortification," he wrote Jacobus. ". . . I trust that a kind Providence will presently send me some sign of guidance which I shall have sight enough to perceive and to interpret."[54]

The providential sign which Wilson wanted turned out to be the same lesson his father had taught him. The response to defeat had to be renewed determination to fight on and remain true to ideals. A week after the Board meeting, Wilson went before the Philadelphian Society on October 24 and spoke on "The Importance of Singlemindedness," taking his text from Ecclesiastes 11:4—"He that observeth the wind shall not sow, and he that regardeth the clouds shall not reap." "The difference between a strong man and a weak one is that the former does not give up after a defeat, but continues the struggle," Wilson told the students. ". . . The work of the world is carried on by the man who lives true to the purpose of his heart, and not to the opinions of other people." When tempted to do the easy thing, one should remember that the best fortification, "although the hardest, is singleness of mind."[55]

Wilson's refusal to accept defeat was encouraged by Melancthon W. Jacobus. "I would fight it out," he wrote, ". . . and in the end you have got to win out." David B. Jones also goaded Wilson on in the language Wilson knew best, telling him that the struggle was for "the ultimate redemption" of Princeton. "If Mr. Pyne thinks it best to withdraw his support," Jones stated, "I shall be very sorry, but I shall be infinitely more sorry to see the University dominated by the club men of New York, Philadelphia, and Pittsburgh."[56]

Convinced now that Princeton must be liberated from "the dictation of the men who subscribe to the Committee of Fifty," and spurred by Jacobus' advice to "make clear not only the issue which is joined, but the money spirit of the opposition," Wilson embarked upon a campaign to convert the alumni.[57] Mindful of Pyne's warning, he never once mentioned the "quad" plan by name. However, at Memphis in

---

[53] M. T. Pyne to A. C. Imbrie, Oct. 23, 1907, *ibid.*, pp. 453-54; D. B. Jones to WW, Nov. 12, 1907, *ibid.*, pp. 495-97.

[54] WW to M. W. Jacobus, Oct. 23, 1907, *ibid.*, p. 451.

[55] News report, Oct. 25, 1907, *ibid.*, pp. 455-56; notes, Oct. 24, 1907, *ibid.*, p. 454.

[56] M. W. Jacobus to WW, Oct. 25, 1907, *ibid.*, pp. 458-59; D. B. Jones to WW, Nov. 12, 1907, *ibid.*, pp. 495-97.

[57] WW to M. W. Jacobus, Nov. 6, 1907, *ibid.*, p. 470; M. W. Jacobus to WW, Jan. 10, 1908, *ibid.*, p. 598.

November 1907, he raised the issue of the undemocratic influence of wealth, adding that students from public schools had better records at Princeton than those from private schools.[58] He admitted that as president his duties had been "almost exclusively political,"[59] and in these speeches, he shifted his emphasis to fit the audience. Before the Baltimore alumni in March 1908, he appeared conciliatory, stressing the need to put intellectual interests above social life at Princeton and expressing his willingness to cooperate in devising a plan.[60] A few days later, before the more enthusiastic Chicago alumni, he dryly noted that when the curriculum was reformed and the preceptorial plan was introduced, no one had protested. But when he had tried to reform the social life, "a storm of excitement swept the body academic, and we knew at last that we had . . . touched the vital matter." The university, Wilson argued, had to be organized by "democratic thinking, not stopping to ask a man's origin, not stopping to ask a man's influence, but regarding a man, every man, as different from his fellows only in capacity, only in trustworthiness, only in character." "Whenever you have shut classes up tight," he warned, "nations have begun to rot, because the individual worth has been checked and individual opportunities denied."[61]

This campaign failed miserably. The panic of 1907, which had begun early in the year and grown to crisis proportions by the autumn, dried up potential financial support. Wilson tried repeatedly to get funds from Andrew Carnegie for his plan "of national importance." Through the YMCA leader, John R. Mott, he attempted to interest John D. Rockefeller, but that effort also met with frustration. Meanwhile, he consistently refused to consider any compromise, even an experimental quadrangle.[62] In April 1908, a trustee's committee reported again on the club situation. Their report was a devastating setback. "Membership in the clubs does not seem to lower academic standing, nor to discourage study itself," the committee found. In general, the clubs were "conducive to the maintenance among their own members of a clean, manly, and fairly studious life."[63]

By the spring of 1908, Wilson was discouraged and physically ex-

[58] News report of a public speech in Memphis, Nov. 9, 1907, *ibid.*, p. 475.

[59] News report of a speech in Memphis to the Princeton Alumni Association of Tennessee, Nov. 9, 1907, *ibid.*, p. 481.

[60] *Princeton Alumni Weekly*, VIII (March 11, 1908), 370-71.

[61] Speech to the Princeton Club of Chicago, March 12, 1908, *PWW*, XVIII, 18, 23.

[62] WW to A. Carnegie, Jan. 12, 1908, *ibid.*, XVII, 599; WW to Frank Arthur Vanderlip, Feb. 1, 1909, *ibid.*, XIX, 18-19; Henry Smith Pritchett to WW, Feb. 18, 1909, *ibid.*, pp. 51-52; C. H. Dodge to WW, March 16, 1909, *ibid.*, pp. 100-101; H. S. Pritchett to WW, May 1 and 5, 1909, *ibid.*, pp. 180-81, 185; WW to C. H. Dodge, Feb. 18, 1910, *ibid.*, XX, 141.

[63] H. B. Thompson *et al.* to the Trustees, April 8, 1908, *ibid.*, XVIII, 229-41.

hausted. He was suffering from another attack of "neuritis," and he confided to Dodge, "I have found the past year go very hard with me. I feel, as you know, blocked in plans upon which I feel the successful administration of the University, both as a teaching body and as a wholesome society, depends, and for which I can find no substitute, and in these circumstances it has been a struggle with me all the year to keep in any sort of spirits." He left again for the lake country of England, promising to divest his mind of the matter altogether at least for the summer.[64]

The "quad" fight had taken an enormous toll on Wilson. It had gravely injured his close friendship with Hibben; it was his first defeat after a string of administrative victories at Princeton; it alienated him from Pyne, the university's largest single benefactor; and it eroded his relationship with the trustees. Throughout the rest of his presidency, he never forsook what he called "my favourite plans."[65] However, by the time he returned from England, the "quad" fight had merged with the struggle over the nature and development of Princeton's graduate school and college.

"The battle of Princeton," as the graduate school and college controversy was later called, is perhaps the most meticulously described quarrel in American educational history, and with the publication of Wilson's papers, the internecine war has received exhaustive documentation.[66] As Booth Tarkington later observed, "The fight at Princeton was one of incredible bitterness. One could get such bitterness only in a school, a church, a town library committee, or a benevolent society."[67] Like most academic fracases, it was a battle fought in terms of great intellectual and moral principles, which obscured the towering egos and personalities of the protagonists. Although the struggle eventually became a battle for control of the university, with Wilson pitted against Pyne, Wilson's public enemy was West. In some respects, their backgrounds were strikingly similar. Both were sons of Presbyterian ministers who had somewhat checkered careers because of involvement in ecclesiastical disagreements.[68] Both pursued secular careers in academia and distinguished themselves far beyond their

[64] WW to C. H. Dodge, June 18, 1908, *ibid.*, pp. 337-38.

[65] WW to Charles Scribner, Sept. 25, 1909, *ibid.*, XIX, 391.

[66] Link, *Road to the White House*, pp. 59-91; Bragdon, *Wilson: The Academic Years*, pp. 353-83; *WWLL*, II, 275-357. Volumes 18 through 20 of *The Papers of Woodrow Wilson* cover the controversy at its peak.

[67] Quoted in Bragdon, *Wilson: The Academic Years*, p. 353.

[68] See Samuel Huston Thompson, Jr., to WW, Feb. 7, 1910, *PWW*, XX, 84-85, n. 2 for a biographical sketch of the Rev. Dr. Nathaniel West, and Chapter I of this study concerning Wilson's father.

fathers' reputations. Both did their best scholarly work as young men, shortly after completing their doctorates, and later turned to more popular writing and college administration.

But for all their similarities, Wilson and West were studies in contrasts. Where Wilson enjoyed a family life of warmth and joy, West suffered tragedy when his wife became insane after the birth of their only son and spent most of her life in an institution. Wilson was lean, angular, and somewhat aloof, while West was short, stocky, and gregarious—a *bon vivant*, the perfect host who cultivated an atmosphere of gentility and breeding around him. Wilson won support for his policies largely through eloquent speeches and compelling ideals; West, in turn, based his power on friendships and personal contacts. The contrast between the two men is illustrated by their role in the university's sesquicentennial celebration in 1896. Wilson commanded the platform with his oration; West made the arrangements for entertaining the dignitaries. Wilson knew that he faced a formidable opponent. Soon after his inauguration as president, he reportedly told Bliss Perry, "If West begins to intrigue against me as he did against Patton, *we must see who is master!*" After he left Princeton, Wilson described West as the best politician he had ever met.[69]

The graduate school-college controversy had its roots in Patton's administration. When Princeton changed its name from the College of New Jersey to Princeton University in 1896, West had encouraged the dream of a well-endowed graduate school. Against Patton's opposition, the Board of Trustees established the school in 1900 with a loose adminstrative structure. West was appointed dean and enjoyed a power base of his own. He was required to consult with the president but reported directly to a special committee of the trustees.[70]

West also dreamed of a handsome residential college, and when Wilson became president in 1902, he accepted the need for a graduate college as part of the development of the university. At the alumni luncheon in June 1902, he announced his hope that funds would be available "to crown this university with a great graduate college."[71] In addition, in his first report to the Board, he stipulated that the graduate school and college were among the top priorities in his $12.5 million plan for Princeton.

From the first Wilson insisted that the residential college should be an integral part of his organic conception of the university.

[69] Perry, *And Gladly Teach*, p. 158; William Starr Myers, "Wilson in My Diary," *Woodrow Wilson: Some Princeton Memories*, p. 47; Bragdon, *Wilson: The Academic Years*, pp. 270-72.

[70] J. G. Hibben to WW, Nov. 25, 1900, *PWW*, XII, 36-37, n. 1.

[71] News report, June 14, 1902, *ibid.*, p. 424.

We shall build it, not apart, but as nearly as may be at the very heart, the geographical heart, of the university; and its comradeships shall be for young men and old, for the novice as well as for the graduate. It will constitute but a single term in the scheme of coördination which is our ideal. The windows of the graduate college must open straight upon the walks and quadrangles and lecture halls of the *studium generale*.[72]

West seemed to agree. In the autumn of 1902, he visited Oxford and Cambridge and came back with a vision of transplanting an English college to New Jersey's soil. Like Wilson, West wanted a graduate college involved in the undergraduate life of the campus. In a promotional brochure published in 1903, he wrote:

To every graduate who lives within its quadrangle, and to every undergraduate who passes it in his daily walks, the College, should in its very beauty and in the completeness of its appointments, be a visible symbol of the nobility of the truth and knowledge that are fit to dwell there, and the very fact that there is within the college world such a body of men devoted to high and serious work should quicken all good purposes.[73]

In a short preface to West's booklet, Wilson labeled the graduate college "undoubtedly our first and most obvious need." "The plans for such a college which Professor West has conceived seem to me in every way admirable. To carry them out would unquestionably give us a place of unique distinction among American Universities."[74]

The seeds of disagreement, however, were revealed in West's 1903 pamphlet. West paid his respects to the need for perpetuating the ideals of liberal education and training competent scholars, but he also promised that provision would be made "for the most important group of cultivated men,—those who have the desire for the studious life without proposing to themselves permanently the scholar's career." In fact, West's ideal student in many respects resembled the ideal Wilson established for his preceptors. Graduate students should be gentleman scholars, and the graduate college should satisfy their tastes. The buildings, wrote West, should be "Gothic of the purest collegiate type" and should include an entrance tower, students' rooms, a dining hall and breakfast room, kitchen and steward's quarters, commons

[72] WW to the Trustees, Oct. 21, 1902, *ibid.*, xiv, 157-58, 160; "Princeton for the Nation's Service," Oct. 25, 1902, *ibid.*, p. 183.

[73] Andrew F. West, *The Proposed Graduate College of Princeton University* (Princeton, N. J., 1903), p. 14.

[74] Preface to *ibid.*, printed at Feb. 17, 1903, in *PWW*, xiv, 361.

room, and "a house for the Master of the College." Each student would have a suite, which would include a study, bedroom, and private bath. Gardens would complement the exterior. "The interior should be furnished in oak, and special care is to be given to the paneling and furnishing of the dining-hall." Gothic windows would provide lighting; the roof would be carved in oak "or perhaps in fan-tracery of stone." The cost for all this, West estimated, naïvely or facetiously, would be "at least 600,000" dollars.[75]

As late as 1904, Wilson considered the graduate college "the necessary crown and completion of the curriculum"; but by 1906, it was clear that he and West had come to a parting of the ways. In a statement drafted for Hibben who represented him at the June 1906 Board meeting, Wilson argued that the chief problem was an administrative one, which was "not a legal or theoretical question." He argued against West's desire for administrative autonomy and seclusion of the graduate college; "seclusion and separation [are] not synonymous."[76] But the issue was never joined because the trustees' committee on the graduate school could not agree upon a site for the graduate college.

In October 1906, two developments brought the graduate college situation into sharp focus. The will of Josephine Ward Thomson Swann delivered her residuary estate of approximately $275,000 to the university for a graduate college.[77] At the same time, West received an offer of the presidency of the Massachusetts Institute of Technology. Like Wilson, West knew how to use such an invitation to his own advantage. At a meeting of the trustees' committee on the graduate school on October 19, West and Wilson engaged in an angry exchange, West detailing for a half-hour instances of Wilson's failure to support his plans for the graduate college. "I am bound to say you have a remarkable memory" was Wilson's meek reply.[78] Still weakened from the effects of his stroke, Wilson failed to use this opportunity to rid himself of West. Instead, he went before the trustees with a resolution imploring West to stay, calling his loss "quite irreparable" and describing him as "one of the chief ornaments and one of the most indispensable counsellors of the place."[79] The Board approved, and West remained at Princeton with an even stronger hand.

Melancthon W. Jacobus, who sensed the political implications of the

---

[75] *The Proposed Graduate College of Princeton University*, pp. 16, 14, 18-19, 20.

[76] WW to the Trustees, Dec. 8, 1904, *PWW*, xv, 566; draft of a letter, WW to J. G. Hibben, June 4, 1906, *ibid.*, xvi, 413-14.

[77] William Milligan Sloane to WW, Oct. 15, 1906, *ibid.*, pp. 457-58, n. 1.

[78] Andrew F. West, "A Narrative of the Graduate College of Princeton University . . .," mimeographed MS (UA, NjP), pp. 25-28. Hereinafter cited as "A Narrative of the Graduate College."

[79] Resolution, *c.* Oct. 20, 1906, *PWW*, xvi, 467.

action, wrote Wilson and expressed the hope that West's decision to stay was "on the basis of a thorough understanding of the position which he occupies in relation to your Presidency of the University." But the situation was not clearly understood. Wilson's reply to Jacobus confirmed his suspicions and fears.[80] West promised "team work" with Wilson,[81] but their relationship fell apart when Wilson launched the "quad" plan.

West had legitimate reasons for resenting Wilson's giving top priority to the "quads." Wilson himself had never mentioned the quadrangle plan as one of his goals prior to December 1906. He had frequently paid at least lip service to the need for a graduate college. In addition, West had supported Wilson's curricular reform, reorganization of the faculty, and preceptorial system. Furthermore, the Swann bequest raised the immediate question of the site of the graduate college, a problem which was temporarily obscured during 1907 by the "quad" controversy.

In 1905, West set up a pilot project for a graduate college at Merwick, a large, elegant house a few blocks removed from the heart of the campus. Wilson immediately praised the new housing for graduate students in his report to the trustees. "The house is comfortable and spacious, stands in beautiful grounds ornamented with delightful shade trees, and . . . has at once become an institution among us," he declared. "We believe that in this graduate house we have a sure prophecy of the Graduate College for which we so largely hope as the crowning distinction of Princeton's later development as a University."[82] West promised the Board that he would devote "the closest attention, perhaps almost daily," to the development of Merwick as a graduate college, and resolved "that Merwick shall not take on anything of the character of a boarding house, a club, or a hotel, but shall preserve at all times the aspect of a quiet studious home."[83]

Despite Wilson's sanguine expectations and West's resolutions, life at Merwick developed along somewhat different lines, and it appears that part of Wilson's opposition to West lay in the milieu created there. Two accounts of student life at Merwick are extant, one written in 1907 and the other in 1914-1915, and they leave the unmistakable impression that "Merwick and its ambience," in the words of one historian, "were elitist."[84] Maxwell Struthers Burt of the Class of 1904

[80] M. W. Jacobus to WW, Nov. 4 and 9, 1906, *ibid.*, pp. 480-81, n. 1, 484.

[81] A. F. West to WW, Oct. 30, 1906, *ibid.*, p. 478.

[82] WW to the Trustees, Dec. 14, 1905, *ibid.*, p. 263.

[83] A. F. West to the Standing Committee of the Trustees on the Graduate School, June 10 and Oct. 16, 1905 (Trustees' Papers, UA, NjP).

[84] Willard Thorp (ed.), "When Merwick was the University's 'Graduate House,' 1905-1913," *Princeton History*, No. 1 (1971), p. 55.

returned to Princeton "quite resigned to undergo the historic hardships of graduate study" and instead found such "material benefits" that he described his reaction as "something dangerously akin to blind enthusiasm."[85]

Burt rhapsodized over the relaxed breakfasts, the light luncheons ("not so heavy as to take the edge off the afternoon's work and play"), and the leisurely, elegant dinners.[86] According to another resident at Merwick, the food was so sumptuous that it was rumored in town that the students dined on peacock's tongues and similar delicacies. Actually, the students' favorites were Virginia ham and beaten biscuits. The Wednesday dinners were the most elaborate. Guest speakers were invited; students wore evening clothes under their gowns; and one resident reported that students carried large candles and escorted Dean West to Merwick from his home across Bayard Lane. Leonard Chester Jones, who lived at Merwick from 1908 to 1910, felt it necessary to defend the residents of Merwick from the then-current charge that they did nothing but play bridge all day. Actually, Jones said, he had never seen more than eight of the twenty-five men at Merwick playing bridge at any one time. Both he and Burt conceded that various sports were very popular and well patronized,.particularly after four o'clock when the students normally stopped their day of studying.[87]

Burt believed that Merwick was founded on "the English theory of education," "that a man must have a sound body as a home for a sound mind, that scholars are gentlemen and should live as such, that the beauty of living can not consist in a single development of mind or material; but in having as much beauty as possible in everything done or seen."[88] Jones concluded that his experience at Merwick was "invaluable." "My fund of facts was, perhaps, not startlingly increased: I doubt if I showed much 'progress.' Yet those two years revolutionized my scale of values and outlook on the world, so much so that everything before them seems to belong to another and a dimmer life."[89]

After Wilson's stroke of 1906 and his confrontation with the alumni over the "quad" plan, his personal opposition to West was fed by his reaction to West's ideals for the graduate college as realized at Merwick. By 1907, West was so delighted with the Merwick experiment that he urged that Merwick become the permanent location of the

[85] Maxwell Struthers Burt, "Life at Merwick," *Princeton Alumni Weekly*, VII (May 8, 1907), 512.

[86] *Ibid.*, pp. 513-14.

[87] See Jones' original manuscript account, "The History of Merwick," in UA, NjP. Substantial portions of this manuscript are reprinted by Thorp, "When Merwick was the University's 'Graduate House,' " pp. 56-71, and it is summarized in n. 2 to Edward Capps *et al.* to WW, Jan. 10, 1910, printed as an Enclosure in H. B. Fine *et al.* to WW, Jan. 11, 1910, *PWW*, XIX, 755-56.

[88] Burt, "Life at Merwick," p. 514.

[89] Jones, "History of Merwick."

graduate college. He defended it as "sufficiently retired to ensure the residential separation of the graduate from the undergraduate students" but insisted that administrative and scholastic control would remain in the hands of the president and the Board.[90] Wilson disagreed, and he based his opposition on the issue of location, not West's ideals. Wilson believed that geographical separation had already "created in the Graduate School a sense of administrative as well as social seclusion" which was "undesirable." He also felt that West had deserted his "original and better conception" by insisting on geographical separation.[91]

The situation was further complicated by the terms of the Swann bequest which stipulated that the "John R. Thomson Graduate College" should be constructed on the grounds of the university. In April 1908, the Board accepted legal advice which ruled out Merwick as a site and designated Prospect, the grounds of the president's home, as the location for the graduate school.[92]

This was ostensibly a victory for Wilson, but he continued to drag his feet and worried about West's continued control over the graduate school and its administration.[93] During the winter of 1908-1909, Wilson started his offensive against West and proposed a thorough reorganization of the graduate school which would strip West of much of his power. A newly constituted faculty committee would be in charge of the administration of the graduate school, and Wilson would control the crucial committee appointments.[94] On February 5, 1909, the trustees' committee on the graduate school met in New York, and West objected that the new scheme conflicted with the Board's resolution of October 1906, urging him to remain at Princeton. Wilson sensed victory and slowly raised his head to reply. "I wish to say to the Dean somewhat grimly that he must be digested in the processes of the University."[95] David B. Jones was concerned that West, "the chief disturber," was not entirely eliminated but felt that he would be eventually when "his absurdity" became more evident.[96]

[90] A. F. West to the Trustees' Committee on the Graduate School, May 13, 1907, *PWW*, XVII, 142-46.

[91] Draft of a report to the Trustees' Committee on the Graduate School, Jan. 9, 1908, *ibid.*, pp. 590-94, n. 1; WW probably did not deliver this report, but it is an indication of his policy at this time.

[92] William Jay Magie to G. Cleveland, March 13, 1908, printed as an Enclosure with Edward Wright Sheldon to WW, March 21, 1908, *ibid.*, XVIII, 64-66; WW to R. A. Cram, April 7, 1908, *ibid.*, pp. 226-27.

[93] WW to M. T. Pyne, Feb. 16, 1909, *ibid.*, XIX, 48-49.

[94] WW to M. W. Jacobus, Nov. 11, 1908, *ibid.*, XVIII, 493-94; E. W. Sheldon to WW, Feb. 4, 1910, with Enclosure, *ibid.*, XIX, 27-28; WW's draft of the reorganization plan, *c.* Feb. 4, 1910, *ibid.*, pp. 28-29.

[95] "A Narrative of the Graduate School," pp. 42-44.

[96] D. B. Jones to WW, March 4, 1909, *PWW*, XIX, 79.

The Board approved the plan reorganizing the graduate school in April,[97] but some trustees and faculty members became increasingly alarmed by what Jacobus called West's "luxurious views" of the graduate college. "If these are carried out," he warned, "it will result in simply making the Graduate School a great big upper class Club." Wilson agreed, describing West's plans as "in every way too costly and elaborate." Edwin G. Conklin, a member of the faculty graduate school committee, insisted that "in general the building be so planned as to minister to the needs of a large number of students rather than to the luxuries of a few."[98] The continuing acrimony took its toll. Discouraged with the graduate school, James Hopwood Jeans announced his resignation and later went on to win a Nobel prize for his research in mathematical physics.[99]

Wilson found his anger becoming more easily aroused. "As I grow older, instead of growing colder, I grow hotter," he declared in March 1909. "I think that of all the unfavorable seasons for heatable persons, the season which we have just passed has been the worst."[100] The trustees' meetings left him exhausted by the constant tension and political haggling. "A week with the trustees of the University wears my spirits out more than it fatigues my body, and after it is over I sadly need sleep and silence." But Wilson vowed to "fight stubbornly and circumspectly on" and saw himself as a Scots-Irishman who would not be conquered.[101]

In the spring of 1909, West's counterattack against Wilson began to surface. In March, Wilson was chagrined by rumors of large gifts which might be forthcoming for the graduate school, and in May, West dropped the bombshell. William Cooper Procter, the wealthy soap manufacturer of Procter and Gamble and an old friend of West's, offered $500,000 for the graduate college under two conditions. First, some site other than Prospect had to be chosen, and second, the university needed to raise a matching amount from other donors.[102] Wilson's initial reaction was cautious. "It is of course deeply gratifying," he told McCormick, "if we can manage to meet his terms." But the

[97] Trustees' Minutes, April 8, 1909, *ibid.*, pp. 153-54.

[98] M. W. Jacobus to WW, March 20, 1909, *ibid.*, p. 114; WW to M. W. Jacobus, March 23, 1909, *ibid.*, p. 116; E. W. Conklin to WW, March 30, 1909, *ibid.*, p. 135.

[99] J. H. Jeans to WW, March 20, 1909, *ibid.*, pp. 115-16.

[100] "Civic Problems," an address to the Civic League of St. Louis, March 9, 1909, *ibid.*, pp. 81-82.

[101] WW to Mary Allen Hulbert Peck, April 13, 1909, *ibid.*, p. 162.

[102] WW to M. W. Jacobus, March 27, 1909, *ibid.*, pp. 124-25; William Cooper Procter to A. F. West, May 8, 1909, *ibid.*, pp. 189-90. Actually, Wilson received West's word of Procter's probable benefaction at a meeting of the Trustees' Committee on the Graduate School on April 2, 1909, but the formal offer was not extended until Procter's letter to West in May. At that meeting, according to West, Wilson and the committee encouraged West to secure the gift. See "A Narrative of the Graduate College," pp. 45-46.

official acknowledgment of the offer was issued by Pyne, and the trustees' committee asked for a conference with Procter concerning the terms of the gift.[103]

Jacobus immediately suspected that Pyne and West were collaborating in an anti-Wilson move to realize West's vision of a graduate college. However, at least initially Pyne saw the problems inherent in Procter's offer. He thought it possible to use the Swann bequest as part of the matching money, but he felt that it was problematical that the gift would be accepted because the terms were "so onerous."[104] At a conference of Wilson, West, Pyne, and Procter in June, Procter abandoned his original preference of Merwick for the site of the graduate college and argued, probably under West's suggestion, for the golf links location, which was even further removed from the heart of the campus. Similarly, the university architect, Ralph Adams Cram, began to espouse the golf links site because if offered no competition from other buildings for an architectural masterpiece, and Pyne wavered in the face of the new arguments and the available funds.[105]

By the summer of 1909, Wilson was extremely discouraged with the developments at Princeton and found himself "very tired and out of tone." He claimed that he found friendships more important than ever before, but without Hibben and with more divisions within the Princeton community, he increasingly made friendship a matter of personal loyalty to him and his policies. When his friend and former classmate, Cornelius C. Cuyler, was killed in an automobile accident, Wilson had an ambivalent reaction. "It is hard to analyze my feelings about Cuyler," he said of the deceased trustee. "He has not been a true friend the last two years. He has done and said many disloyal things." He complained that all his friends went "bad," and the break with Hibben scarred him deeply. "*Some* of the old, familiar faces do not wear the old, familiar expression, do not give back the glance as they used to. What a fool I am to go back to that so often! Can my heart *never* be cured of its hurt?" But by the end of the summer, his combative temperament was restored. "I expect to go back to [Princeton] with normal nerves and a stiffened purpose, while my opponents show signs of weakening if they should be hard pressed a little longer."[106]

Wilson was deluding himself, for West and his forces had stiffened

[103] WW to C. H. McCormick, May 15, 1909, *ibid.*, pp. 196-97; M. T. Pyne to W. C. Procter, May 12, 1909, *ibid.*, pp. 194-95.

[104] M. W. Jacobus to WW, May 18, 1909, *ibid.*, pp. 198-99; M. T. Pyne to R. A. Cram, May 18, 1909, *ibid.*, p. 200.

[105] W. C. Procter to WW, June 7, 1909, *ibid.*, pp. 237-38; R. A. Cram to WW, July 8, 1909, *ibid.*, pp. 303-304; M. T. Pyne to WW, July 27, 1909, *ibid.*, p. 320.

[106] WW to M.A.H. Peck, June 19, July 11, Aug. 8, 22, 29, and Sept. 5 and 26, 1909, *ibid.*, pp. 261-62, 307-10, 330-33, 349-51, 354-59, 392-94. Recollections of Mary Hoyt (R. S. Baker Coll., DLC).

their resolve. Procter, under advice from West and Pyne, adamantly refused to back down from the golf links site, and at the October meeting of the trustees, Pyne moved that the Board reject the graduate school committee's recommendation of a central location and accept Procter's gift. The Board approved Pyne's motion but added an amendment stipulating that the terms of the Swann bequest be satisfied.[107] Infuriated, Wilson toyed with the idea of appealing directly to the general public but rejected it as "a foolish and perhaps demagogic course."[108] He bitterly resented the victory of "that arch-intriguer West" and believed that the Board had placed financial considerations over his policies and authority as president. "It is the second time they have done this," Wilson complained, still smarting over the defeat of his "quad" plan.

> They rejected the plans of mine about which there has been so much debate, rejected them though their judgments approved them, because they feared they would fail to get money from a small group of men who were passionately opposed to them. Twice, therefore, on two questions as important as can arise in my administration, they have refused to follow my leadership because money talked louder than I did. It is really intolerable. I am too angry just now, too disheartened, too disgusted, to think straight or with any sort of coolness about what I ought to do in the circumstances.

He considered resigning but resolved to fight on, "to possess my soul in patience, and keep my powder dry, until the battle is finally won or lost."[109]

Wilson's opposition to the Procter gift was complex. On the level of educational principles, Wilson believed that a central location of the graduate college was essential to preserve his goal of the university as an organic community. He also felt that West's designs for the graduate college were too elaborate and luxurious, producing expensive housing and discouraging qualified graduate students of less than ample means. He further considered West's drive for a graduate college at odds with the instructional needs of the graduate school and preferred to see the fellowships and professional chairs well endowed before living quarters were constructed.

[107] W. C. Procter to M. T. Pyne, Oct. 4, 6, 13, and 20, 1909, *PWW*, xix, 403, 406, 413, 434; Trustees' Minutes, Oct. 21, 1909, *ibid.*, pp. 435-39. The action was taken despite the graduate school faculty committee's recommendation of a central location for the graduate college. The committee's majority report was signed by Conklin, Daniels, Fine, and Capps. A minority report was issued by West and Hibben. A. F. West to WW, with Enclosure, Oct. 19, 1909, *ibid.*, pp. 426-33.

[108] WW to H. S. Pritchett, Oct. 23, 1909, *ibid.*, p. 442.

[109] WW to M.A.H. Peck, Oct. 24, 1909, *ibid.*, pp. 442-43.

In addition, Wilson's opposition was complicated by his antipathy to West. His objections on the grounds of educational principles were not unimportant and were shared by many faculty members, but they disguised what Wilson called the "personal equation." As he told Jacobus in October 1909, West had to be totally eliminated from the administration of the graduate school. He feared that West's elitism would have a bad effect on the graduate students and observed, "His influence upon the graduate students is one of the most serious things of the whole situation." Striking once again the theme of his own authority as president, Wilson maintained, "The choice now is between sustaining West and reorganizing the University, on the one hand, and getting rid of his influence altogether and following our own ideals, on the other. It is only by cutting the issue clear in this way that we can accomplish anything."[110]

West was equally determined not to submit to Wilson's authority and could claim with some validity that he and Wilson agreed on the development of the graduate college in many respects. Wilson had approved the booklet outlining West's dream in 1903; Wilson had drafted the resolution urging West to stay at Princeton in 1906; West had also reluctantly agreed to the reorganization of the graduate college in early 1909. The quarters that West envisioned for the graduate college were probably somewhat more luxurious than Wilson's proposed quadrangles, but the difference was one of degree, not kind. Indeed, the undergraduate dormitories constructed during Wilson's presidency hardly subjected students to primitive accommodations.

The simple fact is that Wilson had changed his mind. Whereas he had formerly seen Princeton as a training ground for an elite group of students, by 1909-1910 Wilson was struggling to develop a more democratic conception of the university education. The defeat over the "quad" plan had clarified his thinking, and when the graduate college controversy reached its peak, Wilson approached it with new ideas. He admitted as much to the New York alumni in April 1910. "I did not understand this matter five or ten years ago as I do now," he declared. ". . . If you had asked me five years ago about this thing I would have told you a different story; because I did not know . . . half as much about the conditions of graduate instruction as I know at the present time."[111]

On the other side, West's fundamental difference with Wilson was his antagonism over being slighted by Wilson's pursuit of the "quad" plan, an action he considered imprudent and immoral. He had taken a proprietary interest in the development of the graduate college, stubbornly resisting as much as he could any incursion on his plans or au-

110 WW to M. W. Jacobus, Oct. 29, 1909, *ibid.*, pp. 458-59.

111 Address to the Princeton Club of New York, April 7, 1910, *ibid.*, xx, 344.

tonomy. This is why the question of the location of the graduate college, so trivial in one respect, could assume such significance. But in
the final analysis both men realized that funds would resolve the issue.
Wilson himself was convinced in February 1910 that "nothing but a
large gift" for the quadrangles would "save the situation."[112] The
Procter gift for the graduate college gave West the upper hand and put
Wilson consistently on the defensive, trying to prove why the university should reject a gift of a half-million dollars.

Throughout the fall and winter of 1909, Pyne found himself increasingly allied with West. Pyne's opposition to Wilson was based in part
on his own opposition to the "quad" plan and his fear that Wilson's
attacks on the undemocratic influence of wealth were alienating financial support from the university. He also believed that rejecting the
Procter gift because of the golf links site would be a stupid tactical
move. "Once we put it out that Princeton was rich enough to refuse
half a million dollars because the giver wishes to put a building a few
hundred yards one way or the other, it would become almost impossible to collect money in any direction and the Alumni subscriptions
would have fallen off woefully," Pyne predicted.[113] As the most powerful trustee, Pyne was probably also alarmed by Wilson's growing
domination of university policy and affairs.

Financial considerations, personal conflicts, and battles over educational ideals characterized the struggle over the graduate college, but
the situation was complicated still further by legal problems. The
Board's action in October 1909, accepting the Procter gift if it could be
reconciled with the Swann bequest, presented an obstacle for West and
Pyne because the golf links were not a part of the grounds of the university when Mrs. Swann signed her will. The executors of the Swann
bequest, who were Princeton alumni allied with Pyne, declared that the
golf links location met the terms of the will, but Wilson received powerful support from William J. Magie, the former chancellor of New
Jersey and the trustee relied upon for authoritative legal advice. Magie
held that the Swann bequest could not be used to construct the graduate
college on the golf links.[114]

Grasping at straws, Wilson used this legal tangle to advance still
another idea involving two separate graduate colleges, one on the golf
links to be built with Procter's money, and another on the campus itself
to be built with the Swann bequest. Pyne reacted vehemently. "This
strikes me as such a ridiculous solution of the question that it does not
seem to me worth considering." But Wilson claimed support for the

[112] WW to C. H. Dodge, Feb. 18, 1910, *ibid.*, p. 141, n. 1.

[113] M. T. Pyne to C. H. McCormick, Nov. 3, 1909, *ibid.*, xix, 481.

[114] W. M. Sloane *et al.* to M. T. Pyne, Nov. 8, 1909, *ibid.*, p. 488; WW to M. T. Pyne, Dec.
25, 1909, *ibid.*, pp. 628-31; William Jay Magie to WW, Jan. 3, 1910, *ibid.*, pp. 707-708.

idea among prominent faculty members,[115] and on December 22 he proposed the idea to Procter who promptly rejected it out of hand.

Wilson was distraught. He penciled a hasty note to Pyne, declaring, "I spent an hour and ten minutes with Mr. Procter this afternoon. He is unwilling to adjust the terms of his offer to my suggestion. The acceptance of this gift has taken the guidance of the University out of my hands entirely,—and I seem to have come to the end."[116] Pyne's reply expressed the hope that the note did not represent Wilson's "well considered conclusions" and that he would "withdraw it upon further consideration."[117]

Instead, Wilson answered in an ultimatum that was a declaration of war. West, he charged, had abandoned his original idea of a graduate college at "the geographical and spiritual centre of the University." West had lost all faculty support for his ideas, Wilson argued, and nothing administered by him in accordance with his present ideas could succeed. "Indeed, nothing administered by him can now succeed." He claimed that his conscience could not permit the use of the Swann bequest for construction of the graduate college on the golf links, and Procter had insisted that the colleges not be separated. Accepting the Procter gift, he angrily told Pyne, had "reversed the policy of the Faculty, and the leading conception of my whole administration, in an educational matter of the most fundamental importance." "I am not willing to be drawn further into the toils. I cannot accede to the acceptance of gifts upon terms which take the educational policy of the University out of the hands of the Trustees and Faculty and permit it to be determined by those who give money."[118]

Wilson sent copies of the letter to every member of the Board, and if there was any question about Pyne's alliance with West, Wilson's letter made it impossible for Pyne to mediate between the two men. For the first time, Wilson had dramatically clarified the issue as a fundamental struggle between West and himself. As he told Dodge, the letter meant that "West must be absolutely eliminated, administratively." "It is our turning point," he added grimly. "It could not have been postponed."[119] Dodge was sympathetic, praising Wilson for taking "the bull by the horns" and forcing the issue. "I knew it must come & don't see how you could have done anything else."[120] But James W. Alexander, another trustee, was mystified. "There is one thing I can-

[115] M. T. Pyne to Joseph Bernard Shea, Dec. 18, 1909, *ibid.*, p. 609; M. T. Pyne to WW, Dec. 20, 1909, *ibid.*, p. 610; WW to M. T. Pyne, Dec. 21, 1909, *ibid.*, pp. 611-12.

[116] WW to M. T. Pyne, Dec. 22, 1909, *ibid.*, p. 620.

[117] M. T. Pyne to WW, Dec. 24, 1909, *ibid.*, p. 627.

[118] WW to M. T. Pyne, Dec. 25, 1909, *ibid.*, pp. 628-31.

[119] WW to C. H. Dodge, Dec. 27, 1909, *ibid.*, p. 631.

[120] C. H. Dodge to WW, Dec. 28, 1909, *ibid.*, p. 649.

not understand, & that is how it comes that West, who has been encouraged & endorsed, & prevented from accepting desirable offices in other institutions, is now regarded as unfit to administer anything," he told Wilson. "I think he should be heard before he is condemned."[121]

Although Wilson's letter mobilized considered support behind him,[122] his position remained in some doubt. John L. Cadwalader thought that the letter indicated Wilson's inability to work with people who disagreed with him. "It has too, an amusing phase—namely, that if the Board of Trustees in any essential point shall differ from the President the Board of Trustees is to give way."[123] Thomas D. Jones, who had joined the Board when his brother David's term expired, warned Wilson not to make too much of the site question because the alumni would not understand such a justification. Wilson replied that the primary problem was West but also Procter's stipulation of the location of the graduate college; he could not make West the central issue because that would make it appear to be solely "a personal matter."[124]

Meanwhile, the political machinations continued. Henry B. Thompson, Jacobus, Dodge, and Sheldon tried to work out some sort of accommodation between Wilson and Pyne.[125] Wilson's allies on the faculty graduate school committee issued a statement supporting Wilson and attacking West's "adherence to dilettante ideals."[126] But the real stroke of political genius was Pyne's. He arranged for Procter to accept Wilson's idea of two graduate colleges, and the result was exactly what Pyne had hoped it would be.[127]

The Board meeting of January 13, 1910, was the arena where the contending groups finally clashed, and the meeting brought out the worst in Wilson. Procter's willingness to accept two different graduate colleges "proved to be the bomb that broke up the meeting" of the trustees' committee on the graduate school on the morning of January 13, and Wilson was obviously put "in a most awkward position."[128]

---

[121] James Waddel Alexander to WW, c. Dec. 28, 1909, ibid., pp. 650-51.

[122] M. W. Jacobus to WW, Dec. 28, 1909, ibid., p. 648; H. B. Thompson to WW, Dec. 28, 1909, ibid., p. 649; E. W. Sheldon to WW, Dec. 28, 1909, ibid., pp. 649-50; D. B. Jones to WW, Dec. 29, 1909, ibid., p. 656; John Aikman Stewart to WW, Dec. 29, 1909, ibid., p. 656.

[123] John Lambert Cadwalader to M. T. Pyne, Dec. 30, 1909, ibid., p. 661.

[124] Thomas Davies Jones to WW, Dec. 30 and 31, 1909, ibid., pp. 659-61, 662; WW to T. D. Jones, Jan. 1, 1910, ibid., pp. 695-97.

[125] H. B. Thompson to C. H. Dodge, Jan. 3, 1910, ibid., p. 711; H. B. Thompson to M. W. Jacobus, Jan. 6, 1910, printed as an Enclosure, with H. B. Thompson to WW, Jan. 6, 1910, ibid., pp. 731-33.

[126] H. B. Fine et al. to WW, Jan. 11, 1910, with Enclosure, E. Capps et al. to WW, Jan. 10, 1910, ibid., pp. 753-55.

[127] W. C. Procter to M. T. Pyne, Jan. 12, 1910, ibid., xx, 3.

[128] H. B. Thompson to C. H. Dodge, Jan. 14, 1910, ibid., p. 14; M. W. Jacobus to H. B. Thompson, Jan. 22, 1910, ibid., p. 46.

At the Board meeting, he claimed that the issue was not one "of geography but of ideals," his versus West's, and that the faculty could make a success of the graduate college "anywhere in Mercer County." He pulled out a copy of West's pamphlet on the graduate college and exclaimed, "The fundamental difficulty with Mr. Procter's offer is that it is specifically intended to carry out the ideals of that book. A graduate school based on those ideals cannot succeed." James W. Alexander then asked Wilson why he had written such a commendatory preface, and Wilson said that he had not seen the book when he wrote the preface.

Contradiction followed contradiction. Wilson signaled Jacobus to introduce a motion rejecting the Procter offer of two graduate schools, and Wilson was immediately asked why he now opposed an offer he himself had made. Although he had earlier claimed faculty support for the idea, he now asserted that he had been convinced by unnamed faculty members that the plan was "unworkable." One trustee, to Wilson's great indignation, reportedly commented that this "did not appear to comport with standards of strict honor." Finally, the Board approved a motion calling for a committee to negotiate with Procter concerning his offer.[129]

It is little wonder that Pyne was exasperated with Wilson. "It is difficult to tell the vagaries of his mind as it changes so," he noted bitterly.[130] Pyne particularly resented the charge that West, Procter, and he wanted "a luxurious or dilettante college" and insisted that all three wanted "a hard-working, broad, democratic institution, very much on the line of the undergraduate life."[131] That was precisely the issue, for Wilson believed that the eating clubs had created an undemocratic climate for undergraduate education. The chasm between Wilson and Pyne was complete, and Pyne began to maneuver for Wilson's resignation by arranging for Procter's withdrawal of his offer and the simultaneous resignation by West.[132] Procter agreed that Wilson should no longer be president but feared that the withdrawal of his gift would have a detrimental effect on university fund-raising. Eventually he accepted Pyne's tactics and on February 6 canceled his offer.[133]

"The jig is up & it now only remains to have decent obsequies," Dodge jubilantly wrote to Wilson. "At last," Wilson exclaimed, "we

[129] Trustees' Minutes, Jan. 13, 1910, *ibid.*, pp. 4-5; the account of this meeting is based on the Editorial Note, Wilson at the Meeting of the Board of Trustees on January 13, 1910, *ibid.*, pp. 6-9.

[130] M. T. Pyne to Charles Wood, Jan. 18, 1910, *ibid.*, p. 29.

[131] M. T. Pyne to Henry Woodhull Green, Jan. 18, 1910, *ibid.*, p. 30.

[132] M. T. Pyne to Wilson Farrand, Jan. 25, 1910, *ibid.*, pp. 56-57.

[133] W. C. Procter to M. T. Pyne, Jan. 31, 1910, *ibid.*, p. 65; W. C. Procter to T. D. Jones, Feb. 6, 1910, printed in T. D. Jones *et al.* to the Trustees, Feb. 10, 1910, *ibid.*, pp. 100-101.

are free to govern the University as our judgments and consciences dictate! I have an unspeakable sense of relief."[134] On February 10 the Board met and approved the special committee's report sustaining Wilson's position that the graduate college should have a central location.[135] But the battle continued. Pyne arranged secretly for Procter to purchase land guaranteeing a better approach to the golf links site,[136] and the Pyne-West forces became further embittered by a *New York Times* editorial describing them as trying "to bend and degrade [students] into fostering mutually exclusive social cliques, stolid groups of wealth and fashion, devoted to non-essentials and the smatterings of culture."[137] Herbert B. Brougham wrote this editorial after Wilson had accepted his offer of support, and while Wilson later claimed he had nothing to do with the editorial, he wrote Brougham after its publication that "every word" was true. He protested that he could not get further involved in a public exchange because the dispute was personal. "The central equation in this whole business is a personal equation."[138]

After the Board meeting, Wilson left for Bermuda to soothe his frayed nerves but not before he launched an attempt to have West removed as dean at the April board meeting. His allies among the trustees and faculty advised against it, warning that in the wake of Procter's withdrawal of his gift, West would simply appear to be a martyr.[139] In Bermuda, the problems of Princeton continued to plague Wilson, giving him bad dreams of the struggle "with college foes, the sessions of hostile trustees, the confused war of argument and insinuation." "I have been fighting a hard fight here with myself," he told Ellen, "and have not succeeded in getting myself in hand as well as I should."[140]

He began to flirt with the idea of resigning and entering politics, because as even Ellen realized, "This thing has strengthened you *im-*

[134] C. H. Dodge to WW, Feb. 6, 1910, *ibid.*, p. 82; WW to C. H. Dodge, Feb. 7, 1910, *ibid.*, p. 83.

[135] T. D. Jones *et al.* to the Trustees, Feb. 10, 1910, *ibid.*, pp. 92-115.

[136] W. C. Procter to M. T. Pyne, Feb. 8, 1910, *ibid.*, p. 90.

[137] *New York Times*, Feb. 4, 1910, reprinted at Feb. 3, 1910, in *ibid.*, pp. 74-76.

[138] Herbert Bruce Brougham to WW, Jan. 31, 1910, *ibid.*, p. 65; WW to H. B. Brougham, Feb. 1 and 5, 1910, *ibid.*, pp. 69-71, 79-80; for Wilson's disavowals, see a memorandum of a conversation with Paul van Dyke, March 16, 1910, and WW to Hiram Woods, March 23, 1910, *ibid.*, pp. 249-51, 285-87.

[139] WW to E. W. Sheldon, Feb. 11, 1910; WW to M. W. Jacobus, Feb. 11, 1910; H. B. Thompson to E. W. Sheldon, *c.* Feb. 15, 1910; M. W. Jacobus to C. H. Dodge, Feb. 15, 1910; T. D. Jones to C. H. Dodge, Feb. 18, 1910; H. B. Fine to WW, Feb. 24, 1910; H. B. Fine to E. W. Sheldon, Feb. 26, 1910; H. B. Thompson to T. D. Jones, Feb. 26, 1910; E. W. Sheldon to WW, March 1, 1910; all in *ibid.*, pp. 118-19, 119-20, 128, 128-29, 142-44, 173-75, 182, 183, 190-91.

[140] WW to EAW, Feb. 17 and 20-21, 1910, *ibid.*, pp. 133, 145.

mensely throughout the whole country; it is said that there have been hundreds upon hundreds of editorials and all *wholly* on your side." Wilson, whose family had adopted a motto of "God save us from compromise," felt that his personal integrity was intact. "We have no compromises to look back on, the record of our consciences is clear in this whole trying business," he wrote to Ellen. "We can be happy, therefore, no matter what may come of it all. It would be rather jolly, after all, to start out on life anew together, to make a new career, would it not?"[141]

However bright the political future may have been, the situation at Princeton was still very tense. In contrast to the "quad" fight which quickly became a public debate, much of the quarrel over the graduate college remained behind the scenes until the public announcement of the withdrawal of the Procter gift. Alumni began to organize,[142] and a bad situation was compounded by the injection of the "quad" issue into the fight. Alumni prepared pamphlets praising Wilson's quad-rangle scheme and his position in the graduate college debate,[143] and Wilson's November 1909 article in *Scribner's Magazine*, "What Is a College For?" clearly indicated that he had not forsaken his cherished vision of reorganizing the social life of Princeton students. He attacked the idea that a college education had become fashionable and expressed alarm over the influx into colleges of "the sons of very rich men" who were "not as apt to form definite and serious purposes, as those who know that they must whet their wits for the struggle of life." The intellectual life of colleges was threatened by "side shows" which did not need to be abolished but subordinated. "The fundamental thing to be accomplished in the new organization is, that, instead of being the heterogeneous congeries of petty organizations it now is, instead of being allowed to go to pieces in a score of fractions free to cast off from the whole as they please, [student life] should be drawn together again into a single university family of which the teachers shall be as natural and as intimate members as the undergraduates."[144]

At this same time, another of Wilson's primary achievements—the preceptorial plan—was in deep trouble. The cost of maintaining the preceptors mounted steadily; the preceptors themselves grew restive with their heavy reading and teaching responsibilities which did not

[141] EAW to WW, Feb. 28, 1910, *ibid.*, p. 189; WW to EAW, Feb. 20-21, 1910, *ibid.*, p. 146.

[142] William Royal Wilder to WW, with Enclosures, Jan. 31, 1910, *ibid.*, pp. 65-68.

[143] Coleman Peace Brown, *The Princeton Ideal: A Permanent Plan To Secure Social and Intellectual Coordination* (copy in UA, NjP), and Robert Fulton McMahon to the Editor of the New York *Sun*, March 21, 1910, *PWW*, xx, 278-82. McMahon also published a pamphlet making essentially the same points as his letter to the *Sun–The Graduate School and the Quads* (copy in UA, NjP).

[144] "What Is a College For?" Aug. 18, 1909, *PWW*, xix, 334-47.

leave them time for their own research; and Wilson faced the problem of either promoting the preceptors to professorial rank, further increasing the costs, or releasing them and hiring new preceptors.[145]

Faced with a steadily disintegrating situation, Wilson returned from Bermuda in March 1910 with a two-pronged strategy for the graduate college fight. First, he intended to urge the trustees at their April meeting to refer the question of the graduate college location to the faculty for a final decision. Wilson knew that he had the votes there to sustain his own position, and he feared that the Board would finally vote with Pyne and West. He was also afraid that Procter would renew his offer in a form which would " 'dish' " him in some adroit way.[146]

The second part of his strategy was to take his case to the alumni, just as he had done with the "quad" plan. By early April, Wilson announced, "My little campaign is over. I have spoken in Baltimore, Brooklyn, Jersey City, and St. Louis, and have tried in the four speeches pieced together to make as complete an impersonal statement of our case as was possible. Each of these meetings was thoroughly encouraging."[147]

Wilson even carried his defense of himself and his policies before the most hostile group of alumni—the Princeton Club of New York. He reviewed the record of his presidency and emphasized that the social and intellectual life of the university, as well as undergraduate and graduate education, had to be unified. "The whole Princeton idea is an organic idea, an idea of contact of mind with mind,—no chasms, no divisions in life and organization,—a grand brotherhood of intellectual endeavor, stimulating the youngster, instructing and balancing the older man, giving the one an aspiration and the other a comprehension of what the whole undertaking is,—of lifting, lifting, lifting the mind of successive generations from age to age!" He told alumni that Princeton had "arrested the attention of the academic world" and asked, "When the country is looking to us as men who prefer ideas even to money, are we going to withdraw and say, 'After all, we find we are mistaken: we prefer money to ideas'?"[148]

The New York alumni were unmoved, but Wilson still had the op-

[145] M. W. Jacobus to WW, April 12 and 19, 1909, *ibid.*, pp. 159-60, 167-68; M. W. Jacobus to H. B. Thompson, April 20, 1909, *ibid.*, pp. 168-69; H. B. Thompson to Jacobus, May 17, 1909, *ibid.*, pp. 197-98; WW to the Trustees' Curriculum Committee, *c.* June 12, 1909, *ibid.*, pp. 242, n. 2; E. W. Sheldon to WW, Oct. 11, 1909, *ibid.*, pp. 407-408. WW to the Trustees' Curriculum Committee, *c.* May 13, 1910, *ibid.*, xx, 445-53.

[146] WW to E. W. Sheldon, March 21, 1910, *ibid.*, pp. 270-71; WW to C. H. McCormick, March 21, 1910, *ibid.*, p. 271; WW to M. W. Jacobus, March 21 and April 2, 1910, *ibid.*, pp. 271-72, 311-12.

[147] WW to M. W. Jacobus, April 2, 1910, *ibid.*, p. 311.

[148] Speech to the Princeton Club of New York, April 7, 1910, *ibid.*, pp. 337-48, esp. p. 348.

portunity to persuade the trustees to refer the whole matter of the graduate school's "character, methods, and administration" to the faculty. The trustee's committee on the graduate school approved the idea, but at the meeting of the entire Board on April 14, a motion to postpone referral was adopted.[149] Henry B. Thompson's report of the meeting indicates the vicious antagonisms which were tearing the Board apart:

> The temper of the opposition was hostile, although nothing was said that was offensive, except old [John] DeWitt, as usual, made an ass of himself. . . . Wilson feels that the opposition is now permanent, and is not governed by reason, but simply by orders. . . . I have tried to approach Momo [Pyne] on two occasions, but he is absolutely implacable, and refuses to talk consecutively two minutes on any subject, but flies back to what happened months ago. Bayard [Henry]'s attitude is one of dignified hostility. He hisses criticisms. . . . Archie [Russell] is really the most disappointing of the lot, as he has simply been fed on a lot of Princeton women gossip, and has swallowed it all. . . . All of the above is not encouraging.[150]

Thompson's conclusion was an understatement, for Wilson was furious with the Board for doing "*nothing.*" "That nothing was hostile (because I urged action upon it)," he concluded.[151]

Wilson left immediately to address the Pittsburgh alumni, and he issued a vehement defense of his policies and a stinging indictment of his opponents and the influence of wealth in American society. He began by declaring that he did not know whom he represented any longer and said he occupied a position of "splendid isolation." "How does the nation judge Princeton?" he asked. "And which judgment should take precedence, the Princeton family judgment or the common judgment of the country?" He charged that the nation's colleges were "looking to the support of the classes, looking to the support of wealth"; "they are not looking to the service of the people at large."

Stung by the continuing opposition of nearly all the clerical members of the Board, Wilson lashed out at the churches as well.

> I believe that the churches of this country, at any rate the Protestant churches, have dissociated themselves from the people of this country. They are serving the classes and they are not serving the masses. They serve certain strata, certain uplifted strata, but they are not serving the men whose need is dire. The churches have more regard

[149] A. F. West to the Trustees, April 14, 1910, *ibid.*, pp. 354-55; Trustees' Minutes, April 14, 1910, *ibid.*, pp. 356-57.

[150] H. B. Thompson to C. H. Dodge, April 15, 1910, *ibid.*, pp. 361-62.

[151] WW to M.A.H. Peck, April 19, 1910, *ibid.*, p. 370.

to their pew-rents than to the souls of men, and in proportion as they look to the respectability of their congregations to lift them in esteem, they are depressing the whole level of Christian endeavor.

The same man who had hailed college men as a kind of intellectual aristocracy now rejected them and saw the true American spirit in "the great mass of the unknown, of the unrecognized men, whose powers are being developed by struggle, who will form their opinions as they progress in that struggle, and who will emerge with opinions which will rule." Concluding with a rhetorical flourish, Wilson warned, "If she loses her self possession America will stagger like France through fields of blood before she again finds peace and prosperity under the leadership of men who understand her needs."[152]

The Pittsburgh alumni were shocked, and Wilson's speech was circulated in the newspapers and through an alumni pamphlet, *That Pittsburgh Speech*.[153] "I let myself go," Wilson admitted.[154] In a letter to the New York *Evening Post*, he tried to undo the damage, arguing that the news reports "conveyed an entirely false impression." He was not opposed to the refining influence of college education but merely wanted a college organized to "produce that subtle atmospheric influence in which culture thrives while the spirit of service and achievement is not dampened or slackened."[155] But if Wilson's letter to Pyne on December 23, 1909, represented a private declaration of war against the wealthy interests supporting the university, the Pittsburgh speech made the break public. Pyne was incensed by Wilson's address but was encouraged by the prospect that Wilson would either resign or be forced out of office.[156]

Wilson realized that the opposition was growing and the situation becoming "rather serious."[157] New negotiations with Procter were initiated to persuade him to renew his offier,[158] and rumors of new gifts for the graduate college began to circulate. Wilson stubbornly insisted that he was "fighting for the very life and integrity of the University" but resolved to keep quiet and maintain "the wisdom of the serpent in

---

[152] News reports, April 17 and 20, 1910, *ibid.*, pp. 363-68, 373-78. Actually, the various news reports leave some doubt about what Wilson actually said because Wilson's words were variously quoted. It seems plausible that Wilson did in fact make some of the more extreme statements that were attributed to him, for he was in an extremely agitated frame of mind.

[153] Copy in UA, NjP.

[154] WW to M. A. H. Peck, April 19, 1910, *PWW*, xx, 370.

[155] WW to the Editor of the New York *Evening Post*, April 21, 1910, *ibid.*, pp. 378-79.

[156] M. T. Pyne to Bayard Henry, April 20, 1910, *ibid.*, pp. 377-78.

[157] WW to Z. C. Felt, April 26, 1910, *ibid.*, p. 392.

[158] C. H. McCormick to T. D. Jones, April 26, 1910, *ibid.*, pp. 393-95; W. C. Procter to M. T. Pyne, April 26, 1910, *ibid.*, pp. 396-97.

this matter."[159] Various compromises designed to reduce West's power were proposed, and Wilson professed to be open to them but added, "Compromise is exceedingly difficult where very deep principles are involved and where deep principles seem to express themselves in every detail of administration when one is dealing with men who cannot quite be depended upon to cooperate effectually."[160]

The denouement came quickly. On May 18, a wealthy, obscure alumnus, Isaac C. Wyman, died in Salem, Massachusetts, leaving virtually his entire estate to Princeton for the graduate college and designating his attorney and West as executors of the will. "I can hardly believe it all!" West exclaimed to Pyne. "Isn't it fine? TE DEUM LAUDAMUS. NON NOBIS DOMINE," he concluded and jubilantly signed himself, "Little Willie."[161] Pyne was similarly overjoyed. "The effect of the announcement was astounding," he told Procter and immediately arranged for the renewal of his offer. Pyne also sensed the political implications of the bequest which West had secured. The future, he declared, was in West's hands, not Wilson's.[162] Wilson knew he was beaten. When he received West's telegram notifying him that the Wyman gift to Princeton would be "at least two millions" and possibly more, he announced to Ellen, "We've beaten the living, but we can't fight the dead—the game is up."[163]

His capitulation was total. He agreed that West could remain as dean; that the Procter gift could be accepted if it was divorced from considerations of academic policy; and that the Swann bequest should be submitted to litigation to determine whether it could be used to construct the graduate college on the golf links site.[164] Wilson's moral and educational objections to the Procter gift were swept away by the enormous gift which neither Princeton nor its president could refuse. On June 6, Procter made his offer again for $500,000 for endowing the preceptorial system, designating $200,000 for the dining hall of the graduate college and the rest for fellowships. On June 9 the trustees accepted the offer and formally thanked West for "his great services to the University in assisting so largely in obtaining the gifts under the will of Mr. Wyman."[165]

[159] WW to E. G. Reid, May 2, 1910, *ibid.*, p. 407; WW to H. B. Brougham, May 9, 1910, *ibid.*, p. 425.

[160] WW to Z. C. Felt, May 17, 1910, *ibid.*, p. 459.

[161] A. F. West to M. T. Pyne, May 22, 1910, *ibid.*, pp. 465-66.

[162] M. T. Pyne to W. C. Procter, May 24, 1910, *ibid.*, pp. 470-71.

[163] John Marshall Raymond and A. F. West to WW, May 22, 1910, *ibid.*, p. 464; Eleanor Wilson McAdoo, *The Woodrow Wilsons* (New York, 1937), p. 101.

[164] WW to C. H. McCormick, May 25 [26], 1910, *PWW*, xx, 472-73.

[165] W. C. Procter to M. T. Pyne, June 6, 1910, *ibid.*, p. 506; Trustees' Minutes, June 9, 1910, *ibid.*, pp. 509-11.

"The end of our controversy here was truly dramatic. I hope that Providence will never be really as funny as it can," Wilson wrote to a friend after the June commencement.[166] He was right in more ways than he knew. A controversy which Wilson characterized as a moral struggle over whether contributors could determine Princeton's educational policy was ironically settled by a munificent contribution from a dead alumnus who could not be fought. Wilson had resisted the Procter gift as part of a larger effort to rid himself of West's administrative influence, but in the face of the Wyman bequest, West, not Wilson, triumphed. A personal battle, complicated by conflicting educational ideals, had been transformed by Wilson into an attack on the deleterious influence of wealth in American society, but money ended the fight. Even more ironic, the Wyman bequest eventually turned out to be far less than the three to thirty million dollars that some had predicted. From 1912 to 1917, West and Wyman's lawyer turned over $171,000 to the university, and of this amount $64,000 was used to build a house for West near the graduate college. In 1917, the balance of the estate, approximately $623,000, was surrendered by the executors of the will.[167]

Wilson recognized that West's victory left open the question of his "future relations to the University." "I reserve for future consideration, therefore, the answer to the question whether my position is now tenable or untenable."[168] He made a startling admission to his former classmate, Hiram Woods: "So many of West's desires and purposes with regard to the Graduate School are the same that are held by all of us that I am afraid it would seem small and petulant if I were to resign in the circumstances, though I must say that my judgment is a good deal perplexed in the matter."[169]

These reflections were somewhat disingenuous, for throughout the spring of 1910 Wilson had been conferring with Democratic leaders in New Jersey about the possibility of his running for governor in November, and although those negotiations were still incomplete, Wilson was clearly disposed toward leaving the scene of what he feared was his surrender.[170] Wilson also knew that his ideals for the graduate school had changed during his presidency and did not agree with West's. As Edwin G. Conklin recalled, Wilson had good reason for his opposition to West, for after Wilson's resignation, West became the unchallenged authority over the graduate school. He barred married

[166] WW to Roland Sletor Morris, June 16, 1910, *ibid.*, p. 534.

[167] J. M. Raymond and A. F. West to WW, May 22, 1910, *ibid.*, p. 464, n. 3.

[168] WW to C. H. McCormick, May 25, 1910, *ibid.*, p. 472.

[169] WW to H. Woods, May 28, 1910, *ibid.*, p. 482.

[170] WW to M.A.H. Peck, June 17, 1910, *ibid.*, p. 535.

students from obtaining graduate training at Princeton, and he saw Princeton's graduate school as the natural complement to an Ivy League education.[171]

Wilson's last four years as president of Princeton contrast so sharply with the first four years that one is forced to conclude that his stroke in 1906 had prompted a decisive change in both his thinking and behavior. He continued to talk the language of common counsel and mutual discussion, but be consulted fewer people and gradually personified the struggle at Princeton as an attack upon himself. He always portrayed himself as open to compromise, but the terms of available compromises were exceedingly narrow. He had always preached the gospel of fidelity to one's ideals, but after 1906 fidelity spelled moral rigidity, stubbornness, and obdurateness. One colleague recalled an incident which is illustrative. Wilson found himself in a hot debate with a seminary professor over a game of pool. Finally, in a gracious gesture, the theologian remarked, "Well, Dr. Wilson, there are two sides to every question." "Yes," Wilson shot back, "a right side and a wrong side!"[172]

The conflict and turmoil of Wilson's last four years as president were marked not only by his personal intransigence but by a number of strategical mistakes. He did not lay a proper foundation for the quadrangle plan with either the trustees, alumni, faculty, or students, and the explosive reaction was predictable. Similarly, in proposing the "quad" scheme, Wilson antagonized his most powerful opponent, Andrew F. West, and by failing to make a clean break with West in 1906, he perpetuated a personal quarrel and administrative strife for his last four years. By ignoring the legitimate claims of the graduate college as a university priority and by remaining remarkably blasé about the university's financial situation, Wilson undermined his long friendship with Moses Taylor Pyne—the man who had told him as late as 1908 that he was "Princeton's best asset."[173] He drove Pyne into West's camp by consistently agitating for the "quad" plan after the Board had rejected it and by insisting on the university's moral right to reject money because the donor wanted to determine the location of the building.

One can scarcely fault Wilson's criticisms of the eating clubs at

[171] Conklin remembered that a student from Hope College applied and "presented an excellent record and recommendations as to his ability for advanced courses in biology." West summarily rejected the application, writing across it, "Ineligible—institution of no account." R. S. Baker memorandum of an interview with E. G. Conklin, June 19, 1925 (R. S. Baker Coll., DLC).

[172] W. S. Myers, "Wilson in My Diary," *Woodrow Wilson: Some Princeton Memories*, p. 43.

[173] M. T. Pyne to WW, Oct. 25, 1908, *PWW*, xviii, 473.

Princeton or his alarms over West's ideals of a genteel graduate program at Princeton. Yet, if Wilson was genuinely concerned about the democratic character of student life at Princeton, as he claimed to be in his initial presentation of the "quad" plan, the place to begin was the nature of the student body itself. Admissions policy remained unchanged throughout his presidency, and although the clubs clearly needed to be reformed, a more radical proposal for altering the undemocratic character of Princeton would have been a transformation of the university's reliance upon students from wealthy backgrounds. Given Wilson's comments about colleges becoming "country clubs" and the academic superiority of public school students, it is possible that if he had remained at Princeton, he might have moved in the direction of revamping Princeton's admissions policy. But Wilson's defeat in the graduate college fight meant that the implications of his emerging democratic thinking would be felt in politics, not in academia.

Wilson's insistence upon an organic conception of the university also prompted him to attempt a coordination of both the intellectual and social life of the students. He may have legitimately feared the competition of "side shows" to the intellectual purposes of an educational institution, but there is no necessarily simple or straightforward relationship between students' social activities and their academic pursuits. Students have long used various social outlets as a release from or a substitute for their formal academic training, and even Wilson as a student at Princeton seemed far more interested in the college newspaper, the debating clubs, and the football and baseball teams than the courses that he was taking. Wilson's desire to reorganize and completely unify all phases of college life was essentially coercive in its attempt to surround the student with what Wilson conceived to be beneficial influences, molding the individual's character along lines that Wilson had ordained.

The "quad" and graduate college controversies were a tragedy—for Wilson and for Princeton University. Under West's leadership, graduate education at Princeton was undistinguished and remained so until after World War II. The club system flourished, searing the lives of students like Leon Levy and Harold Zeiss and contributing to Princeton's reputation of being perhaps the most WASPish and elitist of all the eastern colleges. Nearly a half century after Wilson left Princeton, an undergraduate acknowledged "the very real conflict between the social and academic side of life" at Princeton and went on to confirm one of Wilson's central indictments of the club system. "Yet I knew," the student said, "that, like thousands of Princetonians before me, I would love Princeton not primarily for the academic education, but for my club and my social life."[174] Today the popularity of the

---

[174] Otto Butz (ed.), *The Unsilent Generation* (New York and Toronto, 1958), p. 70.

clubs ebbs and flows, but the system itself is withering—testimony to changes in student attitudes and the increasing diversity of the Princeton student body. The palatial club houses stand as relics of another age—monuments to the pyhrric victory won by the Princeton alumni and artifacts of the tremendous social struggle at Princeton that made Wilson's name a subject of campus controversy for years.

Despite the defects in Wilson's vision for Princeton, he can be credited with what Link has described in a different context as "higher realism."[175] Decades before the rest of American society came to the same realization, Wilson saw that if eductional institutions were to be enlisted "in the nation's service," they could not merely serve a particular strata of society. "We have conceived education in its true terms in Amerca," Wilson observed at the height of the graduate college fight. "It is a public, not a private, instrumentality."[176]

Accordingly, the college became in Wilson's mind a laboratory for a democratic society, a place where ability obliterated the distinctions created by "the spirit of material achievement." "Only that college is democratic whose members take the contacts of life as they come; where men are preferred by conduct and performance rather than by taste and the rivalries of competitive organizations which have nothing to do with the main moral and intellectual business of the place; where there is no childish concentration upon the immediate objects of social success, but where men are tried out as spirits, as sample servants of the country and of the age." Wilson concluded, "Democracy is a field in which the favours are natural, not artificial; and the democracy of the college is to be tested by what it does with its men of parts."[177]

As he consistently preached to Princeton students, education could not be separated from political life or from American society as a whole, and out of his agonizing experience at Princeton he formulated a new understanding of what a democratic society could be. That transferral from academic theory to political life was partial and incomplete, for Wilson never became a radical social democrat but a moderate, reformist progressive. But in his policies at Princeton, Wilson pointed to the truth that every minority group in America has grasped—the importance of eduction in creating a more equal and just society.

Tragically, Wilson pushed ahead with his ideals—blindly, impetuously, and against insuperable odds. In a sense, Wilson was at his best and worst when faced with virulent opposition. His speeches were eloquent, even heroic and prophetic. His tactics were clumsy and con-

[175] Arthur S. Link, *The Higher Realism of Woodrow Wilson* (Nashville, Tenn., 1971), pp. 127-39.

[176] "The Country and the Colleges," *c.* Feb. 24, 1910, *PWW*, xx, 159. Because of the animosities generated by the graduate college fight, Wilson withheld this essay from publication.

[177] *Ibid.*, pp. 160, 161.

tradictory. Particularly after the announcement of the Procter gift, Wilson was consistently on the defensive, and "that arch-intriguer" West proved to be his superior at academic politics. Whether Wilson could have salvaged the situation after the winter of 1909-1910 is doubtful. The entire fracas scarred him deeply, and even during the last years of his life after he left the White House, he encouraged a friend to try to raise money to find him a university presidency where his social ideal—the "quads"—could be realized.[178] By the summer of 1910, Wilson realized that the stakes had been raised too high, the lines too clearly drawn, the wounds too widely opened.

As many have observed, Wilson's college presidency presents startling parallels with his governorship of New Jersey and presidency of the United States. All were characterized by early achievements and then marred by conflict, turmoil, and subsequent defeat. Less noticed is the remarkable similarity between Wilson's behavior during the battles at Princeton and his father's reaction to his troubles at Columbia Theological Seminary. When confronted with opposition, both fused the issues of authority and morality and became absolutely intransigent in their positions. But when Wilson's father retreated to a wealthy pastorate to contemplate his misfortune, he instilled in his son the necessity of fighting on against all opposition. Wilson learned the lesson well, for as he told the seniors in 1910 at their annual dinner, Princeton men were not united by vague ideals but were really "a *little* company" who had "the feeling of an organization, an army corps."[179] Together, they would fight for God's purposes in an alien world.

---

[178] Raymond B. Fosdick to Ray Stannard Baker, June 23, 1926 (R. S. Baker Coll., DLC).
[179] Notes, June 9, 1910, *PWW*, xx, 511-12.

IX

The Moralizer of American Life

When Wilson became president of Princeton in 1902, he was naïve and inexperienced in the wiles of practical political life, but by 1910 the conflicts at Princeton had made him a good deal wiser. "I don't want you to suppose," he told a friend in 1911, "that when I was nominated for Governor of New Jersey I emerged from academic seclusion, where nothing was known of the problems of politics. . . . I'll confide in you—as I have already confided to others—that, as compared with the college politician, the real article seems like an amateur."[1] Wilson gained more than mere political experience during the eight years of his presidency. Indeed, this period of his life is crucial because of the gradual, subtle, but finally dramatic alteration of his political thought.

By 1902, Wilson's numerous articles and books and his ceaseless lecturing throughout the nation had brought him a degree of prominence as a political commentator. His reputation was based on his firm allegiance to the Democratic party, his alarm over its usurpation by the Bryanites, and his conservative misgivings about proposals to reform American life. He believed that if he had lived at the time of the American Revolution, he probably would have been a Tory because he preferred "patient changes." "The dogged pressure of opinion brings reform just as surely, although more slowly than a revolution."[2]

He gradually began to see that William Jennings Bryan's assessment of the wrongs in American society was accurate, but he continued to inveigh against Bryan's ability as a leader. The Great Commoner's chief difficulty, Wilson declared, was that he had "no brains" and regretted "that a man with his power of leadership should have no mental rudder."[3] To a party rent by sectional differences and factional quarrels, Wilson increasingly became an attractive political figure in his own right, and in 1902 "An Old Fashioned Democrat" gave him his first public endorsement for the presidency of the United States. In a letter to the editor of the *Indianapolis News*, he hailed Wilson as "a man of ability and character, one who has a profound conviction of the

---

[1] Henry B. Needham, "Woodrow Wilson's Views," *Outlook*, xcviii (Aug. 26, 1911), 940.

[2] News report of a speech in Syracuse, N. Y., Feb. 17, 1905, *PWW*, xv, 172.

[3] R. S. Baker memorandum of an interview with Roland Sletor Morris, March 7 and 8, 1926 (R. S. Baker Coll., DLC).

truth of Democratic principles, and who has the advantage of knowing what these principles are."[4]

During his early years as Princeton's president, Wilson devoted most of his speeches to educational subjects and avoided direct comment on the political issues being raised by the maturing progressive movement. But he soon realized, as a trustee later advised him, that the presidency of Princeton was "second only to the Presidency of the Country as a pulpit,"[5] and he used his new platform to preach a gospel of order and service to the nation. He conceded that reforms were needed in American society, but he remained studiously vague about specific proposals, declaring instead his faith in the "essential soundness and wholesomeness of this nation."[6] He brought to all of his public addresses a calm assurance that God's special blessing was extended to the American people, for "there is nothing that gives a man [a] more profound belief in Providence than the history of this country."[7] Before the New York Society of Mayflower Descendants, Wilson confidently declared, "The question of the present day to solve . . . is not what new principles discover, but what old ones apply."[8]

To students, alumni, and the general public, Wilson's message remained the same. The old ideals of an agrarian, Protestant America were still valid in an increasingly pluralistic, industrialized, and urbanized society. The university was the conservator of those values, and its function was to preserve the nation's "memorials, to keep in the recollection of the youth the principles, the traditions, the impulses of race, to act as a sort of clearing-house where the indebtedness is cancelled, where the fine balances of thought must be thought out."[9] Students were trained in the "*statesmanship of the mind*" to fulfill their unique calling of disinterested service to society. "There is a difference . . . between success and achievement," Wilson believed, and he held out an idealistic vision of personal responsibility. "Achievement comes to the man who has forgotten himself and married himself and his mind to the task to which he has set himself; success may come to the merely diligent man."[10]

The total commitment to altruistic service, which Wilson's gospel demanded, also made possible a facile identification of religion and pa-

---

    [4] An Old Fashioned Democrat to the Editor of the *Indianapolis News*, May 1, 1902, *PWW*, xii, 356-58.

    [5] D. B. Jones to WW, May 19, 1910, *ibid.*, xx, 459.

    [6] News report of a speech to a women's club in Lowell, Mass., Jan. 3, 1903, *ibid.*, xiv, 316.

    [7] A speech on patriotism to the Washington Association of New Jersey, Feb. 23, 1903, *ibid.*, p. 371.

    [8] News report, Nov. 22, 1902, *ibid.*, p. 210.

    [9] News report of a speech in East Orange, N. J., Dec. 23, 1902, *ibid.*, p. 302.

    [10] Notes for an address to the Twentieth Century Club of Boston, Dec. 29, 1902, *ibid.*, p. 308; speech to the Princeton Club of New York, Dec. 9, 1902, *ibid.*, p. 271.

triotism. Consistently using religious terms to describe allegiance to America, Wilson viewed patriotism as a principle "not of taste" but of "devotion" and "consecration." True to his Calvinist heritage, he insisted that patriotism was not passive but assertive, "a display of energy outside of selfish interest."[11] Since America's patriots were those without selfish motives, the nation was charged with the evangelical mission of spreading its ideals throughout the world. He defended the expansionist thrust of the United States because the nation intended to show people "the way to liberty without plundering them or making them our tools for a selfish end." "We are a sort of pure air blowing in world politics," he declared, "destroying illusions and cleaning places of morbid miasmatic gases."[12]

This moral imperialism became a political imperialism as well, and Wilson viewed America's mission as the particular responsibility of the Anglo-Saxon race. "When you consider what the different nations of the world stand for, keeping in mind the specific purpose of England and America," he proclaimed, "you will see that there is but one course to choose and that is to carry forward in honesty and unselfishness that service to the world which has now been carried too far for us to turn back. The Anglo-Saxon people have undertaken to reconstruct the affairs of the world, and it would be a shame upon them to withdraw their hand."[13]

Wilson buttressed his justification of American imperialism with Frederick Jackson Turner's frontier interpretation of American history, arguing that once the domestic frontier had closed, an international one had to be created. "It was not an accident that we annexed the Philippines," Wilson maintained. "We had to have a frontier; we got into the habit, and needed one. The characteristic American is an exploiter."[14] In spite of Wilson's appropriation of history to sanction American policy, his defense remained fundamentally moral in character. The United States could rule the world, he believed, but would do so wisely only if the people remained idealists, seeking to serve humanity. "America is not great because of the things she holds in her hand," Wilson emphasized.

> but because of the things she holds in her heart, because of the visions she has seen; and she will lose her greatness if in her too

[11] Speech on patriotism to the Washington Association of New Jersey, Feb. 23, 1903, *ibid.*, p. 367; speech on patriotism to the students of the University of Michigan, April 22, 1903, *ibid.*, p. 419.

[12] "The Statesmanship of Letters," Nov. 5, 1903, *ibid.*, xv, 41; news report of a speech in Montclair, N. J., Jan. 28, 1904, *ibid.*, p. 143.

[13] News report of a speech to the Pilgrims of the United States, Jan. 30, 1904, *ibid.*, p. 149.

[14] News report of a toast, "Benjamin Franklin," at the American Philosophical Society banquet, April 15, 1905, *ibid.*, xvi, 57.

sophisticated majority she forgets the visions of her youth. It is not because we will have and hold the fleetest ships and most irresistible armies that we shall deserve the annals we started out to write, but as we use these armies and navies to do the just thing and to serve mankind.[15]

The university played a special role in America's mission, for it was "no longer a place cloistered and set apart" but involved in the affairs of the world. Its task was "enlightenment, the preparation of at least a certain number of men to see life and its affairs with a comprehensive and comprehending view."[16]

Moral statesmanship became Wilson's panacea for every ill in American society. He reminded an audience of bank clerks that "the wise financier" had frequently come "to the rescue of his country in the hour of its direst need." He informed the Pennsylvania State Bar Association that lawyers were "bound in conscience and patriotism" to supply many of the legal solutions to the nation's problems.[17] When it came to specific questions, Wilson glossed over them with moral aphorisms. The conflict between capital and labor should be handled in "a spirit of fairness" to both parties. He declared himself "an enthusiastic labor advocate" and a supporter of all unions "conducted in a proper manner," but found some union rules "unfair and irrational." Mere criticism of existing institutions was "immoral," Wilson felt, because no constructive solutions were proposed.[18]

Wilson sounded conservative and safe, and by restricting his public speeches to evangelical calls for adherence to moral ideals, he was able to avoid public controversy and move his audiences with his eloquence. "In the midst of the sordid commercialism in which I live," a lawyer wrote Wilson, "your address was like the fresh air of the mountains to one dwelling in a low-lying swamp."[19] Wilson delighted even himself with his oratorical powers. "I must say that the audience seemed fooled to the top of my wish," he reported to Ellen after a speech at the University of Michigan. After addressing some school teachers, Wilson brashly announced, "I . . . filled them with a glow that could not possibly help them to do anything I can think of, except make love! Oratory is surely an imaginative art, but who shall explore its sources?"[20] He appeared to his audiences as "the typical Ameri-

[15] "The University and the Nation," Dec. 15, 1905, *ibid.*, p. 268.

[16] "Princeton's New Plan of Study," *c.* Aug. 29, 1904, *ibid.*, xv, 455.

[17] News reports, May 13 and June 30, 1904, *ibid.*, pp. 329, 401.

[18] News report of a speech at New York City's Cooper Union, Nov. 20, 1904, *ibid.*, p. 538; news report of a speech to the New Rochelle, N. Y., People's Forum, Feb. 27, 1905, *ibid.*, xvi, 15.

[19] Francis Fisher Kane to WW, July 1, 1904, *ibid.*, xv, 401.

[20] WW to EAW, April 22, 1903, *ibid.*, xiv, 421; March 21, 1904, *ibid.*, xv, 201.

can," "tall and lank," a combination of "Abraham Lincoln and Uncle Sam." His diction was "beautiful in its simplicity," and he spoke with "perfect enunciation" and sufficient power to be heard throughout large auditoriums.[21] Despite the pressures of work at Princeton, he traveled widely, focusing mainly on cities along the Atlantic seaboard but ranging as far west as Minnesota and as far south as Alabama.

It was, in fact, the South on which Wilson pinned his hopes for a conservative resurgence in the Democratic party and American political life. "The radical element has been allowed to play fast and loose with southern politics," he complained privately, "because the conservative men, as I take it, were disinclined to go into affairs which were complicated by the necessity of handling the negro vote." He hoped that "this latent conservatism," which was stronger in the South than anywhere else, would assert itself and participate in "the reclamation of the Democratic Party."[22]

Publicly, he announced his dream for a restoration of the Democracy in a speech to the Society of the Virginians in New York in late November 1904. Weeks earlier, the conservative Democrat Alton B. Parker had been crushed by Theodore Roosevelt, but Wilson insisted that the Bryanites should not be allowed to regain control of the defeated party. "Populists and radical theorists, contemptuous alike of principle and of experience, these men could never have played any role in national politics but that of a noisy minority," Wilson declared. They had used the Democratic party since 1896, but they were interlopers, standing outside the party's traditions. The solution lay in the South, and Wilson appealed to the Virginians to help lead the way. "Let the South demand a rehabilitation of the Democratic party on the only lines that can restore it to dignity and power," he proclaimed, adding that populists should be read out of the party "as an alien faction." As the arch-conservative New York *Sun* noted, Wilson's speech "was greeted with one of the most remarkable demonstrations of approval that has been manifested at a public dinner in this city for a long time. . . . When he closed, in a voice impressive and earnest in its tone, the applause broke loose like a pent-up torrent."[23]

Increasingly, Wilson sensed that he could play a special role in influencing the politics of the nation. He styled himself as a disinterested observer, advising people on the ideals and principles which ought to guide their thinking and conduct. His emphasis was on "*private statesmanship*," and he clearly thought of himself when he announced, "The best citizens and statesmen are those who ascertain and speak the

[21] News reports of speeches in Minneapolis and Pittsburgh, April 26 and Nov. 6, 1903, *ibid.*, xiv, 427; xv, 46-47.

[22] WW to James Calvin Hemphill, Jan. 26, 1906, *ibid.*, xvi, 288.

[23] News report, Nov. 30, 1904, *ibid.*, xv, 547-48.

truth and have no private axe to grind." He claimed that there was a difference between what men demanded and what they needed. "I find that where a good many men demand good booze, that what they really want is good advice," and he proposed to supply it.[24]

In this respect, Wilson's political speeches represent a contrast to his policies as president of Princeton University. There he insisted upon creating an organic community of those bound by common values and ideals; and while he continued to emphasize the individualistic component of education, in practice his educational vision was a comprehensive, corporate one. Both aspects—the individualistic and the organic—were part of his earlier political and religious thought and heavily influenced by his covenant religious inheritance. The difference between public speeches and educational policy was power. As a private statesman, Wilson could do little more than proclaim the gospel of order and service to the nation's elite. But as Princeton's prime minister, he possessed the resources to create the community of idealists, to arrest the disintegration of contemporary life, to unify knowledge, and to convey the "map of life."

In stressing individualism and morality in public life, Wilson attracted the attention of political and economic conservatives who were alarmed by new proposals for state and federal regulation of the commercial life of the nation. One of these men was Colonel George Brinton McClellan Harvey, prominent journalist and self-styled political king-maker. An avid Cleveland Democrat, Harvey enjoyed the friendships and financial support of wealthy financiers, including William C. Whitney, Thomas Fortune Ryan, and J. Pierpont Morgan; with their assistance he assembled his own publishing empire of the *North American Review* (acquired in 1899), Harper & Brothers (of which he became president in 1901), and *Harper's Weekly*, which he edited himself. As early as 1902, Harvey reportedly thought of Wilson as an excellent presidential candidate, but he delayed in launching his personal campaign until 1906.[25]

The occasion was a dinner of the Lotos Club of New York on February 3, 1906, when Wilson was the guest of honor. Wilson claimed that he felt ill at ease among such prominent men, and using his favorite, hackneyed anecdote, he likened himself to the woman who visited a side show at a circus. There, Wilson said, "she saw, or thought she saw, a man reading a newspaper through a two-inch board. 'Oh, let me out of here,' she cried, 'this is no place for me, with these thin things

---

[24] Notes for a speech to the New Rochelle, N. Y., People's Forum, Feb. 26, 1905, *ibid.*, XVI, 13; news report of a speech in New York to the Sons of the Revolution, Feb. 23, 1905, *ibid.*, p. 12; news report of a speech to the Princeton alumni in Newark, May 16, 1903, *ibid.*, XIV, 461.

[25] Link, *Road to the White House*, pp. 97-98.

on.' " Settling down to more serious observations, Wilson selected enlightenment as the nation's most pressing need. "It seems to me that the only method of guiding ourselves in life is by determining fixed points and steering by them," Wilson stated.

Then he issued another declaration of his religious and moral idealism. Noting that preachers were right in insisting on "a philosophy of life and conduct," Wilson asked,

> Must we not have, gentlemen, some scheme of life, some particular hope, some great set of principles? Shall we forget that our eternal Judge was the judge of men who are convinced of the principles of their life? Must we not always have the spirit of learning, which is the open-minded spirit, the catholic spirit of appreciation, the spirit which desires the best, that is truth; the spirit which is correctly convinced that there are principles at the heart of things, and that things are worth while only in proportion to the sound principles that lie at their heart?[26]

While Wilson took the high road, Harvey got down to specifics. Woodrow Wilson, he declared, "was born in an atmosphere surcharged with true statesmanship" and was "by instinct a statesman." Hailing Wilson as the right man to provide the country with "a period of perfect rest," Harvey added that he contemplated "with a sense of almost rapture . . . even the remotest possibility of casting a ballot for the president of Princeton University to become President of the United States."[27]

Wilson also caught the fever, and the same night he thanked Harvey from the bottom of his heart. "It was most delightful to have such thoughts uttered about me, whether they were deserved or not."[28] After a few days, Wilson saw Harvey's speech in a clearer light and assured one friend that the "Wilson boom" was not serious. Harvey, refusing to let the matter rest, ran a picture of Wilson on the cover of *Harper's Weekly* and printed a portion of his own speech booming Wilson's candidacy.[29]

Wilson grew alarmed, fearing that the idea would be carried too far and become embarrassing,[30] and when St. Clair McKelway, editor of the *Brooklyn Eagle*, suggested that his paper further Wilson's cause, Wilson decided to squelch the idea. "Nothing could be further from

[26] Speech to the Lotos Club of New York, Feb. 3, 1906, *PWW*, xvi, 292-99.

[27] Harvey's address to the Lotos Club of New York, Feb. 3, 1906, *ibid.*, pp. 299-301.

[28] WW to G.B.M. Harvey, Feb. 3, 1906, *ibid.*, p. 301.

[29] WW to Benjamin Wistar Morris III, Feb. 7, 1906, *ibid.*, p. 306; G.B.M. Harvey to WW, Feb. 9, 1906, *ibid.*, p. 307, n. 1.

[30] WW to A. W. Hazen, March 20, 1906, *ibid.*, p. 338; WW to Robert Hunter Fitzhugh, March 19, 1906, *ibid.*, p. 338.

my thoughts than the possibility or the desirability of holding high
political office," insisted the man who had had exactly that dream since
his youth. Wilson said that he interpreted Harvey's speech as merely
suggesting that someone of Wilson's type and beliefs should be President, not necessarily himself. He acknowledged that he appealed to
"conservative men" who could support him "without apprehension."
However, at the present time he found his presidential candidacy a
mere possibility and wished no further discussion which might make
him appear "ridiculous."[31]

Wilson's alliance with Harvey in 1906 had two important results.
First, it put him in contact with powerful men who could advise him
and exert some influence in the affairs of the Democratic party. Second, it made Wilson politically reliant upon the most conservative
wing of the party and effectively foreclosed any sympathy he might
have possessed for the growing progressive movement. At precisely
the time that Harvey was proposing Wilson as a presidential candidate,
Wilson was becoming alarmed about the club situation at Princeton;[32]
yet there was no indication in his political speeches that he had extended his concern about the undemocratic influence of wealth beyond
the Princeton campus to American society at large.

On the contrary, he railed about the dangers of socialism before the
North Carolina Society of New York in late February 1906,[33] and in
April he gave another statement of his conservative beliefs at a Jefferson Day dinner sponsored by the National Democratic Club of New
York. Wilson, who earlier had little use for Jefferson,[34] now found an
exalted place for him and his principles in the American political tradition. He found in Jefferson "two main ideals" to gladden the heart of
any conservative businessman—"the right of the individual to opportunity and the right of the people as a whole to a free development."
What was needed, Wilson insisted, was a moral reformation in politics, not fundamental reform. "It is not even [new] laws that we need,
but a new spirit in the enforcement of existing laws, an enlightened and
purified intention." Simultaneously emphasizing that individual freedom should be recovered and offering himself as an advisor to the nation, Wilson said, "We . . . should believe in the capacity of a free
people to see their own interest and follow it when told the truth and
given leave to choose disinterested counselors." When he approached
specific questions, Wilson remained either ambiguous or safely conservative. The tariff should be reformed for the benefit of the many;

[31] WW to St. Clair McKelway, March 11, 1906, *ibid.*, pp. 329-31.

[32] Memorandum on the club situation at Princeton, Feb. 17, 1906, *ibid.*, pp. 314-15.

[33] News report, Feb. 28, 1906, *ibid.*, p. 320.

[34] "A Calendar of Great Americans," *c.* Sept. 15, 1893, *ibid.*, VIII, 373-74.

railroads should realize that their object was public service; corporations had "come to stay" but might be freed from "the spirit of monopoly" by "scrutiny and regulation"; above all, law was "an umpire," "condescending to assist nobody, but umpiring every move of the contest."[35]

The accent was always on individualism and moral idealism, and Wilson's attraction was his firm faith that despite economic upheaval and social unrest no basic alterations were necessary. "We have come upon no new region of morals," he confidently declared. "The difficulty is only to recognize old principles amidst novel surroundings." Like all potential candidates, he disclaimed interest in political life, modestly describing himself as "remote . . . from public affairs,"[36] but his continuous praise of "disinterested counsel" indicated how deeply Harvey's speech had stirred his political ambitions. He reminded the students at Princeton that "the right temper of mind" was necessary "in the management of national affairs" and consoled himself "that a nation can catch the flavor of a great personality."[37]

Wilson's stroke in May 1906 threatened to limit all his ambitions, political and educational, but his astonishingly rapid recovery during the summer prepared him for a more direct political opportunity when he returned. While Wilson was in Europe, Harvey had concocted a plan to bring Wilson into politics without his knowledge. New Jersey had to elect a United States senator in 1907, and Harvey struck an alliance with the Newark Democratic boss, James Smith, Jr., to support Wilson for the office. In effect, Wilson's senatorial candidacy was meaningless because the New Jersey legislature would probably be dominated by Republicans after the November election. Nevertheless, Harvey believed that Wilson would gain publicity through the move, paving his way for a subsequent presidential bid.[38] When reporters greeted Wilson upon his return from England, Wilson insisted that the entire idea "was without any authority from me, and was a great surprise." He added that as an "old-line Democrat" he would be glad to help the party but was reluctant to give up his work at Princeton.[39]

Wilson naïvely accepted Harvey's assurances that the support would be purely "complimentary."[40] However, the situation was immedi-

---

[35] News release, c. April 13, 1906, *ibid.*, XVI, 358-62; speech text, April 16, 1906, *ibid.*, pp. 362-69.

[36] News release, *ibid.*, p. 362; speech text, *ibid.*, p. 363.

[37] News report of a speech at the *Daily Princetonian* banquet, March 29, 1906, *ibid.*, p. 346; news report of a speech in Washington, D. C., Feb. 23, 1906, *ibid.*, p. 318.

[38] Link, *Road to the White House*, p. 103.

[39] News report, Oct. 15, 1906, *PWW*, XVI, 456-57; see also the news article from the New York *Evening Post*, Oct. 2, 1906, *ibid.*, pp. 454-55, n. 1.

[40] WW to Edwin Augustus Stevens, Jan. 2, 1907, *ibid.*, p. 545.

ately complicated by another candidate, Edwin A. Stevens of Hoboken, who was Wilson's classmate at Princeton and the hope of the progressive Democrats in New Jersey. Wilson assured Stevens that he would not oppose his candidacy, but he made no effort to dissuade Harvey or the New Jersey Democratic bosses from supporting himself.[41] Finally, in December, Stevens impressed upon Wilson the fact that the senatorial fight was more than an empty honor and involved the control of the Democratic party in New Jersey.[42] It was obvious that Wilson did not understand the political situation, but he gradually realized that he had to withdraw in order to avoid being entangled in a factional political quarrel.[43] Notifying Harvey of his decision and expressing deep gratitude for his help, Wilson finally issued a letter of withdrawal, drafted almost verbatim by Harvey.[44] As Link has pointed out, it carefully avoided expressing any support for Stevens or the progressive cause in New Jersey.[45]

Wilson's brief foray into New Jersey politics had exposed his ignorance of the actual workings of practical politics, but in the process he had obtained from Harvey a deeper commitment to his own political future and Harvey's willingness to attract others as well. Wilson told his political adviser in December 1906 that he did not consider himself "a suitable person to be a presidential candidate on the ticket of a party so divided and so bewildered as the Democratic party." Still less did he deem himself "a suitable person to be President." "The party," he added, "should be led at this time by a man of political experience and of extraordinary personal force and charm, particularly if he is to lead as a representative of the more conservative and, by the same mark, less popular section of the party." But he pressed Harvey for additional information about other people interested in him as a political figure.[46]

Harvey's reply listed a galaxy of conservative, wealthy figures—August Belmont, banker and American representative of the Rothschilds; Henry Watterson, editor of the Louisville *Courier-Journal*; William M. Laffan, editor of the New York *Sun*; Adolph S. Ochs and Charles R. Miller of the *New York Times*; Thomas Fortune Ryan, financier and utilities tycoon; James Calvin Hemphill of the Charleston, S. C., *News & Courier*; and Dumont Clarke, president of the Ameri-

[41] E. A. Stevens to WW, Dec. 29, 1906, *ibid.*, pp. 539-41, ns. 1-3.

[42] *Ibid.*; E. A. Stevens to WW, Jan. 5, 1907, *ibid.*, pp. 548-49.

[43] Edward Henry Wright to WW, Jan. 4, 1907, *ibid.*, p. 547.

[44] WW to G.B.M. Harvey, Jan. 7, 1907, *ibid.*, pp. 549-50; G. B. M. Harvey to WW, Jan. 10, 1907, *ibid.*, pp. 554-55; WW to Charles Clarke Black, with Enclosure, Jan. 11, 1907, *ibid.*, pp. 560-61.

[45] Link, *Road to the White House*, pp. 103-106.

[46] WW to G. B. M. Harvey, Dec. 16, 1906, *PWW*, xvi, 531-32.

can Exchange Bank of New York.[47] Wilson immediately did some political calculation of his own on the back of Harvey's letter, dividing the men into three groups—those interested in him, those disposed to his "type," and those favorable.[48] Harvey persevered in his efforts in behalf of Wilson, and in March 1907 he arranged for Wilson to dine at Delmonico's in New York with Dr. John A. Wyeth of the Southern Society of New York, plus Laffan and Ryan.[49]

Wilson had become a new figure for the conservative Cleveland wing of the Democratic party to rally around, and the men intended to press Wilson on his political views. Wilson apparently arranged to set forth his beliefs at a future meeting of the Southern Society, but when he was unable to make the engagement, he prepared a "Credo" in August for Laffan's perusal.[50] During the summer of 1907, Wilson was embroiled in the controversy over his "quad" plan, and although he had forsaken for strategical reasons his attacks on the clubs as undemocratic, there was little in Wilson's "Credo" to suggest his emerging democratic views.

On paper and before his potential political supporters, he remained a conservative, insisting that the object of constitutional government was "the liberty of the individual." "Great trusts and combinations are the necessary, because the most convenient and efficient, instrumentalities of modern business," he wrote. Most were legitimate and honest, and when they disobeyed the law, responsibility should be placed upon the individuals within the corporations, not the corporations themselves. Wilson flatly dismissed the idea that government should "undertake the direct supervision and regulation of business" because the nation could not afford to repeat the mistake of "that fruitless experiment, the experiment of paternalism." Unions were anathema to the principle of individual liberty, and every man ought to have the right to sell his labor to whomever he pleased. No man or class could flout the law, for this bred anarchy or autocracy. The judicial system, rightly conceived, was an umpire between individuals and between government and the individual.[51]

Wilson's "Credo" was a private communication for his supporters, designed to encourage political backing for a possible try for the Democratic presidential nomination in 1908. It is significant precisely because it contrasts so sharply with Wilson's prior statements about the

[47] G.B.M. Harvey to WW, Dec. 17, 1906, *ibid.*, pp. 532-33.

[48] Memorandum, *c*. Dec. 18, 1906, *ibid.*, p. 534.

[49] John Allan Wyeth to WW, March 9 and *c*. 12, 1907, *ibid.*, XVII, 65, 66.

[50] J. A. Wyeth to WW, June 21, 1907, *ibid.*, p. 220; "A Credo," Aug. 6, 1907, *ibid.*, p. 335, n. 1.

[51] *Ibid.*, pp. 335-38.

positive function which government could play in promoting justice and encouraging progress. His emphasis on individualism and a neutral role for government is also contradicted by his own educational policies as president of Princeton. There he had used the power of the presidency in an aggressive fashion, reforming and reorganizing university life along the model of his organic, corporate ideal. Wilson recognized that in 1907 his political future depended upon the distance he could establish between his own views and those of the party's leader—William Jennings Bryan. His "Credo" surveyed that ground and put him safely outside Bryan's camp.

Wilson's political thought must be seen not only in the light of his conservative political backers but against the background of the conflict at Princeton and his own health. His emphasis on individualism encouraged those who were frightened by Theodore Roosevelt's proposals for government regulation of business, but when Wilson spoke of individuals, it was not a Manchesterian liberalism that he was advocating. In fact, only one month before he composed his "Credo," he attempted to strike a middle road between laissez-faire and strong, centralized approaches to government. Acknowledging that individual opportunity was restricted by the facts of modern economic life, Wilson offered two possible remedies. Government could become an umpire, passively administering political institutions but placing as few restrictions on the individual.as possible. "That is hardly our notion," Wilson flatly declared. Or, government could regulate everything, but that would be "too much government," with no added efficiency. The true task, Wilson insisted, was "making a new translation of our morals into the terms of our modern life, where individuality seems for the time being lost in complex organizations, and then making a new translation of our laws to match our new translation of morals." Wilson proposed to find the individual "in the maize of modern social, commercial and industrial conditions" through the "probe of morals" and the "probe of law."[52]

Wilson's individual was not the free, untrammeled individual who sought his own interests but a person who had been transformed, renewed, morally purified to serve others. This theme emerged most clearly in Wilson's baccalaureate address of 1907, and in it he offered evidence that his accommodation to the political winds around him might have caused him some moments of discomfort. "You will see that I but go about to elucidate a single theme," he told the students, "that all individual human life is a struggle, when rightly understood and conducted, against yielding to weak accommodation to the

[52] "The Author and Signers of the Declaration of Independence," July 4, 1907, *ibid.*, XVII, 254, 256.

changeful, temporary, ephemeral things about us, in order that we may catch that permanent, authentic tone of life which is the voice of the Spirit of God." He hailed "the transformed university man, whose thought and will have been in fact renewed out of the sources of knowledge and of love," as "one of the great dynamic forces of the world." To the students he offered an image of Christ, whom he described as the "non-conformity of the perfect individual, unsophisticated, unstaled, unsubdued."[53]

Throughout this sermon, Wilson returned repeatedly to themes and images of renewal and regeneration—"fountains of perpetual youth," "renewal of your minds," "refreshment," "purified" and "sifted" knowledge, "undefiled waters," "the pure, untainted air of free uplands," "the keen breath of the wind that comes out of the hills." This may have been Wilson's means of symbolically compensating for his impaired vision and weakened physical condition following his stroke in 1906.[54]

But Wilson's need for physical renewal also corresponded with what he perceived as the divisive, unhealthy, and undemocratic influences of wealth in the eating clubs at Princeton. He focused on a transformed individual because he began to see that it was the individual student who was most victimized by the exclusive system of clubs. In addition, the stroke had left Wilson with a greater sense of his personal mission. When he was confronted by opposition to the quadrangle plan from the trustees and alumni, his exalted sense of purpose translated itself into an assertion of the moral individual against intrenched interests and institutions.

This language of purification and moralization pervaded Wilson's speeches and writings after his encounter with death. The leader, always at the center of Wilson's political thought, was now portrayed as the transformed, renewed individual, capable of withstanding the corruption of society around him. In an article praising Grover Cleveland's administration, Wilson labeled him as a "man of integrity" and concluded, "Fame still sits serene in her temple, and crowns only those with a stainless crown who come to her with a pure heart and clean hands. The Nation still assesses its public men by moral standards as old as the human conscience, and will not be deceived by any charlatan."[55] Wilson could be critical of Theodore Roosevelt's policies,[56] but he was entranced by the Roosevelt spirit. If the Ameri-

---

[53] Baccalaureate address, June 9, 1907, *ibid.*, pp. 192, 194, 195.

[54] Weinstein, "Wilson's Neurological Illness," pp. 336-37.

[55] "Grover Cleveland, Man of Integrity," March 17, 1907, *PWW*, XVII, 78.

[56] See the news report of Wilson's speech to the Southern Society, Dec. 15, 1906, *ibid.*, XVI, 529-31.

can people "only believe in the essential soundness and integrity of his character," Wilson argued, "they would rather have their President aggressive to the point of recklessness than see the prudent calculations of political managers prevail."[57]

Changes in Wilson's political thought were dramatically revealed in his Blumenthal lectures at Columbia University in the spring of 1907. Later published as *Constitutional Government in the United States*, these lectures demonstrate how the Cleveland and Roosevelt presidencies, as well as America's emergence as a world power, had undermined Wilson's earlier assumptions. As early as 1900, when he wrote a new preface to *Congressional Government*, Wilson conceded that congressional hegemony might have come to an end and its demise might "put this volume hopelessly out of date."[58] By 1907, Wilson apparently believed that his prediction had been fulfilled. In *Congressional Government*, he had attempted to create a common legislative purpose by unifying the interests of the legislative and executive branches and reforming their structure along the lines of the English parliamentary model. He had brushed aside the potential of the presidency, but in these new lectures, the President was exalted to a new position of leadership. Although Wilson had previously seen in Congress the representation of the various interests and needs of the American people, he now personalized that representation in the President. What kind of man do we need to be President? Wilson asked. "A man who will be and who will seem to the country in some sort an embodiment of the character and purpose it wishes its government to have,—a man who understands his own day and the needs of the country, and who has the personality and the initiative to enforce his views both upon the people and upon Congress."[59]

Wilson had discovered an American equivalent to Gladstone, Bismarck, and Pitt, and although he insisted upon the President's reliance upon popular opinion for the sanction of his policies, Wilson reveled in the possibilities of the extensive power of the nation's chief executive.

> His is the only national voice in affairs. Let him once win the admiration and confidence of the country, and no other single force can withstand him, no combination of forces will easily overpower him. His position takes the imagination of the country. He is the representative of no constituency, but of the whole people. When he speaks in his true character, he speaks for no special interest. If he

[57] "Grover Cleveland, Man of Integrity," *ibid.*, XVII, 74.

[58] Preface to the "Fifteenth Edition" of *Congressional Government*, Aug. 15, 1900, *ibid.*, XI, 571; actually, this was not a new edition but another printing.

[59] *Constitutional Government in the United States* (New York, 1908), p. 65. This volume is also published in *PWW*, XVIII, 69-216. All citations are from the original edition of 1908.

rightly interpret the national thought and boldly insist upon it, he is irresistible; and the country never feels the zest of action so much as when its President is of such insight and calibre. Its instinct is for unified action, and it craves a single leader. It is for this reason that it will often prefer to choose a man rather than a party. A President whom it trusts can not only lead it, but form it to his own views.[60]

Exhilarated by his own achievements and leadership at Princeton, Wilson was again advancing a vision of American politics which he saw as particularly adapted to his own aspirations. The goal of organic purpose remained the same. Statesmanship was necessary to bring "the several parts of government into effective coöperation for the accomplishment of particular common objects." But the agency had changed. The President "must stand always at the front of our affairs, and the office will be as big and as influential as the man who occupies it."[61]

Wilson realized that such praise of a strong President sounded like support for Roosevelt, and he carefully avoided any appearance of falling into the insurgent Republican camp. Instead, he consistently stressed the need for a moral reformation in American politics and business, and the focus was always individualistic. In an article for the *Atlantic Monthly*, published in November 1907, Wilson denied "that there is or can be any such thing as corporate morality or a corporate privilege and standing which is lifted out of the realm of ordinary citizenship and individual responsibility." Governmental regulation was "of course socialistic" and could not be tolerated, for a government commission would inevitably undertake "to order and conduct what it began by regulating." Claiming that he sensed "a deep enthusiasm for the old ideals of individual liberty," Wilson contended that dishonest individuals, not corporations, should be punished by the processes of law. "We shall never moralize society by fining or even dissolving corporations . . . ," he wrote. "We shall moralize it only when we make up our minds as to what transactions are reprehensible, and bring those transactions home to individuals with the full penalties of the law."[62]

As opposition to his policies at Princeton mounted and as the election of 1908 approached, Wilson increasingly spoke out on political subjects. In lauding the principled, rigidly moralistic leader, he portrayed his own style of leadership as the nation's principal need. "What the country just now needs and wishes more than anything else is distinguished advice and a clearing of counsel," Wilson declared in

---

[60] *Ibid*., p. 68. [61] *Ibid*., pp. 54, 79.
[62] "Politics (1857-1907)," *c.* July 31, 1907, *PWW*, XVII, 322-25.

Memphis at the height of the panic of 1907. "Above all things we need men who, because they are rendered independent by not seeking office or even desiring it, can hold militant ideals for which they are ready to fight in season and out of season, and which they are ready to expound, though no man at first agree with them."[63]

Everywhere he spoke, the message was the same. "My program is to rediscover the individual," Wilson told the Cleveland Chamber of Commerce. "We founded this government upon principles, and the center of those principles was faith in the individual rather than in the government. . . . If God did not make us honest, the government cannot make us over again."[64] The turmoil of the nation, he told an interviewer from the *New York Times*, was a moral crisis, "a struggle for [moral] supremacy in the affairs of the Nation."[65]

No longer sanguine about the virtue of American life, his rhetoric grew more militant and more pointed. Against the background of exposés of corporate corruption, Wilson piously advised the Commercial Club of Chicago, "The only way you get honest business is from honest men." And in a graphic revelation of how his own attitudes had changed since that morning in May 1906 when he woke up blinded by a ruptured blood vessel, Wilson declared, "There is blood in the eye of the American people now and they are not going to be stopped from wrecking something if you do not guide them into remedying something. You have the choice between wreckage and remedy."[66]

The continuous stress on individualism and morality made Wilson appear conservative, but his rhetoric had the sound of a zealous reformer. Wilson, in fact, enjoyed the enviable public position of advocating less governmental regulation and more moral individualism while simultaneously earning a reputation for attacking the Princeton clubs for their undemocratic character. For example, when he declared that the economic system ought to show "no favor to the sloth, no favor to those who can take care of themselves, but an absolute equality," he was not advocating control of business by the wealthy. Rather, he was insisting upon "democratic thinking,"[67] a refusal to grant special privileges to the wealthy, whether they were students at Princeton or trustees of large corporations.

He felt blocked and frustrated in his plans for Princeton, and, as a result, his public speeches consistently accented the need for individual liberty. In resisting his own weakened physical condition, he fought for what he claimed was the health of Princeton and the nation.

---

[63] News report, Nov. 9, 1907, *ibid.*, pp. 477, 478.

[64] "Ideals of Public Life," Nov. 16, 1907, *ibid.*, pp. 503-505, 506.

[65] Interview in the *New York Times*, Nov. 24, 1907, *ibid.*, p. 514.

[66] "The Government and Business," March 14, 1908, *ibid.*, XVIII, 38, 42.

[67] Speech to the Princeton Club of Chicago, March 12, 1908, *ibid.*, pp. 22-23.

Before the National Democratic Club in April 1908, he put the situation in terms that businessmen would understand. "I have come to the mortifying time of seeing both political parties in the hands of receivers," he stated. "You know how you get in the hands of a receiver—you lose your principal. And, having gone into bankruptcy, some one—not yourself—must run the business. That is the present situation in both National parties. . . . That is, we have lost our principles."[68]

The speech was an important echo of Wilson's hopes for the Democratic presidential nomination in 1908, and when he heard that Bryan would also attend the dinner, Wilson asked if he could withdraw to avoid creating party disharmony. But Bryan refused to appear because he would not be permitted to speak, and Wilson enjoyed an uncontested audience.[69] Adjusting his theme to his only constituency in the Democratic party, Wilson warned that the nation confronted the threat of rule by law or personal power. "Have we given up law? Must we fall back on discretionary executive power? . . . If we return to it, we abandon the very principles of our foundation, give up the English and American experiment and turn back to discredited models of government." Wilson insisted that no one advocated "the old *laissez faire*" or doubted that some kind of regulation of business was necessary. But he argued that government could not undertake the "paternalistic" policies of commission regulation and that "predatory wealth" was made only by stock manipulators—"shrewd wits playing on the credulity of others." His solution was once again to rid corporations of unscrupulous individuals through the processes of law.[70]

If Wilson hoped that his speech would galvanize Democratic support behind his candidacy, he was hopelessly wrong. Bryan had regained control of the party machinery, and Wilson left for a summer vacation in the British Isles to recover from the exhausting "quad" fight. In his absence, Stockton Axson served as his political agent, and Harvey went to the Democratic convention in Denver to see what he could do for his candidate. "I must admit that I feel a bit silly waiting on the possibility of the impossible happening," Wilson wrote to Ellen from Edinburgh. ". . . There is evidently not a ghost of a chance of defeating Bryan—but since Col. H. *is* there I might as well be here."[71] When "the great Inevitable," as Wilson called Bryan, received the nomination, Wilson was not crushed. "It was an amusing convention and a diverting outcome, taken altogether," he observed.[72] Wilson had gambled a little and lost nothing in posing as a possible presidential candi-

[68] News report, April 14, 1908, *ibid.*, p. 270.
[69] *Ibid.*, pp. 269-70; WW to John Robertson Dunlap, April 1, 1908, *ibid.*, pp. 219-20.
[70] Press release, "Law or Personal Power," *c.* April 13, 1908, *ibid.*, pp. 264, 268.
[71] WW to EAW, July 6, 1908, *ibid.*, p. 352.
[72] WW to S. Axson, July 31, 1908, *ibid.*, p. 385.

date in 1908, and when Bryan lost for the third time in November, the way was open for Wilson's voice of "disinterested counsel."

In the midst of his emerging political career, Wilson met Mary Allen Hulbert Peck, and this relationship is an important facet in the development of Wilson's personality and political thought. Their letters, although utilized by Ray Stannard Baker in Wilson's authorized biography, were restricted until the death of Wilson's second wife in 1961 and are only now being published in *The Papers of Woodrow Wilson*. Wilson and Mrs. Peck first became acquainted during Wilson's trip to Bermuda in the winter of 1907, and Wilson was immediately taken by her. In his first letter to her, he confessed that it was not often that he had the privilege of meeting anyone whom he could "so entirely admire and enjoy," and she was similarly drawn to this serious, intense president of Princeton University. An attractive woman in her mid-forties when Wilson met her, she was in the process of being estranged from her husband, Thomas Dowse Peck, a well-to-do woolen manufacturer from Massachusetts. Her first marriage to Thomas Harbach Hulbert in 1883 was apparently happy but brief. Hulbert died of an injury in 1889, and by this first marriage she had her only child, Allen Schoolcraft Hulbert. Her second marriage was less felicitous but gave her the financial resources to live comfortably and entertain often, and she was one of the leading figures in the social scene of Bermuda during her annual winter visits.[73]

Ellen Wilson had encouraged Wilson's friendships with women who were particularly vivacious and intellectually stimulating, including Edith Gittings Reid, Henrietta Ricketts, Jenny Davidson Hibben, and Nancy Saunders Toy. Ellen felt that she was "too grave" or "too sober" and said of herself, "I am not gamesome." "Since he has married a wife who is not gay," she told her cousin Florence Hoyt, "I must provide for him friends who are." Wilson himself believed that all his best friends were women, and in his letters to Ellen he frequently noted the pretty women he met or the ones he found singularly "conversable."[74] Wilson's correspondence with Mrs. Peck, however, suggests that this relationship was quite different from his earlier friendships with women, especially in its intensity and intimacy.

It must also be understood within the framework of Wilson's deepening love for his wife, for whatever affection Wilson demonstrated to Mrs. Peck, it is clear that Ellen had first claim upon his devotion. In 1908, he confessed to Ellen that their love was "the one indisputable reality" of his life and told her that after more than twenty years of

---

[73] WW to M.A.H. Peck, Feb. 6, 1907, *ibid.*, XVII, 29-30, n. 1.

[74] *WWLL*, II, 59; Florence Hoyt, "Recollections," October 1926 (R. S. Baker Coll., DLC); Bragdon, *Wilson: The Academic Years*, p. 220; WW to EAW, Jan. 14, 1907, *PWW*, XVII, 4.

married life, his love continued to grow "deeper and more passionate."[75] And yet, beginning in approximately 1908, Wilson found a
new source of support and encouragement in Mrs. Peck. The friendship quickened particularly after Wilson and Jack Hibben split over the
issue of the "quad" plan, and Wilson's letters to her during the final
years of his Princeton presidency indicate that she had become his new
confidant, the one to whom he could bare his deepest feelings about the
controversies at Princeton and his aspirations for a political career.

The relationship also developed at a critical time for Ellen Wilson.
The family illnesses and the death of her brother Edward had shaken
her deeply, and Wilson encouraged her to take up painting again to
relieve her spirits.[76] In addition, because she identified so completely
with her husband, Ellen found the perpetual acrimony at Princeton extremely painful. Isolated as the president's wife, she must have missed
the Hibbens' old friendship as much as her husband did.

Wilson renewed his acquaintance with Mrs. Peck on his second trip
to Bermuda in January 1908, and dutifully reported to Ellen, "I have
seen Mrs. Peck twice, and really she is very fine . . . I know that you
would like her, despite her free western manner."[77] During October
1908, both Wilson and Ellen visited Mrs. Peck at her home in Pittsfield, Massachusetts. After their visit, Wilson turned to Mrs. Peck repeatedly to describe his feelings and the developments at Princeton. He
complained to her of his nervous exhaustion after a speaking tour;
grumbled about his health; gave a grisly account of the dental extraction of three roots of his teeth and his refusal to take any gas for the
pain; and poured out his feelings of depression. "I am a person," he
wrote, ". . . who observes no sort of moderation in anything, and
when I *do* have the blues I go in for having them with great thoroughness and fairly touching bottom."[78] He apparently delighted her with a
sarcastic description of a luncheon of the trustees. "You can imagine
the scene," he wrote.

> Mrs. Wilson is the only woman at the long table, and is taken in to
> lunch by the senior trustee present, generally some old gentleman
> who is *very* dull to talk to and who makes the whole thing a burden
> to the poor lady. The slow, elderly members gather at her end of the
> table, held together by a certain natural affinity, while the younger
> and livelier ones sit at my end,—most of them former college mates

[75] WW to EAW, Aug. 27, 1908, *ibid.*, xviii, 414; Jan. 4, 1907, *ibid.*, xvi, 546.

[76] Memorandum of an interview with Stockton Axson, Feb. 8, 10, 11, 1925 (R. S. Baker
Coll., DLC).

[77] WW to EAW, Jan. 26, 1908, *PWW*, xvii, 607.

[78] WW to M.A.H. Peck, Oct. 12 and 19, and Nov. 2, 1908, *ibid.*, xviii, 448-50, 466-67,
478-81.

of mine, and as ready for lively talk and jest and badinage as they were thirty years ago.[79]

Very few of her letters survive, perhaps destroyed by Wilson himself or someone else, but it is clear he was charmed by her. He sent her pictures of himself and some of his books,[80] and by the middle of 1909, he was addressing her as "Dearest Friend," rather than "My dear Mrs. Peck," and signing himself, "Your affectionate and devoted friend."[81]

To her he confided his growing ambition to go into politics and his determination to be free of the academic disputes at Princeton. On November 2, 1908, the day after Bryan had met defeat for the third time, he told her that someone must combat the Commoner's influence in the Democratic party. But the man must be different, Wilson contended. "He must devote himself to principles, to ideas, to definite programmes, and not to personal preferment; . . . he must be a man with a cause, not a candidacy." Still angry over the Board's refusal to support his "quad" plan, Wilson announced, "I shall not willingly wait more than two years for the Princeton trustees to do what is their bounden duty to do with regard to the reform of university life. At the end of that time I would be glad to lend my pen and voice and all my thought and energy to anyone who purposed a genuine rationalization and rehabilitation of the Democratic party on the lines of principle and statesmanship!" Yet he still hesitated to commit himself openly.

I am willing to do *this*: I am willing to *seem* to take the initiative, to seem to venture upon the field alone and of my own motion, and then yield the field, with the best will in the world, to some one of the rivals who would certainly be drawn out by my action. . . . Certainly I do not want the presidency! The more closely I see it the less I covet it. The "sacrifice" would be a release from what no prudent man, who loved even his physical life, could conceivably desire! . . . I do not deem myself the man, but was born political and chafe like a dog in leash that I must sit here in academic seclusion and not run the game to cover. The fray would be delightful, and would be free from all the polite restraints of academic controversy! One could say what he really thought and make the fight a fight![82]

Wilson's mood was angry and frustrated; he felt restrained from declaring what he believed and what he wanted to do. In the midst of his

[79] WW to M.A.H. Peck, Oct. 12, 1908, *ibid.*, p. 449.
[80] WW to M.A.H. Peck, Feb. 20, 1907, *ibid.*, xvii, 48; Oct. 12, 1908, *ibid.*, xviii, 448; Charles Scribners' Sons to WW, Nov. 17, 1908, *ibid.*, xviii, 517.
[81] WW to M.A.H. Peck, June 18 and 19, 1909, *ibid.*, xix, 258, 261.
[82] WW to M.A.H. Peck, Nov. 2, 1908, *ibid.*, xviii, 479-80.

Dearest Friend,

   It was such a pleasure, and so delightful a relief to
my spirits to receive your letter,- a letter which, somehow,
seems to breathe a new air I have not noticed in your letters for a long time- the beginning of a new self-possesion
and self-mastery which is no# doubt the result of your freedom and your expected peace and rest. I hope that you will
presently find it a pleasure and a means of "finding" yourself to write a good deal of what you are thinking in letters to me. At every crisis in one's life it is absolute
salvation to have some sympathetic friend to whom you can
think aloud without restraint or misgiving. It is more
than salvation: it does more than save the spirits and give
strength and serenity. It enables one to understand the
crisis itself and one's own thought better, and constitutes
a sort of air in which one consciously develops and frees
oneself of both doubt and fear, as if growing into a new
self. I have proved this for myself more than once; and I
would be so proud and happy if I might render you the same
service. I _will_ understand and I will sympathise as keenly
and entirely as your heart could wish. Will you not use
me and make me _feel_ my use? That is what I am for. I am
happy that I was sent to you at such a time. I am glad you
sent me that unspeakable clipping from Town Topics, for I
am sure I felt when I read it just as you did. It is impossible to put into words the feelings that well up in

Woodrow Wilson to Mary Allen Hulbert Peck, Aug. 1, 1909.
Library of Congress

own troubles at Princeton, he sympathized with Mrs. Peck's marital misfortunes, advising her on possible courses of action[83] and receiving in return her support for his desire to break away from his academic confinement. Freedom, individual liberty, rebellion against artifical restraints, fighting for ideals—these were the themes of Wilson's public speeches during 1908-1910, and they graphically reflected his own desire for freedom and release from the trustees' opposition to his policies.

As he so frequently did, Wilson enunciated these ideas and revealed his deepest feelings in his religious addresses. "Morality is of necessity individual, not corporate," he declared in his baccalaureate sermon of 1908. "Men are bad, not societies. . . . We shall find our reforms, not in law, but in conscience. . . . Look about you with candid eye and you shall find that the malady of the age is lack of individual courage, lack of individual integrity of thought and action." What was necessary, Wilson proclaimed, were individuals willing to fight for their ideals, and he summoned the Princeton graduates to the righteous cause of resisting evil, just as he was combating the trustees and the alumni. "Go out and honor yourselves and Princeton and the standards of Christ by enacting righteousness in the field of affairs; by refusing to put your conscience at the service of any man, of any corporation; by playing a part, at whatever temporary cost, which will not cost you your individual liberty and integrity.[84]

The American Bankers Association heard a similar sermon in September 1908. Assuring them that he did not share the "unreasonable" views of those who criticized the banking industry, Wilson proceeded to use those same attacks as the basis for his own solution. "The banks of this country are remote from the people and the people regard them as not belonging to them but as belonging to some power hostile to them," Wilson charged. The problem was that bankers, like many others in American society, had lost the ideal of serving the public welfare. He urged each banker "to constitute himself a statesman" and held before them his conception of their responsibility. "It is the duty and the opportunity of those who control wealth to pay less attention to the business of making particular individuals rich and more attention to the business of making the country rich."[85]

Wilson suggested no institutional reforms, despite the pressing need for changes in the national banking system following the panic of

[83] WW to M.A.H. Peck, April 13, 1909, *ibid.*, XIX, 160-61.

[84] Baccalaureate sermon, June 7, 1908, *ibid.*, XVIII, 327, 332. Wilson's text suggests his frame of mind: "Let no man deceive you: he that doeth righteousness is righteous, even as He is righteous" (I John 3:7).

[85] "The Banker and the Nation," Sept. 30, 1908, *ibid.*, pp. 429, 433.

1907. And yet the speech was repeatedly interrupted by laughter at his anecdotes and applause for his moralisms. One man turned to a friend of Wilson's after the speech and said, "I have always been a strong Republican, but by Jove if the Democrats nominate Wilson for President, I'll surely vote for him."[86]

Gradually, his remarks became more pointed, and his conservatism showed signs of cracking. In Newark, he remarked that economic problems were not so much due to violations of the law as "pure selfishness," and at a private preparatory school, he announced that he would not serve as a president of a "country club." The attacks on wealth became increasingly obvious, Wilson arguing that college men did not know how to work and that they needed moral and intellectual discipline. The truly successful man did not rely upon social prestige but picked himself out, Wilson maintained. "He is not elected by anybody else to be distinguished; he is chosen by himself to be distinguished; or else condemned by himself to be insignificant."[87]

Wilson's address to the Southern Society of New York on December 9, 1908, represented a partial breakthrough. Still trying to describe himself as a conservative, Wilson sought to distinguish between a "false and bastard conservatism, which is merely reactionary," and a conservatism "which seeks a return to old and well recognized principles . . . in such a way as will give them a new interpretation and a new meaning for the time we live in." The complex problems of the country made the American people impatient with conservatism, he reminded his audience. But conservative principles "will be discredited only by applying them in some inadequate or pedantic way." He set out his program: no special tax privileges for individuals or corporations but a tax system designed to promote "the benefit of the taxpayers as a whole or of the nation as an organism"; some regulation of corporations by commissions to assure equality of competition; dispersion rather than centralization of governmental authority; and finally, safeguards to preserve individual initiative and individual freedom.[88]

Vainly trying to stay within the conservative camp, Wilson was consistently frustrated by the same conservative, wealthy constituency at Princeton that he hoped would be his political support for the future. In January 1909, he finally confessed that he was unable to know whether he was a conservative or a liberal. "I believe that many of the alumni of Princeton would now describe me as a radical; yet I deem myself a

[86] Z. C. Felt to WW, Oct. 1, 1908, *ibid.*, p. 435.

[87] News report of a speech to the Wednesday Club of Newark, N. J., Dec. 17, 1908, *ibid.*, p. 552; "The Meaning of a College Education," speech at the Hotchkiss School, Nov. 12, 1908, *ibid.*, pp. 495-507, esp. pp. 496, 503.

[88] "Conservatism: True and False," Dec. 9, 1908, *ibid.*, pp. 535-40, esp. pp. 537-38.

conservative, for I believe that life is the only thing that conserves, and life is the only thing that does not stand still or retrogress."[89]

Ten days later, he visited the University of North Carolina to give a speech on Robert E. Lee, and he reminded his audience that Lee was not great because of his breeding but because "he was a man who saw his duty, who conceived it in high terms, and who spent himself, not upon his own ambitions, but in the duty that lay before him." In his native South which he had earlier praised for its natural aristocracy, Wilson now insisted that "an aristocratic polity" went "to seed." "The establishment of a democratic nation means that any man in it may, if he consecrate himself and use himself in the right way, come to be the recognized instrument of a whole nation." Obviously wishing to become that instrument, Wilson still insisted that power should not be sought for itself but to serve others. He wished, he said, that a great orator would "make men drunk with this spirit of self-sacrifice." "I wish there were some man whose tongue might every day carry abroad the golden accents of that creative age in which we were born a nation; accents which would ring like tones of reassurance around the whole circle of the globe, so that America might again have the distinction of showing men the way, the certain way, of achievement and of confident hope."[90]

Resentment against wealthy Princeton alumni and political conversion proceeded simultaneously. Indeed, Wilson's emergence as a political progressive is inexplicable except in terms of his experiences in the "quad" and graduate college controversies at Princeton. Denied the realization of what he saw as a democratic means of organizing the social life of the university, he began to see the stratification in the student body as a microcosm of the increasing class divisions in the nation at large. Embittered by the wealthy alumni and trustees, he gradually turned an increasing critical eye toward large combinations of economic power and their malevolent influence. Actual political programs would emerge later, but the important change in Wilson's attitudes and values had taken place. As a result of his bitter confrontation with West, Pyne, and the Princeton alumni, Wilson began to see problems in American society, and thus he turned his anger and considerable rhetorical gifts from the sphere of educational reform to the reshaping of that society.

The process, of course, was gradual, but the changes in many cases were dramatic. Even the pariah, William Jennings Bryan, assumed new stature in Wilson's scale of values. On January 25, 1909, Wilson

---

[89] "The Meaning of a Liberal Education," an address to the New York City High School Teachers Association, Jan. 9, 1909, *ibid.*, p. 593.

[90] An address on Robert E. Lee, Jan. 19, 1909, *ibid.*, pp. 631-45, esp. pp. 634, 638, 645.

told the Princeton students that in the recent campaign Bryan was *"a preacher* whose proposals were accepted by millions because his sermons were indisputable," and on February 6, he lashed out at those opposing his educational dreams for Princeton. The problem facing colleges today, he told the Williams College alumni, was to make students "as unlike their fathers as we can." The hostile Princetonians of New York were his special target. "Take Abraham Lincoln, for example," Wilson said. "He couldn't have been born in the present City of New York. He would have fought New York. Any one who thinks New York today doesn't think American." Insisting that colleges could not simply be country clubs training a leisure class, Wilson exploded, "I don't blame the leisure classes for doing wrong. If I belonged to a leisure class I would try to see how near I could come to getting into jail."[91]

Wilson found it increasingly difficult to restrain himself in public speeches, and in Chicago in a speech on Abraham Lincoln, he elevated his impetuosity to a virtue. "God save a free country from cautious men," he asserted, "men, I mean, cautious for themselves, for cautious men are men who will not speak the truth if the speaking of it threatens to damage them. Caution is the confidential agent of selfishness." No longer worrying about the excesses of popular democracy, Wilson found Lincoln's strength in his common origins and his sympathy for the mass of people. "A man of the people is a man who sees affairs as the people see them, and not as a man of particular classes or the professions sees them." Above all, Wilson declared that a man of the people was a free man. He "has felt that unspoken, that intense, that almost terrifying struggle of humanity, that struggle whose object is, not to get forms of government, not to realize particular formulas or make for any definite goal, but simply to live and be free." Seeing himself embattled on all sides, Wilson was gradually dissolving his traditional social and political allegiances, and, in his combative frame of mind, he began to identify with the victims of society. The man of the people, he maintained, "felt beat in him, if he had any heart, a universal sympathy for those who struggle, a universal understanding of the unutterable things that were in their hearts and the unbearable burdens that were upon their backs."[92]

The Lincoln speech of February 1909 represented Wilson's declaration of ideological emancipation. As he told the Presbyterian Union of

---

[91] Notes for a speech to the Monday Night Club at Princeton University, Jan. 25, 1909, *ibid.*, XIX, 9; news report of a speech in New York to the Williams College alumni, Feb. 6, 1909, *ibid.*, pp. 30-31.

[92] "Abraham Lincoln: A Man of the People," Feb. 12, 1909, *ibid.*, pp. 33-46, esp. pp. 38, 42, 44.

Baltimore on February 19, the speeches on Lee and Lincoln "set me very seriously to meditating upon the responsibilities and the character of my own particular task in life." The president who had argued that college graduates formed an elite to serve the nation now proposed a quite different role for the colleges—giving the new generation "the general consciousness of the country, as distinguished from the general consciousness of any class in the country." "If we are merely going to reproduce after our several kinds," Wilson warned, "we are going to reproduce and intensify the points of view of particular separated interests, and if we do that, every finger of prophecy in our affairs will be directed towards a warfare of classes."[93] Before the Philadelphia alumni in March, he reportedly charged that "the college or university which encouraged social stratification and made a bid for the exclusive patronage of the rich, is de-Americanizing the nation, and is not contributing any part to the real development of the country." Would Lincoln have been of such great service to the nation if he had gone to college? Wilson asked. "It is a question I hesitate to answer."[94]

If Wilson was reluctant to draw the conclusion, he continued to attack wealth as an undemocratic influence in both education and the nation. "The chief enemies of government to-day," he told the Newark alumni in May, "are the men who are using their wealth for predatory purpose. These men are criminals, ingenious criminals, . . . who sooner or later will be brought to the bar." Slowly but perceptibly, Wilson incorporated his covenant mode of thinking into a democratic framework. The inclusive, comprehensive view of the world which a college ought to provide "should fit its graduates not alone for the business world, but for a true citizenship that will work for the nation's good and prosperity." The wealthy "criminals," he claimed, are untutored and unschooled "in that field of statesmanship which makes self-indulgence impossible and which puts country above self, nation above ambition."[95]

As the 1908-1909 academic year came to an end, Wilson was exhausted, but he escalated his criticisms of wealth. He told the Western Association of Princeton Clubs that the nation's colleges were lifting people out of broad sympathy with the vast majority of citizens. In a widely publicized speech at St. Paul's School in New Hampshire, he announced, "Schools like this one and universities like Princeton must pass out of existence unless they adapt themselves to modern life." He warned that education faced "the danger of over-wealth" and declared, "I am sorry for the lad who is going to inherit money. . . . I fear

[93] Speech to the Presbyterian Union of Baltimore, Feb. 19, 1909, *ibid.*, pp. 53-54, 55.

[94] News report, March 20, 1909, *ibid.*, pp. 112-13.

[95] News report, May 6, 1909, *ibid.*, pp. 187-88.

that the kind of men who are to share in shaping the future are not largely exemplified in schools and colleges."[96]

But in his political speeches, Wilson was more cautious and vague. In an address on "Civic Problems" during March, he repeated to a St. Louis audience all the familiar litanies about punishing the individuals in corporations, instituting the commission form of city government to obtain simplicity and control, and resisting the idea of popular initiative in government. He was no longer afraid of a strong president, describing the office as the "one national voice." And in his 1909 baccalaureate address, he leveled a harsh criticism at the labor unions, describing them as regulating the performance of workers to the least productivity possible for the wages received.[97]

Wilson's religious addresses indicate that despite the persistent theme of individualism in his political speeches, he had not forsaken his corporate, organic vision of society and knowledge. In "The Present Task of the Ministry," delivered on May 26, 1909, at Hartford Theological Seminary, Wilson described the church in imperial terms as the center of the spiritual framework of the world. It stands, he said, "at the center not only of philanthropy but at the center of education, at the center of science, at the center of philosophy, at the center of politics; in short, at the center of sentient and thinking life." The minister's task "is to show the spiritual relations of men to the great world processes, whether they be physical or spiritual. It is nothing less than to show the plan of life and men's relation to the plan of life."[98]

Wilson had consistently resisted the claim of the social gospel movement that the church become more involved in social and political issues. In 1908, he gave a complete statement of his position to John R. Mott. "I thoroughly believe in the widest activity for the church," Wilson wrote,

> but I have had the fear in recent years that the ministers of our churches, by becoming involved in all sorts of social activities (of course I use the word "social" in its widest sense), have too much

[96] News reports, May 23 and June 3, 1909, *ibid.*, pp. 212-14, 226-28. A storm of protest broke out among Princeton alumni over this speech, and Wilson tried to discredit the accuracy of the news reports. See Lawrence Crane Woods to WW, June 5, 1909, *ibid.*, pp. 230-31; WW to L. C. Woods, June 10, 1909, *ibid.*, p. 239; interview in the *Princeton Alumni Weekly*, June 9, 1909, *ibid.*, p. 238.

[97] "Civic Problems," March 9, 1909, *ibid.*, pp. 81-97; news report of a speech to the Virginia Society of St. Louis, March 11, 1909, *ibid.*, p. 97; news report of a speech in Philadelphia to the University Extension Society, March 13, 1909, *ibid.*, pp. 98-100; speech in New York to the Friendly Sons of St. Patrick, March 17, 1909, *ibid.*, pp. 102-108; baccalaureate address, June 13, 1909, *ibid.*, p. 245. For labor reactions to Wilson's criticism, see Edgar R. Laverty to WW, June 16, 1909, and Francis Dundon to WW, June 25, 1909, *ibid.*, pp. 255, 269-70.

[98] "The Present Task of the Ministry," May 26, 1909, *ibid.*, pp. 215-22, esp. p. 218.

diverted their attention from the effectual preaching of the Word. The danger seems to be that individual churches will become great philanthropic societies instead of being what it seems to me they ought to be, organizations from which go forth the spiritual stimulation which should guide all philanthropic effort. Many of our modern pastors are so exceedingly busy with the affairs of the communities in which they live that they are not fountains of real spiritual refreshment to their people. The old-fashioned pastor had at least this advantage over the modern pastor, that he gave himself leisure for spiritual contemplation, meditated upon the real needs of the human heart, and associated himself intimately with the families and individual lives under his charge, making himself not the organizer of benevolent power but the spiritual source of it, as the spokesman of his master.[99]

But by 1909, however, Wilson was willing to countenance a larger social role for the church. Still warning about the temptation of making the church "chiefly a philanthropic institution," he said, "Christianity came into the world to save the world as well as to save individual men, and individual men can afford in conscience to be saved only as part of the process by which the world itself is regenerated."[100]

Wilson's growing awareness of the need for reform in American society and his own predisposition to lead that reform are graphically revealed in his baccalaureate address of 1909. His theme was unprofitable servants—those who merely did their duty. As he confessed to Mrs. Peck, "The idea is searching me pretty thoroughly,—that mere duty does not profit, but only that which we volunteer over and above."[101]

His attack on the unprofitability of labor unions generated publicity, but Wilson's criticism ranged more broadly. "If there is any aristocracy of class to be got out of the interesting business [of life]," Wilson told the graduating class, "it lies ahead of us, not behind us, in what we shall do, not in what we have done." The rich had "kept their legal obligations as well as usual and yet came near ruining the country, piled up wealth and forgot how to use it honourably, built up business and came near to debauching a nation." They brought "disaster upon business" because "they ran with blinders upon their eyes, saw only the immediate task under their hands, volunteered no look around, paid no call of thought or wish upon their fellow men, left statesmanship to politicians and public interests to the censors of public morals, attended wholly to their own business." "The secret of

[99] WW to J. R. Mott, May 1, 1908, *ibid.*, XVIII, 279-80.
[100] "The Present Task of the Ministry," May 26, 1909, *ibid.*, XIX, 221.
[101] WW to M.A.H. Peck, May 31, 1909, *ibid.*, p. 224.

what it is to live," Wilson insisted, is an individual's service beyond duty—"what he adds to his duty for his own satisfaction, for the release of the power that is in him."[102]

As Wilson told Mrs. Peck, "I write my sermons to myself. I at least know what *I* need to hear." Frustrated by the opposition of the trustees and alumni, Wilson was seeking the release of the power within him, which he had always known was meant for the political arena. "The perfect moment," he thought, "comes when duty and inclination, obligation and choice, join hands and forget that there is any difference between them."[103] After commencement, he traveled to Harvard where he put what he called "the whole of my academic creed" into his Phi Beta Kappa oration, "The Spirit of Learning." "The college has been the seat of ideals," he argued. Then he inveighed against contemporary education for losing "its definiteness of aim." College life had to be reconceived and reorganized along democratic lines to provide students with a comprehensive conception of the world and their moral duty within it. "The college," Wilson believed, "will be found to lie somewhere very near the heart of American social training and intellectual and moral enlightenment."[104]

While the disputes over educational matters at Princeton preoccupied him, Wilson continued to flirt with the idea of an active political career. He considered it "manifestly undesirable" for a university president to get involved in a partisan political fight, but if he were offered "an invitation," he promised to give it "very careful consideration."[105] He retreated to Old Lyme, Connecticut, and in a remarkable letter to Mrs. Peck, he reflected on how the Princeton battles had changed his thinking. "Certainly it is the same town to a stick that I knew four years ago," he wrote, but "I have changed much more than it has." He detested the "motors" that passed his summer cottage "because they contain for the most part, in all probability, specimens of the sort of people I like least, the restless, rich, empty-headed people the very sight of whom makes me cynical." "I am glad to have them pass by, but very resentful that I must forever have their dust (and odour) in my nostrils." Such people, Wilson complained, "are in the world to deepen all its problems and give it nothing at all that it can profit by. They and their kind are the worst enemies of Princeton, and create for me the tasks which are likely to wear my life out."[106]

Angry, tired, and discouraged, Wilson increasingly turned to Mrs.

[102] Baccalaureate address, June 13, 1909, *ibid.*, pp. 242-51, esp. pp. 243, 247, 249.

[103] WW to M.A.H. Peck, May 31, 1909, *ibid.*, p. 224.

[104] WW to M.A.H. Peck, July 3, 1909, *ibid.*, p. 290; "The Spirit of Learning," July 1, 1909, *ibid.*, pp. 277-89, esp. p. 280.

[105] WW to Adolphus Ragan, July 3, 1909, *ibid.*, p. 292.

[106] WW to M.A.H. Peck, July 18, 1909, *ibid.*, p. 312.

Peck as the conflict at Princeton grew in bitterness and intensity. "All roads of thought lead back to you," he wrote, and when he was unable to visit her, he expressed deep disappointment. "It would have been worth half a vacation for refreshment to see you and spend a few hours in your company." When Mrs. Peck did not write regularly, Wilson asked how a man could have a holiday when his mind was "filled with anxious conjecture about those whom he loves." She was plagued with uncertainty about her marriage, and in offering his friendship, Wilson demonstrated how their relationship had filled a vacuum created by his alienation from Jack Hibben. "At every crisis in one's life it is absolute salvation to have some sympathetic friend to whom you can think aloud without restraint or misgiving," he told her. "It is more than salvation: it does more than save the spirits and give strength and serenity. It enables one to understand the crisis itself and one's own thought better, and constitutes a sort of air in which one consciously develops and frees oneself of both doubt and fear, as if growing into a new self."[107]

Wilson was considerably confused and perplexed throughout the summer and autumn of 1909. He saw "a new self" emerging, one more critical of the wealthy, conservative interests of the country, and one more disposed to active political life. "This is what I was meant for, anyhow, this rough and tumble of the political arena," he told Mrs. Peck. "My instinct all turns that way, and I sometimes feel rather impatiently the restraints of my academic position."[108] At the same time, he knew that he relied upon Colonel Harvey and other rich men to bring him into a position of political leadership.

His confusion is demonstrated by two essays written during the summer of 1909. In "The Man Behind the Trust," Wilson blasted those who misused corporations "to satisfy their own greed for wealth and power" and called them "public enemies."[109] That essay he never published. Instead, he turned to criticizing the Payne-Aldrich tariff of 1909 in "The Tariff Make-Believe," published in Harvey's *North American Review* in October. Wilson criticized the new tariff law for protecting special interests but had praise for the men who constructed the vast American industrial colossus. "They were men of extraordinary genius," he wrote, "many of them, capable of creating and organizing States and Empires." The destructive influence of corporations, he insisted, was due to their scope, not their kind, and any reform must be slow and gradual.[110]

[107] WW to M.A.H. Peck, July 3, 18, and 25 and Aug. 1, 1909, *ibid.*, pp. 291, 312, 317, 321-22.

[108] WW to M.A.H. Peck, Sept. 5, 1909, *ibid.*, p. 358.

[109] "The Man Behind the Trust," Aug. 3, 1909, *ibid.*, pp. 324-27.

[110] "The Tariff Make-Believe," Sept. 5, 1909, *ibid.*, pp. 359-80.

This was a delicate tightrope that Wilson was attempting to walk, appearing conservative in his writings and political speeches and yet criticizing the influence of wealth through his educational addresses. It illustrates once again Wilson's capacity for compartmentalizing his thinking. Caught up in the tremendous pressures of the graduate college controversy, Wilson had very little time for the kind of reflection that might have produced an earlier integration of his democratic educational ideals and his conservative political views. Even if Wilson had been conscious of the dichotomy in his thought, it also would have been politically dangerous for him to give full expression to some of his more liberal democratic ideas, for they would have alarmed and possibly alienated his potential conservative supporters. Consequently, the key to Wilson's emerging progressivism lies in his experience during the "quad" and graduate college fights and the new themes which he sounded in his educational and religious speeches from 1907 to mid-1910. Only after Wilson had secured the gubernatorial nomination, turned his back on Princeton, and thrown himself into the campaign would the transferral of democratic educational principles to political life be achieved in more explicit terms.

Wilson, however, did make a few harmless concessions to the reform movement, assuming the presidency of the Short Ballot Organization and delivering addresses hailing the short ballot as "the key to the whole question of the restoration of government by the people."[111] But his continuous emphasis upon individualism gave him the appearance of a conservative. In a religious talk, "The Ministry and the Individual," delivered at McCormick Theological Seminary in Chicago in November, he again reverted to his spiritual, individualistic conception of the Christian faith. Christianity "did not come into the world merely to save the world," he argued, but to bring salvation to the individual. "The end and object of Christianity is the individual, and the individual is the vehicle of Christianity." Therefore, a minister "must preach Christianity to men, not to society."[112]

However reassuring Wilson's speech might have been, it was not characteristic of his growing desire to preach a more political gospel of morality and service to the nation. Ten days later at the Harvard Church in Brookline, Massachusetts, Wilson, the evangelical reformer, found a different role for Christianity and the church. "I believe that the essence of religion is disturbance, the absence of weak conformity, and that a church that is not a church militant is a church

---

[111] Richard Spencer Childs to WW, Oct. 14, 1909, *ibid.*, pp. 419-20; an address to the City Club of Philadelphia, Nov. 18, 1909, *ibid.*, pp. 509-22; see also his address to the Short Ballot Organization, Jan. 21, 1910, *ibid.*, xx, 32-43; and his article for the *North American Review*, "Hide-and-Seek Politics," March 2, 1910, *ibid.*, pp. 192-207.

[112] "The Ministry and the Individual," Nov. 2, 1909, *ibid.*, xix, 472, 479.

decadent," he stated. ". . . A church that does not go out to wage war, in a Christian way, against existing evils, has forgotten its Christian obligations."[113] Wilson was unwilling to turn the righteous warfare over to the church entirely, for as he told the Chicago alumni, "Princeton is being looked to for a leader now. Other universities have furnished great public men, and we must do the same." He hurriedly left the meeting amidst shouts that Wilson was the "logical successor to Theodore Roosevelt."[114]

Events at Princeton made it even more difficult for Wilson to play simultaneously the roles of political conservative and educational reformer. After the tumultuous January 1910 Board meeting, at which Wilson declared that the graduate college could be built anywhere in Mercer County, he vented his anger in a speech to the New York bankers. "The city of New York does not only not constitute the nation, but does not understand the nation," he said. "The city of New York is a provincial community. . . . If the bankers of the country are to keep their precedence in control of affairs of the nation they must quit their narrower interests and become statesmen." J. P. Morgan angrily puffed his cigar as Wilson charged that the banking interests were concentrated too much in one individual and that the country at large distrusted bankers. "This country will never be satisfied and ought not to be satisfied with any banking reform which does not put all the banking resources at the command of the people."[115]

If Colonel Harvey was alarmed at the opinions of his presumably conservative candidate, he showed little inclination to drop his plans. As early as May 1909 Harvey predicted in *Harper's Weekly* that Wilson would be elected governor of New Jersey in 1910 and President in 1912. In January 1910 he secured the support of the influential Democratic boss of Newark, James Smith, Jr., for Wilson's gubernatorial candidacy.[116] Apparently sometime during January 1910, Harvey went to Princeton and told Wilson that he would not have to make any effort to obtain the nomination. It would be offered to him "on a silver platter." Wilson reportedly paused and finally said, "If the nomination for governor should come to me in that way, I should regard it as my duty to give the matter very serious consideration."[117]

Wilson left for Bermuda to contemplate the worsening situation in

[113] News report, Nov. 13, 1909, *ibid.*, p. 497.

[114] News report of a speech to the Princeton Club of Chicago, Nov. 3, 1909, *ibid.*, p. 479.

[115] See the four news reports from the New York *Evening Post*, New York *World, New York Times*, and *New York Tribune*, Jan. 18, 1910, *ibid.*, xx, 23-27.

[116] Link, *Road to the White House*, p. 127; Editorial Note, Colonel Harvey's Plan for Wilson's Entry into Politics, *PWW*, xx, 146-48.

[117] *Ibid.*; William O. Inglis, "Helping to Make a President," *Collier's Weekly*, LVIII (Oct. 7, 1916), 15ff.

Princeton and his brightening political future in New Jersey. "It would be rather jolly, after all, to start out on life anew together, to make a new career, would it not?" he wrote to Ellen. She seemed to like the idea and suggested that if West were not forced out as dean of the graduate school, it would set him free to leave if he wished—"that is, to accept the nomination for governor and go into politics." Wilson even found that he could joke about his situation, and as he worked on an article on the short ballot, he said, "I shall call it, I think, 'Hide and Seek Politics.' Is not that a pretty good account of myself?"[118]

But Wilson was unable to escape the Princeton situation, and during his stay in Bermuda he wrote letters of virtually equal length to Ellen and Mrs. Peck. Wilson's frustration and resentment about the opposition of the trustees and the alumni prompted him to idealize Mrs. Peck and see in her exactly those qualities which he felt unable to express in his own life. "You are a veritable child of nature," he had told her in September 1909. ". . . I mean not only that there is a splendid naturalness and spontaneity about you, which you have never been able to spoil or cover by any self-defensive mask, but that Nature herself calls to you upon the instant, like a mother to her child, and that always in her presence the fine truth of you comes out, radiant, unmistakable." Wilson missed visiting her in Bermuda and complained, "This is a land without its presiding spirit. . . . I am with her all the time in thought while I am here." His letters to his "dearest, sweetest Friend" grew warmer and more affectionate, and he signed them "with infinite tenderness."[119]

Mrs. Peck, who separated from her husband in late 1908, responded with equally warm letters. She said she missed Wilson "horribly" and asked, "Why, *why* can I not be there—to fling *myself* where I would!" She called him "an adorable person" and counted it "the greatest honor and happiness and privilege" of her life to have Wilson as her friend. However, she did not hesitate to give Wilson some advice about his manners in the social world of Bermuda. "Before I write another word, I want to tell you—best beloved—of a small habit which you have which may cause you to be misjudged," she wrote. "You will laugh when you hear it. *Do not* leave your spoon in your cup when you drink your tea. It is a crime in the eyes of some—no less. You do not mind my telling you? *I* would not care if you lapped it up with your tongue. The king can do no wrong." She pleaded with him, "Write me—write me—I miss you and am your devoted friend." Wilson ef-

[118] WW to EAW, Feb. 21 and 25, 1910, *PWW*, xx, 146, 177; EAW to WW, Feb. 28, 1910, *ibid.*, p. 189.

[119] WW to M.A.H. Peck, Sept. 19, 1909, *ibid.*, xix, 385; Feb. 18, 1910, *ibid.*, xx, 140-41; Feb. 25, 1910, *ibid.*, p. 178.

fused appreciation for her affectionate letters and declared, "God was very good to me to send me such a friend, so perfectly satisfying and delightful, so *delectable*."[120]

It is impossible to determine whether Wilson's relationship with Mrs. Peck moved beyond the expression of verbal affection. Their correspondence continued until 1915, when Wilson married Edith Bolling Galt. Wilson frequently visited Mrs. Peck in New York after her separation from her husband, and in a moment of reverie or playfulness in 1908, while Wilson was in Bermuda at the same time as Mrs. Peck, he started a letter to her in shorthand, which began, "My precious one, my beloved Mary."[121] He apparently caught himself, reconsidered, and never wrote the letter. When rumors of his relationship with Mrs. Peck circulated while he was President of the United States, Wilson told Colonel House that the friendship was merely "platonic," but he admitted that "he had been indiscreet in writing her letters rather more warmly than was prudent."[122] Even his worst enemies refused to believe that Wilson had been physically involved with Mrs. Peck. Andrew F. West observed, "Heaven knows I hated Wilson like poison, but there is not one word of truth in this nonsense. It is simply not in character."[123] Even Theodore Roosevelt snorted that Wilson would be better cast as the Apothecary than as Romeo.[124]

And yet, the stiff, reserved, one-dimensional man that so many of Wilson's contemporaries and subsequent historians saw is a distortion of a much more complex, passionate personality. The strain of the last years of his presidency at Princeton may have prompted Wilson into uncharacteristic and indiscreet behavior. Ellen Wilson is reported to have confided to the White House physician, Dr. Cary Grayson, that while she believed that the relationship was innocent, it was the "only unhappiness" Wilson had caused her "during their whole married life."[125]

---

[120] M.A.H. Peck to WW, Feb. 15 and 18, 1910, *ibid.*, pp. 127, 142; WW to M.A.H. Peck, Feb. 20-21, 1910, *ibid.*, p. 150.

[121] A Salutation, *c.* Feb. 1, 1908, *ibid.*, XVII, 611.

[122] House diary, Sept. 22, 1915, quoted in Arthur S. Link, *Wilson: Confusions and Crises, 1915-1916* (Princeton, N. J., 1964), p. 6.

[123] Margaret Axson Elliott, *My Aunt Louisa and Woodrow Wilson* (Chapel Hill, N. C., 1944), p. 202.

[124] Patrick Devlin, *Too Proud to Fight: Woodrow Wilson's Neutrality* (New York and London, 1975), p. 23.

[125] Diary of Breckinridge Long, Jan. 11, 1924 (Breckinridge Long Papers, DLC). Grayson became a confidant of the Wilson family during the White House years. He told Long that he believed that "the relationship had been quite innocent—but indiscreet for a public man." Mrs. Wilson had told Grayson that she was hurt, not because "there was anything wrong—or improper—about it, for there was not, but just that a brilliant mind and an attractive woman had some-how fascinated—temporarily—Mr. Wilson's mind—and she (Mrs. Wilson) did not want to share his confidence or his inner mind with any one." *Ibid.*

In addition, Wilson's tendency to compartmentalize his thinking may have extended to the separation of his strict morals from his personal life. During a visit to Mrs. Peck in Pittsfield, he delivered a speech in which he made what appears to be a startling admission. "If there is a place where we must adjourn our morals," Wilson declared, "that place should be in what we call private life. It is better to be unfaithful to a few people than to a considerable number of people."[126]

In the final analysis, the extent of Wilson's relationship with Mrs. Peck is shrouded in doubt and somewhat irrelevant. What is clear is that Wilson found in her the qualities of freedom, naturalness, and spontaneity which he needed during the bitter struggles at Princeton. She compensated for his sense of being confined and restricted, and her friendship replaced temporarily the loss of his closest companion, Jack Hibben. As Wilson once exclaimed to her, "How shall I ever say what it has meant to me to find just the friend I wanted and needed." Like Ellen, she offered the constant support which he demanded, especially in his most combative moods. "Your affection," he told her, "seems in some way to restore my tone, to set the courses of my blood straight again, and give me a strange mastery of myself in the midst of distressing circumstances."[127]

When Wilson returned to Princeton in March 1910, he came with stiffened resolve to persevere in his plans for the university. In his public speeches, he made fewer attempts to mask himself as a conservative. Before the Contemporary Club of Philadelphia, he said, "The dangerous radical is that man of middle age who has been hurt in one way or another. He can preach you those blazing sermons that hurt because we all know they are true." Linking his ideal of service to the battle of Princeton, he asserted, "The ideals of war are the ideals of self-sacrifice, and that is why we prize them."[128] He maintained his ties with the conservative wing of the Democratic party by lauding Grover Cleveland at a meeting of the National Democratic Club of New York, but his praise focused on Cleveland as a man of conscience and principle who did not bow to political expediency.[129]

As defeat loomed before him at Princeton during the spring of 1910, Wilson seemed obsessed with the idea of moral integrity. In April he delivered a homily to the Philadelphian Society on the theme of Matthew 16:26 (what shall a man give in exchange for his soul), and he emphasized "the difficulty, and imperative necessity of independence, moral and intellectual." In another religious talk, he showed the

[126] News report of an address in Pittsfield, Mass., Oct. 9, 1908, *PWW*, xvIII, 442.
[127] WW to M.A.H. Peck, Feb. 28 and 20-21, 1910, *ibid.*, xx, 187, 150.
[128] News report, March 15, 1910, *ibid.*, p. 242.
[129] Speech text, March 18, 1910, *ibid.*, pp. 257-62.

students "how despicable it is always to go with the crowd and 'sing the popular tune,' and that is so to-day, as it has always been, that 'he that observeth the wind will not sow and he that regardeth the clouds will not reap.' "[130]

Meanwhile, Wilson's speeches to Princeton alumni took on the appearance of a man looking back over his term of office, justifying his policies and recalling the alumni to his ideal of Princeton in the nation's service. "We are not at liberty to use Princeton for our private purposes or to adapt her in any way to our own use and pleasure," Wilson told the Maryland alumni. "It is our bounden duty to make her more and more responsive to the intellectual and moral needs of a great nation."[131] If Princeton could not be separated from the demands of a growing country, the conclusion was obvious, even to a believer in individualism: "There is nothing private in America. Everything is public; everything belongs to the united energy of the nation; everything is an asset of the nation."[132]

Wilson's rising anger and his attacks on wealth culminated in the famous address to the Pittsburgh alumni in April. He was now convinced that Lincoln would not have served the country as he did if he had gone to college. Great creative forces in society came "from below, not from above." "We should cry out against the few who have raised themselves to dangerous power, who have thrust their cruel hands into the very heartstrings of the many, on whose blood and energy they are subsisting."[133]

Wilson's speeches and the details of the graduate college fight were widely reported in the press, and it is somewhat puzzling why Harvey, Smith, and others continued to look to Wilson as the great conservative hope. Both apparently ignored the implications of Wilson's speeches during the debate over the graduate college and focused instead on Wilson's impeccably conservative political addresses. Similarly, both were presumably intrigued with the possibility of launching Wilson from Princeton to the White House, via the New Jersey governorship. In addition, Smith faced challenges from Democratic reformers in New Jersey, and Wilson provided the opportunity to perpetuate his machine behind the façade of an attractive candidate. In early June, Smith conferred with the Chicago Democratic boss, Roger C. Sullivan, and the two men agreed that Wilson would be a formidable presidential candidate in 1912. Through one of Wilson's former students,

---

[130] Notes for a religious talk, April 3, 1910, *ibid.*, p. 314; news report of a talk to the Philadelphian Society, March 18, 1910, *ibid.*, p. 256.

[131] Speech text, March 11, 1910, *ibid.*, pp. 229-35, esp. p. 235.

[132] Speech to the Princeton Club of New York, April 7, 1910, *ibid.*, p. 348.

[133] News report, April 17, 1910, *ibid.*, pp. 364-65.

Smith was also assured by Wilson that he would not dismantle the Democratic machine in New Jersey and construct his own organization if he were left "absolutely free in the matter of measures and men."[134]

These negotiations, like much of the maneuvering concerning the graduate school, were private, and Wilson made only one speech to New Jersey Democrats prior to his nomination for governor. On March 29 he spoke to the Democratic Dollar Dinner in Elizabeth at the invitation of the state Democratic chairman, James R. Nugent, who was also Smith's chief lieutenant. Wilson gave few hints of his emerging progressive political views. He labeled governmental regulation as "a wholesale invasion by government itself [into] the field of business management"; the government should get out of "the business of granting favours and privileges" and reform the tariff; Democrats should support reforms that "will secure economy, responsibility, honesty, fidelity" in government; and the Democratic party should "challenge the people by every possible means to depend upon themselves rather than upon fostering powers lodged in groups of individuals."[135] Wilson's platitudes kept his political supporters in line, and Harvey and Smith gradually assembled the votes necessary to win the nomination for Wilson.

Privately, Wilson's views were more explicit and more progressive. A measure of his growing political importance, as well as his chameleon political reputation, are two requests that he received to prepare platforms for state Democratic parties. In April, Wilson formulated the issues for the Pennsylvania Democracy and focused on the tariff as the creation of special interests, conservation of public lands, regulatory legislation for the trusts to punish individuals, judicial rather than administrative regulation of public service corporations, corrupt practices acts, state social service examinations, and equitable public taxation. His draft was accepted in many respects, except that the Pennsylvania Democrats added more pointed anti-Republican language and insisted upon government commissions to regulate railroads and water companies.[136] Wilson was also asked by the Democrats of South Carolina to prepare a platform, and although no copy of his suggestions exists, they presumably satisfied the request for something defending state rights.[137] To a fellow Democrat dis-

[134] Link, *Road to the White House*, pp. 142-43; WW to J. M. Harlan, June 23, 1910, *PWW*, xx, 540-41.

[135] "Living Principles of Democracy," March 29, 1910, *ibid.*, 297-303.

[136] Arthur Granville De Walt to WW, March 30 and April 12, 1910, *ibid.*, pp. 307-308, 352; draft of a Platform for the Democratic Party of Pennsylvania, *c.* April 4, 1910, *ibid.*, pp. 315-17.

[137] Richard Irvine Manning to WW, May 13 and 21, 1910, *ibid.*, pp. 453-54, 463; his draft was also received too late to be used by the South Carolinians in formulating the Democratic platform.

turbed by Bryanism, Wilson wrote of his own concern that the party ought to be drawn back "to the definite and conservative principles which it once represented," but he was confident that "new men will take hold of the party and draw it away from the influences which have of late years demoralized it."[138]

The Wyman bequest and the certainty of continuous friction with an even stronger Dean West made the prospect of running for governor of New Jersey increasingly attractive to Wilson. In late June, he dined with Harvey, Henry Watterson, and Smith at Harvey's country home in Deal, New Jersey, and the offer was made plain. If Wilson agreed, they would work to elect him governor of New Jersey in 1910 and then to nominate him for President in 1912. Wilson apparently held off giving a firm commitment, writing to his friend David B. Jones that the political situation had become "acute."[139] He solicited advice from Jones and several other trustees, and they urged him to follow the path of duty as he saw it. Finally, on July 12, at the Lawyers' Club in New York, Wilson again conferred with Harvey and several Democratic leaders in New Jersey. Wilson gave his assurances that he would not gratuitously dismantle the Democratic machine in the state and that he would accept the nomination if it were offered to him without any strings attached.[140]

Wilson notified his friends among the trustees of his decision, thanking them for their continued support during his presidency and declaring, "I have all my life been preaching the duty of educated men to accept just such opportunities; and I do not see how I could have done otherwise; great and poignant as is the qualm it causes me to think of leaving Princeton and all the great duties there to which I have devoted the best years of my life."[141]

The rumors of Wilson's candidacy were given extensive coverage by the New York City and New Jersey newspapers, and on July 15, Wilson issued a telegram to the *Newark Evening News* and the Trenton *True American* announcing his decision. He claimed he was "in no sense a candidate" and would not make an effort to obtain the nomination. "But . . . if it should turn out to be true," Wilson added, ". . . that it is the wish and hope of a decided majority of the thoughtful Democrats of the State that I should consent to accept the party's

[138] WW to Hugh S. McClure, April 9, 1910, *ibid.*, p. 351.

[139] WW to D. B. Jones, June 27, 1910, *ibid.*, p. 543.

[140] Editorial Note, The Lawyers' Club Conference, *ibid.*, pp. 565-66.

[141] WW to E. W. Sheldon, July 11, 1910, *ibid.*, pp. 572-73. See also WW to C. H. Dodge, July 11, 1910, *ibid.*, pp. 573-75; WW to C. H. McCormick, July 14, 1910, *ibid.*, pp. 577-78; WW to D. B. Jones, July 14, 1910, *ibid.*, p. 578; WW to H. B. Thompson, July 14, 1910, *ibid.*, pp. 578-79.

nomination for the great office of Governor, I should deem it my duty, as well as an honor and a privilege, to do so."[142]

Wilson stayed in seclusion in Old Lyme, Connecticut, for most of the summer, obeying Harvey's orders to say as little as possible and leave the political negotiations to him. But Wilson did not remain unopposed. Henry Otto Wittpenn, the mayor of Jersey City, entered the race against Wilson, and Frank S. Katzenbach, a Trenton lawyer and Democratic gubernatorial candidate in 1907, embarrassed Wilson by garnering the support of Wilson's home county.[143] Wilson was attacked as a candidate of the Wall Street interests and for his hostility to labor, and he chafed under the rule of silence imposed upon him. Harvey urged him to keep his peace. "The situation is well in hand," he advised. "There are no breaches in the walls."[144]

But Wilson could not stand it any longer when the New Jersey State Federation of Labor denounced him as an enemy of organized labor. He replied to the attacks, insisting that he had "always been the warm friend of organized labor," that he saw unions as the only way for working people to secure justice from organized capital, and that he feared large corporations more than labor. He also promised his support for labor legislation regulating working conditions, assuring adequate wages, and "reasonable limits" to the working day.[145]

Wilson's labor statement satisfied most of the objections, and six days before the nominating convention, Harvey reported to Wilson, "All reports are good. There will be only one ballot." On the morning of September 15, Wilson wrote, "I look forward to the prospect with many misgivings, but with no doubt as to what my duty in the case is."[146] That afternoon he accepted the nomination, terming the occasion "a day of unselfish purpose" and "confident hope." In his speech, he called for economy in a reorganized state government, equalization of taxes, and regulation of corporations. He hoped that New Jersey would "lead the way in reform" and held before the convention his corporate, organic vision of society, now democratized with a popular element. "Government is a matter of common council,

[142] A Statement, July 15, 1910, *ibid.*, p. 581.

[143] WW to G.B.M. Harvey, July 14, 1910, *ibid.*, pp. 576-77; July 26, 1910, *ibid.*, xxi, 24-25; WW to M.A.H. Peck, Aug. 6, 1910, *ibid.*, pp. 38-39.

[144] G.B.M. Harvey to WW, Aug. 12, 1910, *ibid.*, p. 52.

[145] Edgar Williamson, editor of the Orange, N. J., *Labor Standard*, to WW, Aug. 18, 1910, *ibid.*, pp. 55-56, n. 2; WW to E. Williamson, Aug. 23, 1910, *ibid.*, pp. 59-61. Wilson's letter was published in the *Labor Standard* on Sept. 2, 1910, and reprinted in several New Jersey papers.

[146] G.B.M. Harvey to WW, Sept. 9, 1910, *ibid.*, p. 88; WW to Harold Laity Bowlby, Sept. 15, 1910, *ibid.*, p. 90.

and everyone must come into the consultation with the purpose to yield to the general view, the view which seems most nearly to correspond with the common interests." He entered politics as the Christian soldier, battling for moral principles against special interests and proclaiming his gospel of disinterested public service. "We shall serve justice and candour and all things that make for the right," he confidently proclaimed. "Is not our own ancient party the party disciplined and made ready for this great task? Shall we not forget ourselves in making it the instrument of righteousness for the State and for the Nation?"[147]

[147] Acceptance speech, Sept. 15, 1910, *ibid.*, pp. 91-94.

X

The Covenanter

"The originative power of the individual in affairs must always remain a mystery, a theme more full of questions than of answers,"[1] Wilson once declared, and his verdict is as true of his own life as the people he studied. He was profoundly influenced by the world in which he lived—from the Calvinist religious training of his home to his confrontation with the forces of wealth and privilege at Princeton. Yet throughout his life he stood back from his world, assessed its needs and his own ambitions to lead and guide, modified his ideas when he felt he should, and remained unwavering when he saw fundamental principles at stake. The first fifty-four years of his life are notable because of the development and change which he experienced, particularly in his ideas about how he could adapt his cherished ideals to a rapidly changing American society. Wilson himself described maturity as a process of adjustment and added, "Some men gain it late, some early; some get it all at once, as if by one distinct act of deliberate accommodation; others get it by degrees and quite imperceptibly. No doubt to most men it comes by the slow processes of experience—at each stage of life a little."[2]

For Wilson, the development of his religious, political, and educational thought was doubtless "by the slow processes of experience," a gradual struggle to formulate the gospel of service and order that he hoped to preach to the nation. Those ideals he expected to provide him with a position of power and leadership which he sought through ceaseless work and activity. Animating his thought and spurring his goals was his fundamental faith in the power of the individual to change the course of history and bring order out of the chaos of human affairs. "Organization is not the mere multiplication of individuals," he believed. "It is the drawing of individuals together into a net formed by the conceptions of a single mind, and the greater the organization, the more certain you are to find a great individuality at its origin and center."[3]

Wilson longed to be the great individual and provide the conceptions

---

[1] "John Wesley's Place in History," June 30, 1903, *PWW*, xiv, 511.

[2] "When a Man Comes to Himself," *c.* Nov. 1, 1899, *ibid.*, xi, 265.

[3] Commemorative address in Schenectady, N. Y., Sept. 29, 1904, *ibid.*, xv, 497.

which would be the center of society's understanding of itself and its government. His ideas and personality were decisively shaped by his religious background, and he frequently acknowledged the importance of the Christian faith in his own life. "My life would not be worth living," he declared as President, "if it were not for the driving power of religion, for *faith*, pure and simple. I have seen all my life the arguments against it without ever having been moved by them. . . . There are people who *believe* only so far as they *understand*—that seems to me presumptuous and sets their understanding as the standard of the universe. . . . I am sorry for such people."[4] He had an acute sense of God's judgment of human life, and his brother-in-law Stockton Axson was convinced that Wilson viewed the idea of an all-merciful God as "a piece of soft sentimentality."[5] He relied upon the Bible as the source of God's moral law, or as he typically put it in constitutionalist fashion, " 'the Magna Charta' of the human soul."[6] Prayer was of crucial importance for him, and he said that he could not see how anyone could sustain himself "in any enterprise in life without prayer." "It is the only spring at which he can renew his spirit and purify his motive. God is the source of strength to every man and only by prayer can he keep himself close to the Father of his spirit."[7] Most importantly, Wilson's religious faith gave him a basic assurance that God was controlling and ordering human affairs. "If I were not a Christian," he once confessed as President, "I think I should go mad, but my faith in God holds me to the belief that He is in some way working out His own plans through human perversities and mistakes."[8]

That deep sense of God's order and structure for the world was largely a product of his home and the covenant theological ethos of the southern Presbyterian Church. Wilson frequently expressed his "unspeakable joy of having been born and bred in a minister's family," and once observed, "The stern Covenanter tradition that is behind me sends many an echo down the years."[9] It was a tradition communicated through Wilson's father, who taught his son that a moral foundation undergirded all human life and that an individual was called by

[4] Diary of Mrs. Crawford H. Toy, Jan. 3, 1915 (R. S. Baker Coll., DLC).

[5] R. S. Baker memorandum of an interview with Stockton Axson and George Howe, Feb. 24, 1925 (*ibid.*).

[6] "The Bible and Progress," May 7, 1911, *Public Papers of Woodrow Wilson: College and State*, Ray Stannard Baker and William E. Dodd (eds.), 2 vols. (New York and London, 1925), II, 295.

[7] *WWLL*, I, 68.

[8] Cary T. Grayson, *Woodrow Wilson: An Intimate Memoir* (New York, 1960), p. 106.

[9] "The Minister and the Community," March 30, 1906, *PWW*, XVI, 350; speech at the Mansion House in London, Dec. 28, 1918, *Public Papers of Woodrow Wilson: War and Peace*, R. S. Baker and W. E. Dodd (eds.), 2 vols. (New York and London, 1927), I, 346.

God to realize those moral ideals through work and self-assertion. "In order to advance," Wilson believed, "the Christian must needs strain every muscle."[10]

Raised in the violent atmosphere of the Civil War and nurtured by his combative father, Wilson viewed the world as an alien environment in which moral individuals were forced to fight against evil. This conception of religion as moral warfare remained an enduring force throughout his life, and he consistently viewed himself as a Christian soldier battling for the realization of right over wrong. In his youth he wrote, "As followers of this mighty Prince of Light we are ever under the stern necessity of fighting for our own safety, as well as the general advance of Christian doctrine. He who pretends to fight under the great banner of Love, should rejoice that there is no armor for his back, that to retreat is death, and should thus go forward with an eagerness and will which no slight cause can turn from their object."[11] Nearly thirty years later he continued to speak of the man who was "the true soldier of the Cross" and expressed his belief that "one of the requisite things is that we should cultivate hardness enough of fibre to stand, when it is necessary and right, against the crowd."[12]

This was a creed which brooked no opposition and made Wilson a pertinacious foe in any conflict by encouraging a sense of rigidity and self-righteousness. Particularly after Wilson's stroke in 1906, this aspect of his religious faith played an important role in affecting his policies at Princeton and his behavior as the university's president. He asked himself in 1909 how he could know that his principles were right, but he quickly brushed aside the question, believing that "a connection with a divine providence" established "a firm conviction that in following the principle I am doing right."[13]

Wilson also followed his father in linking such martial devotion to the concept of service, so that what was moral had to be enforced for the benefit of others. The essence of the Christian religion was disinterested service, he repeatedly told Princeton students, but he made that commitment a matter of militaristic assertion. "Men's consciences are awake and crave conquests which are attempted in the spirit of religion if not in its name and under its elder organization."[14] Like so many of his contemporaries, he spoke of America's duty to "Christianize" the world, and what appeared as missionary zeal was easily

[10] "Christian Progress," Dec. 21, 1876, *PWW*, I, 234.

[11] *Ibid.*, p. 235.

[12] News report of a talk at Princeton Theological Seminary, Nov. 23, 1905, *ibid.*, XVI, 232; news report of a speech to St. Andrew's Sons in New York, Dec. 1, 1903, *ibid.*, XV, 59.

[13] News report of a speech at Phillips Exeter Academy, Nov. 13, 1909, *ibid.*, XIX, 499.

[14] Baccalaureate sermon, June 12, 1904, *ibid.*, XV, 370.

translated into political imperialism, stirred by moral ideals. "We have come out upon a stage of international responsibility from which we cannot retire," Wilson declared, not in 1919 but in 1909. ". . . Every nation of the world needs to be drawn into the tutelage of America to learn how to spend money for the liberty of mankind [*applause*]; and in proportion as we discover the means for translating our material force into moral force shall we recover the traditions and the glories of American history."[15]

On the other hand, what often appeared to his opponents as moral obdurateness was also interpreted as fidelity to ideals, and at a time when the corporate structure of American economic and political life was eroding a sense of individual responsibility, Wilson remained steadfast in reminding people of their moral commitments. Integrity became a preoccupation for him, especially during the waning days of his presidency at Princeton. In April of 1910, he asserted, "I believe, as the profoundest philosophy in the world, that only integrity can bring salvation or satisfaction; can bring happiness; that no amount of fortune can, in a man's own consciousness, atone for a lost integrity of the soul."[16] Like his father, Wilson was willing to be defeated rather than risk the possibility of being wrong, and throughout his career he attempted to adhere to the dictum that he proclaimed to the students at Princeton—a person who enters politics "should be careful of his conduct when in office and be ready to sacrifice himself for principle, if need be."[17]

Wilson's religious faith interacted with his political and educational thought in deeper and more subtle ways than his obvious tendency to moralize. At the heart of his Calvinist covenant background was a concern with order, structure, and wholeness. While Wilson was scarcely aware of the intricacies of this theological tradition, it gave him a comprehensive view of the world in which the individual, society, and God were given definite roles and responsibilities. Its advantage for Wilson was its capacity for making the capriciousness of human life seem predictable, for resolving the disorder of the world and giving it structure.

Wilson frequently used the covenant theological emphasis on order and structure to resolve his personal turmoil and the disintegration of the society around him, and the method usually involved a covenant or constitution. During the dreamy, introspective year of his adolescence spent in Wilmington, he organized even the imaginary world of his Royal United Kingdom Yacht Club, with a constitution of elaborate

---

[15] Speech to the Friendly Sons of St. Patrick in New York, March 17, 1909, *ibid.*, xix, 107.

[16] "The Clergyman and the State," April 6, 1910, *ibid.*, xx, 334.

[17] News report of a speech to the Philadelphian Society, May 19, 1899, *ibid.*, xi, 119.

and well-defined rules. As an undergraduate at Princeton, he resolved his anxiety over his professional future by concluding a "solemn covenant" with his roommate that they would unite their powers to realize commonly held principles. With his wife Ellen, the ambiguities of marital love were removed through a compact pledging honesty and openness in their relationship. At various institutions, he seized upon a constitution as the means of organizing his favorite extracurricular diversion—debating clubs.

His imagination, professional goals, emotional life, social activities—all fell under his desire to order them according to a constitution. He once observed that it was "characteristic of my whole self that I take so much pleasure" in the writing of constitutions, and in a revealing statement he confessed that the covenanted order of a debating society gave him power over others without making himself vulnerable to them. "I have a sense of power in dealing with men collectively which I do not feel always in dealing with them singly. In the former case the pride of reserve does not stand so much in my way as it does in the latter. One feels no sacrifice of pride necessary in courting the favor of an assembly of men such as he would have to make seeking to please one man."[18]

Wilson utilized the covenant outwardly as well, and it shaped his assumptions about the nature of society and government. During the 1890's, he responded to political and social upheaval by stressing the need for society to be reknit into an organic unity through common allegiance to moral principles. Politically, his mentor was Burke, but his deeper commitment was to the idea of a society compacted to preserve social order and justice. Similarly, when he became president of Princeton, his educational policies—from reorganizing the curriculum to establishing a graduate college—were based on the ideal of the university as an organic community, unified by clear lines of authority and shared ideals. Education became the means of providing students with an inclusive view of knowledge and the world that defined an individual's place and mission. "My conception . . . of the higher education is a conception broad enough to embrace the whole field of thought, the whole record of experience," Wilson declared as president of Princeton. Characteristically relying on geographical imagery to describe his view of the individual and the world, he added, "[Education] is a process by which the young mind is, so to say, laid alongside of the mind of the world, as nearly as may be, and enabled to receive its strength from the nourishing mother of us all, as Anteus received strength from contact with the round earth."[19]

[18] WW to ELA, Dec. 18, 1884, *ibid.*, III, 552-53.
[19] "The Statesmanship of Letters," Nov. 5, 1903, *ibid.*, XV, 40-41.

The covenant tradition also played a role in Wilson's policies as governor of New Jersey and President of the United States, ranging from reorganizing the government of New Jersey cities with commissions to centralizing the banking system of the nation to establishing an international organization to guarantee peace. All were attempts to make social life predictable and orderly, and Wilson gave explicit tribute to his religious heritage during the negotiations at Paris over the Covenant of the League of Nations. "I wish that it were possible for us to do something like some of my very stern ancestors did, for among my ancestors are those very determined persons who were known as the Covenanters," he told a British audience in 1918. "I wish we could, not only for Great Britain and the United States, but for France and Italy and the world, enter into a great league and covenant, declaring ourselves, first of all, friends of mankind and uniting ourselves together for the maintenance and the triumph of right."[20]

Within the covenant tradition and Wilson's thought was also a deep reverence for the individual, and this tension between society as an organism and the supreme importance of the individual played a contrapuntal theme throughout Wilson's life. After the turmoil of the 1890's began to subside and after collapses in his own health, Wilson moved away from his emphasis on social order and cohesion to an exaltation of individual liberty. Similarly, during his presidency of Princeton, his speeches to alumni on the need for reintegration of social and intellectual life at Princeton were foils to his public addresses attacking the government's restrictions on individual initiative.

The difference, quite simply, was one of power. As the self-styled political adviser to the nation, Wilson could defend the individual against the encroachment of governmental authority, but once in power—whether in Princeton, Trenton, or Washington—he could not avoid exercising his own position of influence to extend the ability of government to realize social order and unity.

Like the covenanters, Wilson demonstrated throughout his life a striking ambivalence toward power. The covenant heritage had argued that God was sovereign but shared his authority with human beings. God predestined people to salvation or damnation but individuals retained freedom. Similarly, Wilson could exalt the capacities of a Gladstone or Bismarck who resisted the popular will to pursue their own policies, and yet he could also insist that the genius of American constitutional government was its reliance upon popular approval. "The freedom of a Democratic [*sic!*] form of government," he de-

---

[20] Speech in Manchester, England, Dec. 30, 1918, *Public Papers of Woodrow Wilson: War and Peace*, I, 355-56.

clared in 1896, "consists in the undictated choice by the people of the things they will accept and the men they will follow."[21]

Wilson attempted to resolve this ambivalence by moralizing power and by linking its exercise to unchanging moral laws, for as he reminded the Princeton graduates in 1910, "There are definite comprehensible practices, immutable principles of government and of right conduct in the dealing of men with one another."[22] The only ethical use of power was in realizing those principles and using authority in behalf of others. Sin, individual or political, was merely "selfishness." "The whole morality of the world depends upon those who exert upon men that influence which will turn their eyes from themselves; upon those who devote themselves to the things in which there is no calculation whatever of the effect to be wrought upon themselves or their own fortunes. For when a man most forgets himself he finds himself—his true relation to all the rest of the spiritual universe."[23]

Wilson consistently made leadership a matter of service by principled, moral individuals on behalf of others. Because leaders possessed that broad, inclusive view of people and the world, they were able to act, not out of their own interests, but in the interests of everyone. Power was never sought for its own sake but only for the sake of using it for the social welfare.

This was the framework that Wilson used to analyze his predicament at Princeton and the crisis in American society during the early twentieth century. Through the conflicts with the trustees and alumni, Wilson came to view their interests as narrow and parochial, bound by their social position and concern with wealth. They were restricting the service of Princeton to the nation as a whole by providing education only to a social elite. Wilson came to see the struggle at Princeton as merely a microcosm of the larger conflict in American society between the special interests of wealth and the larger interests of the nation as a whole, and the result was a dramatic change in his political thought.

This was perhaps evidenced first in his espousal of the common people in the address on Abraham Lincoln in February 1909, but the connection between academic conflict and political conversion is most clearly seen in an article that Wilson never published. Written at the height of the graduate college controversy in February 1910, Wilson's essay, "The Country and the Colleges," demonstrated that he now saw special interests as the enemy in both educational and political life.

[21] News report of an address at the Brooklyn Institute of Arts and Sciences, Oct. 15, 1896, *PWW*, x, 8.

[22] Baccalaureate Address, June 12, 1910, *ibid.*, xx, 523.

[23] "The Clergyman and the State," April 6, 1910, *ibid.*, p. 334.

"Learning knows no differences of social caste or privilege. The mind is a radical democrat," he insisted. ". . . And that, too, is the spirit of American life. It recognizes no privilege or preference not bestowed by nature herself. . . . [A true American college] will recognize uncompromisingly the radical democracy of the mind and of truth itself, will rank its men according to their native kinds, not their social accomplishments, and bestow its favours upon immaterial achievement."[24]

In political terms, Wilson's creed had an enormous appeal to a nation seeking to understand and control an increasingly complex society. When corporations and farmers fought for control over the government, Wilson proclaimed that the national interest was the welfare of all people, not merely some of them. When the ideals of a Protestant, agrarian America seemed invalid in a pluralistic, urban environment, Wilson insisted that the old morality was still viable but had to be translated for a new age. Work and individual initiative were still the routes to individual success, not the manipulation of institutions by special privilege. When segments of society grew increasingly powerful and separated in their outlooks, Wilson argued that government was the arbiter of those interests and the only source of social unity. In describing this larger function of government as the agency of social cohesion, Wilson's use of the language of Christian morality and the American tradition made him appear conservative while simultaneously he was changing the assumptions, expectations, and ideas about government in American life.

In all of this, there was a conspicuous circularity about Wilson's conception of leadership. If power was used on behalf of others and if it was based on moral principles, it could not be challenged. But in Wilson's view and behavior, virtually the only judge of the application of those principles was the leader himself. He alone could determine when compromises involved matters of detail or fundamental principles. This attitude in particular contributed to the cries of hypocrisy from liberals disillusioned by Wilson's negotiations at Paris and also explains how the seemingly principled President could be so adept in political dealings. However, once Wilson decided that basic moral issues were at stake, he became intransigent, and he too often forgot what he once described as "the law of political life"—"the law of compromise—you must see things as others see them."[25]

Because Wilson consistently viewed leadership as the disinterested exercise of power, he ignored the degree of self-interest involved in his own quest for influence and prominence. Because he perpetually iden-

[24] "The Country and the Colleges," c. Feb. 24, 1910, *ibid.*, 160-61.
[25] News report of a speech at the University of Michigan, April 22, 1903, *ibid.*, xiv, 420-21.

tified conflicts as disagreements over principles, he was unable to see his own jealousy, resentment, and pique toward men like West and Lodge. Inherent in his political thought and activity was a tendency to make his personal principles universally valid and an intolerance toward those who disagreed. At the same time, he bequeathed to American politics an ideal of power used not to coerce but to persuade others. "Power, in its last analysis," he believed, "is never a thing of mere physical force; the power that lasts has as its center the just conception to which men's judgments assent, to which their hearts and inclinations respond. An unjust thing is ever ephemeral; it cannot outlast any age of movement or inquiry. The action of the world, if you will but watch it in the long measure, is always based on right thinking, and the thinker must always walk at the front and show the way."[26]

[26] "The Statesmanship of Letters," Nov. 5, 1903, *ibid.*, xv, 36.

Bibliographical Essay

Joseph Ruggles Wilson

I. Primary Sources

A. LETTERS, SERMONS, AND ARTICLES

Because of the extraordinary influence of Joseph Ruggles Wilson on his son, any discussion of Woodrow Wilson's religious and intellectual development must begin with an analysis of his father. The richest source for studying the elder Wilson's personality and the relationship between father and son is the hundreds of letters they exchanged. Unfortunately, most of Wilson's letters to his father have been lost or destroyed, and historians have usually tried to reconstruct his attitudes and thinking on the basis of his father's letters to him. In preparing this study, I have read Joseph Ruggles Wilson's letters somewhat differently, trying first to analyze what kind of man he was and then drawing some conclusions about the nature of his relationship with his son. This correspondence reveals not only the father's somewhat mercurial personality but also illumines many of his values, beliefs, and ideas. In discussing Dr. Wilson's theology, I have relied in part on these letters but also on his sermons and essays. These sources, previously unexploited by Wilson scholars, contain a vast amount of valuable evidence about Wilson's father and the religious and intellectual climate in which his young son matured. Most of the sermons are unpublished; seventeen are located in the Woodrow Wilson papers in the Library of Congress; nine other complete sermons, plus five fragments, are in the Historical Foundation of the Presbyterian and Reformed Churches, Montreat, North Carolina. Some of Wilson's father's sermons and addresses have been published, and all of them are cited in the notes in Chapter I. Most of the manuscript sermons come from a later period in his ministry, but fortunately a few of the printed ones were composed earlier. Two of the most significant are *The True Idea of Success in Life* . . . (Richmond, Va., 1857) and *Mutual Relations of Masters and Slaves as Taught in the Bible* . . . (Augusta, Ga., 1861). For a man who spent a large part of his professional career in academic life, Joseph Ruggles Wilson published very few articles. Among the most important are "In What Sense Are Preachers to Preach Themselves," *Southern Presbyterian Review*, xxv (1874), 350-60, and "The Doctrine of Hell," *Southern Presbyterian Review*, xxix (1878), 459-74. His editorials during his brief tenure (1876-1877) as editor of the Wilmington, *North Carolina Presbyterian* also provide insight into his views on a wide range of subjects.

B. NEWSPAPERS

Since documentation of the details of Wilson's father's life is so sparse, the newspapers of several southern cities were searched for reports of his sermons and professional activities. These papers included the Augusta, Georgia, *Daily Constitutionalist*; Augusta, Georgia, *Chronicle & Sentinel*; Wilmington, North Carolina, *Morning Star*; Wilmington, North Carolina, *Evening Review*; Wilmington, North Carolina, *Daily Journal*; Clarksville, Tennessee, *Democrat*; and Clarksville, Tennessee, *Leaf Chronicle*. In general, this source produced meager results. More profitable and valuable for my research were the church newspapers of the southern Presbyterian Church—the Wilmington *North Carolina Presbyterian*; the *Southern Presbyterian*, published in Columbia, South Carolina; and the *Christian Observer*, published in Richmond, Virginia, and Louisville, Kentucky. These papers were especially valuable for coverage of the southern Presbyterian General Assembly, for they usually provided a nearly verbatim transcript of the debates, as well as extensive reporting on church affairs.

C. ARCHIVAL AND LIBRARY COLLECTIONS

The southern Presbyterian Church's Historical Foundation in Montreat, North Carolina, has the most extensive and valuable holdings containing information about Joseph Ruggles Wilson and provides the researchers the opportunity to do their work in an idyllic setting. Minutes of several presbyteries and synods, many local church histories, ministerial directories, newspapers, and journals are among the productive sources there. Both the Historical Foundation and the Presbyterian Historical Society in Philadelphia have assembled extremely helpful biographical indexes, and these considerably eased the task of uncovering the details of the elder Wilson's life.

II. Secondary Sources

The secondary literature on Joseph Ruggles Wilson is very scanty. L. Joel Swabb, Jr., "The Rhetorical Theory of Rev. Joseph Ruggles Wilson, D.D." (unpublished Ph.D. dissertation, Ohio State University, 1971), contains a good discussion of him as a preacher and rhetoretician and provides helpful biographical information, particularly for Dr. Wilson's college years and early ministry. Ray Stannard Baker, in the first volume of *Woodrow Wilson: Life and Letters*, 8 vols. (Garden City, N. Y., 1927-39), made an effort to chronicle some aspects of the elder Wilson's life, but Baker does not mention Dr. Wilson's devastating experience at Columbia Theological Seminary. Francis P. Weisenburger has assembled a good deal of important biographical material in "The Middle Western Antecedents of Woodrow Wilson," *Mississippi Valley Historical Review*, XXIII (1936), 375-90, but George C. Osborn's work on Woodrow Wilson and his father is generally superficial and sketchy; see "The Influence of Joseph Ruggles Wilson on His Son Woodrow Wilson," *North Carolina Historical Review*, XXXII (1955), 519-43, and *Woodrow Wilson: The Early Years* (Baton Rouge, La., 1968), pp. 3-46. Theological developments in the southern Presbyterian Church have received insufficient attention, but Ernest Trice Thompson's monumental work, *Presbyterians in the South*, 3 vols. (Richmond, Va., 1963 and 1973), chronicles major aspects of the denomination's history. It supplants the outdated and strongly partisan treatment by Thomas C. Johnson in the *American Church History Series* (New York, 1894), XI, 311-479. For the division in Old School Presbyterianism in 1861, see William Junius Wade, "The Origins and Establishment of the Presbyterian Church in the United States" (unpublished Ph.D. dissertation, University of North Carolina, 1959), and Lewis G. Vander Velde, *The Presbyterian Churches and the Federal Union, 1861-1869* (Cambridge, Mass., 1932).

WOODROW WILSON

I. Primary Sources

A. LETTERS

The present study is the first one based on the comprehensive series of *The Papers of Woodrow Wilson* (Princeton, N.J., 1966—), edited by Arthur S. Link, David W. Hirst, John E. Little, John Wells Davidson, M. Halsey Thomas, Jean Maclachlan, Sylvia E. Fontijn *et al*. Most of the documents dealing with the first thirty to forty years of Wilson's life were made available for the first time through the published volumes. In addition, the detailed and chronological presentation of the documents, as well as rich annotation, has given new importance to Wilson's letters, speeches, and essays by supplying a fuller context of his life and thinking. Among the correspondence, the most valuable for the early period of Wilson's life were letters from Wilson's parents to him and the occasional extant letter from him to his parents. His letters to Ellen Axson Wilson during their courtship and marriage are perhaps the most revealing personal documents about Wilson's personality and family life. By printing all of these letters between Wilson and Ellen, the editors have supplanted the highly selective collection of excerpted correspondence edited by Eleanor Wilson McAdoo, *The Priceless Gift* (New York,1962). These letters succeed in destroying the caricature of Wilson as a sexually repressed Puritan, incapable of expressing his emotions and feelings, verbally or physically. The voluminous correspondence between Wilson and his friends—Charles A. Talcott, Robert Bridges, R. Heath Dabney, Cleveland H. Dodge, Melancthon W. Jacobus, David B. Jones, Thomas D. Jones *et al.*— reaffirms the early contention of people like Stockton Axson, who marveled at Wilson's capacity for forming and maintaining friendships. In addition, the remarkable letters between Wilson and Mary Allen Hulbert Peck, as well as the correspondence with Edith Gittings Reid, demonstrate Wilson's warm friendships with women and illustrate Wilson's self-analysis and reflective temperament, as well as his moods of anger, bitterness, and resentment. Considered as human documents, Wilson's letters are striking for their pre-Freudian quality, revealing far more about his attitudes, passions, and temperament than a later and more self-conscious age might produce. Finally, the editors have wisely included a rich selection of collateral correspondence that paints an often colorful picture of how others viewed Wilson. These letters are particularly valuable for the latter years of Wilson's presidency at Princeton, indicating not only the tenacity of the antagonists but also the political machinations which swirled around Wilson within the alumni, faculty, and trustees.

B. DIARIES, NOTES ON READING, NOTES FOR LECTURES

Previous attempts to describe Wilson's intellectual development have been hampered by Wilson's use of shorthand for notations to himself. The transcription of his diary as a student at Princeton and his "Index Rerum" are rich sources for Wilson's beliefs and values as a young man. The editors of *The Papers of Woodrow Wilson* have also transcribed Wilson's sporadic attempts at keeping a diary in later life, and despite their fragmentary quality, they are important evidence of Wilson's vision of his goals and purposes. The editors searched Wilson's personal library in the Library of Congress for the marginal notes that he made in his books, and these reactions are especially fruitful for tracing Wilson's ideas as a student and young professor. Wilson utilized his shorthand in preparing memoranda on various questions of politics, and the only evidence of the contents of his projected *magnum opus*, the *Philosophy of Politics*, are these random attempts by Wilson to spell out the scope of the work and some of its key points. Wilson's lecture notes can be productively studied for the development of his thinking about the individual, society, and the state. The notes for his lectures on administration at Johns Hopkins, as well as the notes for courses in history and politics at Bryn Mawr, Wesleyan, and Princeton, reveal how his political thought changed under the impact of social and political turmoil during the late nineteenth century. These notes formed the core of his lectures, and although they belie Wilson's reputation for classroom eloquence, they indicate the quality of instruction which he provided. One vainly wishes for evidence of Wilson's changing classroom approach to government during the period between 1902 and 1910, but there his thought must be traced through public speeches and addresses.

C. ESSAYS AND BOOKS

During Wilson's early professional career, he considered himself as much an author as a teacher or public speaker. From his earliest essays on "Work-Day Religion" and "Christ's Army" to his later efforts to spell out his educational and political philosophy, these essays are a continuously valuable guide to Wilson's attempt to influence public opinion. The editors have usually been able to determine with great accuracy the date of Wilson's composition, and in some cases this has made a particular essay even more significant. Perhaps the clearest example of this is Wilson's declaration of spiritual maturity, "When a Man Comes to Himself," written in 1899 after another collapse of his health but not published until 1901. Similarly, Wilson's literary essays during the 1880's and 1890's assume additional prominence when read against the background of his lectures on administration, politics, law, and history, rather than as chapters in collections of essays. With the exception of *Congressional Government* and *Constitutional Government in the United States*, Wilson's books have not been included in *The Papers of Woodrow Wilson*, but the editors did include the final and most significant chapters of *The State* and have provided extensive documentation and annotation of the preparation of *Division and Reunion, George Washington*, and *A History of the American People*. In all cases, however, the editors have included a helpful collection of reviews of Wilson's books, which suggests once again that the early critical reaction may not be the most enduring.

D. SPEECHES

Wilson once called his throat "my most used member," and from his days as an orator at Princeton to his efforts to offer himself as the disinterested adviser to the nation, his life is notable for the number of his public speeches on a variety of subjects. In *The Papers of Woodrow Wilson*, these addresses range from short homilies to baccalaureate sermons, informal after-dinner talks to commencement addresses, public orations to quasi-political campaign speeches. His audiences were equally varied—students, faculty, alumni, women's clubs, social organizations, political gatherings, and church congregations—and were located in such different places as New York, Colorado, Alabama, and Massachusetts. The editors have assiduously culled local newspapers for news reports of these speeches, and the result is documentation of Wilson's public opinions in the most comprehensive and accessible form. This study has attempted to make special use of Wilson's religious talks and to integrate them with his political and educational speeches. His baccalaureate addresses are particularly valuable and significant, for they seem to suggest more of the dynamics and development of Wilson's thought than some of his other public speeches. Amidst the turmoil at Princeton, baccalaureate addresses forced Wilson to reflect on his purposes and policies. Their measured, meditative tone contrasts sharply with his other public speaking and demonstrates how deeply his Christian faith had influenced his policies, values, and "principles." In many cases, the editors of *The Papers of Woodrow Wilson* have been able to print complete texts of Wilson's speeches; in other cases they have provided the best news report available. In cases when neither a text nor a news report was extant, fortunately Wilson's speech notes were often preserved, and although these notes are the most suspect evidence of what Wilson actually said, they are at least a reliable guide to what he intended to say.

E. EDITORIAL NOTES

Interspersed throughout the documentary record of Wilson's papers are several extended Editorial Notes, which supplement and enrich the narrative of Wilson's life when primary Wilson documents do not convey the entire story. The editors have made especially constructive use of this device in the early volumes during Wilson's youth and early manhood, when evidence is sketchy and incomplete, and during the latter years of Wilson's presidency of Princeton. Occasionally, the editors have highlighted a particular document, such as Wilson's constitution for the Royal United Kingdom Yacht Club or his lecture on Edmund Burke, but generally these Editorial Notes have been used sparingly and judiciously. Some may quarrel with their conclusions, but the Editorial Notes have been characterized throughout by careful analysis and cautious generalization. Other annotation has facilitated the work of a researcher, identifying correspondents and literary references, clarifying references to contemporary events, and providing helpful cross references. Volume 13 contains a comprehensive table of contents and index to the first twelve volumes. Indeed, due to the publication of *The Papers of Woodrow Wilson*, no other public figure in

American history is as easily accessible to historians, and because of the vast collection and publication of documents for Wilson's early life, a study of his religious and intellectual development is possible under the most advantageous circumstances.

F. MEMOIRS

In contrast to the presidential period of Wilson's life, there are relatively few valuable memoirs. Eleanor Wilson McAdoo's edited collection of letters between Woodrow and Ellen Wilson, *The Priceless Gift* (New York, 1962) provides some interesting and indispensable evidence about the Wilson family life and can be supplemented by her earlier book, *The Woodrow Wilsons* (New York, 1937). Margaret Randolph Axson Elliott, who lived with the Wilsons during his presidency of Princeton, also offers some insight into the Wilson family during a critical period in *My Aunt Louisa and Woodrow Wilson* (Chapel Hill, N. C., 1944), but her reminiscences are frequently gratuitous and irrelevant. Edith Gittings Reid has written a perceptive and articulate study of Wilson, *Woodrow Wilson* (New York, 1934), and its value lies primarily in portraying Wilson as a student and lecturer at Johns Hopkins. Frederic C. Howe in his *Confessions of a Reformer* (New York, 1926), briefly discusses his reaction to Wilson's lectures on administration at Johns Hopkins. The best memoir of Wilson as a professor at Princeton is Bliss Perry, *And Gladly Teach* (New York and Boston, 1935), but during his years as president of the university, more sources are available. The most productive is the collection of essays edited by William Starr Myers, *Woodrow Wilson: Some Princeton Memories* (Princeton, N. J., 1946), which includes reminiscences by important faculty members as well as some of the young preceptors. Hardin Craig, who came to Princeton as a preceptor, has written *Woodrow Wilson at Princeton* (Norman, Okla., 1960), but it is chiefly an attempt to defend Wilson's educational philosophy, rather than to recollect his experiences at the university. Raymond B. Fosdick's graceful essay, "Personal Recollections of Woodrow Wilson," recalls his impression of Wilson as president of Princeton and is included in *The Philosophy and Policies of Woodrow Wilson*, Earl Latham, ed. (Chicago, 1958), pp. 28-45. Mary Allen Hulbert published her memoirs as *The Story of Mrs. Peck: An Autobiography* (New York, 1933), and although her sense of chronology is very confused, her highly discreet discussion of her relationship with Wilson contains some helpful material.

G. ARCHIVAL COLLECTIONS

In a different category, but not strictly qualifying as memoirs, are the numerous interviews which Ray Stannard Baker conducted in preparation for his authorized biography of Wilson. During the 1920's, Baker asked for the recollections of hundreds of Wilson's contemporaries, and as a former journalist, he demonstrated considerable skill in eliciting valuable information from them. These interviews and letters, preserved in the Ray Stannard Baker Collection in the Library of Congress, contain significant material relating to Wilson's early youth, family life, and the controversies at Princeton. Henry W. Bragdon followed Baker's example and has left another collection of interviews and correspondence with contemporaries of Wilson in the archives of Princeton University. Both men have left future historians in their debt by making these materials available for subsequent use. When used with caution, they enrich the documentary sources of Wilson's life and thought. The archives of Princeton University are also helpful for evidence related to the quadrangle and graduate school fights, including Andrew F. West's mimeographed account of the struggle, "A Narrative of the Graduate College of Princeton University. . . ."

II. Secondary Sources

A. GENERAL BIOGRAPHIES

The first two volumes of Ray Stannard Baker's *Woodrow Wilson: Life and Letters*, 8 vols. (Garden City, N. Y., 1927-39), remain the starting point for any description of Wilson's life prior to his entry into politics. As the authorized biographer, Baker was highly sympathetic to Wilson and stressed, but did not analyze, the importance of Wilson's religion in the development of his political and educational thought. Baker is annoyingly erratic in annotating the sources of his evidence, and since at least parts of the first two volumes are based on his conversations with Wilson, his study continues to be a major, though somewhat suspect, source. Baker's work is primarily a narrative of Wilson's life and does not attempt to analyze Wilson's intellectual development. Henry W. Bragdon's *Wilson: The Academic Years* (Cambridge, Mass., 1967) does provide more analysis of Wilson's changing attitudes and ideas and suggests at least one important point about Wilson's political views during the late nineteenth century. For all of his fascination with British institutions and German administrative theory, Wilson retained a deep affection for American democratic institutions and traditions, and although he was critical of reform, he was not as conservative or reactionary as many of his contemporaries. Bragdon is also helpful in describing the settings of the various institutions at which Wilson studied and taught, but he devotes virtually no attention to Wilson's religious faith or its relationship to his political and educational thought. The weakest section of his book is his discussion of Wilson during the 1890's. In many respects, Wilson's stroke, his response to the decade's political upheaval, and the changes in his religious thought prepared the way for his gradual conversion to a political progressive during his presidency of Princeton. The decade was certainly not as idyllic or peaceful as Bragdon has portrayed it. Finally, many errors of fact weaken Bragdon's attempt to surpass Baker or provide the comprehensive narrative of Wilson's life and thought prior to 1910.

The first of Arthur S. Link's multi-volume biography, *Wilson: Road to the White House* (Princeton, N. J., 1947), makes no attempt to cover in detail the early decades of Wilson's life, but the chapters dealing with the quadrangle and graduate school controversies and Wilson's entry into politics remain a reliable narrative of Wilson's life during the last years of his presidency of Princeton. In contrast to his later essays on Wilson's religious faith and subsequent volumes of the Wilson biography, Link does not probe the interrelationship of Wilson's political, educational, and religious thought and overestimates the extent of Wilson's early conservatism. But as a political biography, Link's *Road to the White House* is a model of careful scholarship and lucid prose, and the testimony to its virtues is its endurance for more than twenty-five years as the best study of the pre-presidential Wilson.

Arthur Walworth's two-volume biography, revised and issued as one volume, *Woodrow Wilson* (Boston, 1965), is a brilliantly written narrative but has practically no annotation and is marred by numerous mistakes. Patrick Devlin's incisive study, *Too Proud to Fight: Woodrow Wilson's Neutrality* (New York and London, 1975), is primarily devoted to Wilson's diplomacy from 1914 to 1917, but Devlin has many perceptive insights into Wilson's thought and personality. John M. Blum's short, interpretive study, *Woodrow Wilson and the Politics of Morality* (Boston, 1956), is critical of what Blum sees as Wilson's tendency to reduce all problems to moral issues, but it should be read with Blum's other work on Theodore Roosevelt, *The Republican Roosevelt* (Cambridge, Mass., 1954), in which he is more sympathetic to another style of moralizing in politics. For figures such as William Jennings Bryan, Roosevelt, and Wilson, the question is not so much one of moral reductionism but how moral values and religious beliefs influenced and were influenced by their political thought and activities.

Three older biographies of Wilson provide some additional details of Wilson's life. The most valuable is William Bayard Hale's campaign biography, *Woodrow Wilson* (Garden City, N. Y., 1912), because Wilson provided Hale with most of the information about his early boyhood. Less helpful are William Allen White, *Woodrow Wilson: The Man, His Times, and His Task* (Boston and New York, 1924), and

Josephus Daniels, *The Life of Woodrow Wilson, 1856-1924* (Chicago, 1924).

B. SPECIALIZED STUDIES

Arthur S. Link's essays on Wilson's religious faith, buttressed by his work on Wilson as a politician, have been pioneering initial attempts at demonstrating the importance of Wilson's Calvinistic heritage on his policies as President. These essays include "Woodrow Wilson: Presbyterian in Government," *Calvinism and the Political Order*, George L. Hunt, ed. (Philadelphia, 1965), pp. 157-74; and "Woodrow Wilson and His Presbyterian Inheritance" and "The Higher Realism of Woodrow Wilson," in *The Higher Realism of Woodrow Wilson* (Nashville, Tenn., 1971), pp. 3-20, 127-39. Without formal training in theology, Link astutely perceived some of the distinctive aspects of Wilson's Calvinistic Presbyterian faith but overlooked the pervasive influence of the covenant theological tradition. Two studies have aimed, without much success, at some integration of Wilson's political and religious thought—Herbert Roscoe Howard, "The Social Philosophy of Woodrow Wilson" (unpublished doctoral dissertation, Southern Baptist Theological Seminary, 1944), and David Wesley Soper, "Woodrow Wilson and the Christian Tradition" (unpublished doctoral dissertation, Drew Divinity School, 1945). In relying solely on Wilson's public speeches and addresses and in failing to utilize any manuscript collections, these studies are superficial and inadequate. Harry Rine DeYoung, "A Study of the Religious Speaking of Woodrow Wilson" (unpublished Ph.D. dissertation, Wayne State University, 1965), ignores the important question of how Joseph Ruggles Wilson's homiletical style might have influenced Wilson's own rhetorical approach.

William Diamond, *The Economic Thought of Woodrow Wilson* (Baltimore, Md., 1943), is best for the early period of Wilson's life, but Diamond fails to appreciate Wilson's hostility to economic theory *per se* and his tendency to treat economic questions as part of larger political, social, and moral problems. Kazimierz Grzybowski was the first to analyze Wilson's lecture notes for courses in law at Princeton ("Woodrow Wilson on Law, State and Society," *George Washington Law Review*, XXX [1962], 808-52), but the result was a rather prosaic analysis of Wilson's views on various legal problems, not a broad examination of the larger questions with which Wilson was attempting to deal. Link demonstrated for the first time the importance of Wilson's lectures on administration at Johns Hopkins in his short essay, "Woodrow Wilson and the Study of Administration," in *The Higher Realism of Woodrow Wilson*, pp. 38-44, but since Wilson abandoned so many of his political ideas of the 1890's, it remains an interesting question whether as President Wilson implemented any of his theories of administration.

Besides Bragdon, only Laurence R. Vesey has attempted to describe Wilson's educational thought ("The Academic Mind of Woodrow Wilson," *Mississippi Valley Historical Review*, XLIX [1963], 613-34), and his chief contribution is placing Wilson's educational reforms at Princeton against the larger background of trends in American higher education. In at least one crucial area, Vesey misunderstood the core of Wilson's educational philosophy by arguing that Wilson saw college education as a withdrawal from the affairs of the world. On occasion, Wilson did describe the university as separated from the world, but the purpose of education was consistently the same—preparation of students for service to society. In addition, neither Bragdon nor Vesey appreciates how Wilson's organic view of society and the university shaped his reforms as president of Princeton.

Several attempts have been made to study Wilson's personality. The earliest was William Bayard Hale's embittered, neo-Freudian analysis, *The Story of a Style* (New York, 1920), which used Wilson's worst book, *George Washington*, as the basis for the argument. Sigmund Freud and William C. Bullitt, *Thomas Woodrow Wilson: A Psychological Study* (Boston, 1967), has been roundly condemned as both bad history and bad psychology. A better reception has been granted to *Woodrow Wilson and Colonel House: A Personality Study* (New York, 1956), by Alexander L. and Juliette L. George. This work, like Freud and Bullitt's, focuses on the relationship between father and son as determinative of Wilson's later personality development. Several problems plague the Georges' analysis. First, they did not utilize any of Wilson's early papers in arriving at conclusions about the father-son relationship; second, they demonstrated no knowledge of the developments in Wilson's father's life; third, they failed to appreciate the importance of Wilson's emotional relationship with his wife in the development of his maturity; and they ignored the way in which Wilson's religion produced a moral rigidity and sense of personal righteousness that made relationships with John G. Hibben and Colonel House difficult to preserve. Wilson's personality must be studied within the context of his physical health, and Edwin A. Weinstein has clarified many important developments in Wilson's life in "Woodrow Wilson's Neurological Illness," *Journal of American History*, LVII (1970), 324-51. Another possibly fruitful approach would be the application of Erik Erikson's stages of the "life cycle" to Wilson's life, for Wilson himself clearly saw his own life as a process of development and maturation.

C. BACKGROUND STUDIES

It is evident that this work relies on several studies dealing with the covenant theological tradition. I have found Michael Walzer's interpretation of the covenant as a response to social disorder extremely useful in my own understanding of Wilson; see *The Revolution of the Saints* (Cambridge, Mass., 1965). Fred J. Hood, "Presbyterianism and the New American Nation, 1783-1826: A Case Study of Religion and National Life" (unpublished Ph.D. dissertation, Princeton University, 1968), was very helpful in probing the religious and cultural milieu created by Presbyterianism in the aftermath of the revolution. The continuing influence of covenant modes of thought, particularly in interpreting American nationhood during the nineteenth century, is demonstrated by George M. Marsden in his excellent study, *The Evangelical Mind and the New School Presbyterian Experience* (New Haven and London, 1970). Paul A. Carter's survey of late-nineteenth-century American Protestantism, *The Spiritual Crisis of the Gilded Age* (DeKalb, Ill., 1971), was fruitful in providing a background for Joseph Ruggles Wilson, whose struggle with the gospel of success was much more agonizing than that of some of his northern contemporaries. Richard Hofstadter's classic, *Social Darwinism in American Thought* (Philadelphia, 1944), probes an important but not dominant intellectual movement, which had some impact on Wilson; Social Darwinism merged easily with Wilson's Protestant ethic consciousness and merely reaffirmed his faith in an inevitable progress. My conclusions about the organic character of Wilson's political thought are reinforced by George M. Frederickson's *The Inner Civil War: Northern Intellectuals and the Crisis of the Union* (New York, 1965) and by Robert H. Wiebe's broad survey of populism and progressivism, *The Search for Order, 1877-1920* (New York, 1967). The concept of "civil religion" might be fruitfully employed to interpret Wilson's political career, but it lacks sufficient conceptual clarity to be used within the context of this study. See Robert N. Bellah, "Civil Religion in America," *Daedalus*, XCVI (1967), 1-21, and the excellent collections of essays edited by Elwyn A. Smith, *The Religion of the Republic* (Philadelphia, 1971), and Russell E. Richey and Donald G. Jones, *American Civil Religion* (New York, 1974).

Index

Publication of Supplementary Volumes to *The Papers of Woodrow Wilson* is assisted from time to time by the Woodrow Wilson Foundation in order to encourage scholarly work about Woodrow Wilson and his time. All volumes have passed the review procedures of the publishers and the Editor and the Editorial Advisory Committee of *The Papers of Woodrow Wilson*. Inquiries about the Series should be addressed to The Editor, Papers of Woodrow Wilson, Firestone Library, Princeton University, Princeton, N.J. 08540

Raymond B. Fosdick, *Letters on the League of Nations. From the Files of Raymond B. Fosdick* (Princeton University Press 1966)

Wilton B. Fowler, *British-American Relations, 1917-1918: The Role of Sir William Wiseman* (Princeton University Press 1969)

John M. Mulder, *Woodrow Wilson: The Years of Preparation* (Princeton University Press 1978)

George Egerton, *Great Britain and the Creation of the League of Nations* (University of North Carolina Press 1978)

LIBRARY OF CONGRESS CATALOGING IN PUBLICATION DATA

Mulder, John M., 1946-
  Woodrow Wilson: the years of preparation.

  (Supplementary volume to The papers of Woodrow Wilson)
  Bibliography: p.
  Includes index.
  1. Wilson, Woodrow, Pres. U. S., 1856-1924.
2. Presidents—United States—Biography.
3. Historians—United States—Biography.   4. Princeton
University—Presidents—Biography.   I. Series: Wilson,
Woodrow, Pres. U.S., 1856-1924.   Papers: Supplementary volume.
E767.M75   973.91'3'0924 [B]   77-72128
ISBN 0-691-04647-6